Foundations of European Politics

Foundations of European Politics

A Comparative Approach

Catherine E. De Vries

Sara B. Hobolt

Sven-Oliver Proksch

Jonathan B. Slapin

OXFORD
UNIVERSITY PRESS

OXFORD
UNIVERSITY PRESS

Great Clarendon Street, Oxford, OX2 6DP,
United Kingdom

Oxford University Press is a department of the University of Oxford.
It furthers the University's objective of excellence in research, scholarship,
and education by publishing worldwide. Oxford is a registered trade mark of
Oxford University Press in the UK and in certain other countries

Published in the United States of America by Oxford University Press
198 Madison Avenue, New York, NY 10016, United States of America

British Library Cataloguing in Publication Data
Data available

Library of Congress Control Number: 0000000000

ISBN 978-0-19-883130-3

Printed in Great Britain by
Bell & Bain Ltd., Glasgow

Preface

The idea for this textbook goes back to a sunny afternoon in bustling Milan in June 2017. The four of us were participating in the annual conference organized by the European Political Science Association and we met in a street café to exchange views about our ongoing research projects. The conversation moved on to a more general discussion of teaching European politics at our various universities. Each of us regularly teach classes on European politics, albeit in four different countries, including general introductions but also seminars and lectures focusing on elections and voting behaviour, political institutions, and European Union politics. Over the years, we had come to realize that existing textbook resources to teach these classes had become increasingly difficult to use for two reasons.

First, explaining patterns in national politics in Europe without an understanding of the developments at the European Union level was becoming nearly impossible. Brexit may be the most obvious example, but there are many other instances where EU politics matters increasingly for national politics. For instance, the emergence of new political parties in national elections may have roots in European level politics. Second, explaining interactions at the European Union level between governments and supranational actors is increasingly difficult without understanding the domestic politics behind action at the European level. National parties, for example, continue to play an important role in the political framework of the European Union.

On that day, sitting in the Milan street café, we decided to write a new textbook that bridges the national and European levels of government by adopting a rigorous analytical approach in the hope that such a resource will be useful for university teachers and students alike in learning about the fundamentals of contemporary European politics. This book is the culmination of our efforts.

In addition to providing the theoretical foundations necessary to understand national and European political actors and institutions, the textbook aims to expose students to various political data in Europe. The book offers many data visualizations, as well as extensive online materials that introduce major political science datasets currently being used by academics to study European politics. The online materials allow students to answer exercise questions using interactive data visualizations based on these datasets. In combination, we hope that the book and the online materials will be used by the next generation of scholars of European politics.

This textbook would not have been possible without the help of numerous scholars and colleagues. First, we like to thank Pit Rieger and Jens Wäckerle for excellent research assistance along the way. Pit created the many data visualizations found throughout this book. Jens has done an outstanding job in developing the online materials, including all of the interactive data exercises. Both Jens and Pit provided many helpful suggestions to make the textbook even more approachable to students. The book would not be what it is without their invaluable help.

In addition, many colleagues have read various chapters of this book, and some even the entire manuscript, and they gave us valuable feedback and comments. These intrepid souls include: Chitralekha Basu, Bruno Castanho Silva, Michele Fenzl, David Fortunato, Daniel Kelemen, Lucas Leemann, Lanny Martin, Stefan Müller, Verena Reidinger, Lennart

Schürmann, and Christopher Wratil. We also thank the numerous anonymous reviewers who have furthermore helped us to be more concise and precise with our arguments. We are grateful to Oxford University Press, in particular Sarah Iles and Katie Staal, who have always believed in this project and who have kept us (mostly) on schedule! Finally, we would like to thank our many wonderful students over the years who have taught us so much and inspired us to write this book. We dedicate this book to them and the next generation of European politics scholars.

Catherine E. De Vries
Sara B. Hobolt
Sven-Oliver Proksch
Jonathan B. Slapin
February 2021

Brief Contents

Detailed Contents

PART THREE Elections and Parties

List of Figures

List of Tables

List of Boxes

How to Use this Book

Box 4.4 METHODS AND MEASUREMENT: Measuring Eurosceptic Attitudes

Early studies of attitudes towards European integration focused on support for European integration, but the focus in the last decade has shifted to opposition to European integration, or so-called **Euroscepticism**. Moreover, people's attitudes towards the European Union were traditionally captured along one single dimension ranging from a Eurosceptic pole, indicating a rejection of the European project, to a Europhile pole, indicating support for the European project (Hobolt and De Vries, 2016a). In her book *Euroscepticism and the Future of European Integration*, De Vries (2018) challenges this classical approach in two ways. First, attitudes towards the EU might reflect the multifaceted nature of European integration. For example, people might generally support their country's membership in the EU, but at the same time show little appreciation for the policies that the EU pursues. Due to the complex nature of their attitudes, people cannot be easily classified as either Eurosceptic or Europhile. Rather, they are often conflicted and ambivalent about the EU and simultaneously like and dislike certain aspects of European integration. Second, people's attitudes towards the EU should not be conceptualized in isolation from their attitudes towards the nation-state. National institutions and policy performance provide an essential benchmark for how citizens view the EU. Eurosceptic attitudes are more likely to develop in country contexts in which national institutions perform well and yield

Methods and Measurement Boxes

Provide more detailed information about methodological concerns, or examine questions about how to measure particular facets of politics.

Box 12.3 CASE STUDY: European Responses to the Covid-19 Outbreak in 2020

The devastation of Covid-19, beginning in Spring 2020, proved an existential threat to shared ways of life across the European continent, and across the globe. Deaths mounted, economies shut down, jobs evaporated, and social isolation became the new norm. National governments struggled to address the pandemic, and their efforts varied widely in effectiveness. At the initial time of the outbreak, the EU proved particularly challenged in its capacity to respond. A pandemic that does not stop at the border begged for a collective response across a highly interdependent Europe. Yet, the first responses were primarily national. From nationwide lockdowns in Italy, France, and Spain to partial shutdowns in the Czech Republic, Germany, Netherlands, Poland, and Slovakia to only partial school closures in Sweden, member state governments decided on very different measures to stop or slow down the spread of the virus. National governments went as far as to erect barriers to each other through the reintroduction of border controls. The fact that member states brought in border checks initially created some problems in terms of the movement of pharmaceuticals and food within the single market.

What explains the EU's lack of coming together to work through the Covid-19 crisis? For its first

Case Study Boxes

Case study boxes foreground particular examples in greater detail to demonstrate a concept, or to show how it applies in real-world politics.

Box 7.2 CONTROVERSIES AND DEBATES: Is the European Union Responsive to Voters?

The European Union has been traditionally regarded as relatively unresponsiveness to voters. Historically, governments in the Council have been been able to negotiate and legislate away from the glare of public scrutiny and their actions in the EU have little impact on their chances of re-election domestically (Bailer et al., 2015). Without public attention, there are few incentives for politicians to respond to public opinion. According to this view, public opinion plays a limited role in shaping the positions of governments and politicians in EU policy-making, which is driven instead by economic, partisan, and geo-strategic interests.

Moreover, as multiple institutions are involved in decision-making at the European level—the Council, the Commission, and the European Parliament as well as the member state—it is also characterized by low clarity of responsibility, making more difficult for voters to hold their representatives to account in national and European Parliament elections. Studies have shown that voters in European Parliament elections do not punish or reward parties on the basis of economic performance, as retrospective models of voting would suggest (Hobolt and Tilley, 2014). One reason is the lack of clarity about who

Controversies and Debates Boxes

Controversies and debates boxes highlight disagreements in the academic literature about both theoretical concepts and empirical findings.

Presidential systems offer an alternative form of democratic governance, characterized by a 'mutual independence' (Stepan and Skach, 1993) between parliament and the executive (the president). Citizens participate in two elections: the parliamentary election which determines which candidates and parties represent the country in the legislature, and the presidential election which determines the chief executive. The parliament and the president thus have two separate electoral mandates and their own legitimacy. They are independent from one another: neither can the president dissolve parliament, nor can the parliament re-call the president—at least not for purely political reasons. The most well-known presidential democracy is the United States of America. In Europe, Cyprus has adopted a presidential political system. And according to the classification scheme by Cheibub et al. (2010), Switzerland also should be considered a presidential system. However, Switzerland differs from the other countries in the sense that parliament delegates executive power to a collective government, composed of representatives of several parliamentary parties, for a fixed term in office. Parliament elects this government, composed of seven individuals representing different parties, regions, and linguistic backgrounds, at the start of a parliamentary term. But once elected, the

Glossary Terms

Key terms appear emboldened in the text and are defined in a glossary at the end of the book, helping you to understand technical terms as you learn, and acting as a useful prompt when it comes to revision.

Guided Tour of the Online Resources

Description

An analytical approach to the study of comparative European politics with a unique focus on the interaction between national and European-level politics.

⬇ CC v1.0

⬇ Simple CC v1.0

Resources for Foundations of European Politics: A Comparative Approach

Foundations of European Politics: A Comparative Approach Instructor Resources

Catherine E. De Vries, Sara B. Hobolt, Sven-Oliver Proksch, and Jonathan B. Slapin

Instructor resources to accompany *Foundations of European Politics*

Foundations of European Politics: A Comparative Approach Student Resources

Catherine E. De Vries, Sara B. Hobolt, Sven-Oliver Proksch, and Jonathan B. Slapin

Student resources to accompany *Foundations of European Politics*

For student Multiple-Choice Questions, Web Links, and lecturer resources go to: www.oup.com/he/DeVries1e

For Dataset Descriptions and Exercises, go to: www.foundationsofeuropeanpolitics.com

For Students

Multiple-Choice Questions

Self-marking multiple-choice questions for each chapter reinforces students' understanding of the key points of each chapter, and provide a useful prompt for revision.

Web Links

Web links to further relevant information to help students take their learning further.

Dataset Decriptions

An interactive guide to important datasets that can be used by students to analyse European politics.

Interactive Data Exercises

Explore key concepts from each chapter with activities which encourage you to manipulate and engage with data.

For Registered Adopters

Essay Questions

Ready-made essay questions for each chapter have been designed to use in assessment, or to stimulate class debate.

Test-Bank Questions

A bank of multiple-choice questions to be used for assessment purposes, to help test students' understanding of the key concepts explored in each chapter.

PowerPoint Slides

PowerPoint slides accompany each chapter, and can be used and tailored by lecturers in their teaching.

About the Authors

Catherine E. De Vries is a Professor of Political Science at Bocconi University. She is the author of several books on European politics, including Euroscepticism and the Future of European Integration (OUP, 2018) and Political Entrepreneurs (Princeton UP, 2020).

Sara B. Hobolt is the Sutherland Chair in European Institutions and professor at the London School of Economics and Political Science. She is the author of four books on European politics, including Europe in Question (OUP, 2009), Blaming Europe? (OUP, 2014) and Political Entrepreneurs (Princeton UP, 2020).

Sven-Oliver Proksch is a Professor of Political Science and Chair in European and Multilevel Politics at the University of Cologne. His research interests include political representation, party politics, parliaments, and political text analysis. He is co-author of the book The Politics of Parliamentary Debates (CUP, 2015).

Jonathan B. Slapin is a Professor of Political Science and Chair in Political Institutions and European Politics at the University of Zürich. His current research focuses on European parliamentary and party politics, and his most recent book is Roll Call Rebels (CUP, 2019).

Introduction

On 23 June 2016, the United Kingdom held a referendum in which the country voted to leave the **European Union** (EU). At the time, few figures loomed larger over British politics than Nigel Farage, the leader of the United Kingdom Independence Party (UKIP). Farage and UKIP had been campaigning for the UK to leave the EU for many years. And ahead of the general election of 2015, the threat of UKIP encouraged Conservative Prime Minister David Cameron to commit to a referendum on EU membership. Throughout the referendum campaign, Farage made regular appearances in the media, including as a panellist on the BBC's popular weekly political show *Question Time*, and he continued to be a regular thorn in the side of the Prime Minister. Ultimately, the campaign to leave the EU won the day. UKIP and its charismatic leader were an important force in pushing the UK towards this outcome.

Meanwhile, across the English Channel, another populist politician was having similar success in France. In 2011, Marine Le Pen became leader of the National Front (which is now known as the National Rally), a radical right party. She took over the party helm from her father, Jean-Marie Le Pen, who had founded the party and led it since 1972. The elder Le Pen, in particular, was known for his anti-Semitic and anti-Muslim views. Like UKIP, the National Rally has opposed French membership in the European Union and other international organizations. The party also strongly opposes immigration, especially from outside of Europe. Marine Le Pen secured reasonably strong political backing and managed to enter the second round of the 2017 French presidential elections against Emmanuel Macron. Even though she eventually lost, she put up a strong electoral showing.

Besides their similar positions and well-known public personas, Nigel Farage and Marine Le Pen have something else in common. Their parties have never performed particularly well in national parliamentary elections. UKIP has only ever won one single seat in the British House of Commons—a seat held by the formerly Conservative MP Douglas Carswell. Nigel Farage, himself, has never won a seat in the House of Commons despite standing for election seven times. Marine Le Pen has only done slightly better. In her fifth attempt to become a deputy in the French National Assembly, she finally won a seat in 2017. Her National Rally party, however, remains a fringe phenomenon in the French parliament, holding only eight seats out of 577 in the National Assembly following the 2017 election.

In contrast, both UKIP and the National Rally have performed exceedingly well in the European elections that elect deputies to the European Parliament (EP)—the directly elected parliament of the European Union. UKIP and its successor party—the Brexit Party—finished as the largest British party in both the 2014 and 2019 EP elections and the second largest in 2009. Nigel Farage held a seat in the EP from 1999 until 31 January 2020, the day the UK left the EU. During that time, he made a name for himself as someone prone to outlandish speeches in which he would insult both European institutions and politicians. Likewise, Le Pen's party was the first-place finisher in the EP elections in France in both 2014 and 2019, and, like Farage, Le Pen used her role as a member of the European Parliament to project an image of herself as someone willing to fight European institutions back in France.

Beyond the UK and France, the rest of Europe has also been experiencing dramatic political change. Many smaller parties, sometimes holding radical views, have come to national prominence, having had greater electoral success at the European level than the national level. Throughout the 1980s and 1990s, for example, the German Green party consistently polled better in European elections than at home. Even when parties holding radical views first experienced success nationally, this success was often validated in subsequent European elections. The Five Star Movement, an Italian party founded by comedian and blogger Beppe Grillo, came to prominence by winning almost 26 per cent of the votes and becoming the second largest party in Italy following the 2013 national elections. The party's platform was very critical of European integration, expressing support for holding a referendum to leave the EU's common currency, the Euro (although it has since softened its tone). In the subsequent 2014 EP election, the party repeated its success, securing 21 per cent of the vote and again finishing as the second largest party.

In the 2019 EP election, smaller parties across many countries and at both ends of the ideological spectrum continued their string of successes, winning a record number of seats. In Germany, the far-right Alternative for Germany (AfD) won 11 per cent of the vote, similar to their vote share in the previous national election and more than double their vote share from the 2013 national election; in Sweden, the Green Party likewise captured over 11 per cent, more than doubling their previous national vote share; and in Greece, the Coalition of the Radical Left (Syriza) won 23 per cent of the vote, finishing as one of top two parties in every Greek election since 2010, when previously they had tended to win less than 5 per cent of the vote. When these parties sustain their European-level success at the national level, as the German AfD, the Italian Five Star Movement, and the Greek Syriza have done, it creates particular challenges for more moderate, traditional parties, who must decide how to compete against these upstarts. The decisions they make impact voters' choices at the ballot box. And the success of new parties nationally has concrete consequences for the formation of governments. Most countries across Europe use a form of **parliamentary system**, in which the formation of government occurs within parliament after an election, and governments need the support of a majority in parliament to make policy. New types of coalitions have formed and governed, including an all-populist government in Italy comprised of the Five Star Movement and the League Party (Lega), and a novel coalition government in Austria of the centre-right Austrian People's Party and the Greens. Numerous governments haven been unable to muster stable parliamentary majorities, including in Spain, the Czech Republic, Belgium, and Ireland due to increasingly fragmented parliaments.

So why are some politicians prominent in national politics when the national parties that they lead have never had much success at the national level? Why do some parties experience relatively more, or earlier, success in European Parliament elections? Why are parties able to generate electoral buzz by criticizing the European Union or Brussels elites? What should mainstream, established parties do when competing against these parties? And what are the implications for government formation, policy-making, and political representation?

These questions touch on important themes that lie at the very heart of European politics today. They get at the interplay between national and European politics. They ask why populist and anti-EU views have become so omnipresent in European politics. They even touch on why voters feel disenfranchised or unrepresented by mainstream political parties and politics. And they ask how parties compete in elections, especially when smaller parties that challenge the system experience electoral success.

Given their importance, we must carefully consider how best to answer these and many other similar questions surrounding European politics. That is precisely what this book seeks to do. In addition to offering answers to these questions and many others, this book aims to discuss the *tools* and *approaches* necessary to understand politics systematically. That way, when new questions about politics and policy arise, readers of this book will be able to answer them even when this book does not. In other words, we hope to introduce students to the research on European politics and the reasoning that underpins that research so they can engage in research themselves. In doing so, our book covers the foundations of European politics.

We argue that to understand European politics we must accept two premises. First, we must take the interplay between European and national-level politics seriously and study the two levels simultaneously. We would not be able to understand the prominence of politicians like Nigel Farage and Marine Le Pen, and thus important trends across European politics, without understanding the interplay of national and European politics. Second, we must take guidance from a theoretical **model of politics**. A theoretical model helps us to make our assumptions about politics explicit, and ensures that our arguments are logically consistent. A model allows us to zoom in on essential parts of politics—e.g. how electoral systems work, how voters choose to support political candidates and parties, how parties compete, and how laws get made. Models provide us with an understanding of similarities and differences across political systems and levels of government. They allow us to make comparisons and to test arguments about how politics works. Such an approach is more general than one that simply looks at the politics of individual countries, e.g. France, Germany, Poland, or the United Kingdom. Indeed, the examples so far show that similar patterns can occur in more than one country and that we can learn about general phenomena through comparison.

But why focus on Europe? Why read a whole book, or take a whole class on European politics? Again, we believe there are two reasons related to the stories we have just told. First, Europe is home to the largest number and variety of democratic governments anywhere in the world. If we want to understand democracy, its nuances, even its fragility in supposedly stable systems, Europe is the place to look. And second, we can see EU integration as an experiment in supranational governance—democratic governance above the level of the nation-state—that requires explaining and understanding. Even for students living in other areas of the world, understanding how European democracy works is extremely important for understanding how the EU influences world politics. It can provide insights into how democracy and international integration work all over the world.

The remainder of this introductory chapter discusses our comparative analytical approach to the study of European politics. It then introduces the core concept of democracy, which is fundamental to our understanding European politics, and discusses how democracy has developed across the European continent over time, paying attention to theories that seek to explain its development. Finally, we provide a road map for the remainder of the book and explain its organization. In this chapter and throughout the book we will take a theoretical and topic-based, rather than country-based, approach. But, of course, we will repeatedly refer to politics in different countries across Europe to offer examples of the concepts and ideas that we introduce.

1.1 Political Analysis as Model-Building

We have said that our approach to European politics will be comparative in nature, but that means that we require a basis for comparison. For that we require **theory**. Theory offers a simplified version of reality—we can think of it as a model—that allows us to tell a logically consistent story about how different social and political factors relate to one another. It involves making assumptions about the world. A generalizable theory, or model, provides a basis for comparison across different cases and for the testing of different ideas, or hypotheses, about how politics works. With a comparative model-based approach, we can explore political phenomena by comparing people's actions within and across countries and political systems.

To better understand why we require a model, we must first consider the purpose that models serve. We can start by imagining a visit to a shop where we purchase a kit of a model airplane. The model plane may resemble a real plane in some ways, but diverge from it in others. Some model kits seek to precisely replicate to scale the visual aspects of a plane, but the model may not fly. Other kits may be less true in scale and detail while enabling the model to actually fly. All of these representations of airplanes fulfil a particular function for understanding aspects of a real plane, but the process of simplification means that some aspects are lost. None of the airplane models is wrong, but they are useful for different purposes—the first for understanding what an airplane looks like and the second for understanding flight. With our model in hand, we could go to an airport and observe actual airplanes. If we have a flying model, we could compare our model to the actual airplanes to help us understand what makes real planes fly. If we have a scale model, we could use our model to identify different parts of a plane and compare across airplane types.

Political scientists are much like model builders constructing a model plane. They build models of decision-making within societies to understand the nature of politics. **Politics** can be conceived as a subset of human behaviour in which a set of individuals uses power to influence decisions that affect both themselves and society as a whole. Many political interactions are strategic, meaning how one person behaves influences the choices and actions of others in society. These interactions can become very complex, so we need to create models to simplify reality and better understand various facets of these relationships. Political science model builders, just like model airplane builders, seek to construct models that preserve the most important aspects of the world as they see it, and they strip away the parts that are less necessary to answer the questions they wish to ask. And different models can help to answer different questions.

Once a particular model has been developed, it can be used to understand politics in many different settings and environments. Using models allows us to take a comparative approach. We can examine how the model fits in some contexts, and how it might need to be tweaked in others. This book will first introduce a theoretical model of democracy and democratic government, and we will then apply the model repeatedly to understand different aspects of democracy in different settings across Europe. The model will discuss the basic linkages between voters and politicians. In particular, we will assume a **delegation** model of democracy, in which citizens possess ultimate political authority, but delegate decision-making authority to politicians by electing them to office, who in turn delegate authority further to specific politicians holding positions in governments, the bureaucracy, or to the EU. The process of delegation is determined by **institutions**—the rules and norms that shape social interactions—such as those that govern elections or that determine the relationships between the branches of government. This process is often organized and guided by political parties. In other words, we view democracy as a **chain of delegation** that links voters to the political decision-making process. But the precise details of how the chain of delegation works differ across countries and political systems. It is these differences that make European politics so interesting, and we explore them throughout this book. In the next chapter, we present the main theoretical tools that we will use, together with our model of democracy, but we first discuss the nature of democracy and its development across Europe.

1.2 Democracy and Democratization

Democratic governance lies at the heart of European politics, but there is no single agreed-upon definition of democracy. We can, however, distinguish between two basic conceptualizations: a minimalist conceptualization and a maximalist one. **Minimalist conceptualizations of democracy** focus on the presence of free and fair elections and electoral turnover. Schumpeter, an early proponent of this view, considers democracy as "free competition for a free vote" (Schumpeter, 1942, 271). Maximalist definitions, such as the one put forward by Dahl (1971), do not dismiss electoral competition, but additionally stress participation, broad inclusion in political processes, guarantees of basic rights, and the rule of law.

From a minimalist perspective, electoral democracy is a form of government in which ultimate authority, at least in theory if not always in practice, lies with citizens who then empower politicians to make decisions on their behalf. The principles of electoral competition and the legitimacy of a political opposition separate democracy from autocracy at the most fundamental level. Empirically, countries can be considered a democracy from this perspective if the chief executive is elected, the parliament is elected, there is more than one party competing in elections, and there has been alternation in power under identical electoral rules (Cheibub et al., 2010).

Maximalist conceptualizations of democracy require more from a political system before calling it a democracy. Notions of **liberal democracy** come into play; these include guarantees regarding civil rights, minority protection, equality before the law, associational rights, and the ability of the judiciary to constrain the executive. Politicians must protect the basic human rights of citizens, including those of the people who did not vote for them as leaders. Citizens must also be able to participate freely in politics, usually by electing leaders in free and fair elections, but also through protest and speech. Moreover, elected politicians are supposed to represent the views of citizens. There are many different forms that representation can take, which will be discussed in detail in subsequent chapters, in particular in Chapter 7. Politicians may seek to determine the will of voters and turn it into policy, they may make decisions that they feel are in the best interest of all voters, or they may represent voters merely by the fact that they come from a similar background to the voters who elected them. Liberal democracy has recently been challenged in Europe, with a few countries experiencing **democratic backsliding**. Hungary's Prime Minister Viktor Orbán, in a speech in July 2014 talked of turning Hungary into an 'illiberal state', while Poland's president has engaged in attacks on the judiciary (see Chapter 14.2). For now, though, we simply wish to ask how, when, and why basic features of democracy arose in Europe in the first place. This, of course, is no small question.

Discussions of democratization often focus on the interaction between politics and economics (e.g. Lipset, 1959; Acemoglu et al., 2019), and the gradual development of the nation-state (e.g. Tilly, 1990; North and Weingast, 1989). Many have argued that the ability of citizens to restrain political leaders and to exert control over would-be dictators lies at the heart of both economic and democratic development. Ruling over a country comes with a tremendous amount of power; if rulers are to produce economic growth for their country, they must be able to reliably promise not to confiscate property and to protect property rights. Citizens must feel that their wealth is safe if they are to have an incentive to generate more wealth and to invest in a country. As Olson (1993) has famously written, democratic institutions can offer a mechanism to governments for creating **credible commitments**—reliable promises that citizens can believe—offering citizens the security that they need to invest, safe in the knowledge that the government will not expropriate their wealth.

Box 1.1 METHODS AND MEASUREMENT: Measuring Democracy

To understand how democratization has progressed, we must measure levels of democracy over time. This is not an easy task and there is no single, correct method for doing so. Different political scientists have taken different approaches. To measure democracy, we must first decide how to conceptualize it. Some scholars, most notably Przeworski et al. (2000), conceive of democracy as binary—an either/or prospect. Either a country is a democracy or it is not. Often this judgement is made on the basis of a minimalist definition. There is a set of countries that most observers would agree are democratic, and another set that most would agree are not. Of course, there are some cases that truly lie in the middle, which makes a classification difficult. Moreover, the binary classification can be criticized for glossing over important details.

In contrast to Przeworski and his colleagues, other scholars seek to measure the degree of democracy, not just its presence. A project dedicated to measuring the degree and depth of democracy—the V-Dem project—asks country experts to rate their country on different aspects of democracy. The V-Dem project also seeks out experts on the historical development of countries to gain insights back in time. This approach can produce rich, fine-grained information on democracy. However, these measures require us to believe that experts are able to accurately judge democracy levels on these specific indicators going back over many decades.

Lastly, there are other projects run both by academics and think tanks that seek to use coders to code levels of democracy on the basis of set criteria. The Polity project is an example of such a project run by academics and Freedom Scores are produced by the Freedom House think tank. For these scores to be accurate, different experts must apply the same rubric to very different countries in the same manner. In sum, there are many different ways of conceiving of democracy and measuring it, and there is no definitive answer as to which approach is best.

To understand how a government's ability to make credible commitments can lead to economic growth, consider the following story. Imagine a monarch, a ruler with absolute power, who commands a strong military and seeks to conquer more territory abroad. The monarch will need money to pay for his wars—he must buy weapons, transport his troops, and pay them their wages—and this gives him an incentive to steal wealth from his citizens. Indeed, there is a strong relationship between the development and transformation of the state and war, as outlined by Tilly (1990): state institutions, including a bureaucracy, taxation system, and conscription, developed as a consequence of the need to fund expensive warfare.

Moreover, as an absolute dictator, the monarch has the power to confiscate wealth. If he tries to promise his citizens that, if they just help him out, he will not to take more of their wealth, they will not believe him. They know that he needs as much money as he can get and he has the power to take whatever he wants. In turn, they have an incentive to hide any wealth that they possess, or simply to not create any in the first place, as they know that it will just end up in the monarch's hands. In other words, it is not enough for a powerful monarch to say that he will not steal wealth from his citizens; he has to make them believe him. If citizens have reason to believe the government, the government may be better able to raise revenue through taxation and borrowing because citizens do not fear that the government will steal their wealth. Instead, citizens can expect a return on their investment in the state through the provision of public infrastructure, or repayment of their loans with interest.

So how can a monarch credibly commit to not stealing citizens' wealth? Something must happen to reduce the power of the monarch relative to the citizenry. North and Weingast (1989) have argued that just such a transition occurred in England during the seventeenth century following the English Civil War and the Glorious Revolution. The House of Stuart took control of the English crown with the coronation of King James I in 1603, but immediately faced financial difficulties and trouble repaying debts incurred during previous wars. Eventually the crown, after effectively trying to steal wealth from citizens, faced an uprising. The resulting English Civil War led to the beheading of King Charles I and the 'Republican Period' under the leadership of Oliver Cromwell. Following Cromwell's death from natural causes, the monarchy was restored, first under Charles II and then James II. However, James II was himself overthrown in 1688 in the Glorious Revolution, leading parliament to put William III and Mary II on the throne, but with stricter limits on the power of the monarch, making the monarch subordinate to a ruling class represented in parliament.

North and Weingast argue that, after the Glorious Revolution, William and Mary were much more successful at raising money and could borrow at much lower interest rates than monarchs before them. Presumably, the fact that two of the three previous monarchs had been executed or forced into exile would have given William and Mary pause before attempting to exert too much power. In other words, according to North and Weingast, it took decades of political upheaval, executions, civil war, and the threat of exile to create a form of restricted monarchy capable of credibly committing to not usurping wealth. Gradually, this form of government would transform into the British democracy we know today.

The North and Weingast story suggests that the presence of political institutions that create credible commitments (and at least move in the direction of democracy) lead to conditions conducive to wealth creation. Indeed, there is now substantial evidence that democracy leads to increased wealth across countries (see e.g. Acemoglu et al., 2019). However, the story also suggests that increased wealth may have helped solidify England's new democratic institutions. The development of a wealthy English middle class, represented in parliament, is key to understanding how credible commitments and institutions eventually led to the establishment of democracy. Democracy may help lead to wealth creation, but wealth also seems to be a requirement for democracy to flourish.

Indeed, another set of literature suggests that the causal arrow runs from wealth to democracy, as well. In his book on the social origins of dictatorship and democracy, Moore (1966) argued that the existence of a middle class is a prerequisite for the emergence of democracy. Succinctly and memorably, Moore wrote 'No Bourgeoisie, No Democracy'. He quite simply meant that democracy cannot emerge in societies without a stable, wealthy middle class. Power divided across a stable middle class with the ability and incentive to rein in autocratic leaders is necessary for democracy to flourish. **Modernization theory**, first posited by Lipset (1959), also suggests that democracy can only take hold in a society that is sufficiently wealthy, urban, and educated. Only in such a society do citizens have the ability and time to pay attention to and become informed about politics. Democracy requires knowledgeable citizens who can hold political elites to account, and who have enough wealth and leisure time that they are no longer solely concerned with surviving, giving them time to pay attention to politics.

Arguably, many of these conditions only appeared in Europe during the late nineteenth century following the Industrial Revolution. Some of the major political parties across Europe, as well as other political institutions, can trace their origins to this time. The German Social Democratic Party, for example, traces its roots to 1863, while the UK Labour Party was founded in 1900. These parties grew out of efforts to organize labour in the factories. The Industrial Revolution brought working classes together into the same spaces, where labour activists could inform and organize them, forming nascent parties and political organizations.

Research on democracy and wealth—regardless of whether we conceive of wealth causing democracy or democracy leading to wealth—suggests that stable democracy takes time to develop. Support for democracy and democratic attitudes among citizens must develop and grow. As a result, researchers have made a distinction between **consolidated** and **unconsolidated democracy** (see Rustow, 1970; Linz and Stepan, 1996; Svolik, 2008). When countries first transition to democracy, we may assume that their democracy is unconsolidated. The possibility that the country could slip back into an authoritarian regime is still reasonably high. Over time, as democracy takes hold in a country, the likelihood of the country slipping back into autocracy diminishes. Democratic norms become entrenched among the citizens and political elites. We can say that these countries have become consolidated democracies.

Democracy first began to emerge across Europe during the late nineteenth century. While the path to democracy was relatively smooth in some places, it was much rockier in others. The United Kingdom, along with Denmark, the Netherlands, and Sweden, followed a rather straightforward path, steadily and incrementally increasing rights of citizens. Other countries experienced more ups and downs, with some movement towards democratization and then movement back in the other direction. Germany is perhaps the most notable example, having had several years of democratic governance during the interwar years—a period known as the Weimar Republic—before the rise of the Nazi party and Hitler's dictatorship responsible for starting the Second World War and for the Holocaust, the genocide of European Jews. But Germany is not alone in following this pattern. Indeed, Italy, France, Greece followed an uneven path towards democratic government. Many central and eastern European countries, such as the Baltic states, Hungary, and Poland, also experienced some aspects of democracy during the interwar years, only to fall under the Soviet Communist umbrella after the Second World War.

We can plot these different paths to democracy using data on levels of democracy over time. Figure 1.1 uses data from the V-Dem project, based on surveys of country experts, to show democratization in several European countries including France, Germany, Greece, Hungary, Poland, Spain, Sweden, and the United Kingdom. Higher values indicate higher levels of democracy. Each panel shows a different trajectory towards democracy. The upper-left quadrant shows the linear path followed by Sweden and the UK. The upper right shows the rapid democratization of France and Germany following the Second World War. The bottom left panel depicts the rockier paths followed by Greece and Spain, with Greece experiencing periods of military government, and Spain not fully democratizing until the death of the long-term dictator Francisco Franco. Finally, the lower right depicts Hungary and Poland, rapidly democratized following the collapse of Communism, but which have recently experienced backsliding, a pattern that we will discuss in more depth in the final chapter of the book.

Inspired by these disparate patterns of democratic development, Ziblatt (2017) has argued that the path that countries followed was, in part, due to the development of political parties, and in particular the success of the conservative right in organizing electorally successful parties. When the societal elites, who were most likely conservative and seeking to protect their privileged position, were able to organize electorally successful parties and had confidence that

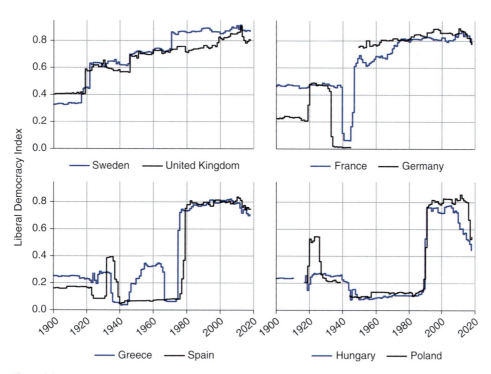

Figure 1.1 Paths to Democracy for Several European Democracies

they could maintain power via electoral politics, even as more people were allowed to vote, democracy fared well. Where this did not happen, democracy faced a harder road.

Although many European nations developed fledgling democracy in the wake of the First World War, their democracy was largely unconsolidated, and the Second World War snuffed out much of that progress. But in the aftermath of the war, with the financial and military support of the US, democracy emerged across much of western Europe. Nevertheless, authoritarian regimes still held sway in Portugal and Spain; Communist regimes took hold across eastern and southeastern Europe; and Greece suffered a military coup and military government from 1967 to 1974. But by the mid-1980s, democratic government had arrived in Greece, Portugal, and Spain. And the collapse of Communism, starting in 1989, led to a spread of democratic regimes across central and eastern Europe.

The EU has played a particularly important role in fostering democracy. In the late 1980s, even as cracks began appearing in many countries' Communist facades, few people anticipated the depth and breadth of change that the autumn of 1989 and its aftermath would bring. In November 1989, the Berlin Wall, which had divided East Berlin from West Berlin for nearly thirty years, and which had symbolized the divisions between Communist central and eastern Europe and the democratic free-market societies of western Europe, came crashing down. West and East Germany reunified in 1990, and by 1992, post-Communist countries from across central and eastern Europe were adopting democratic institutions (with varying degrees of success), clamouring for access to western European markets, and hoping to join the EU. The EU saw its appeal to these newly democratic countries as a carrot that it could use to entice them to fully embrace democratic change.

This was not the first time that the EU had seen itself a force for bringing democracy to European countries. Arguably, the entire raison d'être of European integration, since its inception following the Second World War, has been to secure peace and democracy in Europe, through the process of economic and political integration. But even putting aside the grand visions of the 'founding fathers' of European integration, European institutions had found themselves previously dealing with the fall of authoritarian regimes in their own backyard, even if not on such a scale. Greece first applied for membership in the fledgling **European Economic Community** (EEC)—the precursor organization to the EU—in 1959, and signed an association agreement in 1961. But cooperation between the EEC and Greece was put on hold during the period of Greece's military dictatorship from 1967 until 1974. Following the restoration of democracy, Greece eventually joined the EU on 1 January 1981. Likewise, Spain and Portugal were not allowed into the 'club' until they fully embraced democracy. With the collapse of the authoritarian Franco and Salazar regimes in Spain and Portugal, both countries joined the European Community on 1 January 1986. The EU viewed the prospect of membership for these countries as a mechanism to entice them to fully embrace democratic change.

The assumption among academics and non-academics alike is that the European integration has been a force for fostering and consolidating democracy across Europe, both in western Europe, and across the post-Communist countries of central and eastern Europe. Indeed, the European Union as an organization won the Nobel Peace Prize in 2012 and the EU's official stance is that 'The prospect of membership is a powerful stimulus for democratic and economic reforms in countries that want to become EU members' (European Commission, 2020a). For western European countries that developed or revived democratic institutions in the immediate aftermath of the Second World War, European integration has helped to increase wealth, which has likely led to a quicker consolidation of democracy. For countries looking to join the EU, the EU sets out requirements for democratic governance that prospective member states must meet. These requirements were formalized after the fall of Communism and before the newly free states of central and eastern Europe could join. They are known as the **Copenhagen Criteria** because they were decided at a summit meeting of member state governments in Copenhagen in 1993 and they include:

1. Political criteria: stability of institutions guaranteeing democracy, the rule of law, human rights, and respect for and protection of minorities;

2. Economic criteria: a functioning market economy and the capacity to cope with competition and market forces;

3. Administrative and institutional capacity to effectively implement the acquis (the entire corpus of EU law) and ability to take on the obligations of membership.

But even before 1993, it was clear that member states had to be democracies with free-market economies. In central and eastern Europe, the assumption has been that the allure of membership in a 'rich nations' club like the EU led governments to undertake democratic reforms and to do what was necessary to gain entry. Many scholars of EU expansion have argued that the EU provides both carrots and sticks to potential member states to undertake reforms that foster democracy, and that these have largely worked (Vachudová, 2005; Schimmelfennig and Sedelmeier, 2004).

The EU has developed tools for punishing countries that do not meet these standards, although many question their effectiveness. It has the power to sanction governments that fail to live up to democratic standards and can even suspend them from participation in European-level government. However, no member has ever actually been suspended. Austria was briefly sanctioned by other EU states in 2000 after the far-right Freedom Party, led by Jörg Haider, joined a coalition government as a junior partner with the main centre-right Austrian People's Party. Haider was known for his tendencies towards neo-Nazi, anti-immigrant, and anti-Muslim rhetoric. But the sanctions were lifted after a few months.

While the EU has developed legal mechanisms to punish member states for engaging in undemocratic behaviour, in practice, sanctioning members is difficult. Suspension of a member state's voting rights in the Council requires the unanimous consent of all other remaining member states. If the rogue member state has just one ally, that ally can block any sanctions. In short, it is much easier for the EU to wield power over candidates for membership than over member states. Once a state becomes a member, it can **backslide** or engage in undemocratic actions, and it is difficult for other member states to punish the offending government (Kelemen, 2017). Indeed, we have witnessed some backsliding in some states in central and eastern Europe, most notably Hungary and Poland. We will discuss the issues with democracy in these and other countries throughout the book, and return to questions on the future of democracy in Europe in the concluding chapter.

1.3 Citizenship and Participation

One of the key features of democracy is the right of citizens to participate in politics, in particular through voting. Who has the right to vote in elections and when they achieve this right is a core question in the development of democratic government. In many nascent nineteenth-century democracies, only a small percentage of male landowners were considered citizens with the right to vote. Over time, the **franchise**, or right to vote, was often granted first to all men, and then to women. In the early nineteenth-century United Kingdom, the franchise was primarily limited to wealthy, male landowners. By the late nineteenth century the voter rolls had expanded significantly, and many more citizens were eligible to vote. Still many potential voters remained excluded from politics, including all women. Universal suffrage for all adults was finally established in 1928 in Britain.

In 1906, Finnish women became the first European women to gain the right to vote and to stand for parliament, at least at a national level. Denmark, Norway and several other countries followed soon after. Women in both Germany and the UK (but only those over the age of 30 and meeting certain property qualifications in the case of the UK) were given suffrage rights in 1918. However, women in some other parts of Europe had longer to wait. In France, women first gained the right to vote in 1944, and women in Switzerland were not allowed to participate in federal elections until 1971. In one Swiss canton, Appenzell Innerrhoden, women were not permitted to participate in local elections until 1991 when the Swiss constitutional court finally forced the canton to allow women to take part. While today we find the notion that women would be excluded from voting or politics unacceptable, there are still many arguments about who should be a citizen and, therefore, also have the right to vote, for example second-generation immigrants.

Much like issues surrounding gender, issues of identity and culture, especially regarding citizenship and voter participation, often tap an emotive reaction in people. These issues raise questions about whether people who look, act, and speak differently than a majority group have a right to participate. These are fundamental questions about democracy—can societies exclude people from public services or politics based upon heritage, ethnicity, or race? In some instances, exclusionary policies may be supported by a substantial majority of voters, but they clearly trample on the rights of minorities. Moreover, while some policies may be unambiguously racist and illegal, other policies may fall into a grey area. For example, many countries in Europe (e.g. Austria, Denmark, and France among others) have had public debates over banning clothing and veils worn by some Muslim women, including the so-called Burqa bans. Such policies are often couched in general terms around public safety, saying that no one, Muslims and non-Muslims alike, may wear clothing in public which conceals one's face as it may interfere with law enforcement. But, of course, the effects of such policies fall disproportionately on certain communities, namely Muslim women.

More generally, who has a duty to pay taxes and a right to receive the benefits of state services? Who can be a citizen of a country? Many would decry policies that exclude entire classes of people from political participation or access to public services on the basis of race, religion, gender, or culture as wrong, discriminatory, and anti-democratic. Nevertheless, such policies have a long and odious history in many countries around the world, including many European countries, perhaps most notably, and insidiously, during Nazi Germany culminating in the genocide of European Jews.

The European Union today is based on common values that include the respect for human rights and dignity as well as the principles of equality and non-discrimination, incorporated in the Charter of Fundamental Rights of the European Union. At the same time, people are excluded from political participation and public services on the basis of citizenship all of the time. Such exclusion is perfectly legal and few people are particularly upset by it. Nor are such practices viewed as particularly undemocratic. People who are not deemed to be citizens of a country often cannot participate in politics even if they reside in the particular region. New immigrants to a country, for example, are rarely eligible for citizenship immediately, and depending upon the country, citizenship can be very difficult to attain. Even children born in the country where their parents currently reside may not be automatically eligible for citizenship. Countries across Europe now provide paths to citizenship for immigrants, but the process can be difficult. Often it requires one to demonstrate an understanding of the local culture and language through citizenship tests or interviews, as well as many years of residence in the country. Thus, the citizenship process is also about building new national identities and attempting to ensure integration into the community. There is a direct link between the legal concept of citizenship (and therefore the right to participate), and culture, religion, ethnicity, language, race, and identity.

The process of European integration has begun to change notions of citizenship and rights for participation. Since 1993, the notion of European Union citizenship has existed in addition to, but not as a replacement of, national citizenship. Citizens of any EU member state have the right to live and work in any other EU member state, with the same access to benefits and state services as citizens of that state. They may also participate in local and European, but not national, elections. Thus, EU citizens have some participatory rights all across European Union member states regardless of which European citizenship they hold.

1.4 Our Approach and Scope

In addition to taking a theoretical approach, this book also seeks to understand European politics through the use of data. We draw on data about the attitudes that voters hold, the positions that parties take on issues, and who wins seats in parliament following elections to name just a few examples. In fact, we have already used data in this chapter to compare trajectories of democratization across several countries. Whenever possible, we will seek to visualize politics using data, which we believe will lead to deeper understanding of political phenomena. Using data in this manner also follows directly from our comparative approach. However, this means that we have to decide on which countries to present data for and which not.

Europe is a large continent without clearly defined borders, especially on its eastern edge. To take just one example, some would consider Turkey a part of Europe, while others would not. Turkey clearly straddles two continents no matter how one looks at it—geographically, culturally, and politically. It borders Greece and its largest city, Istanbul, is split down the middle by the Bosporus Strait, often considered the geographic dividing line between Europe and Asia. Its history is deeply intertwined with that of western Europe, but today, in contrast to western Europe, its primary religion is Islam, and it holds much in common culturally with Middle Eastern countries. It has experienced periods of democratic governance and aspects of electoral democracy, but it has also experienced military coups and authoritarian regimes.

Nor is Turkey the only borderline case—we could also ask similar questions about Russia, Ukraine, Belarus, Georgia and many other countries. We decide to draw the border for our selection of countries further west. Our reasoning is twofold. First, as we move east, democratic governance has been weaker and slower to develop. This book focuses on questions of democratic governance, and while it touches on questions of democratization, exploring such questions with respect to many of these eastern European countries is beyond the book's scope. The second concern is more pragmatic, namely data availability.

Many of the types of data that we will rely on throughout the book are simply not available for these countries. Primarily for this reason we exclude the Western Balkan countries from the book. When we present data, tables, and visualizations, we will focus on the twenty-seven member states of the European Union[1] along with Iceland, Norway, Switzerland, and the United Kingdom. These four countries are closely tied to the European Union through their membership in the European Economic Area (Iceland and Norway), through other similar arrangements (Switzerland), or are a former member state (the UK). Additionally, there is similar data availability for these countries as for EU member states. The countries we cover are highlighted on the map presented in Figure 1.2. We are not always able to include all of these countries in every table and figure due to data availability. Nevertheless, we strive for full coverage of these countries whenever possible.

1.5 Plan for the Book

The structure of this book flows from our theoretical approach to politics. The chapters are arranged in the order of the democratic chain of delegation from the beginning to the end—from citizens, the principals, who vote for politicians, their agents, acting within political parties, through to parliaments and governments, who make policy, and on to bureaucracies and courts, which implement and interpret laws. Figure 1.3 shows the basic thematic structure of the book.

We begin in Chapters 2 and 3 by presenting our general theoretical approach and the theoretical tools that we need to study democracy. Chapter 2 focuses on the nature of delegation in democracies, while Chapter 3 covers the multilevel nature of European politics. We then proceed to examine citizens and how they vote for the politicians who will represent them. We first focus on the ideologies and issues that help to structure political decision-making for voters in Chapter 4, and then discuss how voters make decisions about who to vote for in Chapter 5. Following these chapters, Chapter 6 moves on to discuss electoral systems—the rules that link voters' choices at the polls to parties and politicians that hold office—and also direct democracy—the rules that sometimes allow citizens to bypass these elected politicians. We discuss how these rules impact political representation—in other words, how the political system reflects voters and their attitudes—in Chapter 7. We then move to examine political parties (Chapter 8), organizations which are instrumental in structuring the chain of delegation, and we discuss how they compete for office (Chapter 9). Finally, we discuss the process of government formation, and the relationship between elections to parliaments and the formation of the executive branch in Chapter 10. We discuss how governments make policy in Chapter 11 and what types of policy actually get made in Chapter 12. Lastly, we discuss the role of courts in overseeing the political system and examine how law functions across European states in Chapter 13. We conclude in our final chapter by examining challenges and possibilities for the future of European democracy.

---

[1] Austria, Belgium, Bulgaria, Croatia, Republic of Cyprus, Czech Republic, Denmark, Estonia, Finland, France, Germany, Greece, Hungary, Ireland, Italy, Latvia, Lithuania, Luxembourg, Malta, Netherlands, Poland, Portugal, Romania, Slovakia, Slovenia, Spain, and Sweden

Figure 1.2 Map of Europe: Countries Covered in the Book

The book also includes a few noteworthy features. First, key terms and concepts appear in boldface the first time that they are mentioned in each chapter. Each boldfaced term is also defined in the glossary at the end of the book. Second, the book includes breakout boxes that go deeper into some aspect of politics or how to study it. We will use three types of boxes—**Methods and Measurement**, **Case Studies**, and **Controversies and Debates**. Methods and Measurement boxes will provide more detailed information about methodological concerns or examine questions about how to measure particular facets of politics. Case Study boxes will discuss particular examples in greater detail to demonstrate a concept or to show how it applies in real-world politics. Finally, Controversies and Debates boxes will discuss disagreements in the academic literature about both theoretical concepts and empirical findings. The information contained in these boxes is useful for gaining a deeper understanding of European politics, how to study it, and the academic debates that have arisen.

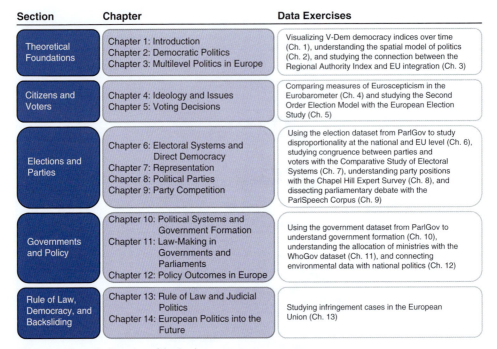

Section	Chapter	Data Exercises
Theoretical Foundations	Chapter 1: Introduction Chapter 2: Democratic Politics Chapter 3: Multilevel Politics in Europe	Visualizing V-Dem democracy indices over time (Ch. 1), understanding the spatial model of politics (Ch. 2), and studying the connection between the Regional Authority Index and EU integration (Ch. 3)
Citizens and Voters	Chapter 4: Ideology and Issues Chapter 5: Voting Decisions	Comparing measures of Euroscepticism in the Eurobarometer (Ch. 4) and studying the Second Order Election Model with the European Election Study (Ch. 5)
Elections and Parties	Chapter 6: Electoral Systems and Direct Democracy Chapter 7: Representation Chapter 8: Political Parties Chapter 9: Party Competition	Using the election dataset from ParlGov to study disproportionality at the national and EU level (Ch. 6), studying congruence between parties and voters with the Comparative Study of Electoral Systems (Ch. 7), understanding party positions with the Chapel Hill Expert Survey (Ch. 8), and dissecting parliamentary debate with the ParlSpeech Corpus (Ch. 9)
Governments and Policy	Chapter 10: Political Systems and Government Formation Chapter 11: Law-Making in Governments and Parliaments Chapter 12: Policy Outcomes in Europe	Using the government dataset from ParlGov to understand government formation (Ch. 10), understanding the allocation of ministries with the WhoGov dataset (Ch. 11), and connecting environmental data with national politics (Ch. 12)
Rule of Law, Democracy, and Backsliding	Chapter 13: Rule of Law and Judicial Politics Chapter 14: European Politics into the Future	Studying infringement cases in the European Union (Ch. 13)

Figure 1.3 Thematic Overview of the Book

Finally, we believe that a state-of-the-art investigation of the fundamentals of European politics should come with a basic foundation in data-driven analysis. Thus, we have created an extensive set of online materials, focusing on the diversity of political data that can be used to study European politics. Each chapter is accompanied by material that allows for more in-depth study of the concepts in it, including many interactive data visualizations, discussion questions, and activities. These activities are described in a box at the end of each chapter. We encourage all students to use these data and activities to get a more complete picture of the contemporary study of European politics.

Online Data Exercise: V-Dem Dataset

In the interactive online exercise accompanying this chapter, you can explore the V-Dem democracy indices that are presented in this chapter. The exercise will expand on two things you learned in this chapter: the concepts of minimalist and maximalist conceptualizations of democracy and how democracy is related to EU integration.

 Take your learning further with this interactive data exercise, available at
www.foundationsofeuropeanpolitics.com

 For additional material and resources, including multiple-choice questions, web links, and more, please visit the online resources: **www.oup.com/he/devries1e**

Part 1

Theoretical Foundations

2 Democratic Politics

This chapter introduces a theoretical toolbox for studying democracy in Europe. The analytical concepts of this toolbox will be useful for understanding many of the different aspects of democratic politics in Europe that are discussed throughout the book. Later chapters will continually refer back to the model that we present here.

To understand democratic governance in Europe, we must model it. In this chapter, we build our model of democracy that will serve as an analytic tool to be used in the chapters that follow. Our goal is not to convey every possible detail of the democratic process. Making our model every bit as complicated as the real world would both be impossible and defeat the purpose of the model. Rather we focus on what we believe to be the essential elements for understanding democratic **politics** in Europe. Having a model in mind will help us to make sense of political events and developments. The model provides a single, coherent framework for comparison and analysis and yields tools that we can apply to understand voting, elections, government formation, policy-making, and outcomes.

2.1 A Model of Democracy: The Median Voter

We take as our starting point the premise that societies constantly need to make collective choices. People must jointly decide about what goes on around them. For example, people living together within a community might need to decide whether they should have access to communal resources, e.g. parks, drinking water, or roads. If they decide that they need or want these resources, several questions arise. How should the community pay for them? Should people be taxed, and if so how? How should the resources be distributed across groups within society? How should different economic activities which may rely on these communal resources—such as business and farming—be regulated? There are many different answers to these questions and different governance structures for making these important decisions. We begin by thinking about a few possible ways to arrive at answers to these questions.

One, decidedly undemocratic, option would be to have a single person who makes all decisions on behalf of everyone. We could imagine that this person is simply able to dictate outcomes, stating what the decision is, and then implementing it. We could imagine a benevolent dictator, a person with absolute power, who makes decisions by seeking to maximize the welfare of all individuals in society. But we could also envision a less benevolent dictator, making decisions to maximize personal gain, extracting as much from society as possible and leaving little for others.

Even under a benevolent dictator—a leader who exercises absolute political power with the interests of the population in mind—members of society may raise questions of fairness.

They may ask whether it is fair that one person gets to determine policies that affect all of society. Any autocrat, benevolent or not, will likely arrive at decisions that make some in society better off while leaving others worse off. The autocrat may make decisions with the best of intentions and those decisions could be best for society as a whole. Nevertheless, citizens who are left worse off could reasonably question the authority of the autocrat to make such decisions. They may view the process that led to a decision, no matter how reasonable the decision itself, as unfair.

So what might a fair process look like? There is no simple or right answer to this question— political theorists have debated this question for, without exaggeration, thousands of years. It could be a process that ensures that every citizen has a voice, such as the principle of one-person-one-vote, where everyone's vote counts equally and the majority rules. Or it could be a system that puts greater value on protecting the rights of minority groups. Of course, in certain instances, systems that protect minority rights could undermine majority rule, even if these systems are perceived by others as more fair. Another fair process may be the involvement of as many actors and interests as possible to achieve outcomes that are accepted by as many in society as possible. In other words, decisions should be consensual. A common denominator is the desire to design a system in which every member of society gets to have input into a decision, no matter how small their input may be. Thus, we will start building our model of democracy from the premise that citizens vote on policies that they would like to see become law, what we will call policy outcomes, and their vote impacts the collective decision arrived at through the policy process.

But how do citizens' **preferences** feed into the democratic process of making collective decisions? Imagine that our society is trying to collectively decide how much money to spend on constructing a new park on a currently vacant plot of land. On the one extreme, the society could leave everything as is, spend no money at all, and allow the plot of land to grow wild. The land would not be usable for recreation, but no one would have to contribute any money towards construction costs. On the other extreme, the society could agree to build an elaborate park with playing fields, swimming pools, tennis courts, and other amenities, but it would mean charging every citizen 100 Euros more in taxes. And we could imagine the entire range of possibilities lying between these two extremes. We could arrange these possibilities along a line according to the amount of money they cost from 0 to 100. For simplicity (remember we are building a model) we will assume that the quality of the park increases linearly with the amount of money spent. In other words, for every additional 1 Euro in tax income collected, the park gets an additional 1 Euro worth of amenities. We assume some people prefer to spend no money while others prefer to pay the full 100 Euros to fund the park project, and many more lie somewhere in the middle.

We can depict this scenario graphically by drawing a line going from high on the left (say 100 Euros tax per individual for a fully equipped communal park) to low on the right (no taxes and an empty lot). We draw the line backwards from high to low so that the high taxation-high spending outcome lies on the left of the line and the low taxation-low spending outcome lies to the right. As we will discuss later in Chapter 4 when we talk more about **ideology**, left-wing politicians are generally thought to be willing to tax citizens more in return for providing them with more state services, while right-wing politicians generally prefer to tax less in return for less involvement from the state. In many countries, this economic trade-off between taxing and spending represents the primary conflict between parties and voters, and we often refer to it as the general **left–right dimension** of political conflict. With this model of ideology in mind, we can then make tick marks along this line to represent the preferences of each of the voters in our society. Figure 2.1 does just this.

The figure shows five individuals (A through E) each with policy preferences on the level of spending on the public park. Individual A prefers to spend the most on the park and individual E prefers to spend the least. When individuals in society want to spend different amounts of money, as they do in Figure 2.1 (and in virtually any conceivable real-life political situation), we have a political conflict. How does the society decide how much money to spend? Which park gets built? The society could have a vote and decide by **majority rule**. They could look for the policy that a majority of members of the society (voters) prefers to all other potential proposals. This proposal would match the position of the voter in the middle—the voter with an equal number of voters on one side preferring to spend less money and on the other side preferring to spend more. This voter is called the **median voter**. In Figure 2.1, this individual is voter C.

Note that the median voter does not necessarily support a policy in the middle of the line, but rather holds a position that lies in the middle of all other voters. In fact, in our example, the position of the median voter is closer to B than to D. For any set of policy outcomes that can be depicted along a line—what political scientists refer to as a one-dimensional policy space—a policy located at the position of the median voter is stable and cannot be changed by majority rule. If all possible policy proposals were to come up for a vote, the policy outcome supported by a simple majority of voters against all other possible policies would be that position of the median voter. This is known as the **median voter theorem** and was originally developed by Black (1948) and applied to the study of parties and elections by Downs (1957), as we will discuss later in Chapter 4 on ideology, Chapter 5 on voting, and Chapter 9 on party competition.

The centrality of the median voter in the study of democracy means that we should understand the conditions under which such a median voter exists. First, we need to assume that people have preferences over different policy outcomes and that they can rank outcomes in a rational manner. **Rationality** implies, for example, that when faced with three policy alternatives x, y, and z, an individual can compare each of these alternatives to each other (e.g. x is preferred over y) and rank all of them—the individual's preference ordering is complete. Moreover, the person's preferences should be logically consistent in the sense that, if the individual prefers x over y, and y over z, then the individual also should prefer x over z. We call this a **transitive preference** ordering. Individuals should strive to attain their most preferred outcome, and take actions that are likely to lead to the best possible outcome for them, contingent on what others are doing. Coincidentally, rationality does not mean that individuals

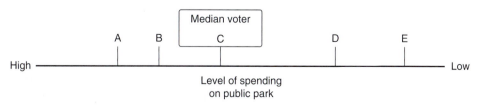

Figure 2.1 Policy Preferences on a Single Issue

are selfish, but that they pursue their own interests in a consistent way and act according to them. Such interests may, of course, include empathy towards others. Rationality also does not mean that individuals only ever act rationally. In fact, we should think about rationality as a subset of behaviour, and more of an approximation to how individuals act in politics under certain circumstances. Other considerations, such as emotions or habit, also play a role in political decision-making.

We can transfer the idea of transitive preferences to the **spatial model of politics** introduced in Figure 2.1. Implicitly, we assume in this figure that each individual prefers policy outcomes closer to their own most preferred policy compared to those policies that are further away. In other words, individuals have single-peaked preferences: the value that an individual places on a policy outcome reaches a maximum at the individual's ideal policy position and slopes away from this maximum on either side. When this assumption holds true, we will always have a median voter (with an unequal number of individuals) on a single issue or dimension.

The median voter theorem then posits that the ideal point of the median voter will win against any other policy alternative in a pairwise majority rule contest. There will always be a majority for the policy most favoured by the median voter when this policy is pitted against any other policy alternative. This position is privileged over other preferences. According to the model, policy outcomes should be close to the median voter's ideal point because this is a stable outcome. One important assumption that we have to make, though, is that political conflict is, indeed, one-dimensional. We will relax this assumption later by assuming that political decisions are often taken on several issues at the same time, and show that stable political outcomes are not guaranteed unless we make further assumptions about the political process.

We could argue, and many political scientists have, that representative democracy works well when the policy that a society decides to implement mirrors the position of this societal median voter, i.e. when there is **congruence** between the policy that the government sets and the preference of the median voter; they are one and the same. However, we also need to think carefully about what such representation implies. When the position of the median voter shifts we might expect policy to shift as well. If policy does shift with the position of the median voter, we could say that the political system is characterized by **responsiveness** to changes in the preferences of voters.

But is a highly responsive and congruent system always desirable? On the one hand, we want a system that reflects and responds to the wishes of voters. On the other hand, such a system could lead to a rapid change and policy instability if voters' preferences change unexpectedly. Going back to our example of building a park, imagine the city is halfway through building the park and all of a sudden, a group of new people move into town, making the position of the median voter shift to desire a less ambitious park. Should construction immediately halt, or should some of the structures already built be dismantled? Such actions might result from a highly dynamic, responsive, and congruent system, but it might not be desirable. We will discuss these models of **political representation** in much more depth in Chapter 7.

Generally speaking, however, we do want our democratic system to be reasonably responsive and to represent voters' interests. So how can we get there? One possibility might be direct democracy where all citizens participate and any proposal can come up for a vote. This may even happen in small communities. The Swiss cantons (federal states) of Appenzell

Innerrhoden and Glarus, for example, both still hold cantonal assemblies where all eligible voters turn up to vote on issues of local politics. In Glarus, the assembly is held every year on the first Sunday in May and it may decide certain issues including the cantonal tax rate. The Appenzell cantonal assembly holds the more dubious distinction of excluding women from participation until the late date of 1991.

Direct democracy, though, is no guarantee that the policy position of the median voter will prevail. We engage in another simple thought experiment to see why. Imagine that one person holds a position of privilege within the assembly and can decide what policy proposals can come up for a vote and can determine the number of votes taken. We will call this individual 'the Mayor'. Imagine that the Mayor wants to spend less money on the park than then median voter. Perhaps the median voter is willing to tax and spend 65 Euros per citizen to construct the park, but the Mayor prefers a less ambitious park and is only willing spend 45 Euros per voter. Maybe high spending on the park would imply that the Mayor has to significantly cut spending on other policies.

Because the Mayor sets the assembly agenda, she proposes that the assembly hold one vote on park spending and she asks the assembled voters whether they prefer to build a park at the price of 45 Euros per citizen or to leave the lot in its current vacant state—the **status quo** option (where the status quo simply refers to the current policy). Because a majority of citizens prefer a park at the price of 45 Euros per citizen over the current vacant lot, the Mayor's proposal passes and her policy for the park is implemented. However, this procedure does not lead to a congruent outcome: the policy deviates from the position of the median voter. If the policy to raise park taxes to 65 Euros were allowed to come up for a vote, a majority of voters would prefer it over the 45 Euros policy. But the Mayor, through her position of privilege, is able to ensure that the 65 Euros proposal never comes up for a vote. Political scientists refer to this tactic as **gatekeeping**. Effectively, the mayor held the gates closed on the expensive policy alternative, so it was never a viable option for voters to choose. Through **agenda setting**—the ability to make proposals that can either be defeated or passed, but not amended—and gatekeeping—the ability to keep policy proposals from coming up for a vote at all—the Mayor is able to move policy away from the position of the median voter and towards her own preferred position, reducing congruence between the policy outcome and the position of the median voter. We will discuss direct democratic policy-making in Chapter 6 on elections and agenda-setting power when we examine law-making in Chapter 11.

2.2 Delegation and Representative Democracy

If the addition of a representative, such as a mayor, to our model of democracy may reduce congruence between the median voter and policy outcomes, we may question why have representatives at all. Perhaps in our example, the town would be better off doing away with the position of mayor. But without someone to formulate the list of proposals to vote on, how would the community decide what comes up for a vote and when? There would need to be someone to organize and keep order at the meeting. There would need to be some set of rules that determines how to conduct business. In the absence of such rules, the meetings could break down into chaos. Nothing would get decided. Essentially, the citizens of our community have engaged in **delegation**. They have delegated authority to the Mayor to set the rules of the political process to ease the process of decision-making. This has clear benefits for the community, namely more efficient decision-making. But it also provides the Mayor with a significant amount of power and responsibility.

So perhaps delegating responsibility to a mayor is necessary, but why select one who seeks to move policy away from the median voter? Again, there are at least two possible reasons. One could be that community needs to decide on multiple items, not just the park, and the preferences of the Mayor match the median voter on average across all of the items that must be decided. This is the more optimistic scenario—the Mayor is representative on average, even if not on every issue. The more pessimistic, and perhaps more realistic, scenario is that the Mayor has information about her preferences for the park and maybe even about public opinion that no one else has—private information. Perhaps, in campaigning for the position of mayor, she told voters that she would support a more ambitious park proposal, but then once in office she reverted to her thrifty ways. We call this **shirking**—failing to uphold one's end of a bargain, or deviating from an agreed upon position.

The voters could punish the Mayor for shirking; they could vote her out of office. But they may not. Why? The voters may not even know that the Mayor has shirked. To know that the Mayor has not implemented the will of the median voter, the public would need to know who the median voter in society is, and they may not. Imagine that the Mayor conducted a private opinion poll and has good information on what the public wants, but has not shared this information with the public. She might have a good idea about just how much she can get away with. In short, the Mayor has an informational advantage over the voters—she may have better information about her own desires and those of the public than the public does. She can use that information to her advantage to get policy outcomes that she likes.

This little tale of decision-making in our village, again, acts a as model. It demonstrates some key features of democratic politics while abstracting away from many others. First, it suggests a way for us to determine if a democratic system is representing the will of the voters. We can examine whether policy matches the position of median voter (of course, this is only one of many ways of determining how representative a democracy is). It also highlights how delegation of authority is necessary and desirable because it eases the process of decision-making. Without the Mayor, our community meeting may have devolved into a shouting match. Moreover, the Mayor possesses the necessary expertise to calculate the actual costs for the park project and consider all the different things that need to be done in order to complete the project, and delegation therefore reduces **transaction costs**—namely the costs associated with doing business, such as the time taken to gather information and make decisions. However, delegation also comes with risks—the possibility of mayoral shirking. Citizens may be willing to overlook some degree of shirking. Some may even like it, namely those who prefer an outcome more in line with the preferences of the Mayor than the median voter. Others may not even know that it is occurring. That depends on the informational advantage of the Mayor over the citizens. But if the shirking becomes too great, the citizens may look to vote the Mayor out of office and replace her.

In short, our example demonstrates that democracy, even at the most basic level, involves making collective choices about policy, often involving the delegation of authority and all the costs and benefits that stem from delegation.

2.3 Principals and Agents in Representative Democracy

We now begin to expand our model by adding in yet more delegation. Suppose that the members of our community are very busy. They have jobs and families. They do not have time to spend thinking about how much money to spend on parks or to figure out how much it costs to build a decent park and how much tax revenue would be needed to cover the construction. In the end, they may decide that they would be better off doing away with the town meeting altogether. Instead, voters agree to delegate authority to a town assembly via elections. Voters retain ultimate control as the final principals—the individuals with whom ultimate authority rests—but they delegate authority to agents—individuals tasked with completing a task on behalf of the principals—through elections. These agents (politicians) are elected to make decisions on behalf of the principals (voters).

We refer to actors—or participants in a political game—as principals when they possess authority over others. Principals often delegate tasks to their agents to carry out. Agents are responsible to principals and generally expected to do what the principal wants. But they may have better information about how to carry out a task, or about the amount of effort required to complete the task. This informational advantage may allow them to shirk, or to deviate from the principal's plans or desires. They may put less effort into carrying out a task than the principal desires, or they may perform the task in such a way that the outcome does not quite match what the principal originally intended. In politics, voters can act as principals and elected representatives as their agents. But we can also think about party leaders as agents of party members, or any number of other **principal–agent relationships**. There are many different principal–agent relationships in democratic political systems.

But just like the mayor discussed above, these elected politicians likely have more information about public policy and also more interest in community affairs than voters do. This is why they become politicians to begin with, and it gives them an advantage in getting things done. But their informational advantage over voters, as we have already noted, can lead to shirking. If the voters perceive the politicians to be bad agents (because, for example, they don't fulfil the voters' wishes when in office), they can vote the politicians out of office at the next election.

In representative democracy, where voters elect politicians who then make political decisions on voters' behalf, voters may both try to elect the politicians who are most likely to support the policies they agree with, and also seek to vote out of office politicians who have enacted policies they dislike (or who have failed to enact policies they do like). Where voters select politicians on the basis of their policy promises (as here), we call it **prospective voting**. But when voters sanction politicians on the basis of their performance we term it **retrospective voting**. Prospective decision-making refers to looking into the future to determine what choice will lead to the best outcome, while retrospective decision-making refers to looking backwards into the past to assess whether decisions already taken have been wise. In each election, elected politicians can be held accountable for their actions. **Electoral accountability** is thus a crucial component of electoral democracy: voters can reward incumbents they like based on their performance in office, but remove those that they think have performed poorly. We will discuss these motivations for voting in much greater detail in Chapter 5. The hope is that this will produce high-quality representation, but our model shows how it could deviate from it as well.

Additionally, we have to think carefully about the quality of representation. What does 'good' or 'bad' representation look like? How do we even know when shirking has occurred? Politicians and voters could perceive electoral victories to mean different things. Elections only come around every so often, and in the interim, voters may not pay close attention to politics. Many voters do not constantly monitor the actions of politicians. After all, that is why they delegated responsibility to begin with. The lack of constant monitoring means that elected politicians can interpret their roles differently. A newly elected politician may perceive themselves to have an electoral mandate. They were elected on a particular policy platform—a set of specific proposals, say to build a new park, or improve roads. Having won the election, they will seek to carry out these plans. And they expect voters to evaluate them on the basis of their ability to fulfil promises, in other words to stick to what they perceive their mandate to be.

Alternatively, politicians could view their role as custodial. They are elected to take the best possible decision for voters, regardless of the views of voters. If voters want to engage in harmful policies, particularly those which may deprive a minority of a fundamental right, it is the duty of a custodial representative to prevent these harmful policies from coming to pass. Note that both of these views of representative democracy could lead to deviations in congruence between policy outcomes and the median voter. Even if we assume that the election outcome perfectly reflected the preference of the median voter, a politician following their electoral mandate will drift from the position of the median voter as that position shifts and changes. A custodial representative will feel it their duty to deviate from the median voter's position if they disagree with the position or view it as reducing social welfare.

2.4 Multidimensional Politics

Up until now, we have discussed democratic decision-making on one issue at a time. The voters in our direct democracy, for example, only had to choose the level of spending for our park. But politics in the real world is rarely about a single issue; in other words, it is almost never so one-dimensional. Often voters and politicians have to decide on multiple, often related issues at the same time—they may decide on the amount of money they wish to spend on their park, but also the issue of who is allowed to use the park as a second dimension. Before, we complicated our model by allowing for delegation to politicians, but now we wish to complicate our model by allowing for decisions on multiple, related issues. Rather than a uni-dimensional space, we now assume a multidimensional policy space.

Returning to our example of park construction, we are going to add decision-making on a very specific dimension—who has the right to be included or excluded from public affairs, and who can benefit from access to state resources. Imagine that, just as our town is deciding what type of park to build, someone at the meeting raises a hand and asks whether the people from the neighbouring village would be given access to the park. They do not live in the town, do not participate in the decision-making process, and do not pay the local taxes that contribute to the construction of the park. This issue quickly divides the participants at the town meeting, and a rancorous discussion ensues. People who are in complete agreement about how much money to spend and what the park should look like are now divided on this question of access. Some feel that the park should be open to all, while others feel that only those who have contributed by paying taxes should enjoy the park. The notion that the park should be gated, with guards checking the addresses of people wishing to enter, infuriates some, while the idea that non-paying neighbours should have the same rights as local taxpaying residents angers others.

The choice to allow neighbours to enter appears binary at first glance—either they are granted access or they are not granted access. But we could also think of various gradations of access between these two stark choices. For example, non-taxpayers could be allowed access for a fee. That fee could vary from 0 Euro (free access for all) to some astronomical amount that would effectively mean no access for non-taxpayers. Again, we could arrange voters along this line according to the outcome they desire. To capture this fight, we need to add another line to our Figure 2.1, perpendicular to the existing economic dimension. This is now shown in Figure 2.2.

Voters in the upper left quadrant of Figure 2.2 wish to spend more on the park, but exclude anyone who is not a local resident. Voters in the lower right prefer to spend less on the park, but allow access for all. The voters in the upper right wish to keep the neighbours off their undeveloped field, and those in the lower left wish to build an elaborate park for all to use. The figure shows the five voters from before (A through E). Each voter now holds a preference over both issues. For instance, voter C prefers a moderate amount of spending, but no access to the park to guests from outside.

Note that once we portray the complexity of politics in such a **two-dimensional policy space**, the median voter on the original tax-spending dimension is not necessarily the median voter on the second access dimension. In fact, in the specific configuration of preferences in

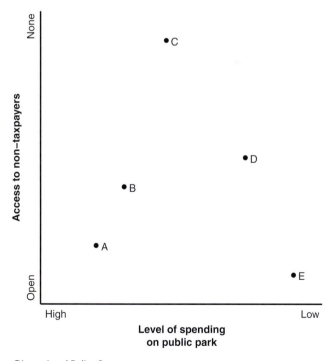

Figure 2.2 A Two-Dimensional Policy Space

Figure 2.2, voter C is the median voter on the tax-spending dimension (the horizontal axis), but voter B is the median voter on the access dimension (the vertical axis). The lack of a single median voter complicates both decision-making and representation. With respect to decision-making, the lack of a single median voter means that we cannot identify what society wants because there is no one policy that will be supported by a majority of voters over all other policies. Instead, for any policy that comes up for vote, there will always be another policy that is supported by a different majority.

Now imagine that two of these voters, B and D, hold elected office and have the power to veto any proposal that is put forward. Figure 2.3 shows the set of points that these actors prefer over a hypothetical status quo (SQ) policy—the current policy that any new policy would replace—with moderate spending for the park and limited access to non-taxpayers. Actors always prefer policies closer to their ideal point than to the SQ, namely those points within the shaded circles, the so-called **indifference curves** which mark the set of points which are equidistant between the actors' ideal points and the SQ. The circular indifference curves are centred at B and D's ideal points with a radius equal to the distance between B and the status quo. The actors are indifferent to the SQ for all points that lie on their circle. Any policy inside their circle is preferred, shown by the coloured area. The overlap of the two circles represents the policies that both B and D prefer over the SQ. If both B and D must agree to change policy, then the only policies that can come into effect are those represented by this overlapping region. This region is known as the **winset of the status quo**. We can refer to both B and D as **Veto Players**. A veto player, according to Tsebelis (2002), is any actor whose agreement is required to change the SQ. In other words, a veto player has the authority to veto, or

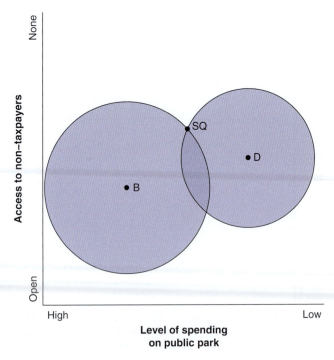

Figure 2.3 Indifference Curve Example

Box 2.1 CASE STUDY: Cyclical Majorities in Politics

To better understand cycling of policy outcomes under majority rule, imagine that a town is deciding whether to construct a park, build a road, or refurbish the community centre. There is only enough money for one of these tasks. We have three elected politicians who must decide what to do—Mohammed, Sofija, and Emma. Unlike with the park example, it is not possible to line up the politicians' preferences on a line from left to right. Instead, they have the following preferences:

Mohammed	Park	>	Road	>	Centre
Sofija	Road	>	Centre	>	Park
Emma	Centre	>	Park	>	Road

where > indicates a preference for one option over another. Each politician's preference ordering is perfectly reasonable, but if they try to resolve their differences by voting using majority rule, they would quickly discover a problem. Imagine that Mohammed proposes that they vote the centre against the road first and then the winner of that vote against the park. If they were to do this, the road would defeat the centre (Sofija and Mohammed both prefer the road to the centre; only Emma prefers the centre). Then when pitted against the park, the road would go down in defeat and the park would be built. Both Mohammed and Emma prefer the park to the road. But seeing her least preferred proposal moving forward, Sofija screams foul. She suggests that they vote again. This time, she suggests they pit the centre against park first. The centre wins this vote (both Sofija and Emma prefer it to the park). In the next round the road defeats the centre (Sofija and Mohammed against Emma). But now Emma is the one who is fuming. She proposes that they vote between the park and the road first. In this instance, the park would win out, only to be defeated by the centre in the second round.

In this example, it is easy to show that any option can defeat any other option. If the politicians were to keep voting, the outcome of the process would continue to cycle through the three options. This simple vignette demonstrates a phenomenon known as Condorcet's Paradox, named for the Marquis de Condorcet, an eighteenth-century French philosopher and mathematician who first wrote about vote cycling. Essentially, the paradox is that a group of rational actors may be incapable of making a rational group decision because the collective preference ordering is intransitive. Much later in the twentieth century, political scientists would demonstrate that almost any time that we are unable to place options along a line in a single dimension, vote cycling of the type described by Condorcet will occur. McKelvey (1979) proved the existence of **cyclical majorities**, that is the absence of a Condorcet winning alternative, for a multidimensional setting, unless there is a very specific configuration of preferences (for example, if one actor holds the median position on all dimensions, then this position will beat all other alternatives in a pairwise contest (Plott, 1967)).

The outcome of the "multi-option referendum" on the "deportation initiative" in Switzerland in 2010 offers an illustration of a Condorcet paradox in practice (Bochsler, 2010). Switzerland features the most opportunities for, and use of, direct democratic procedures, which include popular initiatives and government-initiated referendums. Swiss direct democracy occurs at all levels of government: national, cantonal, and municipal. In 2010, the populist radical right Swiss People's Party, the largest party in Switzerland, was able to collect enough signatures at the national level to place an initiative on the ballot that, if accepted, would expel foreigners who have committed crimes automatically from Switzerland. The multi-option referendum, however, allowed the Swiss government to place a moderate counterproposal on the ballot. Voters were able to express a preference on both options on the ballot, which looked like this:

(continued...)

a)	**Popular initiative:** Do you want to accept the popular initiative on the **deportation of criminal foreigners?**	Answer: 'Yes' or 'No' _____
b)	**Counterproposal:** Do you want to accept the federal decision of 10 June 2010 on the **deportation of criminal foreigners within the framework of the federal constitution?**	Answer: 'Yes' or 'No' _____
c)	**Tie-breaker question:** In case both the popular initiative and the counterproposal are accepted: Should the *popular initiative* or the *counter proposal* enter into force?	Popular initiative Counterproposal ☐ ☐

Note: Ballot translated by the authors

The ballot structure forced Swiss voters to first decide if they preferred the initiative or the status quo (vote a), second, if they preferred the counterproposal or the status quo (option b), and, third, if they preferred the initiative or the counterproposal (vote c). After all votes were counted, the popular initiative prevailed. It was preferred by a majority of voters in vote a), whereas only a minority of voters voted for the counterproposal in vote b). This meant that the third (tie-breaker) question was not considered, since only the initiative, but not the counterproposal, was adopted by majority. However, the results of the, in the end irrelevant, tie-breaker question led to the revelation of a cyclical majority: a majority of voters would have preferred the moderate counterproposal to the initiative. The intransitive collective choice was as follows: SQ > counterproposal > initiative > SQ. There is some evidence that some voters acted strategically, in particular supporters of the Swiss People's party (Bochsler, 2010), rejecting the moderate counterproposal over the SQ even though it would have been closer to their preferences. In sum, the example illustrates that majority cycles may occur, and second, that direct democratic instruments do not guarantee that the preferences of the majority ultimately prevail.

block, policy change. Tsebelis puts forward a theory in which the number of veto players in a political system and the ideological distances between them can explain policy change and political outcomes. We will discuss this theory in much greater depth in Chapter 11.

2.5 Summary

The chapter has introduced the basic tools needed to study and understand democratic politics in Europe. This toolbox includes analytical concepts, such as spatial modelling, the median voter, and principal–agent theory, that we can apply flexibly to understand the fundamentals of European politics. We have kept the discussion deliberately abstract and introduced a very basic model of democratic politics and then made it more realistic in a variety of different ways. In doing so, we have discussed delegation, representation, shirking, decision-making, and cooperation, along with other topics. These are essential elements of representative democracy. We have built a toolbox for studying democracies in Europe focused on attitudes, preferences, and institutions. Indeed, a prominent political scientist, Charles Plott (1991), has argued that to explain political outcomes we must consider the interaction of political institutions (or the rules of the political game) and the preferences of the relevant political actors. This formula, *preferences × institutions = outcomes*, has become known as the **'fundamental equation of politics'** (Hinich and Munger, 1997, 17). In other words, we can expect changes in political outcomes when preferences change but institutions remain constant, when institutions change but preferences remain constant, or when both change. In the following chapters, we will make use of these tools and insights to understand how democracy in Europe works and what challenges it may face.

So far, we have explored delegation from voters to politicians, the foundation of representative democracy, and addressed how this delegation impacts representation. We have discussed the addition of different types of issues and have shown that this complexity may actually make collective decision-making unstable, but also create more room for solutions. Our discussion underlines the importance of the design of democratic political institutions, such as voting rules and agenda-setting rights, in generating stable policy outcomes in democracies.

But in fleshing out the model in these ways, we have only explored a few of the many avenues we could go down in using our model to understand politics. For example, we have yet to consider the role of political parties, even though they are a core part of democratic political systems in Europe and elsewhere. We also only discussed one basic type of delegation—from voters to politicians. But within European politics, there are many different layers of politics from local, to national, to European. Indeed, many of the choices about the level at which an issue should be decided revolve around issues of delegation and representation.

The goal of this chapter is not to introduce all of these different extensions to our model of democracy, but rather to construct a framework that we can repeatedly return to throughout the book as we introduce new concepts in European politics. Once familiar with these basic concepts, we can use them to help us understand the intricacies of European politics that we explore throughout the remainder of the book.

Online Data Exercise: Cyclical Majorities

The interactive online exercise for this chapter explores how multidimensional decision-making influences the feasibility of majority decision-making. By altering the position of the status quo in a multidimensional space and observing how indifference curves change, you will come to better understand how cyclical majorities occur, and also when policies are more stable.

Take your learning further with this interactive data exercise, available at **www.foundationsofeuropeanpolitics.com**

For additional material and resources, including multiple-choice questions, web links, and more, please visit the online resources: **www.oup.com/he/devries1e**

Multilevel Politics in Europe

This chapter explores the territorial nature of European politics. It suggests that policy-making in Europe resembles a system of multilevel governance in which policy authority at the national level is increasingly shared with European Union (EU) institutions at the supranational level, and regional governments at the subnational level. In order to understand the complex relationships between these different levels of government, this chapter familiarizes students with the key concepts to understand multilevel politics, such as the pooling and delegation of policy authority as well as federalism and decentralization.

In the previous chapter, with our model of democracy we explored **delegation** from voters to politicians, the foundation of representative democracy. In this chapter, we explore a different form of delegation. Over the last several decades, national governments have voluntarily delegated policy authority to the **European Union** (EU) at the supranational level, and many have also delegated authority to regional governments at the subnational level. European countries have given up aspects of their **sovereignty**—their sole authority to make decisions on policies—shifting policy authority away from centralized national governments.

Political systems in Europe thus increasingly reflect governance structures in which policy authority is shared and structured across multiple territorial levels, all of which interact with one another. While we tend to think of nation-states as the basic building blocks, or units, of politics, more and more we must consider both how these building blocks interact with each other and also what comprises them. Scholars of European politics sometimes use the term **multilevel governance** to characterize the complex relationships of policy authority between political actors situated at different territorial levels of government (Hooghe and Marks, 2001). The term highlights that the act of governing, or policy-making,—namely governance—requires interactions across these levels, often resulting in lesser control over policy for national governments. These interactions can lead to networks of policy-makers that cut across or even bypass some level, and the nation-state in particular.

The number of levels across which policy authority is shared varies significantly across countries and issues. For most people living in Europe today policy authority is shared across at least three levels—subnational, national, and supranational—of which the first two exist within their nation-state. However, the precise mix of power sharing across levels of government varies both across countries as well as within countries over time. For example, some countries in Europe, like Norway and Switzerland, are not members of the EU, while many other European countries are. In some countries, like France and the Netherlands, policy authority is **centralized** at the national level and fiscal autonomy of subnational governments is low, while in other European countries, like Germany or Spain, policy authority is highly **decentralized** and subnational governments have considerable autonomy when it comes to public spending. Finally, there is also considerable variation in the degree of centralization of policy authority within countries over time. In recent decades, the United Kingdom, for example, has seen a significant shift with more policy authority devolved to the regions—in particular Wales, Scotland, and Northern Ireland.

The crucial question now becomes what explains this variation in multilevel politics across countries in Europe? And why have some countries shared policy authority with supranational and subnational levels of government, while others have not? These are fundamentally questions about delegation, which lies at the heart of our framework for analysing democracy developed in Chapter 2. While these questions are important, they are also difficult and therefore are far from settled in the literature. In this chapter, we provide an overview of some of the key approaches to multilevel politics in Europe that have developed to understand the complex relationships between different levels of government. The first part of the chapter discusses the pooling and delegation of policy authority to the supranational level, to the EU. In doing so, it introduces the key steps in the process of European integration. The second part introduces the ways in which policy authority is shared with subnational levels of government. It distinguishes between two distinct ways of territorial power sharing within countries: federalism and decentralization.

3.1 Supranational Politics in Europe

The experience of fighting two devastating world wars on the European continent led a generation of politicians to engage in the creation of a supranational level of government. Since the early 1950s, we have observed extensive delegation of policy authority from the national level to the EU. Member state governments can be considered as the principals in this delegation, and the supranational actors, EU institutions, as the agents.

The founding generation of the EU had two goals in mind: first, to avoid another devastating war between European countries, and second, to foster the economic reconstruction of the continent. All of this took place in the countries that were not under the influence of the Soviet Union. While there were early plans for a far-reaching federal EU—put forward in a manifesto during the Second World War by Italian politician Alterio Spinelli—the actual impetus for integration was a plan drafted in 1950 by a French administrator Jean Monnet, which became known as the Schuman Declaration after the French foreign minister Robert Schuman. Jean Monnet and Robert Schuman proposed that France and Germany delegate authority over the coal and steel industry—the 'war' industry—to new a supranational entity.

Through the Treaty of Paris from 1952, member state governments gave significant powers to a **supranational organization**, the **European Coal and Steel Community** (ECSC), which is seen as the predecessor of what we now call the EU. The ECSC comprised six member countries—Belgium, France, Italy, Luxembourg, the Netherlands, and West Germany—that sought to bind themselves through economic cooperation in two industrial sectors, coal and steel. These sectors were crucial to reconstruction following the devastation of the two world wars. The ECSC allowed its members to pull down tariff barriers, abolish subsidies, fix prices, and raise money for reconstruction by imposing levies on steel and coal production. Trade and economic cooperation were seen by national and European politicians as important deterrents against war and state aggression.

Following the success of the ECSC, member state governments shifted even more policy authority to the supranational level. In 1958 the Treaties of Rome established the **European Economic Community** (EEC). Like the ECSC, the EEC included six countries, Belgium, France, Italy, Luxembourg, the Netherlands, and West Germany, as its members. The EEC was an important step in the process of European integration in that it set out the goal of achieving a single market in Europe and created a constitutional framework for the European polity. The different communities (ECSC and EEC together with the Euratom Treaty) were henceforth known as the **European Communities**. The European Economic Community established key EU institutions such as the European Commission, the Council of Ministers and the European Court of Justice (which today is formally known as the **Court of Justice of the European Union**), which are responsible for making and interpreting EU policy and law. The powers and responsibilities of all of these institutions were initially laid down in the Treaty of Rome, and have been modified in subsequent treaties. Later treaties have created other bodies, such as the **European Council** in which heads of government meet on a regular basis, and the **European Central Bank**, which oversees monetary policy and implementation of the Euro, Europe's common currency. The European Communities were consolidated into a single legal entity in 2009 with the Treaty of Lisbon. Table 3.1 presents a chronological overview of all European Treaties together with their main purpose.

The EU's long-term objectives are set by the European Council, but this institution has no formal powers to pass laws. The European Council is led by a president and comprises the national heads of state or government as well as the President of the European Commission. In effect, it directly represents member state governments at the highest level. It was in emergency European Council meetings, for example, that the very final details of the agreement over the United Kingdom's exit from the EU were hammered out.

When it comes to making EU legislation, three main institutions are involved: the European Parliament, the Council of the EU (not to be confused with the European Council), and the European Commission. The **European Parliament** (EP) consists of directly elected members who represent EU citizens. These members belong to national political parties and are elected to the EP in national elections that occur once every five years across all EU member states simultaneously. Once they enter the European Parliament, these national parties cooperate with like-minded parties from other member states in European political groups, which organize parliamentary activities, such as debate and committee membership.

The **Council of the EU** represents the governments of each of the member states at the ministerial level and votes on legislative proposals. The composition of the Council changes depending on the type of legislation under discussion. For example, when discussing agricultural policy, the agricultural ministers meet to discuss and vote. But when discussing economic policy, the economic or finance ministers meet. Lastly, the **European Commission** represents the interests of the EU as a whole. Each member state has a single Commissioner, but this Commissioner is not supposed to represent a particular member state. Instead, national identities are supposed to matter less in the Commission. The composition of the Commission is subject to approval of both the European Council and the European Parliament.

Table 3.1 Overview of European Treaties

Treaty	Main purpose	Signed	Entry into force
Treaty of Paris	Founding Treaty of the European Coal and Steel Community (ECSC)	1951	1952
Treaty of Rome	Founding Treaties of the European Ecomomic Community (EEC) and European Atomic Energy Community (Euroatom)	1957	1958
Merger Treaty	Created a single Commission and a single Council for all three European Communities (EEC, Euratom, ECSC)	1965	1967
Single European Act	Changed political institutions with the goal to complete the single market	1986	1987
Treaty of Maastricht	Renamed European Economic Community to European Community and established the European Union (EU). Roadmap for an economic and monetary union (EMU), change of decision-making procedures, including more powers for European Parliament, and introduction of elements of a political union	1992	1993
Treaty of Amsterdam	Changed decision-making procedures in anticipation of Eastern enlargement, including more powers for European Parliament	1997	1999
Treaty of Nice	Further changes to decision-making procedures in anticipation of Eastern enlargement, including more powers for European Parliament	2001	2003
Treaty of Lisbon	Changes to institutional framework to allow an enlarged EU to work more effectively, including changes to Council voting rules, enhanced legislative powers of the European Parliament and the introduction of a permanent President of European Council. Renamed Treaty on European Community the Treaty on Functioning of the European Union.	2007	2009

Today, these three institutions together primarily legislate through a procedure that is called the **Ordinary Legislative Procedure** in which the Commission proposes legislation and the European Parliament and Council of EU propose amendments and ultimately vote on whether to adopt the (amended) Commission proposals. The member states are responsible for implementing legislation, while the Commission ensures that the EU laws are properly applied. If there are disputes over EU law or its implementation between the Commission and a member state, between individuals and a member state, or between member states, the Court of Justice of the EU can issue rulings, interpreting EU law.

Given this institutional structure, we can think of the EU's political system as a chain of delegation just as we can the political system of any nation-state. Figure 3.1 depicts the EU's chain of delegation. Voters across Europe vote both for Members of the EP as well as members of their national parliament. National parliamentarians elect national governments, which are represented in the European Council and the Council of the EU. In some national systems a directly elected president represents the country in meetings of the European Council.

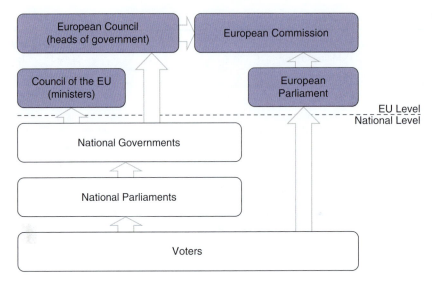

Figure 3.1 European Union Chain of Delegation

The governments, through the European Council, appoint the President of the Commission and the Commissioners, subject to the approval of the directly elected EP.

In addition to outlining the role of the EU's institutions, the Treaty of Rome also founded the Customs Union and established the four freedoms—free movement of people, goods, services, and capital—that guide the constitutional framework for the **Single Market** to this day. Ultimately in 1993, member state governments through the Maastricht Treaty transformed previous efforts of integration into an institutional and constitutional entity that we now know as the EU. The Maastricht Treaty also established the blueprint for **Economic and Monetary Union**, paving the way for a common currency, the Euro, which was introduced in 2002 in nineteen member states, and allowed for deeper political cooperation in the areas of foreign and security policy and justice and home affairs. The Maastricht Treaty thus moved European integration from predominantly economic integration to more and more integration in the political realm. The Treaty of Lisbon which came into force in 2009 serves as the EU's constitution and legal basis for EU policy-making today. It introduced a whole set of institutional innovations, such as a President of the European Council and High Representative of the Union for Foreign Affairs and Security Policy.

Since the foundation of the EU (then the EEC) in 1958, member states have expanded the level of integration, that is they have delegated more and more powers from the national to the supranational level, a process known as **deepening**. And the EU has proven attractive to other countries, with its membership increasing from six to twenty-eight states over time, a process known as enlargement and sometimes referred to as the **widening** of the EU. While the EU's predecessor organizations had six member states—Belgium, France, Italy, Luxembourg, the Netherlands, and West Germany—there were twenty-eight member states at the time of the signing and ratification of the Treaty of Lisbon. Figure 3.2 provides an overview of these different waves of enlargement.

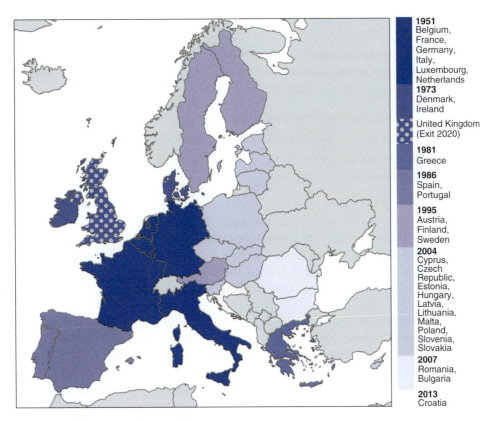

1951
Belgium,
France,
Germany,
Italy,
Luxembourg,
Netherlands

1973
Denmark,
Ireland

United Kingdom
(Exit 2020)

1981
Greece

1986
Spain,
Portugal

1995
Austria,
Finland,
Sweden

2004
Cyprus,
Czech
Republic,
Estonia,
Hungary,
Latvia,
Lithuania,
Malta,
Poland,
Slovenia,
Slovakia

2007
Romania,
Bulgaria

2013
Croatia

Figure 3.2 Widening of the European Union

The increase of political authority at the EU level has been accompanied by increased wariness among some politicians and citizens regarding integration, and questions about whether it should go further or whether it has already has gone far enough. In 2016, the United Kingdom decided by popular referendum to leave the EU, and the UK formally left on 31 January 2020. Thus, while initially the European integration project was confined to a particular industrial sector and limited in its membership, the EU today is a supranational political system that takes decisions that are of great importance to the citizens of its twenty-seven member states. The debate between member states always has been about how much authority to delegate and how to decide policy at the supranational level.

3.2 Delegation and Pooling

Because they have agreed to share policy authority with a supranational level of government, national governments in EU member states no longer have the sole capacity to take binding policy decisions. As we mentioned, we can conceive of delegation from member states to the EU in the form of **principal–agent relationship**. Member state governments can be viewed as the principals, and the supranational actors, for instance the European Commission, as the agents.

When two levels of government have the authority to make policy, we can speak of a federal political arrangement. A minimalist definition for federalism proposed by Riker (1964, 11) includes three elements (see also Riker, 1975; Bednar, 2009):

- two levels of government rule the same land and people,
- each level has at least one area of action in which it is autonomous, and
- there is some guarantee (even if merely a statement in the constitution) of the autonomy of each government in its own sphere.

This definition of federalism as an institutional arrangement can be applied not only to countries and their subnational regions, but also to the EU as a whole, since both member states and the EU have areas in which they have sole responsibility (e.g. the Euro and monetary policy for the EU, education for the member states), but they rule the same land and people and thus share responsibilities. The responsibilities are laid down in both the national constitutions and in the EU treaties. Thus, the EU can be conceived of as a federal political system.

Delegation of decision-making power from the national to the supranational level begs the question why countries have done so and how it changes our framework for analysing politics in Europe. To acquire the theoretical tools to begin to answer these important questions, we return to our two neighbouring villages from the previous chapter—the village constructing the park and their neighbours who want to use it. Imagine that the villages have had a violent past with each other that has caused their economies to be weak. Both villages have a desire to avoid another conflict and to foster economic development. Suppose that the neighbouring village has a factory that specializes in the construction of playground equipment that would be perfect for the new park in the first village. Meanwhile, the agricultural land in the first village is perfect for growing a crop that is considered a delicacy in the second village. Each village could produce the product they need and want. The first village could open a new factory and train new workers to produce playground equipment, and the second village could plant their favourite crop, even though the growing conditions are less than ideal and crop yields lower. However, doing so would be costly and come at the expense of producing other goods that they are better at producing. The villages would each be much better off specializing in the production of the good that they are relatively good at making and then trading with the neighbouring village. Economists have long shown that there are benefits to specialization and trade using the theory of **comparative advantage**. Overall levels of economic output are higher when countries specialize in the production of goods that they are relatively efficient at producing, trading with other countries for the rest.

However, a problem arises, namely the villages do not trust each other. The first village does not trust their neighbours to build high-quality playground equipment. They fear that their neighbours will scrimp and save, building cheaper, less safe playground equipment likely to break a few months after installation. Even if the neighbours produce high-quality equipment for themselves, there is no guarantee that they won't try to pass off a cheaper, inferior product on the other village. To use language from Chapter 2, they may shirk their obligation to make a high-quality product to save some money on production costs.

And the same is true for the second village looking to buy the food delicacy. They might fear that the first village could provide them with tainted produce. The purchasing village in both instances is at an informational disadvantage. Because they do not produce the product and have less information about the production processes, they have a hard time distinguishing between high-quality and low-quality goods, making it easier for the experts to fool them with less than adequate products. It is this informational asymmetry that leads to an inability to trust one another. But, of course, the distrust could be made worse by the fact that they view each other as being culturally different. Not only does the other village have an informational advantage, but they also have reason to exploit the informational advantage because 'they are not like us'.

If this fear of being a victim is sufficiently great, they may not trade at all, even though both villages would be better off if they did trade. We can analyse the relationship between these two villages using **game theory**. A game-theoretic model is one that assumes that actors (individuals or groups playing a game) interact strategically with one another to try to maximize their benefits, conditional on what every other actor does in the game. Imagine that both villages would be best off if they could engage in trade, trusting each other to provide high-quality products. However, they are the worst off if they provide a high-quality product to the other village while receiving a low-quality product in return. They have spent a lot of time, money, and effort on production but the other village has not. To avoid the costs of being cheated, the villages only have an incentive to trade low-quality goods, or perhaps to not trade at all.

To give a simple numerical example, imagine the villages trade for each other's products at a set rate—x amount of playground equipment for y amount of food. A village spends 3 Euros to produce a high-quality version of a product that they specialize in, 1 Euro to produce a low-quality version of that same product, and 4 Euros to produce the product they do not specialize in. They receive 6 Euros worth of benefit from consuming a high-quality version of the other village's product, 0 benefit from consuming a low-quality version, and 5 Euros benefit if they use a product that they have manufactured themselves.

The villages can now choose to either trade a low-quality good or a high-quality good, and their trading partner has no mechanism for determining the type of good being traded until they have it in their possession and the other trader has left, making it impossible to return it or to seek redress. If both villages choose to trade high-quality goods, they each get 3 Euros (6 Euros worth of consumption minus 3 Euros worth of production costs). This is the outcome that makes everyone collectively best off. However, each village could improve its situation by 2 Euros (receiving 5 Euros) if it trades a low-quality product and receives a high-quality product in return (6 Euros of benefit minus only 1 Euro of costs). The problem is that the village receiving the low-quality product is much worse off, receiving no benefits and paying 3 Euros worth of costs. Regardless of what the other village does, each village is better off by trading the low-quality product. In other words, each player has a dominant strategy to trade low-quality goods, leading to a bad outcome for all—spending 1 Euro to produce an inferior product and getting no benefit in return, leading to a negative net benefit of -1. This hypothetical scenario is referred to as a **prisoners' dilemma**, named for the story that was initially used to describe the game. Figure 3.3 depicts this scenario using a table. Village 1 is depicted in the rows and Village 2 in the columns. The numbers in the cells are payoffs, the value of each outcome for each player. In this case, the first number is the payoff for Village 1 in the rows, and the second number is the payoff for Village 2 in the columns.

		Village 2	
		Trade High Quality	Trade Low Quality
Village 1	Trade High Quality	3,3	-3,5
	Trade Low Quality	5,-3	-1,-1

Figure 3.3 Collective Action Problem: Prisoners' Dilemma

In this case, the two villages would be better not trading at all. If they simply were to pro-duce the good they want themselves, they would spend 4 Euros on production to get 5 Euros worth of benefit and come out 1 Euro ahead. They still would have been much better off trading if they could be assured that their trading partner would send a high-quality good. But since they cannot be assured of the quality of their trading partner's good, they have to settle for producing everything themselves.

So how does sharing sovereignty help solve this collective action problem? How can a supranational organization (or in this instance, a supra-village organization) help these two communities realize the benefits of free trade? Well, imagine that both villages could spend 1 Euro to pay an independent monitor to set up production standards and monitor quality. The independent monitor could verify the quality of the products before a trade takes place and provide a quality assurance certificate for high-quality products. Villages would not have to worry about becoming the victim of low-quality goods because they would know at the time of trading the type of goods they are receiving. The supranational monitor has set the stand-ards for quality and verified that the products meet those standards. The villages have both paid into this system, and perhaps sacrificed the ability to determine for themselves what 'high quality' means, but in doing so they have become better off. They have paid an additional Euro, meaning they only see 2 Euros worth of benefit, but that still makes them better off than not trading at all, and they never have to worry about being a 'sucker', receiving a low-quality good when they have sent a high-quality good.

Through the ability to trade, and confident in the knowledge that they are receiving good value from their trading partners, the villages may come to have increasingly close interac-tions. As they interact more, they may become more accustomed to each other's dialects, customs, and culture. This newfound understanding could lead to a more trusting and peace-ful relationship, furthering opportunities for cooperation. This type of increasingly close interaction, initially through fostering trade relationships, was clearly what the politicians founding the European Community, now the European Union, hoped for. Indeed, there is a strong argument to be made that cooperation through trade has made Europe a much safer place in the aftermath of the Second World War.

When it comes to sharing policy authority with a supranational level of government, as our villages have done or as EU member states do, it is important to distinguish between the delegation and the pooling of authority. In the context of the EU, delegation is understood as the conditional granting of authority by the principals, the member states, to the agents, the EU institutions. **Pooling of sovereignty** refers to the joint decision-making among the prin-cipals themselves, consisting of the rules under which member states make decisions, how those decisions are ratified, and the extent to which they are binding. Through delegation,

Box 3.1 METHODS AND MEASUREMENTS: Using Game Theory to Analyse Politics

Game theory is the formal study of strategic decision-making. Its use is prevalent in both economics and political science, and it has generated useful insights into the strategic interactions of political actors. A game aims to model a particular political situation (e.g. delegating power to a bureaucracy, intergovernmental bargaining, etc.) and it is defined by actors, their strategy sets, and their payoffs. Actors are the players in a game (e.g. political parties, government representatives, etc.), while a strategy is a complete description of what a player does at every possible point in the game, regardless of whether a particular move actually occurs. A strategy set is a set of all possible strategies available to a player. Payoffs define what players receive at each possible outcome of the game. Thus, game theory forces an analyst to work formally, i.e. to explicitly state who is involved, what potential actions actors can take at any given point, and what benefits or costs actors derive from all possible outcomes.

Games can be simultaneous or sequential, that is, the actors either take some decisions simultaneously (without knowing what the other players are deciding) or they take the decisions sequentially (after having observed what the other players have done). Actors are supposed to behave rationally. A game is solved to find optimal strategies for all players such that no player has an incentive to deviate from the chosen strategy, given what other players have done. When no player can benefit by changing strategy given what the other actors do, then this constitutes a **Nash equilibrium**, named after the Nobel prize-winning mathematician John Nash. This equilibrium analysis allows for a prediction of what the players might do in a particular interaction. Once a game is solved, analysts can perform a **comparative statics** analysis. The analyst can predict if equilibrium strategies of actors change when particular elements of the payoffs change (e.g. for instance, how international negotiations change as the result of one participating government being more responsive to public opinion than others).

The trade cooperation game between the two villages is one example of a famous game in politics known as the prisoners' dilemma. It is a simultaneous game where both actors decide which action to take at the same time. Its extension to multiple players is also known as the Tragedy of the Commons, in which all actors have an incentive to preserve a common resource, but have dominant strategies to deplete that resource for their own gain. This game demonstrates a 'cooperation' problem, where cooperation is defined as a player engaging in an action that could involve short-term sacrifice for the overall benefit of the group or the other player in the game. This game has only one Nash equilibrium in which both villages trade low-quality goods, even though collectively the villages would both be better off if they could agree to cooperate and trade high-quality goods. We could imagine turning this game into a sequential game where Village 1 moves first, offering a particular good for trade, followed by Village 2. However, this does not change the outcome of the game. Regardless of the move that Village 1 makes, Village 2 has an incentive to trade the inferior good. Knowing this, Village 1 trades the inferior good in the first move.

Another canonical class of games involves coordination. Rather than having one equilibrium, these games have two or more equilibria. And instead of trying to achieve an out-of-equilibrium but preferable outcome, the problem that actors face in these games is choosing among different equilibrium outcomes. Such a game may involve choosing standards for products. For example, imagine that two countries are seeking to set out the information that companies must print on their product labels when selling them in shops. The first country prefers one set of criteria while the second country prefers a second set of criteria, but they both prefer adopting the same criteria over using different criteria, and thus hampering cross-border trade. We can represent this scenario in the following simultaneous game.

(continued...)

		Country 2	
		Standard A	Standard B
Country 1	Standard A	2,1	0,0
	Standard B	0,0	1,2

The game has two equilibria—both countries choose standard A and both countries chose standard B. However, in the absence of communication when deciding simultaneously, the countries could still end up failing to coordinate. Both could mistakenly 'play nice' and chose the other country's preferred standard, or they could both choose their own, in the mistaken belief that the other country will be accommodating. Unlike cooperation games, though, coordination problems can be solved by making the game sequential. If Country 1 moves first, it will choose its preferred Standard A. Knowing that Country 1 has already chosen Standard A, when it comes time for Country 2 to choose, it will also choose Standard A. Whichever country chooses first will see its preferred standard adopted.

The discussion in the previous chapter about **agenda setting** can be recast as a sequential game where, in the first stage, the agenda setter gets to choose a policy proposal in the policy space. In the second stage, the voters get to compare that proposal to the status quo and vote on it.

member states grant the EU institutions authority to perform certain tasks. For example, the European Commission negotiates trade agreements on behalf of the member states with countries that are outside the EU, so-called third countries. Through pooling, member states transfer the authority to make binding decisions from themselves to a collective body of states within which they may exercise more or less influence. In the case of the EU, these are the European Council and the Council of the European Union.

Delegation is designed to ensure the development of policies that tackle cross-border problems, and could not have been achieved by member states on their own; think for example of trade and environmental policy. It also ensures that all relevant information is provided and shared in areas where member states might otherwise not have been willing to share it. Pooling is designed to simplify collective decision-making while at the same time ensuring that member state governments, as principals, continue to have a say. Whereas the strategic problem in delegating authority to the EU is shirking, in which the agent follows its own agenda, the strategic problem in pooling authority is collective decision-making where a member state may be outvoted by other member states once the principle of **unanimity** is abandoned. These two forms of transferring sovereignty, delegation and pooling, are of course closely related. For example, **qualified majority voting** (QMV) in the Council of the EU not only makes the formal decision-making of any single member state government more dependent on the votes of other member states (pooling), but also more dependent on agenda setting by EU institutions (delegation).

Ever since the Treaty of Rome, integration in Europe has increased through consecutive treaties. These different EU treaties, that have been voluntarily and democratically approved by all member states, are binding documents that provide the legal basis for the EU to act. For example, they set out the EU's objectives, decision-making procedures, and structure the relationship between the EU and its member states. To illustrate the importance of treaties, if a policy area is not cited in a treaty, the European Commission cannot propose a legislation in

Box 3.2 CASE STUDY: The History of Qualified Majority Voting in the EU

The Council of the EU makes the vast majority of its decisions today by Qualified Majority Voting (QMV). This means that policy can pass with less than unanimity support among countries, but more than a simply majority. The voting rule stipulates that policy requires the support of 55 per cent of member states representing 65 per cent of the EU's population (a double majority). This rule means that member state governments can get outvoted, but that it is harder to pass policy without the support of the EU's largest states. Two questions have characterized the institutional development of the EU's political system. First, member states have argued at length whether each member state should be able to veto legislation or whether decisions can be taken according to a majoritarian principle. Second, the exact definition of the qualified majority threshold, and thus the potential coalitions that can form a majority, has been contentious over the course of European integration. In fact, member states have changed the voting rule in the Council frequently over time. The initial voting rule laid out in the Treaty of Rome, gave Germany, France, and Italy four votes each; Belgium and the Netherlands two votes; Luxembourg one vote. To pass into law, a proposal required twelve votes. This weighted voting scheme meant that a supermajority of approximately 70 per cent of weighted votes was required to adopt legislation.

Although provisions for QMV, including the voting weights listed here, were included in the Treaty of Rome, in practice most policies were initially decided by unanimity. The Treaty foresaw the move from unanimity to qualified majority voting in the mid-1960s, however it encountered fierce resistance from French President Charles de Gaulle. In 1965, de Gaulle brought the European integration process to a virtual standstill because he feared that the introduction of QMV would encroach upon French sovereignty. He also feared changes to the Common Agricultural Policy, which transferred large sums of money to French farmers through subsidies. Consequently, President de Gaulle withdrew from the Council of Ministers, bringing business to a halt, in what would come to be known as the Empty Chair Crisis. This crisis would ultimately become resolved through the so-called Luxembourg Compromise, named for the country in charge of the Council presidency at the time. The compromise stipulated that, if a member state government viewed its vital interests to be at stake, negotiations would have to continue until a compromise receiving the unanimous support of all member states was reached. The Luxembourg Compromise meant that member state governments could continue to exercise a national veto for many more years. As a result, the plan envisioned in the Treaty of Rome to establish a common market across Europe came to a standstill.

It was not until the European Commission and member state governments agreed to finish the completion of the common market in the 1980s that qualified majority became the de facto voting rule in the Council on legislation concerning the common market. Since then, QMV has been progressively extended to more and more policy areas with each treaty reform. With the Treaty of Lisbon, the EU member states finally agreed to introduce a double majority QMV that lowered the threshold significantly. QMV is now the standard voting rule and it applies to all policy areas, with the exception of sensitive areas such as family law, foreign policy, social security systems, and tax policy. Thus, the Council of the EU has moved from an institution that enshrined veto power for all member states towards a majoritarian system. In practice, however, around 80 per cent of votes are unanimous, meaning that few member states vote against a proposal. Scholars disagree about the exact reason for this phenomenon. While some suggest that a culture of consensus exists in the Council (Heisenberg, 2005), the Council's rules of procedure stipulate that only successful votes on legislation are recorded, thereby providing an incomplete picture about the true level of disagreement. There is, however, evidence that governments' voting decisions are increasingly tied to domestic public opinion and used to send signals to national audiences (Hagemann et al., 2017). If so, contested decisions are likely to increase in the future as the importance of the EU in national politics continues to rise.

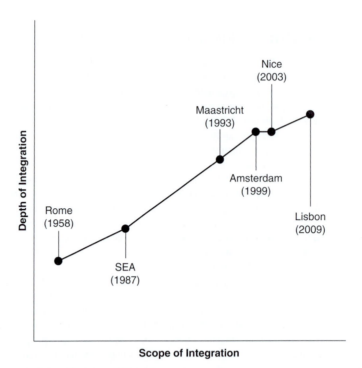

Figure 3.4 Development of European Integration

Data source: Börzel (2005)

this area. Figure 3.4 provides an overview of the increase in the level of European integration between the Treaty of Rome of 1958 and the Lisbon Treaty of 2009. It charts both the scope and depth of European integration based on data developed by Börzel (2005). Scope relates to the expansion of EU authority within policy areas, and captures the extent to which the EU plays a role in a policy area. Depth refers to the level at which decisions are formally taken, and captures the relative importance of European decision-making processes as compared to national processes. Both measures range from 1 low to 5 high and are based on the coding of formal rules as laid down in EU treaties. The figure shows a gradual increase in both the scope and depth of policy authority at the EU level. Since the Treaty of Rome, policy authority has shifted from the national level to the European level (scope) in more areas, and supranational EU decision-making processes have become more important (depth) in these policy areas.

While Figure 3.4 shows a general increase on both dimensions, meaning the process of European integration has led to an expansion of policy authority at the European level, the levels of both delegation and pooling differ considerably across policy areas. For example, taxation and culture remain largely a responsibility of national governments, while monetary and trade policy are largely a European responsibility. Traditionally, there has been much more delegation and pooling in the economic realm compared to security and military co-operation, for example.

Box 3.3 **CONTROVERSIES AND DEBATES:** Theories and Explanations for European Integration

Political scientists have studied European integration for decades and have put forward several explanations for the path of integration that member states of the EU have taken. While there are many schools of thought, there are two theoretical approaches that have gained major prominence: (a) neofunctionalism or supranationalism, and (b) liberal intergovernmentalism.

The first explanation for European integration emerged quickly after the far-reaching goal of establishing a common market was formulated in the Treaty of Rome. It highlighted the functional nature and the importance of the new supranational actors for the process of integration. In 1958, Ernst Haas proposed the theory of **neofunctionalism** (Haas, 1958), which would later be adapted by others to become the theory of **supranationalism**. The idea was to explain the strategies of political elites in post-war Europe. Neofunctionalism poses that integration starts in those policy areas in which countries deem cooperation necessary (e.g. coal and steel). Over time, however, countries would realize that more transfer of power is necessary in other areas to reach the desired goals. This process is known as **spillover**: an economic union eventually develops into a political union. Neofunctionalism and supranationalism furthermore highlights the role of supranational actors, which would act to push European integration even more forward. Critics of neofunctionalism have pointed out that integration actually did not develop as foreseen by neofunctionalists. For instance, the single market was not completed until thirty-five years after it was declared as a goal. There seemed to be a stalemate in the process of integration that could not be overcome by the activity of supranational actors alone.

The theory of **liberal intergovernmentalism**, put forward by Moravcsik (1998), highlights the national interests of the member states rather than those of supranational actors. According to this view, member states remain in control over the process of integration and will always protect their sovereignty. According to Moravcsik, the EU constitutes simply an international regime for effective policy coordination. Thus, if we observe integration, then it is only because it is in the interest of member states. Not all member states are equally powerful, however. Liberal intergovernmentalism suggests that integration is the result of intergovernmental bargaining in which some member states are more powerful due to asymmetrical interdependence between them. European integration is then a series of rational choices made by the leaders of member states. Which interests are then important? In contrast to classical realism, in which security concerns are paramount, Moravcsik proposes a liberal theory of national preferences in which economic interests are of great importance. The EU then is created to serve a particular function that member states do not or cannot execute anymore on their own. Thus, liberal intergovernmentalism follows the logic of a principal–agent model. Member states are the principals, EU actors are the agents. EU institutions, in this view, however are no more than mere necessary institutions for technocratic government to secure credible member state commitments. Liberal intergovernmentalism was also not immune to criticism. Its main focus rests on major integration steps, rounds of bargaining in intergovernmental conferences where member states have written or amended the treaties that define the EU polity. This ignores the EU's daily policy-making processes.

The comparative turn in European integration research has led to the use a framework termed **rational choice institutionalism**. It combines both perspectives; it takes national interests into account, but it also theorizes how supranational actors might influence the process of integration. Institutionalism studies the consequences of political institutions for policy-making, that is, how member states and supranational actors take decisions in the EU's political system and what it means for the potential for policy change. Many scholars nowadays adopt this model, associated with seminal works by Tsebelis and Garrett (2001).

3.3 Subnational Politics in Europe

As section 3.1 has made clear, the scope and depth of policy-making at the EU level has increased immensely, allowing member states the reap the benefits of scale by trading together and jointly tackling other cross-border issues. Yet, sovereignty of nation-states in Europe has not only been eroded from above, but also from below.

Multilevel governance in Europe is not only about the sharing policy authority with a supranational level of government above the state, the EU, but also about delegating authority downward to the subnational level, to **regional governments** (Hooghe and Marks, 2001). Regional governments are sets of legislative and executive institutions responsible for authoritative decision-making in a coherent territorial entity, such as a *Land* (state) in Germany or a *comunidad autónoma* (autonomous region) in Spain. They are intermediates between local and national governments. Within the member states of the EU, regional governments have significant powers in key sectors, such as education, the environment, economic development, urban and rural planning, transport, and public services. They also play an important role in the implementation of national and European legislation. Even in countries that cannot be considered federal by the definition introduced previously, regional authorities may have significant powers. Strictly speaking, neither Spain nor the UK is federal, while Germany is. The regions of Spain and the United Kingdom do not enjoy the strong constitutional protections that the German *Länder* do. Nevertheless, Spanish and British regions, like Catalonia or Scotland for example, often have significant powers to make policy and it would be politically difficult to eliminate these regions.

Hooghe and Marks (2001) point out that the process of European integration has played an important role in deepening and widening of regional authority within EU member states, regardless of whether they are strictly speaking federal, for example through providing financial aid for regions—so-called regional development funds—as well as by granting them political influence. The Maastricht Treaty of 1993 was especially important because it formally enshrined the principle of **subsidiarity** in law and established the **Committee of Regions**. The subsidiarity principle states that policy should be made by the level of government closest to the citizens, given the level of coordination and cooperation required to effectively govern in that policy area. Within the EU, it means that the EU can only take action if the goals of a particular policy proposal are better achieved at the EU level than at the member state level. Subsidiarity seeks to safeguard the ability of the member states, and regions within them, to take decisions and actions in the policy areas in which the EU does not have exclusive policy authority. EU institutions should only intervene when the policy objectives cannot be sufficiently achieved by the member states themselves, but can be better achieved at EU level due to scale advantages. The Committee of the Regions is the political assembly of regional and local representatives across the EU. It seeks to safeguard the principle of subsidiarity. By involving subnational governments, from regions, cities, and municipalities, in the EU's policy cycle, the Committee of the Regions is an institutional representation of the EU's multilevel governance structure.

Although European integration has strengthened regional governments within EU member states, the authority of regional governments differs tremendously both across and within countries. Regional governments in some EU member states, in particular federal countries such as Belgium, Germany, and Spain, have considerable authority over decision-making, policy implementation, and public spending, while in other countries, such as Denmark, the Netherlands, and Portugal, regional governments have much less independent authority. To quantify this variation, Hooghe et al. (2010) have developed the regional authority index (RAI). RAI captures policy authority of regions in two domains relating to self-rule and shared rule. Self-rule is the capacity of a regional government to exercise authority autonomously over those who live in its territory. It includes: the extent to which a regional government is autonomous; the range of policies for which a regional government is responsible; the extent to which a regional government can independently tax its population; the extent to which a regional government can borrow; and if the region has an independent legislature and executive. Shared rule is the capacity to co-determine the exercise of authority for the country as a whole. It includes: the extent to which regional representatives co-determine national legislation; the extent to which a regional government co-determines national policy in intergovernmental meetings; the extent to which regional representatives co-determine the distribution of national tax; the extent to which regional governments co-determine national or subnational borrowing constraints; the extent to which regional representatives co-determine constitutional change.

Figure 3.5 provides an overview of the average authority of regional governments within EU member states over time based on the RAI scores. It shows that considerable variation exists between EU member states when it comes to the extent of regional authority. In Denmark, Ireland Portugal, and Slovenia, countries shaded light blue, regional governments on average have a low level of independent authority, while in Belgium, Germany, and Spain, countries shaded dark blue, the average level of regional authority is very high.

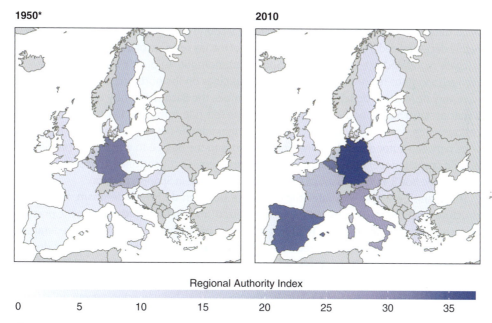

1950* **2010**

Regional Authority Index

0   5   10   15   20   25   30   35

Figure 3.5 Regional Authority within the EU

Data source: Hooghe et al. (2010)

Notes: The figure displays the average regional authority for subnational governments within a country. Lighter shades signify countries in which the average level of regional authority is low, while darker shades signify countries in which the average level of regional authority is high. It shows the regional authority index for two time points. * The map on the right-hand side displays the value of a regional authority index in 2010, while the map on the left-hand side displays the value of the regional authority index in 1950 or the first year included in the Hooghe et al. dataset after the transition to democracy.

Figure 3.5 displays the average level of RAI in two time points, 1950 (or the first year included in the RAI data set after the transition to democracy) and 2010. The comparison of RAI scores at both time points shows that the policy authority of regional governments is much higher recently compared to previous years. Only in Sweden is regional authority on average lower in 2010 compared to 1950, albeit that the difference is not great. In all other member states, the authority of regional governments, as measured through the average RAI scores, has increased over time. This underscores the notion that multilevel governance in Europe is not only about power sharing of national governments with a supranational level, but also with the subnational level. In order to understand this trend of sharing policy authority between national and regional governments and the variation that exists between and within countries, we will now further discuss the concepts of federalism and decentralization.

3.4 Federalism and Decentralization

As the formal definition in section 3.3 suggests, most political scientists conceive of federalism as a power sharing arrangement that combines self-rule—the capacity of a regional government to exercise authority autonomously over those who live in its territory—and shared rule—the capacity to co-determine the exercise of authority for the country as a whole. Yet, the countries that are listed by experts as federal often differ. Why? These discrepancies are largely due to the fact that some countries that are not defined as federal on the basis of their constitution behave as if they had federal structures in practice. Spain is a case in point here. According to its constitution, Spain is not a federal country. Yet, in practice policy authority is highly decentralized. For example, a large share of the tax revenue of the central government is legally mandated to be transferred to Spain's autonomous regions. Spain consists of seventeen autonomous regions (plus two autonomous cities on the northern coast of Africa) that have varying levels of policy autonomy. For example, the Basque Country and Navarra have a special status as autonomous regions with more self-rule compared to other autonomous regions when it comes to tax collection and certain administrative prerogatives. This difference between autonomous regions when it comes to the degree to which they can decide, act and spend independently of the central government is a touchstone of dissent in Spanish politics (see Box 3.4 on the issue of Catalan independence in Spanish politics).

The Spanish example illustrates the difference between **de jure federalism**, the federal structure of a country as constitutionally recognized, and **de facto federalism**, the practice of decentralized policy-making. The term federalism most often refers to de jure federalism, while de facto federalism is referred to as **decentralization**. Countries that are not de jure federal are known as **unitary states**. While federalism is a constitutional issue, decentralization is often seen as a budgetary one. In order for a regional government to act, it not only needs the legal authority to do so, but also the ability. The ability to act in a given policy area is highly conditional on budgetary constraints. In order to implement a policy, a government must be able to collect tax revenue and decide how to spend it. A country is considered decentralized when, next to the central government, the regional government is able to collect a share of the tax revenue. This refers to the degree of **fiscal decentralization**. The share of tax revenue collected by the central government is generally used as a measure of decentralization. Indeed fiscal centralization forms one key part of the RAI measure introduced in the previous section.

On the basis of the formal definition of federalism provided above, only three EU member states can be currently classified as federal—Austria, Belgium, and Germany. Switzerland is also a federal country, albeit not a member of the EU, and historically the former Yugoslavia was also considered federal. While Austria and Germany adopted a federal structure in their constitutions after the Second World War, Belgium became constitutionally federal through several state reforms between 1970 and 2001. Interestingly, when we compare the average level of regional authority of the *Bundesländer* in Austria and Germany or the *gemeenschappen* and *gewesten* in Belgium in Figure 3.5 considerable variation exists. Regional governments in Belgium and Germany have a much higher degree of policy authority compared to their Austrian counterparts. In fact, the average policy authority of Spanish autonomous regions is higher than of Austrian *Bundesländer* even though Spain is not a de jure federal country according to its constitution.

Spain and the United Kingdom have transferred a considerable amount of policy authority to regional governments over the years. In both countries, however, the ultimate power lies with the national government. Neither country qualifies as federal, mainly because the national governments in Madrid and London retain the unilateral right to recall and reshape the powers they have granted to the regional governments. The process by which a unitary state grants more authority to regional governments, but holds the right to revoke these rights is called **devolution**. Devolution differs from decentralization in that it refers to the characteristics of the constitutional arrangement of power sharing between the national and regional governments, while decentralization refers to the practice of it. The importance of the right of the national government to recall the authority it granted to regional governments is clearly illustrated by the relationship between the national government in London and the Assembly in Northern Ireland. After the Northern Irish assembly was created in 1998, the national government in London has suspended it on five separate occasions. The last suspension occurred in January 2017 after the Northern Irish government collapsed due to a lack of trust between Unionists, advocating Northern Ireland to remain in the United Kingdom, and Nationalists, advocating unification with the Republic of Ireland. Since then decisions on funding allocations have been in the hands of the Northern Ireland Civil Service, and budgets will need to be passed through the British Parliament in Westminster.

Federalism is seen as a way to diffuse regional or ethnic tensions within a given geographical area or country, and create a political structure that can facilitate cooperation in the economic and security realm. When it comes to the reasons why countries become federal, political scientists often distinguish between coming-together and holding-together federalism. Riker (1964) conceived of federalism as an institutional bargain in which political communities seek to reap the benefits of scale in some areas, for example by regulating trade and providing military security, while at the same time safeguarding autonomy in other spheres. This process of territorial power sharing is called **coming-together federalism**, and signifies the coming together of previously independent political entities in a bigger territorial unit. Our trading villages in the previous section offer an example of coming-together federalism. In the European context Switzerland is a clear example of coming-together federalism. The experience of EU member states pooling and delegating policy authority to the supranational level also resembles a process of coming-together federalism.

Stepan (1999) distinguished coming-together federalism from holding-together federalism. **Holding-together federalism**, according to him is the result of a process in which the central government of a country chooses to decentralize its power to subnational governments to ameliorate tensions among various ethnic or linguistic groups seeking more say over their own affairs. Here devolution of power is necessary to preserve the state. In Europe, Belgium is an example of holding-together federalism. Federalism was enshrined in law in the 1970 Belgian constitution, and is seen as an attempt to hold the country together despite its internal divisions between the three linguistic groups: Flanders with a majority of Belgian Dutch-speakers, Wallonia predominantly populated by French-speakers, and a small German-speaking community in the east of the country. The capital, Brussels, is a separate political entity which is both Dutch- and French-speaking. Within Flanders there has been a movement for greater autonomy of the region and protection of the Dutch language. Between 1954 and 2002, these demands were advocated by a political party called the People's Union (Volksunie) and after its collapse by the National Flemish Alliance (Nieuw-Vlaamse Alliantie)—and to some extent the far right Flemish Interest (Vlaams Belang). The introduction of federalism to Belgium can be seen as a way to reconcile the scale advantages associated with greater territory and the desire for self-government of those regions that have distinct cultural and linguistic identities.

The tension between a sense of regional identity leading to demands for self-rule, and the functional benefits that are associated with a larger scale of economic and political co-operation crucially shape territorial politics in Europe. The wish of regions to exercise more self-rule—something that often coincides with the presence of linguistic, ethnic, or religious minorities with strong communal ties—in order to circumvent that laws are imposed from the outside often leads friction between national law and minority norms. This in turn generates demands for territorial reform. The issue of Catalan independence discussed in Box 3.4 clearly illustrates this. Decentralization is, moreover, a highly political process and can involve partisan considerations. The transfer of policy-making authority to the subnational level may not only be a concession to vocal regional demands or an instrument to keep peace, but it may be in fact a rational choice of parties at the national level who are ideologically proximate to regional parties who demand authority (Röth and Kaiser, 2019).

Box 3.4 CASE STUDY: The Issue of Catalan Independence

Catalonia is an autonomous region in Spain with a strong independence movement. The beginnings of the movement can be traced back to the mid-19th century, but it became politically organized in 1922 through the founding of the political party called the Catalan State (Estat Català) — now known as the Republican Left of Catalonia (Esquerra Republicana de Catalunya). During the Spanish Civil War, the Spanish fascist dictator General Francisco Franco abolished Catalan autonomy. Following the Spanish transition to democracy, Catalan political parties have demanded autonomy rather than independence.

Recent demands for Catalan independence can be traced to the 2010 ruling of the Constitutional Court of Spain on the 2006 Statute of Autonomy. This legal arrangement was agreed with the Spanish government and passed by a referendum in Catalonia, but eventually ruled unconstitutional by the court. This court decision fuelled mass demonstrations. This popular movement for independence soon translated into parliamentary seats. The 2012 election resulted in a pro-independence majority for the first time in the region's history. The new parliament adopted the Catalan Sovereignty Declaration in early 2013 claiming that the Catalan people had the right to self-rule.

The Catalan government announced a referendum on independence to be held in November 2014. The Spanish government referred it to the constitutional court, which ruled that the referendum was unconstitutional. The Catalan government changed the referendum to a non-binding consultation, which the constitutional court also banned. The Catalan government pressed ahead with the consultation nonetheless. The vote on 9 November 2014 resulted in a majority for independence, although turnout was only 42 per cent of eligible voters. Following the result, the Catalan government called another election for September 2015, which was to become a vote on independence. The pro-independence parties fell short of a majority, winning 47 per cent of the vote.

The new Catalan parliament passed a resolution to start the independence process in November 2015. The following year, the Catalan government announced another binding referendum on independence, which was again ruled as unconstitutional by the constitutional court. The referendum was held on 1 October 2017, nonetheless, but the anti-independence parties boycotted the vote. The turnout was 43 per cent, and of those who voted 90 per cent favoured independence. Following the result, the Catalan parliament approved a resolution to unilaterally declare an independent Catalan republic on 27 October 2017. However, this declaration was ruled illegal by the lawyers of the Catalan parliament as it violated the rulings of the Spanish constitutional court.

The issue of Catalan independence remains unresolved and has polarized national politics in Spain, with the parties on the right of the political spectrum—the Popular Party (Partido Popular), Vox, and Citizens (Cuidadanos)—fiercely opposing independence, while the two main parties on the left, the Spanish Social Democratic Party (Partido Socialista Obrero Español) and We Can (Podemos) supporting a political resolution.

3.5 Summary

This chapter has introduced the basic theoretical ingredients needed to study and understand territorial politics in Europe. It introduced the concept of multilevel governance to describe patterns in power sharing between different territorial levels of government. We have shown that policy authority at the national level is increasingly shifting to EU institutions at the supranational level as well as to regional governments at the subnational level. In order to understand the variation in the extent to which policy authority is shared across policy areas, countries, and over time, we have introduced the concepts of pooling, delegation, federalism, and decentralization among others.

The goal of this chapter has also been to highlight the tension between territorial self-rule and the advantages of scale that stem from cooperation across national and regional borders. This tension is at the heart of change and conflict over territorial politics in Europe, past, present, and most likely in the future. The way in which policy authority is shared among territorial jurisdictions is not a stable equilibrium, but rather subject to contestation and change.

Online Data Exercise: The Regional Authority Index (RAI)

The interactive online exercise introduces one of the most important datasets for studying multilevel politics: the regional authority indices. These indices provide country-level data on how authority is distributed between political levels. In the exercise, you will be able to explore the development of subnational authority over time with a specific focus on Europe and accession to the European Union.

Take your learning further with this interactive data exercise, available at **www.foundationsofeuropeanpolitics.com**

For additional material and resources, including multiple-choice questions, web links, and more, please visit the online resources: **www.oup.com/he/devries1e**

Part 2

Citizens and Voters

Part 2

Citizens and Voters

4 Ideology and Issues

This chapter considers the changing nature of ideology and voter preferences in Europe. We often think of voters and parties residing along a single ideological left–right continuum. This chapter discusses the origins and changing nature of left–right ideology and the emergence of new salient issues, such as immigration, the environment, and European integration. We also discuss how populism is challenging the traditional left–right structure of politics by focusing instead on the division between the people and elites.

Shared **ideology** is the glue that binds citizens and their political representatives. Citizens have **preferences** over policies that guide them when they choose between political parties and candidates in elections, and these preferences, in turn, are structured by political ideology, which we define as a relatively stable and consistent set of ideas about the world that justify and organize political attitudes and beliefs. Ideologies thus simplify otherwise complex political choices; parties compete along ideological lines and voters can choose the parties whose ideology is the closest to their own. In the simple uni-dimensional model of democracy introduced in Chapter 2, parties and voters are located on a single ideological dimension. One way to think about the link between voters and their governments is to examine the match between government policy and the ideology of the **median voter** (see discussions in Chapters 2 and 7).

In the European context, the dominant ideological dimension is typically labelled as the **left–right dimension**, which is centred on the role of the state in the economy, although the content of this dimension may be shifting over time. In this chapter, we consider the nature of citizen ideologies and how they structure political behaviour. We then introduce the notion of left–right politics and discuss whether electoral contestation is becoming multidimensional with the rise of new salient 'cultural' issues, such as immigration and European integration. Finally, we discuss populism as a thin-centred ideology and examine how it challenges our model of democracy.

4.1 Ideology and Elections

A core idea in the model of politics presented in this book, as in most spatial theories, is that both voters and parties can be located on a single ideological dimension. Each voter has a position on this ideological dimension, which they use to decide which parties best represent their interests and who to vote for. In the example introduced in Chapter 2, citizens had to choose how much money to spend on constructing a new park on a vacant plot of land. On the one extreme, they could leave everything as is, spend no money at all, and the plot would not be usable for recreation. On the other extreme, they could agree to build an elaborate park with playing fields, swimming pools, tennis courts, and other amenities, but it would mean charging every citizen more in taxes. We also imagined a range of possibilities lying between these two extremes. Each citizen would vote for the mayoral candidate with the preferences most similar to their own on the issue of the park. The mayor elected with the majority of the votes would therefore represent the preferences of the 'median voter' and implement the park policy that corresponded with their preferences.

Politics in real-world representative democracies is, of course, more complicated than this simple example. Elected representatives have to take views on a vast number of complex issues, and few citizens have detailed knowledge of their preferences on each and every one. Ideology is therefore a crucial tool which voters use in elections to detect differences between representatives and determine their preferences for parties and candidates. Political ideology is a stable and consistent set of ideas about the world that provides a guideline for political action (see Box 4.1). By identifying their own ideological position and that of the parties, voters can choose the party that best represents their preferences. Thus, ideology as a belief system includes a wide range of attitudes that are consistent with one another given the political context, while the belief system itself remains abstract (e.g. liberal or conservative).

Ideology and preferences are not quite the same. While ideology is conceived of as a stable set of ideas, citizens have preferences over specific policies or political candidates. For instance, a citizen might prefer paying a higher tax in order to fund more generous unemployment benefits rather than a lower tax that would limit the number of persons who would be eligible for such benefits. Or a citizen might prefer one candidate over another. Preferences are closely linked to **attitudes**, that is people's beliefs (likes or dislikes) about specific ideas, individuals, or objects. In a sense, when faced with a choice (e.g. several policy proposals or

Box 4.1 **CONTROVERSIES AND DEBATES:** Converse on Belief Systems and Ideology

In his seminal contribution to the study of ideology, *The Nature of Belief Systems in Mass Publics*, Converse (1964) examines whether citizens actually hold consistent and clear ideological views. He introduced the concept of 'belief systems', defined as 'a configuration of attitudes and ideas in which the elements are bound together by some form of constraint or functional interdependence' (Converse, 1964, 206). Without such a 'constraint', or coherence of attitudes, it is impossible to argue that people adhere to consistent belief systems, or that they hold ideologically consistent views. On the basis of his analysis of responses to a set of survey questions, Converse argues that such belief systems are quite rare in the American public and restricted to politically sophisticated citizens. He demonstrates that most respondents express random responses or 'non-attitudes' to political questions. He therefore concludes that the few people hold consistent liberal–conservative (left–right) belief systems that structure their political attitudes and opinions. In other words, most people do not interpret politics through an ideological lens.

Converse's conclusions have been criticized by many scholars who argue that individuals do display ideological 'constraints', especially on salient issues and when politics is more polarized. Numerous studies have shown that people's political predispositions are essentially stable, which suggests that ideology does shape political preferences. A key result from Converse's study that still stands, however, is that ideological constraint is strongly related to political sophistication and education: better educated and more politically sophisticated citizens have more stable and coherent ideological belief systems.

candidates), citizens compare and rank these choices in order of preferences based on their attitudes. Thus, preferences are connected to ideology, and belief systems are abstract aggregations of specific preferences. We use the term policy preferences when citizens and parties rank various policy proposals against the policy that is currently in place—the **status quo**.

When we study democracies in more detail, we learn about various types of political actors that participate in politics: individual candidates, political parties, elected representatives, or cabinets and governments. When candidates and parties campaign in elections and governments propose new laws, then we talk about these revealed preferences as **policy positions**. Fundamentally, the ideology and preferences of politicians are unobservable, or latent. However, politicians reveal them through their actions: they give speeches during election campaigns and in parliament, they vote in parliament on bills and amendments, or they give interviews and post on social media. Such revealed preferences, however, are most often strategic in nature. That is, politicians adopt particular positions because they think the positions may win them support. But such positions may change over time, for instance, if a political party has lost an election and, as a consequence, the party shifts some of its positions in a direction that it hopes will help it win more votes in the next election.

Many different political ideologies exist. In the simplest terms, we can distinguish between three classic political ideologies: Liberalism, Conservatism, and Socialism. In brief, **liberalism** puts emphasis on freedom, individualism, equality, and the rule of law, while **conservatism** places greater value on the maintenance of traditional institutions and norms and promotes respect for authority. In contrast to both of these ideologies, **socialism** challenges the inherent inequalities in capitalism and advocates social/collective ownership and a greater role for the state in the economy.

The origins of these schools of thought can be traced to different responses to the transition from a feudal to an industrial society. Broadly speaking, liberalism, conservatism, and socialism reflect different ways of thinking about historical developments, such as the Reformation, the Industrial Revolution, and the development of the nation-state. Liberalism can be viewed an attack on feudal privilege and absolute rule by monarchs and emperors in Europe. The English philosopher John Locke was a key thinker of early liberalism. Locke's thinking is associated with advocating constitutional rather than absolutist rule based on a belief of people's natural right to life, liberty, and property (Locke, 1690/1980).

Conservatism arose as a reaction to the growing challenges to absolutist rule in Europe, especially during the French Revolution. It is often associated with the writings of the Dublin-born statesman Edmund Burke (1790/1987) who was deeply critical of the way the French Revolution unseated monarchic rule in France. Conservatism as a political school of thought rejects radical social change. Rather conservative political thinkers advocate the preservation of the existing social order, which should only undergo incremental change aimed at conserving that order.

In contrast, socialism developed as a reaction to the Industrial Revolution and the growing of an industrial working class in Europe. Socialists tend to analyse society in terms of the distribution of wealth and means of production that give rise to certain social classes in society. It is associated with the aggregation and articulation of the interests and rights of an oppressed and exploited working class against the privileged class of factory owners and the independently wealthy. A more radical version of socialism, also referred to as **communism**, is associated with the idea of the need for radical change within societies through the means of a revolution of the working class, the proletariat. The idea of proletariat revolution that would overthrow capitalism is associated with the writings of the German philosopher and economist Karl Marx (1867).

Liberalism, conservatism, and socialism, thus, represent three different ideological perspectives on how society should be organized. The differences between these viewpoints are relevant for our understanding of political ideology to this day. For example, the political programmes of Conservative or Socialist parties include key elements of conservatism and socialism respectively. In Europe, for much of the late nineteenth and twentieth centuries, the primary ideological cleavage in electoral competition formed along the so-called **left–right dimension**, named for the seating arrangement in the French National Assembly at the time of the French Revolution (see Box 4.2). It pitted Socialist parties against Conservative parties. Socialist parties forged close alliances with labour unions and emphasized workers' rights and economic redistribution by the state in their policy platforms. Conservative parties, on the other hand, maintained strong ties to capital owners and tended to advocate for less redistribution and for conditions favourable to businesses and capital investment. As a consequence, ideology is often referred to in terms of 'left' and 'right' in European electoral politics. In its classic form, the left–right dimension is concerned with state intervention in the economy and redistribution, with a more left-wing position favouring greater state intervention and more redistribution and a right-wing position favouring a free market with less state involvement, redistribution, and spending. In practice, the left–right ideological dimension also structures attitudes on a wider range of policy issues.

Citizens tend to be able to express their views on this left–right dimension. Figure 4.1 presents density plots of voters' left–right positions across twenty-three European countries when they are asked to place themselves on a left–right scale ranging from 0 to 10, where 0 is most left and 10 is most right (Huber, 1989). This is one of the most commonly asked questions in public opinion surveys in political science. As we would expect, when we simply average over the positions of all survey respondents in a country, the average respondent everywhere is rather centrist, indicated by the black vertical lines for each country in Figure 4.1. Nevertheless, there are significant differences in the distribution of voters within the left–right space across countries. For example, in countries like Lithuania and Slovakia, most voters report that they are centrist with few voters at the extremes, as indicated by the large hump in the middle of the plot and the thin tails at the extremes. In contrast, Danish, Finnish, Italian, and Spanish voters

Box 4.2 CASE STUDY: The French Revolution and the Origins of Left–Right Politics

The labels of 'left' and 'right' in politics date back to the French Revolution. In 1789, members of the French National Assembly met to begin drafting a new constitution. The delegates were deeply divided over the issue of how much authority King Louis XVI should have. Supporters of the king's right to an absolute veto sat on the presiding officer's right in the Assembly, the noble side. The anti-royalist supporters of the Revolution, who wanted a highly restricted veto, seated themselves on the left.

These seating arrangements in the French parliament during the French Revolution took on lasting political significance: to the right, supporters of a monarchy that sought to preserve many of the king's powers; to the left, those who wished to reduce them. Even today, the 'right' is associated with more traditional, conservative values and the 'left' with more progressive ones.

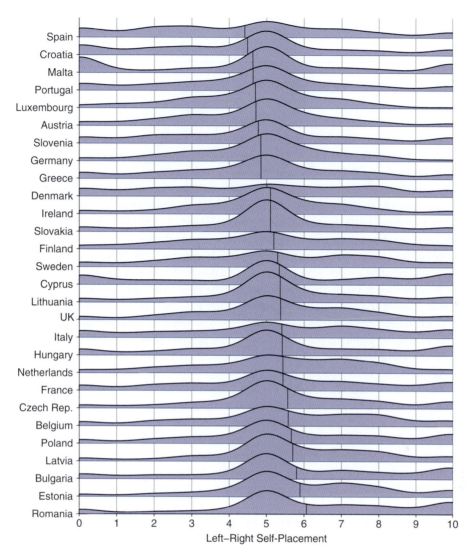

Figure 4.1 Voter Ideological Self-Placement on a General Left–Right Scale

Data source: EES (Schmitt et al., 2019). The black vertical line shows the mean left–right self-placement in each country.

display a much flatter ideological distribution, with similar numbers of voters across all parts of the ideological spectrum. Meanwhile, Cyprus and Malta seem to have extra voters on both extremes. We also see that Spanish, Croatian, and Portuguese voters seem to trend to the left, while Belgian, Bulgarian, Estonian, Polish, and Latvian voters, among others, position themselves further to the right. To some extent, we also see this reflected in the strength of parties in those countries, with parties on the centre-left traditionally performing better in Spain and in Portugal than in Poland and Hungary, where parties on the centre-right and radical right dominate politics (see Chapter 8).

Voters can use their left–right ideology as a basic reference point, or informational short-cut, to choose the party with which they share preferences. In other words, they vote for the

Figure 4.2 Uni-dimensional Electoral Competition

party in closest proximity to their own ideological position. This is shown in Figure 4.2 where the voter with a centre-left ideology will vote for the left-wing Party A rather than the right-wing Party B, since Party A's ideology is more aligned with the voter and the party is more likely to implement policies in line with the voter's preferences, if elected.

This uni-dimensional model depicted in Figure 4.2 follows from Downs's spatial model of electoral competition (Downs, 1957). Downs adapted theoretical arguments originally developed by Hotelling (1929) to account for the relationship between the location of competing stores on a high street or ice cream vendors on a beach and the behaviour of their customers. Just like customers, Downs argued that voters will choose the party that is located the closest to their own position on the left–right ideological dimension. In a two-party contest, parties have the incentive to locate themselves close to the median voter in order to gain as many voters as possible and win office (see Chapters 2 and 9). In this abstract model, ideology thus creates a common frame of reference for voters and parties that should ensure that the party elected to office implements policies that mirror the position of this societal median voter, i.e. that there is **congruence** between the policy programme that the government implements and the preference of the median voter.

The depiction of voter ideologies in Figure 4.2 assumes that the important policy questions can be reduced to a single dimension in a meaningful manner. Indeed, left–right ideology encompasses many of the key public policy debates. What proportion of people's income should be taxed? Should the state redistribute from the wealthier to the poorer in our society? How should the state spend the money on education, welfare, and health or on the military and law enforcement? And, to what degree should the state intervene in how businesses operate? People's views about such questions are structured by their left–right ideological position.

There are three main explanations for how people develop these left–right ideological positions: a social, value, and partisan explanation. The social explanation relates to the idea that social structures, chiefly occupation, religion, and location, determine people's left–right identification. For example, factory workers are more likely to identify as left-wing, while shopkeepers, managers, and entrepreneurs are more likely to identify as right-wing. The value explanation singles out the importance of people's deep-seated value-orientations, such as the role of the state in the economy or the role of religion in public life, that develop during childhood and adolescent socialization and shape people's left–right ideological position. Finally, the partisan explanation suggests that left–right ideological positions mirror the partisan loyalties that people have developed. For example, people who support Conservative or Christian Democratic parties generally place themselves on the right of the ideological spectrum, while people who support Socialist or Social Democratic parties are more likely to place themselves on the left of the ideological spectrum. People who support the far right do so largely based concerns about national identity and immigration, while those who support the far left are generally more worried about rising inequality and unbridled capitalism

(De Vries and Edwards, 2009). Of course, the different explanations are not necessarily mutually exclusive, and may be complementary. For example, it is possible that socio-economic position and socialization influence an individual's values and party affiliation, which may in turn lead to a particular ideological outlook.

History may also play an important role in the development of left–right ideology, especially in new democracies. During the mid-twentieth century dictatorships ruled many parts of Europe, for example the right-wing dictatorships in parts of southern Europe—namely, Greece, Portugal, and Spain—and the left-wing Communist regimes in central and eastern Europe. After democratization, the ideology embraced by these authoritarian regimes was often negatively evaluated by many citizens and elites; the ideology of authoritarian regimes leaves a mark on contemporary ideology (Dinas and Northmore-Ball, 2020). Citizens in new democracies may display a bias in their left–right self-identification with respect to the ideological slant of the previous regime. If the authoritarian regime was ideologically right-wing, like in southern Europe, citizens may self identify as more left-wing and display an anti-right bias. This seems to be the case for Greece, Portugal, and Spain based on Figure 4.2 and could account for the support for radical left parties in these countries, like Syriza in Greece or Podemos in Spain. If the authoritarian regime was ideologically left-wing, like in central and eastern Europe, citizens may display an anti-left bias and self-identify as more right-wing. Figure 4.2 suggests that this is indeed the case for citizens in central and eastern Europe who self-identify more strongly as right-wing compared to many other countries.

4.2 New Political Issues and Multidimensional Politics

Notwithstanding the importance of left–right ideology in Europe, many politically salient issues cannot be easily located on a single ideological dimension. Part of the reason that the uni-dimensional model of democracy based on left–right ideology has been so popular as a way to describe the relationship between political parties and voters stems from the dominance of class politics in Europe. Historically, voters in Europe have been tied to specific political parties, the ideologies that they espouse, through their social class. Working-class voters have traditionally identified with parties on the left, and the self-employed and managers with parties on the right. But other divisions have also shaped voters' political attachments, and therefore their beliefs, notably religious or regional identification. For example, Christians who go to church often are also more likely to vote for Christian Democratic parties than atheists, whereas people who identify strongly with their sub-state nation or region, such as those who feel very Scottish or Catalan, are more likely to vote for regionalist and separatist parties.

These enduring lines of conflict, arising out of social structural characteristics—chiefly, class, religion, and geographical location—are often called **cleavages**. According to the **cleavage theory** developed by Lipset and Rokkan (1967), for a societal division to constitute a cleavage, the groups involved must be conscious of their collective identity, and the divisions must have an organizational expression, such as a political party that expresses the views of the group. Lipset and Rokkan argue that the different societal cleavages are at the root of many of the parties have dominated European politics for decades, something discussed in greater detail in Chapter 8.

What matters for ideology and electoral competition is the degree to which social cleavages are reinforcing or cross-cutting (see also the discussion in Chapters 5 and 8). When social cleavages are reinforcing, the politically relevant social categories that people exhibit, such as their class, religion, or regional identities, are correlated with each other. In other words, they overlap. In the case of cross-cutting social cleavages, these politically relevant social categories are not correlated. To illustrate the importance of **reinforcing** or **cross-cutting cleavages**, imagine a country where both class and religion are the most dominant social cleavages. In this country, people who are religious belong to the upper class in society, whereas the people who are not religious identify as lower class. In such a scenario, even though both religion and class are important in politics, the uni-dimensional model of electoral competition as portrayed in Figure 4.2 suffices to describe voter and party ideology. Because religion and class identity are highly correlated, the two attributes combined form a single ideological dimension on which voters and parties can be placed. Now imagine a country in which religion and class are again the dominant social cleavages, but the cleavages are cross-cutting. People who are religious identify either with the upper or lower class in society, whereas people who are not religious could also identify with either the upper or lower class in society. In this scenario, people's religious and class identity are not linked, and the religious cleavage cuts across the class divide. This gives rise to multidimensional politics; we cannot distil people's beliefs down to a single line.

Big societal transformations may also lead to the development of multidimensional politics, especially if these changes increase the importance of ideological divides not covered by the traditional four cleavages discussed already. In a seminal book, Inglehart (1977) argues that younger generations in post-war western Europe were socialized in an environment where existential material security was taken for granted and this led to a change in political values from materialism to **postmaterialism**. Whereas older generations, who had experienced the economic devastation following the world wars in Europe, were predominantly concerned about economic growth and physical security, the affluence experienced by the post-war generations let them to care more about postmaterialist issues, such as the environment, gender equality, democracy, self-expression, and human rights. Inglehart argued that, with increasing prosperity, younger generations would be more postmaterialist and less materialist, as they experienced relative peace and prosperity during their formative years. Through a process of generational replacement, postmaterial attitudes would become increasingly important (see Box 4.3 for a discussion of how to measure postmaterial values).

Many today do speak of a second **'cultural' dimension** that structures European politics alongside the traditional left–right dimension of conflict. However, not everyone agrees on the content of the second dimension. For some it relates primarily to value divisions based on tradition, religion, sexuality, or the environment; for others it also relates to more recent politically salient issues like attitudes towards immigration and European integration. This 'cultural' dimension of politics has been given a number of different labels, including libertarian–authoritarian (Kitschelt, 1994), transnational (Hooghe and Marks, 2018) or integration–demarcation (Kriesi et al., 2008). What the different understandings have in common is that they highlight the importance of issues that are largely non-economic in nature (although the conflict may have economic roots) and relate to more 'cultural' aspects of politics and polarized responses to the challenges of an increasingly globalized world: immigration,

Box 4.3 METHODS AND MEASUREMENT: Measuring Postmaterialism

Inglehart (1977) suggests that the post-war generations in Europe held more postmaterialist attitudes than previous generations. Postmaterialism is measured by asking survey respondents to rank the following possible goals in order of priority for their country.

1. Maintaining order in the nation
2. Giving the people more say in important government decisions
3. Fighting rising prices
4. Protecting freedom of speech

   If people prefer items 2 and 4 to items 1 and 3 then they are classified as postmaterialist. Although the measurement of postmaterialism has been widely used, it has also been criticized. The measurement fails to include some of the core characteristics of postmaterialism as defined by Inglehart, such as the environment, and for its reliance on only four items, which may make it very sensitive to short-term changes.

borders, identities, and international governance. These cultural aspects of politics juxtapose culturally progressive libertarians against more culturally conservative authoritarians, where the former embrace transnationalism and globalization while the latter emphasize the values of a demarcated national community.

The development of Green or New Left parties in the 1970s and 1980s can be viewed as a response to the increasing political importance of postmaterialism. The rise of the Green Party in Sweden offers an example. The party was founded in 1981 in the wake of the anti-nuclear movement and the nuclear power referendum in 1980. It emerged out of a sense of discontent with the existing parties' environmental policies. The party became the first new party to enter Swedish parliament in seventy years, gaining 5.5 per cent of the vote in 1988. While Old Left parties are closely tied to the industrial working class and mobilize an economic position on the left of the left–right ideological dimension relating to state intervention in the economy, New Left and Green parties privilege issues such as the environment or gender equality that are not necessarily associated with traditional ideological left–right positions. A country's political space can be characterized as two dimensional when both the left–right economic dimension as well as the divide between materialists and postmaterialists are important for describing people's political views.

Within western Europe today generally two dimensions are used to explain the structure of electoral competition: a left–right and a 'cultural' libertarian–authoritarian dimension. Figure 4.3 displays a model of a two-dimensional electoral politics. Both voters and parties can be located in a two-dimensional space based on their positions on the economic left–right dimension and the cultural libertarian–authoritarian dimension. If the two dimensions are cross-cutting, this would most likely produce four 'types' of parties and voters: left-authoritarians, right-authoritarians, left-libertarians, and right-libertarians. The voter shown in Figure 4.3 with a left-authoritarian ideology will vote for the left-authoritarian Party A rather than the right-authoritarian Party B, the left-libertarian Party C, or the right-libertarian Party D. This is because the ideological positions of the voter and Party A's ideology (Left Authoritarian) are more aligned, and therefore Party A, if elected, is more likely to implement policies in line with the preferences of the voter.

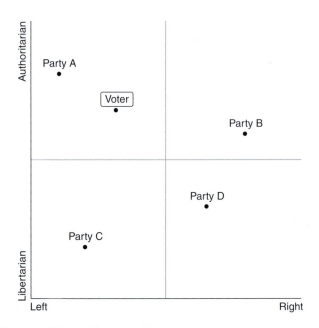

Figure 4.3 Two-Dimensional Electoral Competition

Kriesi et al. (2008) argue that societal conflicts over globalization, such as growing interna-tional market integration and migration flows, have led to the mobilization of cultural issues, such as immigration and European integration, within political competition. They refer to this second dimension as the **integration–demarcation dimension**, which they argue pits the winners of globalization against the losers. While the winners are characterized by high levels of education and occupational mobility and favour closer integration and open borders, the losers of globalization have lower levels of education, lesser occupational skills, and cannot fully profit from the blurring of state and market boundaries. They tend to oppose European integration and open borders.

Attitudes towards European integration, in this account, are thus a core component of the second ideological dimension. However, the degree to which the European integration issue fits into the two-dimensional model of electoral politics is a matter of debate. While conflict over Europe was initially seen as largely independent of the left–right dimensions of political conflict, in the early 2000s experts of party competition suggested that positions on left–right and European integration became linked, albeit in a specific way. When it comes to political parties, Hooghe et al. (2002) have described the relationship between positions on the left–right ideological dimension and support for European integration as an 'inverted U-curve'. The inverted U-curve indicates that parties of the ideological mainstream, that is Conserva-tive, Social, and Christian democratic parties, are generally supportive of the integration pro-cess, as they have frequently been part of governing coalitions throughout western Europe and were therefore largely responsible for the course of integration. Extreme left- and right-wing parties, however, most strongly oppose it, albeit for different reasons. While left-wing extremist parties oppose integration in Europe on the basis of the neoliberal character of the project and its negative influence on the welfare state, the extreme right opposes intra-EU migration and aims to protect national sovereignty. The more recent work by Kriesi et al. (2008) suggests that positions towards immigration, European integration, and international politics have become increasingly linked and part of the second 'cultural' dimension.

A burgeoning literature on public attitudes towards European integration has developed (see Box 4.4). For a long time, public opinion was seen as a form of passive support for the activities of national government leaders in Brussels based on the belief that they would safeguard national interests. Public opinion was characterized by a permissive consensus; in other words, citizens held a generally favourable prevailing attitude towards integration, but it was not an issue they cared about much. Yet, times have changed. Eurosceptic parties have made some of their strongest electoral gains in recent European and national elections, and the outcome of the referendum on EU membership in the United Kingdom in 2016 is perhaps the clearest example of consequences of growing Eurosceptic sentiment.

Figure 4.4 shows the average support for EU membership in four regions in the EU using Eurobarometer data, following the approach by Hobolt and De Vries (2016a): countries in

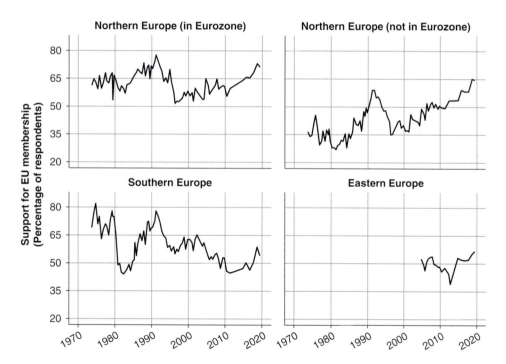

Figure 4.4 Support for EU Membership across Europe

Data source: Eurobarometer Surveys. The following member states are included in each region. Northern Europe (Eurozone): Austria, Belgium, Ireland, Finland, Germany, Luxembourg, and the Netherlands; northern Europe (not in Eurozone): Denmark, Sweden, and the United Kingdom; southern Europe: Cyprus, France, Italy, Greece, Malta, Portugal, and Spain; eastern Europe: Bulgaria, Croatia, Czech Republic, Estonia, Hungary, Latvia, Lithuania, Poland, Romania, Slovakia, and Slovenia.

northern Europe that are in the Eurozone, those that are in the north but not in the Eurozone, countries in southern Europe, and those in eastern Europe that have joined the EU in 2004 and later. The figure shows that membership approval has been, on average, the highest in the northern Eurozone and lowest in southern Europe and eastern Europe. However, there have been notable fluctuations over time. Peak support for membership occurred in the early 1990s, after the end of the Cold War, with the completion of the single market and the plans for economic and monetary union. Support then dropped, increasing again in recent years, in particular in northern Europe. On average in all four regions, a majority of citizens supports the membership of their country in the European Union, but approval is lower in the south and east.

It would be wrong to conclude, however, that citizens in southern and eastern Europe are more sceptical of integration. Figure 4.5 again uses Eurobarometer data and shows support for integration in 2019. The survey regularly asks respondents at what speed they currently think the European Union is being built, where 1 equates to standing still and 7 is running as

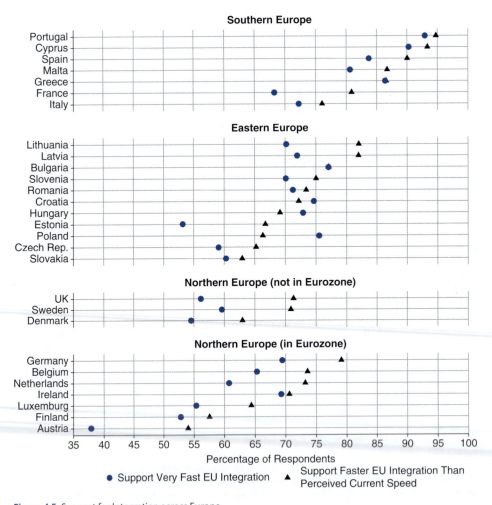

Figure 4.5 Support for Integration across Europe

Data source: European Commission (2020b)

> ### Box 4.4 **METHODS AND MEASUREMENT:** Measuring Eurosceptic Attitudes
>
> Early studies of attitudes towards European integration focused on support for European integration, but the focus in the last decade has shifted to opposition to European integration, or so-called **Euroscepticism**. Moreover, people's attitudes towards the European Union were traditionally captured along one single dimension ranging from a Eurosceptic pole, indicating a rejection of the European project, to a Europhile pole, indicating support for the European project (Hobolt and De Vries, 2016a). In her book *Euroscepticism and the Future of European Integration*, De Vries (2018) challenges this classical approach in two ways. First, attitudes towards the EU might reflect the multifaceted nature of European integration. For example, people might generally support their country's membership in the EU, but at the same time show little appreciation for the policies that the EU pursues. Due to the complex nature of their attitudes, people cannot be easily classified as either Eurosceptic or Europhile. Rather, they are often conflicted and ambivalent about the EU and simultaneously like and dislike certain aspects of European integration. Second, people's attitudes towards the EU should not be conceptualized in isolation from their attitudes towards the nation-state. National institutions and policy performance provide an essential benchmark for how citizens view the EU. Eurosceptic attitudes are more likely to develop in country contexts in which national institutions perform well and yield good policy outcomes, or at least among people that perceive national institutional performance and policy outcomes in a positive light. Using this two-dimensional concept of attitudes towards European integration, we can identify loyal supporters of the EU as those citizens who are more satisfied the EU democracy than with national democracy and more satisfied with EU policies than with national policies. Conversely, strong Eurosceptics are those for which the relationship is reversed (so-called exit sceptics). Finally, there are two types of moderate sceptics: regime sceptics are content with EU policy, but not with the EU's institutions (relative to the nation-state) and policy sceptics are satisfied with EU institutions, but not with EU policy. Measuring Euroscepticism this way allows us to explain unexpected patterns of Euroscepticism. For example, even when economic and political conditions are favourable in the EU, citizens may become Eurosceptic if their relative regime and policy assessment of the EU changes in comparison to that of their own member state.

fast as possible. The survey also asks at what speed respondents would prefer Europe to be built. The figure shows the percentage of respondents per country who wish integration to proceed at a faster pace than they think that it currently is (black dots), and also the percentage who support very fast integration (5 or greater on the seven-point scale) (blue dots). Citizens everywhere want EU integration to proceed faster than they perceive it, but especially so in some parts of southern and eastern Europe, where more than three out of four citizens want faster EU integration than the perceived speed. And the percentage of respondents desiring very fast integration is higher in almost every southern and eastern European country compared to northern Europe, in particular in Portugal, Cyprus, Spain, Malta, Greece, Bulgaria, Croatia, and Poland. The only exceptions are the Czech Republic, Estonia, France, and Slovakia. Southern and eastern countries are perhaps less satisfied with EU membership because the EU is not moving fast enough for them.

4.3 Populism and Anti-Elite Attitudes

Changes to the European political landscape are not only about the rising salience of new issues and a second 'cultural' dimension, but also the increasing appeal of populism. **Populism** is seen to be a key component of the electoral appeal of a number of politicians and new political parties, ranging from the Alternative for Germany and the National Front in France to Syriza in Greece and the Five Star Movement in Italy. Moreover, the British electorate's vote to leave the EU has been described as evidence of the growing appeal of populism. Yet, there is no academic consensus on the fundamental question of just what populism is. Most attention has been given to populism on the radical right. But populism can also be a feature of politics on the left or of parties and movements that defy left–right classification. The concept of populism has been employed in a variety of ways in the academic literature, for example as a political strategy (Laclau, 2005), a political style (Jagers and Walgrave, 2007), an organizational style (Taggart, 2000), a thin-centred ideology (Canovan, 1999; Mudde, 2004).

The most influential approach to populism as an ideology is that put forward by Mudde (2004). He defines populism as a thin-centred 'ideology that considers society to be ultimately separated into two homogeneous and antagonistic groups, "the pure people" versus "the corrupt elite", and which argues that politics should be an expression of the volonté générale (general will) of the people' (Mudde, 2004, 543). The first element of populism is that it is a thin-centred ideology, which means that it is malleable and can be easily integrated to any other more complex and host ideology, such as socialism, fascism, or liberalism. Thick-centred ideologies, such as liberalism, conservatism, or socialism, offer comprehensive answers to the organization and purpose of society, whereas populism can take different shapes as it borrows elements from these ideologies in combination with its fundamental views of the 'elite' and 'the people'.

At the core of populism lies a basic dualist **Manichaean** worldview that envisions society to be divided into two antithetical camps of an 'evil' elite and a 'good' homogeneous people. Populism is thus the opposite of **pluralism**, which holds that society is divided into a broad variety of heterogeneous and overlapping groups and individuals that often entertain fundamentally different views. It also differs from elitism, since elitists believe that the 'elite' are superior to the people in moral, cultural, and intellectual terms. The elite is defined on the basis of power, but often goes beyond attacks on the political establishment to also involve criticism of the media, the cultural elite, and the economic elite and 'global capital'. Populists on the right of the political spectrum often focus their attacks on the political and cultural elites, while those on the left are more critical of the economic elite.

The notion of 'the people' with a general will is also central to populism. The people represent the pure in opposition to the corrupt elite, and according to populist ideology the people are sovereign. This means that populists tend to favour reforms that strengthen 'the general will of the people', such as direct democracy. Given the emphasis on the people, populism also places great value on the nation. Populism on the right is also sometimes referred to as national populism, given its emphasis on nationalism. This form of populism, which is advocated by radical right-wing parties such as the French National Front, the Austrian Freedom Party, and the Danish People's Party, is also characterized by its nativist definition of the nation in ethnic terms and xenophobia towards ethnic minorities and immigrants.

Populism as an ideology is not necessarily anti-democratic and it puts great emphasis on the will of the people and institutions that allow the people to decide. But as we discussed in Chapter 2, it is not always evidence that a general 'will' exists. Unless we make strong

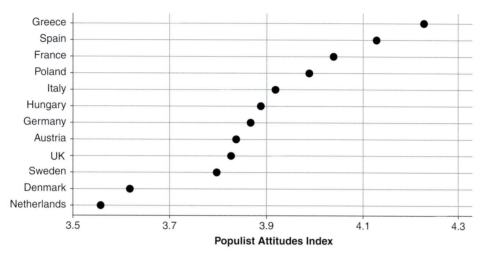

Figure 4.6 Populist Attitudes across Twelve European Countries, 2019

Data source: Kaltwasser et al. (2019)

assumptions about the nature of the policy space, aggregating societal preferences is not straightforward. Moreover, populism, in certain circumstances, can represent a challenge to core principles of liberal democracy, such as pluralism or independent non-majoritarian institutions (e.g. courts and human rights treaties) that protect the rights of minorities and fundamental rights. Because populism differs from the other forms of ideology discussed, much effort has gone into developing measures of populist ideology (see Box 4.5). Figure 4.6 presents levels of populism across twelve European countries using one of these measures.

Figure 4.6 shows that populist attitudes vary quite significantly across countries, with Greece and Spain showing the highest levels of populism and Denmark and the Netherlands showing the lowest levels. Greece and Spain have experienced relatively high levels of corruption, poor governance, and poor economic performance, whereas countries with lower levels of populism—Sweden, Denmark, and the Netherlands—are generally seen to perform better across all of these dimensions. Indeed, Rico and Anduiza (2019) find that the explanation for citizens' populist attitudes is their perception of the government's economic performance. Moreover, people with populist attitudes are also more attracted to vote for parties with a distinct populist ideology.

In addition to populist attitudes, anti-establishment sentiment, more generally—defined as people's general disengagement from politics and distrust of political leaders and the political system—is an important area of ongoing research. In one of the most comprehensive analyses of anti-establishment sentiment, a team of British researchers have examined responses to British public opinion surveys, alongside diaries and letters about politics by ordinary citizens, since the 1940s (Clarke et al., 2018). The data show that negative sentiment towards politics and political elites has grown in both scope and intensity within the British public since the 1940s. This negative sentiment in part reflects people's changing preferences about the desired traits of politicians. While traditionally British respondents wanted politicians to be 'clever' and 'wise', by the end of the time frame of investigation, in 2017, 'honesty', 'trustworthiness', and 'meaning what one says' were viewed as the most

> ## Box 4.5 **METHODS AND MEASUREMENT:** Measuring Populist Attitudes
>
> Researchers have started to measure populism as a set of attitudes individuals hold about politics and society. Such attitudes may be rooted in people's political experiences, but may also be activated by populist rhetoric of political parties. How to measure populist attitudes is a matter of contention. One of the most widely used measures was developed by Hawkins et al. (2012). The authors developed a way to measure populist attitudes in the United States context based on people's level of agreement with four statements:
>
> 1. Politics is ultimately a struggle between good and evil.
> 2. The politicians in Congress need to follow the will of the people.
> 3. The power of a few special interests prevents our country from making progress.
> 4. The people, not the politicians, should make the most important policy decisions.
>
> When people display stronger agreement with these statements, they are classified as holding more populist attitudes. Akkerman et al. (2014) adjust this measure to the European context, specifically the Netherlands, and suggest using the following six statements:
>
> 1. The politicians in the Dutch parliament need to follow the will of the people.
> 2. The people, and not politicians, should make our most important policy decisions.
> 3. The political differences between the elite and the people are larger than the differences among the people.
> 4. I would rather be represented by a citizen than by a specialized politician.
> 5. Elected officials talk too much and take too little action.
> 6. What people call 'compromise' in politics is really just selling out on one's principles.
>
> While people who score highly on such 'populist attitude scales' are also more likely to vote for populist parties, it is still unclear whether many individuals adhere to a consistent and coherent 'populist ideology'.

important traits that a politician should have. These conclusions fit the notion that the trustworthiness of politicians is becoming crucially important to voters (for more discussion see Chapter 5).

4.4 Summary

In this chapter we have considered the role that ideology plays in European politics. Ideology helps to form linkages between voters and political parties. The ideological positions of both political parties and voters are often defined along a single ideological left–right continuum. Yet, the importance of left–right ideology is changing. This is the result of the emergence of new salient issues, such as immigration, the environment, and European integration, as well as the rise of populism. These developments carry some important implications for electoral competition in Europe today. First, electoral competition has become increasingly structured along two dimensions, a left–right and a 'cultural' libertarian–authoritarian dimension. Second, political rhetoric not only focuses on the choice between different policy positions, but also on the divisions between the people and elites, as we see with the rise of populist attitudes.

Online Data Exercise: The Eurobarometer

The interactive online exercise accompanying this chapter explores different operationalizations of Euroscepticism using Eurobarometer surveys. The Eurobarometer provides a rare comparative dataset across European Union member states that allows for a detailed analysis of public opinion in all member states. You will then use these surveys to examine how Eurosceptic attitudes are related to voting decisions.

 Take your learning further with this interactive data exercise, available at **www.foundationsofeuropeanpolitics.com**

 For additional material and resources, including multiple-choice questions, web links, and more, please visit the online resources: **www.oup.com/he/devries1e**

5   Voting Decisions

This chapter addresses how citizens vote in elections across Europe. Elections are the cornerstone of democracy as they allow citizens to shape collective decision-making in their favor. The chapter considers why it is so difficult to explain why people vote in the first place. We also discuss the inequality in turnout between citizens. We then turn to different explanations of vote choice. We first introduce the proximity model of voting which assumes that voters and political parties can be aligned on one ideological dimension, and voters will vote for the party that most closely resembles their own ideological position. Subsequently, we add complications to this model by highlighting the role of retrospective performance evaluations and affective attachments to social groups and political parties. Finally, we discuss how the institutional context may influence voters' decision-making.

The classical notion of democracy is based on the idea of direct and continuous participation of citizens. Yet such high levels of citizen participation are impractical in modern societies. One of the ways in which we come closer to this ideal is through citizen participation in elections. Free and fair elections held at regular intervals have become the vehicle through which citizens' preferences feed into the democratic process of collective decision-making. Participation through **voting** can be an expression of just how meaningful and effective citizens find elections to be as a channel for embedding their preferences within the democratic process. Elections are thus viewed as the cornerstone of a modern democratic political process. Yet, electoral **turnout** has been on the decline in most European countries over the last four decades. For example, in Germany turnout in federal elections has gone from highs of over 90 per cent in the 1970s to just over 70 per cent in the early 2010s. Turnout is generally much lower in European Parliament elections at 62 per cent in the first elections in 1979, and declining by more than 10 percentage points in three decades (IDEA, 2020). Moreover, **electoral volatility** across Europe has been on the rise, meaning when citizens do vote, they are more likely to switch between parties now than ever before (De Vries and Hobolt, 2020).

Political scientists have spent considerable time and effort trying to understand why and how citizens vote. The study of electoral behaviour has centred around two key questions. The first question focuses on turnout in elections: why do people vote? This has proved to be a difficult question to answer, mostly because the benefits from voting rarely outweigh the time and effort necessary for voting. The second question focuses on vote choice: how can we explain specific choices that people make about whom to support? One answer to this question has been to view vote choice as a form of individual decision-making whereby citizens compare the political parties or candidates on offer and vote for the party that most closely resembles their policy preferences. A second explanation views vote choice as an expression of a voter's social group membership and attachment to a particular political party.

While the scholarly debate about which of these factors drive electoral decision-making is ongoing, most scholars agree that, after a period of stability and continuity, electoral behaviour of European voters has become much more volatile in recent years.

This chapter proceeds by considering the nature of electoral behaviour by first discussing the explanations for why citizens vote in elections. We introduce the paradox of voting to explain why relatively high turnout in elections has been somewhat of a challenge for students of electoral behaviour. We also highlight the inequality in turnout between citizens based on age, income, and education. We then turn to the reasons why citizens choose to vote for one political party rather than another at election time. We introduce the proximity model of voting that is rooted in the simple uni-dimensional model of democracy introduced in Chapter 2. Based on this model, parties and voters can be located on a single ideological dimension, and voters are expected to vote for the party that most closely resembles their own ideological position. We then add to this model by introducing the role of retrospective performance evaluations, such as the evaluations of the state of the economy, and group attachments based on class, religion, or partisanship. Finally, we discuss how the institutional context in which voters have to make up their minds affects their vote choices, a topic covered in much greater depth in the next chapter on electoral systems.

5.1 Why Citizens Vote

Why do people vote in elections? Trying to explain why people go to the polls in elections has proven difficult. A key reason for this difficulty is that the costs that an individual incurs when going out to vote, such as the money and time spent getting to the voting booth, normally exceed the benefits of voting, even if those costs are low. This is because the likelihood of an individual voter being a **pivotal** voter, i.e. changing the outcome of an election, is exceedingly small. In real-world elections, when a considerable number of people vote, a rational, self-interested citizens should not bother. This inconsistency—the gap between high levels of actual voter turnout and the theoretical expectation of low turnout based on the notion of a rational, self-interested voter—has been coined the **paradox of voting**. It is also called the **Downs paradox**. While the French philosopher Nicolas de Condorcet noted that voting constitutes an irrational act because the costs of doing it most likely do not outweigh the benefits, Downs (1957) applied this intuition to study of elections more generally.

Let us consider the paradox of voting in more depth. Imagine an election in which two political parties, party X and party Y, compete for office. There are three possible outcomes of the election: party X wins, party Y wins, or there is a tie. Imagine that voter i prefers party X over party Y. Casting a ballot in an election constitutes an investment on the part of voter i to achieve their desired outcome. This is the **benefit of voting** coined B—the value to voter i of party X winning rather than party Y. Yet, the act of voting also involves a cost to voter i, formalized as C, coined the **costs of voting**. These costs can include having to go to the polls, having to obtain information about each of the parties, etc. Voter i is expected to vote when the benefit of doing so exceeds the costs ($B > C$). They will not vote when the costs of voting are larger than the benefits ($C > B$).

Importantly, however, voter i is not the only voter casting a ballot in the election. Voter i will receive benefit B even if they stay at home if their preferred party can win without their support. What matters is whether their vote is pivotal to changing the election outcome in their favour. The probability that voter i casts the decisive ballot in an election is very small in any election with a reasonable number of voters. We call this probability P. In Downs's thinking the reward R for voting to voter i is equal to $(B * P) – C$. In other words, the reward for voting is a function of the benefit of Party X winning (voter i's preferred outcome) multiplied by the probability that voter i's vote is pivotal to bringing about that outcome, minus the costs that voter i has to endure in order to vote. The expected benefit $(B * P)$ associated with voting is therefore almost always close to zero. Hence, assuming even the smallest cost of voting, the reward for turning out is negative. As a consequence, many have argued that it is not rational for citizens to vote. However, the equation also suggests that voter perceptions about being pivotal may matter. Voters living in a district where one party has no realistic chance of winning may think that their vote is unimportant, and that the costs of voting do not outweigh the benefits. But in close elections, voters may believe that they are more likely to be pivotal, and indeed voter turnout does increase when elections are tight.

Yet, the paradox of voting arises because actual turnout levels in elections are much higher than we would expect based on this rational voter model. To illustrate this, the left panel of Figure 5.1 shows the turnout in the 2019 elections to the European Parliament (EP) and the right panel shows the turnout in the last national parliamentary elections held before the 2019 EP election in the twenty-eight member states of the European Union. Higher turnout figures are marked by darker shades in the figure. While turnout in national parliamentary

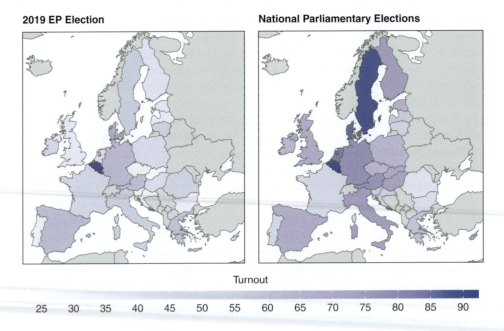

Figure 5.1 Turnout in European and National Parliamentary Elections

Data Source: ParlGov (Döring and Manow, 2019)

Note: Turnout in the national parliamentary elections refers to the last election held before the 2019 European Parliament elections.

elections is overall much higher, European-wide turnout in the 2019 European parliamentary elections was just over 50 per cent, with considerable variation across member states. The turnout was the highest in Belgium with roughly 88 per cent and the lowest in Slovakia with just under 23 per cent. In national parliamentary elections turnout is particularly high in Belgium, where voting is compulsory, but also Sweden. Generally speaking, if voters act rationally and in the self-interested manner of Downs's equation, we would expect to see much lower levels of turnout in all of these elections. The fact that on average one in two European voters decided to cast a ballot in the 2019 European parliamentary elections is especially surprising given that these elections are usually characterized as **second order elections** in which there is less at stake compared to national parliamentary elections. These elections are discussed in more detail later.

One possible explanation of the paradox of voting stems from the work by Riker and Ordeshook (1968) and focuses on **civic duty**. The idea is that most people derive some non-instrumental utility from voting, such as satisfaction with fulfilling a civic duty or from affirming one's partisanship by voting. Although the benefits that voter i would derive from their preferred party X winning remains close to zero, because their vote is unlikely pivotal, they will derive additional benefits from duty D which should be added to the costs of voting. According to Riker and Ordeshook the reward of voting for voter i (R) is equal to $(B * P) - C + D$.

Empirically establishing if a voter's sense of civic duty matters for their decision to turn out in an election is difficult, especially because asking people about their sense of duty will most likely result in socially desirable answers. Respondents in a survey are likely to report that

Box 5.1 **CASE STUDY:** Voter Turnout and Postal Voting in Switzerland

The implementation of postal voting in Switzerland provides an interesting opportunity to learn about the effects of social norms around participating in elections. Between 1971 and 2003, postal voting was introduced at different times in different Swiss cantons. Generally, we might expect postal voting to decrease the cost of voting. A decrease in the costs of voting should increase overall levels of turnout. But research by Funk (2010) highlights that the introduction of postal voting makes the act of voting unobservable. It allows citizens to escape social pressure because both not voting and postal voting mean that the voter does not show up to the polling station. The decline in social pressure should be felt especially strongly in small tight-knit communities in which people know each other and can observe each other's behaviour more easily. Civic duty norms have also been shown to work stronger in these contexts. Following this logic, the introduction of postal voting should reduce turnout as people can now get away with abstaining, and this effect should be especially pronounced in small communities.

The reduction of the cost of voting through the introduction of postal voting seems to have had little effect on turnout in Swiss federal elections. Turnout only increased by 2 percentage points overall. Interestingly, however, Funk finds huge differences across communities. Small tight-knit communities reacted very differently to introduction of postal voting than larger cities. Although postal voting led to slightly increased turnout on average, it led to a decrease in turnout in cantons with a large share of citizens living in small communities. Funk suggests that social pressure to comply with the **social norm** of civic duty provides an explanation for these findings. This study provides a nice example that civic duty may indeed be important in explaining turnout levels. It may also be interesting for policy-makers, as making it easier for people to vote may not always have intended consequences.

they think that all people should to vote in order to demonstrate their adherence to the social norm that voting is important.

An additional explanation for the paradox of voting is provided by Aldrich (1993). He suggests that voting constitutes a low-cost, low-benefit action. Voting is low-cost, because voters may use all kinds of shortcuts for getting informed about the political parties competing in the election. They might always vote for the same party because they feel close to that party. Voting is low-benefit, because voters may perceive that there is little difference between one or another party winning in terms of their individual benefit. Due to the fact that turnout is a low-cost, low-benefit action, small changes in costs or benefits can make a significant difference. Aldrich draws our attention to role of strategic politicians in this respect. When small changes in costs or benefits can make a difference, politicians have every incentive to invest in getting people out to vote. Efforts to increase turnout by strategic politicians may explain why turnout is higher in close races even if voters themselves do not care about an election being close. When strategic politicians invest more when races are close, a voter will be more exposed to campaign information and the cost of voting is decreased ($< C$). In these races politicians will also spend more time and effort in explaining why they are better than their opponents, so the benefit of voting increases ($> B$). Moreover, strategic politicians will inform voters that not voting would constitute a wasted vote and increase their sense that their vote is pivotal ($> P$).

Empirical examinations of why some people vote while others do not also highlight the importance of other factors. For example, voting may simply constitute a habit. People who vote become accustomed to voting and perhaps even acquire a taste for it. The act of voting itself increases the probability of voting in future elections. Franklin (2004) suggests that the type of election that a person is eligible to vote in for the first time crucially shapes habit formation. Elections that do not stimulate high turnout among young adults leave a 'footprint' of low turnout in the age structure of the electorate. In the European context, this means that turnout throughout life is lower for those citizens who first became eligible to vote in the run-up to a EP election (Franklin and Hobolt, 2011). This is because European parliamentary elections tend to matter less to citizens and attract lower turnout compared to national elections.

Age more generally is shown to be important for understanding who votes. Younger voters are less likely to turn out than older voters. Yet, the effect of age is curvilinear. As voters grow older, their probability of voting increases, but it levels off or even decreases again when they reach old age. Smets and van Ham (2013) have conducted a meta-analysis—a study that examines and aggregates the results of all previous studies on a particular topic—of the individual-level determinants of voting and find that 75 per cent of studies on turnout find evidence of a curvilinear relationship between age and turnout.

Voting is also related to social and economic inequality. Historically, the right to vote in most nations in Europe was restricted to males, property owners, and native born citizens (see Chapter 1). Reflecting polarized social divisions in Europe, many conservative politicians were hesitant to grant the working class the right to vote. Yet, even as voting rights were extended, empirical studies have shown that citizens who are poorer and less educated are overall much less likely to turn out in elections compared to the rich and highly educated, who display higher levels of political interest (Verba et al., 1995; Gallego, 2015). The difference in turnout levels between the highly and less educated is shown to be more pronounced in countries with market-orientated media systems and less access to public broadcasting (e.g. Sørensen, 2019; Gallego, 2015). Presumably this is because it is harder for lower educated citizens to gain access to political information. Inequality in turnout may have considerable policy implications. Studies conducted both in the American and European context, for example, suggest that the interests of higher socio-economic strata are better represented in policy-making (Gilens, 2012; Schakel, 2019). Unequal participation in elections may be one of the drivers of unequal representation.

In an attempt to find ways to remedy the inequality in turnout, Lijphart (1997) recommended a system of **compulsory voting**, meaning citizens are legally required to vote in elections. He argued that this would contribute to a high and relatively equal turnout through which the political views of all eligible voters would be represented in parliament. Many, however, have made arguments against compulsory voting. For example, voting may be seen as a civic right rather than a civic duty. Compulsory voting may lead to uninformed choices, or may prove difficult and costly to enforce. While in many countries in Europe voting used to be compulsory, the continued use and enforcement of compulsory voting is rare. One exception is Belgium, which has the oldest existing compulsory voting system in the world. It was introduced in 1893 for men and for women in 1948. Belgian citizens aged 18 and over and registered non-Belgian voters are obliged to present themselves in their polling station on Election Day or otherwise receive a moderate fine. Voting is also compulsory in Luxembourg, where non-voters can face a fine. In Greece, voting is compulsory, but this not enforced.

5.2 How Citizens Vote

When voters do turn out to vote, what explains their specific vote choices? The model of democracy presented in this book (see Chapter 2) assumes that the policy preferences of both voters and parties can be located on a single ideological dimension. In most elections in Europe more than two political parties compete in elections (see also Chapter 9). How does this voter decide which political party to support? The **proximity model of voting** suggests that a voter would vote for the political party that most closely resembles their own policy positions.

Elections are usually fought on a multitude of policy issues. Most political parties in Europe compete in elections based on an electoral manifesto. An **electoral manifesto** is a public declaration of general political aims as well as specific policy proposals issued by a political party ahead of an election campaign. Electoral manifestos comprise a host of detailed policy proposals. Theoretically, all of these policy issues could come to define an electoral campaign. Yet, there are practical limits to the amount of issues parties can mobilize. Important, perhaps, is the limited ability of voters to process all of this information. Most voters do not read electoral manifestos and only a few consider every policy proposal a party puts forward. Rather voters use broad-based ideological labels, such as left and right for example, as a way to help them decide which party to vote for at election time. As we have highlighted in Chapter 4, ideology is a crucial tool which voters use in elections to detect differences between parties and determine which of them to vote for. Reducing the number of policy issues to competition over ideological profiles is also beneficial to parties themselves as it facilitates voter mobilization. While traditionally left–right ideology in Europe pits a more redistributive

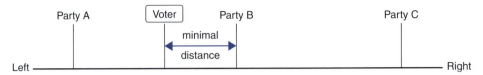

Figure 5.2 Ideological Positions of Voter and Parties on a Single Dimension

role of the state against a more free market role, it is increasingly seen as the ideological super-dimension that bundles policy preferences that happen to be most salient in society.

Figure 5.2 plots the positions of a voter and parties A, B, and C in an unidimensional space based on the left–right ideological positions of the voter and parties. The voter holds a centre-left ideological position. While party B is located in the centre of the left–right ideological space, party A holds an outspoken left-wing position, and party C holds an outspoken right-wing position. Based on the proximity model of voting, we would expect the voter to cast a ballot for the party that holds the most proximate position to her own. In Figure 5.2, this is party B, even though party B holds a slightly more centrist position than the voter. While party A is also clearly on the left of the ideological spectrum, the voter's position is further removed from party A compared to party B. Party C holds a right-wing position and is thus the farthest removed from the voter's ideal position. Hence based on the notion of proximity, i.e the smallest distance, the voter is expected to cast her ballot for party B.

The proximity model of voting is based on a specific understanding of which factors feature into citizens' voting decisions, namely citizens vote for the party that best represents their policy issues. Arguably, the lowest common denominator of any theory of democracy is that there should be some link between a voter and a representative when it comes to deciding on policies. Manin (1997), however, reminds us that elections serve two key functions: **representation** and **accountability**. They ensure representation by allowing voters to select political representatives, who are mandated to implement the set of policy proposals on which they campaigned. The selection of representatives based on their policy proposals for the future is called **prospective voting**. The notion of prospective voting lies at the heart of the proximity model of voting.

Elections also allow for accountability as citizens can sanction political representatives for their time in office. The sanctioning of political representatives based on past performance is coined **retrospective voting**. Retrospective voting assumes that voters use evaluations of past performance as a means to hold political representatives accountable for their time in office. Perceived this way, elections are, at least in part, referendums on the performance of incumbents. By casting a retrospective vote, citizens can incentivize their elected officials to enact policies that favour a majority. While voters could consider a whole range of past performance on which to base their vote (see also Box 5.2), the state of the economy is one of the key aspects of government performance that voters care about. The study of **economic voting** examines the extent to which economic performance evaluations shape voters' choices as the ballot box. Classic empirical studies by Lewis-Beck (1990) and Duch and Stevenson (2008) provide strong evidence of economic voting in western European democracies. In other words, voters are more likely to re-elect the incumbent when the economy has been improving, and more likely to 'throw the rascals out' when economic conditions have worsened.

Box 5.2 CASE STUDY: The Lack of Electoral Punishment of Corruption

Corruption is a complex phenomenon often deeply rooted in the cultural and political practices of societies. It has been particularly widespread in central-eastern and southern Europe (CPI, 2020). Although the precise costs of corruption are hard to quantify and vary greatly from country to country, research suggests that corruption is bad for economic and social development. Therefore, we might expect voters to punish politicians for corruption at election time.

Free, fair, and competitive elections that allow citizens to sanction politicians in a periodic manner are widely believed to have a constraining effect on corruption. Although some evidence suggests that corrupt activities indeed take a considerable electoral toll on incumbents, we often observe that voters fail to punish corrupt politicians. A paradox of unpopular corruption but popular corrupt politicians exists. The re-election of President Jacques Chirac in France in 2002 provides an example. The incumbent president was embroiled in corruption scandals that made headlines during the campaign and for which he was later convicted. Yet, a majority of French voters decided to re-elect him despite these severe allegations.

So why do voters often fail to punish politicians for corrupt activities? In their review of the literature, De Vries and Solaz (2017) suggest that sanctioning elected representatives for corrupt activities is much more difficult than assumed. It is not merely due to a lack of information, as many suggest, but largely due to the fact that voters have to balance many different considerations when casting their ballot. Additionally, voters must correctly assign blame for corruption to individual politicians and parties. Political facts about corruption are hard to come by because politicians aiming to sway public sentiment in their favour to secure re-election often have incentives to spin information and play a blame game. Voters' loyalty to their party or social group makes their attributions of blame biased and overall less likely. Voters may also be willing to overlook corruption for other policy benefits. It may well be the case that poor performance in one area, corruption, is compensated for performance in some by other area, economic growth.

While the proximity model assumes that voters base their choices on ideological considerations, both prospective and retrospective voting can encompass non-policy **valence** considerations, such as the perceived competence of governments or leadership qualities, too. Valence considerations are not about choosing between different policy choices, but instead relate to the question of 'which party is best at delivering?' (Stokes, 1963). Such performance evaluations are generally based on perceptions of how well incumbents have governed, a form of retrospection. This being said, it is of course also possible that voters use their evaluations of the current government and other potential governments to inform their expectations about performance in the future, a form of prospective voting.

Traditionally, the perception among political scientists has been that retrospective voting is relatively easy as it poses few cognitive demands on voters. This sentiment is perhaps best captured in the writings of Fiorina, who has made considerable contributions to the study of retrospective voting. Fiorina (1981, 5) wrote:

> In order to ascertain whether the incumbents have performed poorly or well, citizens only need to calculate the changes in their own welfare. If jobs have been lost in a recession, something is wrong. If sons have died in foreign rice paddies, something is wrong. If thugs make neighbourhoods unsafe, something is wrong. If polluters foul food, water, or air, something is wrong.

Yet, recent work suggests that holding politicians accountable for past performance is more difficult than often assumed. Healy and Malhotra (2013) suggest that retrospective voting ensures accountability through a four-step process. First, voters need to observe a change in their own or societal welfare, for example through a specific event, political action, or policy outcome. Second, they need to attribute responsibility for this change in welfare to particular elected office holders and adjust their evaluations of the performance of these elected officials accordingly. Third, on the basis of these responsibility attributions voters need to adjust their vote choices. Fourth, all of this needs to be translated into specific election results that incentivize office holders to adjust their policy proposals. Casting a ballot based on retrospective performance will involve these steps, and when one or more of these steps breaks down electoral accountability will be breached.

Prospective and retrospective voting models both assume that vote choice is the result of an individual weighing up the costs and benefits of voting for one party rather than another. This individual-level perspective is challenged by two explanations that highlight the group aspect of voting and stress the importance of citizens' attachments to social or political groups. The first one focuses on the role of **social group identification** that is embedded in societal divisions, while the second one stresses the importance of **partisanship**, the loyalty of voters to a given party.

With the introduction of their **social cleavage theory** (see Chapter 4), Lipset and Rokkan (1967) have argued that partisan allegiances are rooted in historical developments, such as national revolutions, the Reformation, and the Industrial Revolution, that produced enduring lines of conflict, or **cleavages**, that continue to shape the structure of politics, political organization, and the content of political conflict, as well as determining political preferences (see also Chapter 8). Within this framework, vote choice is based on long-lasting loyalties to parties rooted in shared social group identification and group interest. Voters are expected to vote for the party that most closely resembles their social group and represents their socio-economic position or religious denomination. For example, working-class voters are expected to vote for communist or social democratic parties, while Catholic voters vote for Catholic or Christian democratic parties.

Cleavages provide one explanation for how group attachments matter for vote choice. A second explanation stresses the role of **partisanship**. Campbell et al. (1960) published a seminal book with the core thesis that voters' psychological attachment to a political party guides their political preferences and evaluations of candidates or past policies. The theory of vote choice developed by these authors is known as the **Michigan model of voting**. According to this model, partisanship—which the authors define as an enduring attachment to a party rooted in group attachments formed through family socialization during early childhood—is a core driver of vote choice. Partisanship is causally prior to vote choice, because the psychological bond to a given party is assumed to predate the conscious political awareness of voters and the evaluations of specific policies or candidates stemming from a specific election contest. The Michigan model introduces the notion of the funnel of causality. The idea is that long-term factors, such as group identification and parental socialization, create a stable loyalty to a party that shapes short-term factors, such as candidate evaluations or policy preferences.

Partisanship also plays an important role because it acts as a 'perceptual screen' that filters out unfavourable information about a voter's partisan leaning. As a result, partisanship is expected to persist, or even strengthen, over time. An observational implication of partisanship as defined here is the relative stability of political preferences. Since partisanship is part of one's identity and key group attachments, short-term fluctuations in preferences are possible, but should not be common. A partisan should display a high degree of continuity in their voting patterns and policy preferences. Yet, patterns of voting in Europe have become less stable over time as we discuss in the next section.

5.3 Stability of Vote Choices

Understanding vote choice through the lens of cleavage theory and partisanship has allowed researchers to account for the high degree of continuity in electoral outcomes and resistance to change of voters' party choices in western Europe. From the 1960s onwards, however, higher degrees of social mobility, wider access to education and the participation of women in the labour force increasingly blurred the boundaries between social groups. This resulted in the decline in importance of social group identification rooted in societal cleavages for understanding electoral behaviour in Europe. Voters switching parties between elections became more frequent. Figure 5.3 displays the trends of electoral volatility in national and European parliamentary elections within Europe over time. **Electoral volatility** is a measure of the degree of change in vote choice between elections. It is usually measured as the change in the vote shares between elections averaged across all political parties. The trends displayed in Figure 5.3 demonstrate that electoral volatility has been increasing over time in both national and European parliamentary elections.

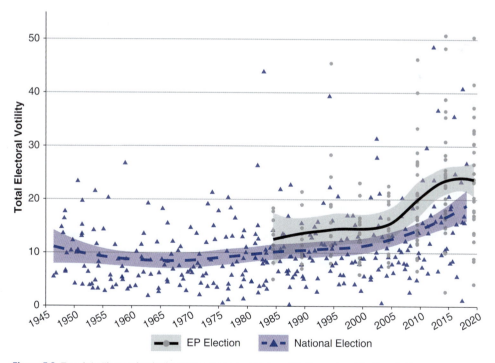

Figure 5.3 Trends in Electoral Volatility in European and National Parliamentary Elections in Europe

Data sources: Emanuele (2015); Emanuele et al. (2019)

While many west European countries have witnessed the blurring of class identification and a decline of church attendance, this does not necessarily mean that class and religion no longer matter for the vote. The dynamics of religious and class voting are not uniform and often nation-specific. Just to provide an example, the religious cleavage still structures vote choice in a largely secular society like the Netherlands. Here pockets of Protestant voters are still tightly linked to confessional parties, and due to a low **electoral threshold** these parties have maintained representation in parliament. The cross-national variation in the impact of the religious and class cleavage on vote choice also suggests that the programmatic offerings of political parties matter (Evans and De Graaf, 2013). Evans and Tilley (2017), for example, suggest that the weakening ties between class identification and vote choice in the United Kingdom are not necessarily the result of increased class heterogeneity, but rather due to the shift to the centre of the Labour Party under the leadership of Tony Blair. When parties fail to provide the programmatic vehicles to express the social group identification of voters, party–voter linkages are likely to become more fluid as a result.

Increasing electoral volatility has also raised questions about the strength and nature of **partisanship**. Challenging the Michigan model of voting, Fiorina (1981) developed the

Box 5.3　METHODS AND MEASUREMENT: Measuring Electoral Volatility

Electoral volatility is relatively straightforward and easy to measure. Pedersen (1979) developed a volatility index for capturing voters moving between parties, which is simply:

$$Volatility = \frac{\sum_i^n |P_{it} - P_{i(t+1)}|}{2}$$

where P_{it} is Party i's vote share in election t and $P_{i(t+1)}$ is Party i's vote share in the subsequent election. The changes in vote share for all parties competing in the elections are summed and then divided by two. They are divided in half because losses for one party are clearly gains for another, so this avoids double-counting.

There is, however, a problem with this conceptualization of volatility, in that it does not distinguish between desirable volatility and undesirable volatility. Some level of volatility is necessary and required for effective democracy. If there were no volatility, there would be no democratic change-over in government. The same parties would always win. However, if there is too much volatility, existing parties may rapidly die and new parties may rapidly gain support, only to lose it again. Such instability can create uncertainty in politics and make it difficult for voters to make informed choices.

Powell and Tucker (2014) distinguish between what they call Type A and Type B volatility, where Type A is volatility that arises due to birth and death of parties and Type B is volatility is change in vote shares among existing, stable parties. Type A and Type B volatility added together give the total volatility calculated using the Pedersen index. Formally Type A volatility is:

$$Type\ A\ Volatility = \frac{|\sum_{o=1}^n P_{ot} + \sum_{w=1}^n P_{w(t+1)}|}{2}$$

where P_{ot} refers to the vote share of an old party o in election t that disappears by election $t+1$ and $P_{w(t+1)}$ refers to the percentage of vote won by a new party w in election $t+1$. While Type B volatility is, generally speaking, good for democracy, Type A volatility can be destabilizing. Powell and Tucker find that, in 1989–2009, a very high proportion of electoral volatility in post-Communist central and eastern European countries came from Type A volatility.

notion of partisanship as a 'running tally'. Voters, so his argument goes, constantly evaluate the performance of political parties and their candidates, and update their assessment of parties accordingly. Partisanship is perceived as something other than an emotional attachment rooted in socialization, rather based on continued assessment of how political parties have performed or are likely to perform in office on the policy issues that are most important to voters. While it may become more stable as people grow older, partisanship can change as a consequence of scandals or shocks. Perceived in this way, partisanship serves as a cognitive shortcut and allows voters to make vote choices based on party labels without having to devote a large share of time or degree of effort to inform themselves about each candidate or policy proposal. Political ideology, policy issues, and past performance now become more important than socialization experiences. The debate between these two views on partisanship, a 'perceptual screen' versus a 'running tally', and its role in shaping vote choice remains relevant to this day.

In central and eastern Europe, the legacy of Communism has meant weakened links between societal groups and parties, less programmatic party platforms, and parties with much shorter histories, resulting in weaker partisanship. As a consequence, these countries have witnessed very high electoral volatility, so much so that parties that do well in one election may fail to enter parliament in the next, while brand new parties can do exceedingly well in their first election (see Haughton and Deegan-Krause, 2021). So how are vote choices structured in this context? Coming to grips with voters' ballot choices in these new democracies is a particularly difficult endeavour given the uncertainties accompanying processes of political transition and democratic consolidation. Have core determinants of the vote, such as left–right ideology, retrospective performance evaluations, or attachment to social groups, gained equal importance in these societies compared to the West? Or do central-east European citizens follow completely different patterns when it comes to electoral behaviour given the relatively short period of time that has elapsed since their societies embarked on the road to democratic and market-driven government? The literature suggests that, despite the fragile nature of party–citizen linkages, weak party organization, and the frequent lack of continuity of particular parties, political parties have succeeded in simplifying the choices for voters, at least to some degree (Evans, 2006). Although the high degrees of party instability characterizing the post-transition period may have initially left voters struggling to make sense of the political landscape, over time citizens have become more able to draw cues from their social and political environments, parties, or social groups, in order to form policy preferences and vote choices.

Economic voting also matters in central and eastern Europe. Tucker (2006) has proposed a transitional identity model of economic voting. He argues that economic voting is not structured by the punishment of incumbent parties for bad performance, but rather associated with so-called 'new regime' parties which guided much of the transition away from communist rule to the development of a market economy. Consequently, his work suggests that these parties perform better electorally when economic conditions improve. For 'old regime' parties which are largely associated with the old communist rulers, the opposite pattern emerges. By contrast, they perform better when economic conditions worsen. The transitional identity model thus extends traditional models of economic voting to suggest that within consolidating democracies certain types of parties distinguished on the basis of their loyalty towards the previous regime will fare better or worse in good economic times.

5.4 Institutional Context and Second Order Elections

The institutional context in which elections are fought and voters have to make up their minds also affects their decision-making. One example of this is provided in the work by Kedar (2009), who examines the degree to which post-electoral coalition bargaining, common within many countries in Europe (see Chapter 10), affects electoral decision-making. She suggests that voters may endorse parties whose ideological positions differ from their own in order to move government coalition bargaining in their favour. The extent to which voters are not only committed to policy preferences, but also care about policy outcomes, makes them divert from their ideal party preference and work around power-sharing institutions, such as governing coalitions. Kedar also suggests that federalism provides voters with incentives to adjust their sincere vote preference (see also Chapter 3). In order for voters to balance policy outcomes at both the federal and regional level, they may split their votes between these two levels of government. She shows that non-simultaneous elections that often characterize federal polities provide important occasions for voters interested in policy performance to adjust vote preferences between several layers of government in order to balance policy outcomes.

Elections to the **European Parliament** also make clear the importance of institutional context, and the multilevel nature of politics, for electoral behaviour. Since 1979 European voters have the ability to express their political preferences in both in national as well as EP elections. Members of the European Parliament (MEPs) are directly elected every five years in national elections held during the same week across all EU member states. Because EP elections take place in all EU member states and because the European Election Studies (EES) have made survey data available since 1979, scholars of electoral behaviour have been able to examine the effects of differing institutional structures across countries. EP elections are often described as **second order national elections** (Reif and Schmitt, 1980), meaning that they are considered less important than national elections by both citizens and national political parties. The crucial difference between 'first order' national elections and 'second order' European elections is that European Parliament elections do not (directly) determine the composition of a government, and therefore less is at stake for voters (see Chapter 10). The lower perceived importance of European Parliament elections has two important consequences for how citizens vote. First, citizens are less likely to vote in EP elections compared to national elections, as we have already mentioned. And second, citizens often use these elections to voice their discontent with domestic politics.

The second order nature of European elections means that voters frequently punish governing parties, especially when they are at the midpoint of the national elections cycle. Large parties also tend to perform worse in European elections, while smaller opposition parties do better (Hix and Marsh, 2007). In addition, analyses of vote switching between government and opposition parties show that Eurosceptic voters are more likely to defect from government parties than voters who are more pro-EU (Hobolt et al., 2009). Hence, while early research on EP elections suggested that voters based their choices predominantly on domestic considerations, more recent research has shown that concerns about European integration increasingly matter to voters, especially in contexts where information about European matters is more widespread (De Vries et al., 2011). This has mainly benefited non-mainstream parties with Eurosceptic positions. Interestingly, research also shows that EU considerations increasingly affect voters' decisions in national elections (De Vries, 2007). As the European Union has started to encroach more and more on domestic policy-making and the integration process

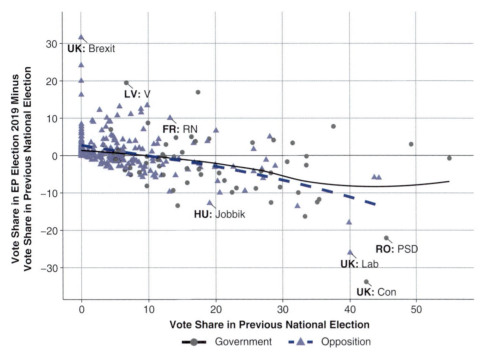

Figure 5.4 Electoral Performance of National Parties in European and National Elections

Data Source: ParlGov (Döring and Manow, 2019)

itself has become more politicized, Eurosceptic political entrepreneurs have been able to capitalize on the persistent gap between the more pro-European position adopted by mainstream parties and the more Eurosceptic attitudes of a large proportion of the electorate (Hobolt and Spoon, 2012).

Figure 5.4 follows Hix and Marsh (2007) and shows the electoral performance of national political parties in the EP election in 2019 compared to the respective previous national parliamentary election. Parties that have gained vote shares are displayed above the horizontal line at zero, whereas parties that have lost vote shares are shown below the line. The visualization distinguishes between parties that were in government at the time of the EP election in 2019 and those that were in parliamentary opposition or not represented in the national parliament.

Three aspects stand out. First, the vast majority of governing parties lost votes. In fact, two-thirds of all governing parties did worse in the EP elections in 2019 compared to the previous national election, while around two-thirds of non-governing parties increased their vote shares. Although this corroborates the government sanctioning implication of the second order election model, it is important that the relationship is not deterministic. Some government parties, such as the conservative New Unity Party in Latvia, performed better in the EP election compared to the previous national election. Second, larger parties tend to perform worse in the EP elections compared to national elections independent of their government status. The larger the vote share in the previous national election, the larger the vote loss for the parties. For instance, the Romanian Social Democratic Party (PSD) and the British Conservatives, at the time in national government, lost substantially in the EP elections. However, even opposition parties such as the Hungarian far right party opposition party Jobbik or the Labour Party in the UK lost support. The third and final noteworthy aspect is that the biggest gains in EP elections appear to be made by many small, oftentimes new, parties. For example, in the UK, the newly formed Brexit Party, under leadership of Nigel Farage, was able to attract almost a third of voters in the UK with the promise to continue to push for a quick withdrawal from the EU. In France, the far right National Rally (RN) led by Marine Le Pen performed better than in the previous national parliamentary election. Overall, while the figure indicates that the main predictions of the second order national election model still hold, the same patterns are also consistent with the explanation that EU sentiments matter to many voters in EP elections and consequently Eurosceptic parties often perform better than they do in national elections.

5.5 Summary

The most straightforward way for citizens to feed their policy preferences into the political process is by participating in elections. In this chapter, we have considered how citizens vote in Europe. We discussed both their reasons for casting a ballot in the first place, and which party they support when they do. The reasons why some people vote while others do not is still a matter of contention in the literature. Nevertheless, most political scientists agree that turnout matters; unequal participation may lead to unequal representation of policy preferences in the political process.

And when citizens do decide to vote, what decides which party they support? The proximity model of voting suggests that voters vote for the party that most closely resembles their ideological position. This constitutes a form of prospective voting in which voters demand that a party implement the set of policy proposals on which it campaigned. Retrospective voting assumes voters support a party based on past performance. Both prospective and retrospective voting view vote choice as a form of individual decision-making. Another approach is to understand vote choice as an expression of a voter's social group membership, based on class or religion for example, or an attachment to a political party. The scholarly debate about which factors are the most important drivers of electoral decision-making is far from settled, but evidence suggests that voters have become more volatile in their choices.

Online Data Exercise: The European Election Study

The interactive online exercise introduces the European Election study, specifically the voter study that relies on a general population survey after the European Parliament elections. In the exercises, you will explore which topics were the most salient for voters in the European elections in 2019. Additionally, you will examine the second order election model, in particular how it relates to vote-switching between national and European elections.

Take your learning further with this interactive data exercise, available at **www.foundationsofeuropeanpolitics.com**

For additional material and resources, including multiple-choice questions, web links, and more, please visit the online resources: **www.oup.com/he/devries1e**

Part 3

Elections and Parties

6

Electoral Systems and Direct Democracy

This chapter provides an overview of the institutions that determine how citizens cast ballots both in elections (e.g. electoral systems) and directly for policy (e.g. direct democracy). We examine the implications of these institutions for party systems and political representation from the perspective of the principal–agent framework. First, we present an overview of the variety of electoral systems in use in Europe. Even though most elections in Europe are held using proportional representation, there are important institutional differences across countries. Second, we examine the effects of electoral systems on the party system and discuss electoral system changes in Europe. Finally we turn to direct democracy and discuss the use of referendums and initiatives, specifically with regard to questions about the European Union.

Electoral systems forge the link in the delegatory chain that most directly connects voters to their representatives. These are the rules that determine how elections work—who can vote, who can stand as a candidate, how candidates' or parties' names appear on the ballot, and how votes get counted and turned into seats in parliament (Cox, 1997). Electoral systems impact how voters think about politics and how politicians behave, the importance that people place on the actions of individual representatives relative to parties, the strength of parties, the behaviour of legislators in parliaments, and the ways that societal views are represented in the political system. How citizens cast ballots during elections, what these ballots look like, and how votes are counted can vary quite drastically across countries, and sometimes even within a single country. Because these rules can shape the allocation of political power in democratic societies, changes to electoral rules often provoke intense conflicts among political parties.

But sometimes, on the path to making policy, the link in the chain between voters and representatives can be bypassed entirely. This occurs when voters vote directly on policy outcomes themselves, rather than for representatives. Institutions determining when and how voters get a direct say over policy at the ballot box through referendums and initiatives also vary significantly. These institutions have had a tremendous impact on policy in some countries, and on European integration, in particular.

In this chapter, we examine the mechanics of the electoral systems, their impact on representation and party systems, as well as the rules governing direct democracy. Our discussion of electoral systems focuses primarily on the rules governing parliamentary elections across Europe and for the European Parliament. We conclude the chapter by examining direct democracy in Europe and the provisions for and importance of referendums and initiatives.

6.1 Objectives of Electoral Systems

Electoral systems have two primary objectives: to foster **political representation** and to ensure government **accountability**. Representation refers to the selection of agents (politicians) who act and speak on the principal's behalf (citizens), expressing views and making policy. Accountability refers to the ability of voters to correctly reward and punish politicians for policy choices. Representation may be enhanced by electoral systems that allow more parties to enter parliament, potentially representing a greater range of views (see Chapter 7). But, at the same time, more parties can make accountability difficult. In political systems where the composition of the executive is determined by parliament (see Chapter 10), more parties in parliament may make the government formation process more cumbersome, and may make it difficult for voters to hold individual parties accountable in elections for government policy. In contrast, governments composed only of single parties with majorities in parliament have high accountability.

Before we can discuss how electoral systems resolve the contradictory goals of representation and accountability, we need to understand a few technical details of electoral systems. Following the seminal work by Rae (1967), we start by defining a central institutional feature of an electoral system referred to as the electoral formula. The **electoral formula** is the set of mathematical rules that determine how votes cast get transferred into parliamentary seats. The precise nature of these rules can matter a lot for political representation, and there is no single right answer as to which set of rules a democracy should use. Broadly speaking, we can group electoral formulas into three groups—those using majoritarian rules, proportional rules, or a mix of both. Figure 6.1 shows the varieties of electoral systems used in national parliamentary elections in Europe. Proportional

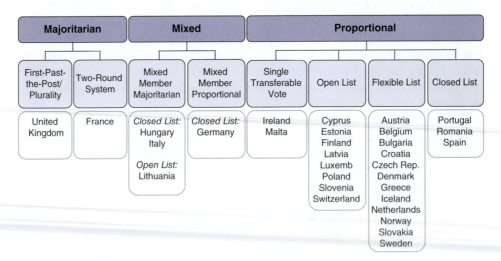

Figure 6.1 Varieties of Electoral Systems in Europe

Data sources: Pilet et al. (2016); Passarelli (2020)

systems clearly dominate in Europe. Majoritarian electoral systems exist only in France and the UK. Four countries (Germany, Hungary, Italy, and Lithuania) use mixed systems, which combine elements from majoritarian and proportional systems. These countries can be divided into those that use systems producing more proportional and more majoritarian electoral outcomes. It is important to note that political actors sometimes change electoral rules. In fact, some European countries have changed their electoral systems frequently during the last decades, an aspect that we address in section 6.5.

6.2 Majoritarian Systems

Majoritarian electoral systems are designed to produce clear winners and they favour accountability and stability over representation. Majoritarian rules tend to produce legislative majorities for a single party, even when that party receives less than a majority of the votes cast. This is sometimes referred to as a manufactured majority. Following the UK general election of December 2019, for example, the Conservative Party won 56.2 per cent of seats in parliament having won only 43.6 per cent of the votes. Majoritarian systems in both France and the UK use single member districts (SMDs), meaning that only one person is elected to parliament from each electoral constituency, so the number of members of parliament equals the number of constituencies in the country. Therefore, these systems are also referred to as single-seat district systems (Herron et al., 2018). The UK uses a **first-past-the-post**, or plurality formula, meaning that the candidate in a district who wins more votes than any other candidate captures the seat. In districts where more than two candidates are competing, it is possible for someone to win a seat with significantly less than a majority of the votes. For instance, in the 2019 UK election, the Conservative Party candidate won the Ashfield constituency in Nottinghamshire, a seat long held by the Labour Party, having only captured 39 per cent of the vote. The second highest vote total was for a candidate running as an 'Ashfield Independent', a local political party, and the third highest was for the Labour candidate, with other parties such as the Brexit Party, the Liberal Democrats, and the Greens capturing smaller fractions of the vote. The fracturing of the vote across so many candidates made it likely that any winner would capture the seat with significantly less than a majority of the votes.

To ensure the winner has support among a majority of voters, France uses a slightly different majoritarian formula—the **two-round system**. In National Assembly elections, any candidate capturing votes totalling 12.5 per cent of the registered electorate in the first round can move on to compete in a second round that takes place two weeks later. When only one candidate (or even no candidate) has polled more than 12.5 per cent of registered voters, then the top two candidates from the first round move on to the second round. The winner of the second round captures the seat. Because the threshold applies to registered voters, rather than to votes cast, the chances of having more than two eligible candidates in the second round is significantly reduced. Moreover, when more than two candidates do qualify, parties often coordinate and the candidate with weaker support withdraws. This means that the second round almost always has just two candidates, with one capturing a majority of votes in the second round.

Box 6.1 CASE STUDY: Presidential Elections in Europe

Majoritarian rules also apply to popular elections of presidents. Direct presidential elections take place in Austria, Bulgaria, Croatia, Cyprus, Czech Republic, Finland, France, Iceland, Ireland, Lithuania, Poland, Portugal, Romania, Slovakia, and Slovenia. Just like in a majoritarian system in single member constituencies, presidential elections generate one winner with the entire country constituting the constituency. All but two countries employ a two-round runoff system. The exceptions are Iceland, which employs a single-round plurality system, and Ireland, which uses a single-round instant runoff system in which voters rank candidates. We briefly discuss the two-round system in France and the instant runoff system in Ireland, both of which are meant to produce a president elected by a majority of voters.

The Two-Round System in France

Similar to electoral system used for the French parliament, the French presidential elections use a two-round system, but only the top two candidates from the first round move onto a second round, guaranteeing a majority of votes for the winning candidate. However, the splitting of the elections across two rounds can lead to some odd results. During the 2017 French presidential election, the field of candidates during the first round was very crowded, with no single candidate polling particularly strongly. The candidate put forward by the traditional left-wing Socialist party, Benoit Hamon, never gained much traction, and he faced competition from Jean-Luc Melenchon, a former Socialist who left the party to form his own left-wing group. The right-wing candidate Francois Fillon, on the other hand, faced a corruption scandal. This left openings for other candidates including Emmanuel Macron, a young politician and former cabinet minister, who had started his own centrist movement, and Marine Le Pen of the far-right populist Front National party. In the end, Macron and Le Pen made it into the second round, shutting out the traditional left and right parties of French politics. In the second round, Macron won relatively easily with 66 per cent of the vote.

Instant Runoff in Ireland

Instead of holding two separate elections, Ireland conducts its presidential election in a single round using the instant runoff method. Voters rank all candidates, and a candidate is immediately elected if she receives a majority of first-choice votes. However, if no candidate wins a majority using the first-choice votes, then the candidate with the fewest first-choice votes is eliminated from the contest. The votes from the eliminated ballots are added to the remaining candidates based on the second ranked candidate choice on each ballot. This process is repeated until one candidate achieves a majority of votes. Thus, a second round is not required to achieve an absolute majority. In the presidential election in 1990, the leading candidate after the first round, Brian Lenihan (Fianna Fáil), eventually lost to the candidate with the second most first-choice votes, Mary Robinson (Labour Party). The reason was that the third placed candidate, Austin Currie (Fine Gael), was eliminated and his votes were reassigned to the next choice ranked on the ballots. This resulted in the vast majority of second-choice votes from his ballots going to Robinson, who managed to win an absolute majority on the second count.

6.3 Proportional Systems

In contrast to majoritarian systems, proportional electoral formulas produce seat shares in parliament that generally reflect the proportion of votes cast for political parties. If a party wins 40 per cent of the votes in an election, it can expect to hold roughly 40 per cent of the seats in parliament. First and foremost, proportional systems are designed to produce parliaments that reflect a wide variety of views rather than stable majorities to support governments. In contrast to majoritarian systems, multiple seats are awarded in each electoral district—the number of seats per district is referred to as **district magnitude** and, as this number grows large, electoral systems can be more proportional. However, no electoral system is perfectly proportional, and all tend to over-represent large parties and under-represent small parties. The degree of proportionality is a function of both the precise mathematical formula used to translate votes into seats, as well as the district magnitude. For example, following the 2017 election in the Netherlands, a country with one of the most proportional electoral systems, the largest party—the centre-right VVD (People's Party for Freedom and Democracy)—won 21.3 per cent of the vote, which translated to 33 of 150 seats in parliament, or exactly 22 per cent, just slightly more than their vote percentage. This contrasts with a system like Portugal, where following the 2019 election the PS (Socialist Party), the largest party, won 38.2 per cent of the vote, which translated into 47 per cent of the seats in parliament.

Electoral thresholds are an important element of proportional systems. These are hurdles that parties have to clear in order to receive any seats at all. Electoral thresholds can be mandated in the constitution or electoral law, requiring, for example, that a party receives 5 per cent of all votes cast, in order to win any seats at all. Their use is usually justified by a desire to limit the number of parties in parliament, and thus potential **fragmentation**. Thresholds tilt the balance from representation in the direction of clarity and government stability. Importantly, thresholds need not be formal in nature. They can exist simply as a natural consequence of the district magnitude. For instance, if a country uses twenty-five four-seat constituencies to elect a 100-seat parliament, a party needs to receive at least 25 per cent of the vote in a constituency to win a seat. In contrast, if the country were to use one 100-seat constituency, it would be sufficient to win 1 per cent of the vote to receive a seat. Therefore, the district magnitude directly impacts the electoral threshold in an electoral system. Electoral engineers can use this feature to make a PR system more or less proportional, depending whether one wants to favour representation or stability. As the district magnitude grows, the system becomes more proportional overall as the quota necessary to win a seat decreases. Equally important, the number of seats allocated per electoral district can vary within a country (see Box 6.2).

We can visualize the proportionality of the electoral formulas by plotting the average discrepancy between seats and votes across countries. Several scholars have proposed various ways of quantifying the **disproportionality of an electoral system**. Figure 6.2 shows the Gallagher Index of Disproportionality (Gallagher, 1991). It is based on the sum of squared differences between vote and seat shares for each political party in an election. The data reveal that the most disproportional systems are two majoritarian systems (France, UK) and one mixed system with a strong majoritarian component (Lithuania), whereas the most proportional systems in Europe are found in the Netherlands, Denmark, Malta, and Sweden. The figure also shows the levels of disproportionality in European Parliament (EP) electoral results. Because all countries use a variant of proportional representation for EP elections, the EP results are much more proportional than national results in majoritarian countries. In smaller, highly proportional countries, EP results are generally less proportional than national results. Even if these countries use the same electoral system for both elections, the EP elections have de facto smaller district magnitudes because these countries have smaller delegations in the EP compared to the size of their national parliament.

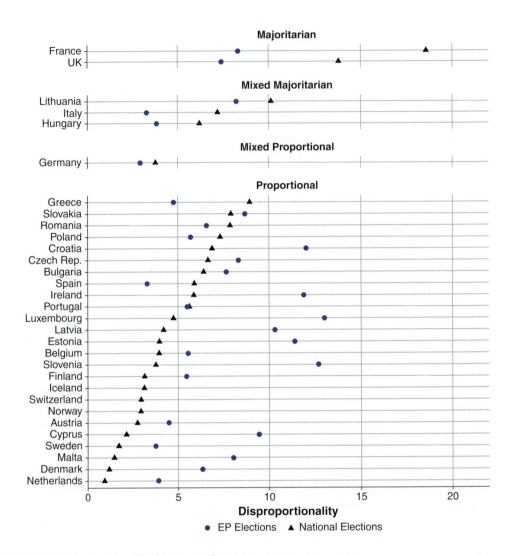

Figure 6.2 Disproportionality of Elections in Europe

Data source: ParlGov (Döring and Manow, 2019)

As always, there are advantages and disadvantages to whichever electoral system a country employs. Proportional systems may lead to seat shares in parliament that better reflect the underlying preferences of the population, but they tend not to produce a single winning party. When no party controls a majority of seats in parliament, coalitions are required to pass policy, and the coalition formation process can blur the link between votes, seat shares, and the government that eventually forms as we will discuss in Chapters 10 and 11. Majoritarian systems, in contrast, often produce a majority for a single party, but the preferences of a sizeable portion of the population are under-represented in parliament. Thus, with electoral

Box 6.2 **CONTROVERSIES AND DEBATES:** The Complexity of District Magnitudes in PR Systems

District magnitude is a key parameter in designing a proportional electoral system. Electoral system scholars have examined both district magnitude variation within and across countries. Some have even asked if there is an 'ideal' district magnitude. While scholars typically focus on countries' average district magnitudes, Kedar et al. (2016) point out that district magnitudes can actually vary quite substantially within a single country. The reason is that electoral district boundaries often coincide with those of administrative ones. In rural areas, where centre-right parties are electorally strong, such communities— and districts—are small. As a consequence, few MPs are elected in each district. In contrast, in urban areas, where centre-left parties have stronger electoral support, districts tend to be larger. For example, Spain has a median district magnitude of five seats. However, in practice it ranges from one seat (in the two Spanish enclaves in Ceuta and Melilla) to thirty-two (Barcelona) and thirty-seven seats (Madrid). Kedar and co-authors find that having many rural electoral districts with smaller district magnitudes creates inequalities by disproportionately benefiting centre-right parties in parliament. Small to moderate average district magnitudes in PR systems may, however, be normatively desirable to resolve the representation-accountability trade-off question. Carey and Hix (2011) advocate for low magnitude PR systems because they achieve a so-called electoral sweet spot. Analysing disproportionality and accountability, they argue that systems with a median magnitude between four and eight seats not only have highly representative parliaments (low disproportionality) but also only a moderate number of parties in parliament and in government (high accountability). In Europe, countries with district magnitudes in this range include Hungary, Ireland, Portugal, and Spain.

results there is often a trade-off between proportionality, on the one hand, and clarity and government stability, on the other.

Majoritarian and proportional systems also tend to have different ballot structures. By ballot structure, we refer to how the ballot actually looks and what appears on it, for example, the names of individual candidates or parties. Ballot structure determines how people cast a vote, for example by making a check mark next to a candidate or party name. In majoritarian systems voters cast votes for individual candidates whose names appear prominently on the ballot paper. Of course, these candidates campaign as individuals representing a particular party, but voters may recognize the candidates as individuals. Voters feel that they have their own individual representative in parliament. In contrast, many proportional systems with larger district magnitudes use party lists. Political parties usually rank order their candidates on a list, and seats are filled with the individuals starting from the top of the list.

We can distinguish proportional systems by whether they allow voters to cast a vote for a preferred candidate (preferential voting) or whether voters can simply vote for a party (Shugart, 2005). In **closed-list proportional representation** systems such as in Portugal, Romania, and Spain, voters can only cast one vote for a party, and not for any individual candidates on the list. Suppose a party receives 40 per cent of the vote and there are 100 seats to be filled in parliament. Ignoring for now the exact mathematical formula used to calculate the number of seats, we simply assume the party would gain forty seats. Thus, the first forty candidates on the party's list are elected (assuming the country has a single electoral district). In short, voters cannot influence the ranking of candidates in closed-list systems, and parties are in full control over who they nominate to the lists prior to the election.

In the vast majority of proportional systems in Europe, however, voters have an opportunity to express preferences for individual candidates. The defining feature of **flexible-list proportional systems** is that the order of candidates on the list is partly determined by parties and partly by voters. This is, in fact, the most prominent electoral system type in Europe, as shown in Figure 6.1. While parties present their list on the ballot, voters may overturn the party's ordering by casting votes for specific candidates or crossing out candidates' names. In practice, the hurdles to reordering the list may be quite high, thus flexible list systems still give parties a greater say over which candidates are ultimately elected than voters. **Open-list proportional representation** systems give voters the most say over list ordering. In these systems, parties continue to propose candidates, but the names are not pre-ranked as in flexible list systems. Thus, voters can only cast preference votes for individual candidates and these votes alone determine which candidates from the parties are elected to parliament. Open-list systems are the second most common electoral system type in Europe. The level of personalization of the ballot thus differs across these three variants of proportional representation. Parties and their members of parliament who intend to run for re-election are aware of these differences, creating incentives to cater more to the party overall (in closed systems) or to personal vote-seeking behaviour of members of parliament (in flexible and open list systems). The incentives of electoral systems create different patterns of behaviour in parliament, something we discuss in detail in Chapter 7.

The **single transferable vote** system is another variant of proportional representation used in Ireland and Malta. The system uses multi-seat electoral districts, just like a proportional system. Rather than casting a vote for a party or simply checking one candidate, voters are asked to rank the candidates running in the district. All votes are added and a quota is calculated which is equal to the number of votes required to win a seat in the district. If a voter's first-rank candidate clears the quota, the candidate is elected. If more candidates than seats remain in the contest, the candidate with the fewest votes is eliminated. The votes of this candidate are transferred to other candidates based on the back-up preference by the voters. This is repeated until all seats in the district are filled. The system offers clear advantages by allowing voters to express ranked preferences and by preventing second ranked alternatives from being considered in determining winners in each district. However, it also places a higher informational burden on voters, who need to compare and rank candidates.

Elections to the European Parliament are also fully proportional. However, member states are free to implement their preferred version of PR. Some member states use closed lists whereas others use open lists or the single transferable vote, but the vast majority of countries use flexible-list PR. Two countries (Ireland and Malta) rely on the single transferable vote system. Given that all countries use PR, the choice of electoral thresholds has important effects on the disproportionality of the results. Among the large member states, France, Poland, and Italy use a threshold of 4 or 5 per cent, whereas no threshold exists in Germany and Spain. This means that it was particularly easy for small parties to win a seat in the 2019 European Parliament election in Germany and Spain. In fact, fourteen German parties won at least one of the seats reserved for German parties and eight parties did so in Spain. The absence of a threshold in the largest member state

Germany was due to a decision of the German Constitutional Court that ruled the existence of a threshold for EP elections in Germany unconstitutional. However, the member states and the European Parliament agreed that, as of the EP elections in 2024, member states in which a party list system is used must use a minimum threshold for the allocation of seats for constituencies which comprise more than thirty-five seats. This would apply to Germany and Spain. Thus, it can be expected that future EP elections will have fewer parties with only one seat.

6.4 Mixed Systems

Some electoral systems attempt to combine the benefits of both types of electoral formulas, electing some members of parliament using a proportional system and others using majoritarian rules. Some scholars have suggested that **mixed electoral systems** may constitute a good compromise or 'the best of both worlds' (Shugart and Wattenberg, 2003). In these systems, voters cast two votes—one for an individual candidate in a single member district and a second for a party in a multi-member district. The precise nature of how this combination works varies across countries, with different implementations yielding large differences in disproportionality. The most proportional version of a mixed system is the German mixed-member proportional system. It is considered a mixed system since half of the Bundestag members are winners of single member district contests, whereas the other half is filled with candidates of the parties from closed party lists. The system yields proportional outcomes, as the seat shares in parliament are allocated only based on the second proportional tier. Box 6.3 explains the ballot and way in which candidates are elected in the German mixed system in more detail.

The three other countries that use a mixed system in Europe—Italy, Hungary, and Lithuania—use a mixed member majoritarian system (also known as a parallel system). In such systems, the party list vote does not compensate for any disproportionalities created in the majoritarian tier. The two votes, or tiers, run in parallel, and the electoral outcomes are less proportional as a result. In Italy, the proportional tier dominates. In the current electoral system, implemented in 2017, there 630 members of the Italian Chamber of Deputies, 232 of which are elected in single member district contests (around 37 per cent) and 386 are elected by proportional representation (61 per cent). The remaining twelve seats are elected by Italians living abroad. In contrast, in Hungary, the majoritarian tier dominates over the proportional one. More than half (53 per cent) of the 199 members of the Hungarian National Assembly are chosen in single member district plurality elections, and the remaining 47% in party lists.

In sum, if the objective of electoral engineers is to maximize the parties and views represented in parliament, and not necessarily accountability, then choosing a proportional electoral formula clearly works. Figure 6.2 shows that the average disproportionality is much lower in mixed member proportional (compensatory) and list PR systems. In contrast, mixed systems of the parallel nature and majoritarian electoral systems have higher levels of disproportionality. Single member plurality (UK) is on average around three times more disproportional than a list PR system.

Box 6.3 CASE STUDY: The German Mixed-Member Proportional System

Germany has a two-tiered electoral system in which voters cast two votes at the same time in Bundestag elections. They cast one vote for a candidate running in a single member district (the first tier), and a second vote for a closed party list (the second tier). The federal states (*Länder*) act as the electoral districts for the second party list vote, and each party nominates a state list. Only the second list vote is relevant for parties' parliamentary seat share. Moreover, this proportional tier is designed to compensate for any disproportionality that arises as a result of voting in the first SMD tier.

The illustration shows an example ballot from the German federal election in 2017 for the district of Berlin-Friedrichshain, illustrating this two vote system. The left column of the ballot lists the names of the candidates for this district together with their party affiliation and profession. The right column shows the parties for the list vote as well as the top five candidates on the party lists. In this election, the Greens won 8.9 per cent of the national vote in the proportional tier, yielding them a total of sixty-seven seats in parliament. They won one single member district, thus one Green MP came from an SMD and the remaining sixty-six candidates were filled from the party's lists. The ballot shown here was from the district won by the Green candidate Canan Bayram, who obtained the seat with a plurality of 26.3 per cent of the first votes.

Ballot
for the German Bundestag elections in district 83 Berlin-Friedrichshain-Kreuzberg-Prenzlauer Berg Ost on 24 September 2017

You have 2 votes

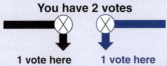

| 1 vote here for electing a Member of Parliament for your district | 1 vote here for electing a state list (party) -decisive vote for the allocation of seats to parties- |

First Vote	**Second Vote**
1 **Husein, Timur** — **CDU** Christlich Demokratische Union Deutschlands — Lawyer/Consultant — Berlin ○	○ **CDU** — **Christlich Demokratische Union Deutschlands** — Monika Grütters, Kai Wegner, Dr.Jan-Marco Luczak, Thomas Heilmann, Dr.Gottfried Ludewig — 1
2 **Kiziltepe, Cansel** — **SPD** Sozialdemokratische Partei Deutschlands — Economist/MP — Berlin ○	○ **SPD** — **Sozialdemokratische Partei Deutschlands** — Dr. Eva Högl, Swen Schulz, Cansel Kiziltepe, Klaus Mindrup, Mechthild Rawert — 2
3 **Meiser, Pascal** — **DIE LINKE** DIE LINKE — Political Scientist — Berlin ○	○ **DIE LINKE** — **DIE LINKE** — Petra Pau, Stefan Liebich , Dr.Gesine Lötzsch, Pascal Meiser, Evrim Sommer — 3
4 **Bayram, Canan** — **GRÜNE** BÜNDNIS 90/DIE GRÜNEN — Lawyer — Berlin ○	○ **GRÜNE** — **BÜNDNIS 90/DIE GRÜNEN** — Lisa Paus, Stefan Gelbhaar, Renate Künast, Özcan Mutlu, Dr.Laura Dornheim — 4
5 **Schmidt, Sibylle** — **AfD** Alternative für Deutschland — Business economist — Berlin ○	○ **AfD** — **Alternative für Deutschland** — Beatrix von Storch, Dr.Gottfried Curio, Dr. Götz Frömming, Dr.Birgit Malsack-Winkemann, Dr. Nicolaus Fest — 5
	○ **Piraten** — **Piratenpartei Deutschland** — Dr. Martin Haase, Ute Laack, Dr.Franz Josef Schmitt, Simon Kowalewski, Alexander Spies — 6
7 **Rousiamani-Goldthau, Athanasia** — **FDP** Freie Demokratische Partei — Homemaker — Berlin ○	○ **FDP** — **Freie Demokratische Partei** — Christoph Meyer, Daniela Kluckert, Hartmut Ebbing, Juliane Hüttl, Roman-Francesco Rogat — 7

Source: Amt für Statistik, Berlin-Brandenburg (2017, own translation).

Several features of this ballot and electoral system are noteworthy. First, voters can split their ticket by choosing a district candidate from one party on the first vote, while using their second vote to support a different party's list. Second, not all parties choose to run district candidates. For instance, the Pirates Party did not to run a candidate in this district, focusing instead on the closed party list vote. Third, most German voters cannot vote directly for the top politicians in their country because the electoral system uses the *Länder* as electoral districts for the second, party list electoral tier. Thus, the voters in Berlin could not vote for a party list headed by Chancellor Angela Merkel. Instead, Merkel ran in a district in her home state of Mecklenburg-Vorpommern, where she was also the lead candidate on the CDU's party list.

A final consequence of the German mixed-member proportional system is that the size of the Bundestag is flexible, as parties may win a number of single member districts even though they fare poorly in the party list vote. When a party wins more single-member districts, and thus seats, than they ought to receive given the party list vote, all other parties are 'compensated' and receive additional seats so that the overall seat distribution in parliament remains proportional to the second vote. Proportionality is only possible by increasing the size of parliament. Therefore, rather than the 598 seats called for in the German electoral law, the Bundestag is often much larger. In 2017, after allocating these compensatory seats, a record number of 709 MPs entered parliament, almost 20 per cent over the target size.

6.5 Electoral Systems and the Party System

Using the electoral system classification as a foundation, we can now examine the reciprocal relationship of electoral rules and **party systems**—a description of all the parties within a country, the number of parties that compete in elections, and their ideological leanings. We first discuss how the number of parties in a party system may be a consequence of electoral rules. We then elaborate on how electoral rules are shaped by political parties.

The link between a country's electoral system and its party system has long been a focus of study in the field comparative politics. Maurice Duverger famously stated that SMD plurality electoral systems tend to produce two-party systems while proportional systems often lead to **multi-party systems** (Duverger, 1951). The first statement regarding the association between SMD plurality and two-party systems is known as **Duverger's Law**, while the second statement about proportional systems is known as Duverger's hypothesis. Duverger talked about two reasons for the relationship between SMD plurality and a two-party system. The first he termed the mechanical effect. Because there is only one seat to win in any given constituency, the threshold for obtaining a seat is rather high, namely a candidate must receive more votes than anyone else. There are likely no more than two candidates that have a realistic chance at winning the seat within a constituency. The second reason for the relationship was called the psychological effect by Duverger. Voters know the mechanical effect and tend not to cast their votes for smaller parties that have very little chance of winning the seat. They might view such a vote as a waste of their ballot. In fact, we can consider this as a form of strategic voting (i.e. voting not for the most preferred party due to strategic considerations).

While the one SMD plurality system in Europe, the UK, has only two main parties, the relationship between the electoral system and the party system is far from perfect. In the UK, the Liberal Democrats perform well in some constituencies, while even the Greens hold a seat in Westminster. The Scottish Nationalist Party dominates in Scotland, and other regional parties, such a Plaid Cymru in Wales and several Northern Irish parties, win seats, too. Duverger's law seems to work best at the constituency level, rather than the national level. At the constituency level, there may only be two parties with a realistic chance of winning, but if these two parties are not the same across the entire country, and in the UK they are not, then the national party system may, indeed, have more than two parties. The geographic concentration of British voters for some parties in different regions means that some small parties can win a relatively large number of seats, while others are particularly poor at translating votes into seats. In the 2019 general election, the geographically concentrated Scottish Nationalist Party won forty-eight seats with only 3.9 per cent of the UK-wide vote, while the geographically diffuse Liberal Democrats won only eleven seats, losing one seat that they had previously held, despite increasing their nationwide vote total by 4.2 per cent up to 11.5 per cent.

Meanwhile, more proportional systems tend to have more parties. As district magnitude increases in list systems, more parties have a realistic chance of winning seats, and the geographic distribution of voters matters less. Proportional systems allow for more parties because the threshold for winning a seat is lower, meaning parties can enter parliament with much lower support than they would need in a SMD plurality system. Proportionality, though, is not necessarily sufficient for more parties to appear. Both Germany and Austria have relatively proportional electoral systems, but have had effectively 2.5 party systems for much of the post-Second World War era. There may be both institutional and societal reasons why these countries did not have more parties for so long. Institutionally, both of these countries have an electoral threshold that parties must pass to gain representation in parliament— 5 per cent in Germany and 4 per cent in Austria, meaning small parties need more support than in countries with no, or a low, threshold, such as the Netherlands.

As new issues developed in politics that the traditional parties did not cover effectively, such as the environment, new parties arose. More proportional systems create a permissiveness to allow new parties to enter the political landscape. The Greens were the first new parties to gain national prominence, in particular in PR systems, but other parties have done well, too. In Germany, these have included the Left Party, and the populist radical right AfD (Alternative for Germany). In general, a country's party system is an interaction between its electoral rules and the cleavages found within society. When numerous cleavages exist in a society and the electoral rules allow for multiple parties, multiple parties may arise. The effects of electoral systems on the party system are thus conditional: as long as electoral systems are permissive in the sense that they allow new parties to enter the landscape easily, then an increase in social diversity or the emergence of new issues may lead to a translation into more parties (Neto and Cox, 1997; Clark and Golder, 2006).

Figure 6.3 shows the relationship between disproportionality and the effective number of parliamentary parties. The **effective number of parties** refers to an adjusted number of political parties in a country's party system, here weighted by their relative strength in terms of seats in parliament. The most proportional systems have on average four and a half parties in parliament, whereas the number decreases to below three parties for the most disproportional systems. The figure also reveals the conditional relationship: there is variation in the number of parties for any given disproportionality level. When a system is proportional (left side of the figure), there may sometimes indeed be many parties in parliament, reaching in a few instances more than nine effective parliamentary parties (as in Belgium in 2019 or in Poland in 1991). However, there are a number of elections in which even the most proportional systems led to only two parliamentary parties (as Malta or in Austria in the 1960s and 1970s).

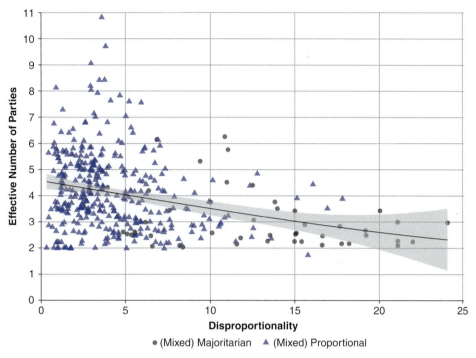

Figure 6.3 Relationship between Disproportionality and Effective Number of Parliamentary Parties

Data source: ParlGov (Döring and Manow, 2019)

Higher levels of disproportionality, in contrast seem to act as a strict barrier to party entry: there are no instances in which there are more than effectively four parliamentary parties in highly disproportional electoral systems.

Duverger's Law seems to imply that electoral rules 'cause' the party system, but of course it is not that simple. The causal arrow may also point in the other direction, with pre-existing social cleavages and existing party systems determining the nature of the electoral system. Countries with many cleavages may opt for more proportional electoral systems. Initially, nineteenth-century European democracies started out with majoritarian electoral systems, but then many switched to PR at the start of the twentieth century. Belgium was the first country to move to PR in 1899. The reasons for the move to PR have been much studied and debated. Rokkan (1970) first argued that PR emerged following the emergence of socialism, and demands from workers for greater representation. PR was thus introduced as a way for established conservative parties to remain electorally viable.

However, Boix suggested that Rokkan's argument was underspecified. Socialists never had enough votes or representation to implement change on their own. Rather, Boix (1999) argues that PR emerged only in places where conservative (bourgeois) parties saw the switch as necessary to preserve their dominance. Electoral systems thus changed as a result of an electoral threat, which itself is a consequence of new parties emerging. If SMD majoritarian electoral systems meant that two right parties might split their vote, handing victory to a unified socialist left, the right was better off switching to PR as a means to preserve their electoral

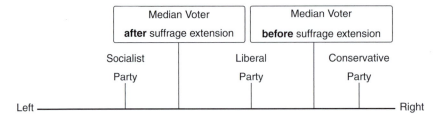

Figure 6.4 Moving to Proportional Representation: The Electoral Threat Model by Boix

advantage. While the political considerations for introducing electoral reform operate both at the party level—how will the party fare overall under different electoral rules—as well as on the district level—how are individual legislators affected by electoral rule change (Leemann and Mares, 2014)—we present a simplified visual illustration of the strategic situation, as examined by Boix, in Figure 6.4.

Suppose that, before suffrage expansion to the working class, the median voter in society was on the right of the political spectrum. Two existing parties, shown here as Liberal Party and Conservative Party, competed for votes in single member district plurality elections. Neither of them were dominant. With the expansion of the suffrage to the working class, the median voter shifted to the left as workers demanded more redistribution. A new party, the Socialist Party, forms and enters the political landscape. If the electoral system were to remain a first-past-the-post system, the Socialist Party would likely be successful since the parties on the right would split the electorate, while many voters would support the Socialist Party in each district. Anticipating a sweeping victory of the new party under the old electoral rules, the Liberal and Conservative Party jointly can agree to a move to proportional representation, thus securing representation in parliament even with a strong Socialist Party. This is, in fact, the situation that occurred in Denmark and Sweden at the beginning of the twentieth century. Conversely, in situations where there is one dominant party on the right, there is no incentive to switch to PR, a situation that occurred in the UK. The political argument for adoption of PR in Europe thus puts multipartyism before institutional choice, and renders 'Duverger's Law upside down' (Colomer, 2005). Multipartyism becomes the cause rather than the consequence of electoral systems.

Following the move from majoritarian to proportional electoral systems across most European countries at the beginning of the twentieth century, most electoral systems have been stable. They constitute the rules of the game and countries usually do not change the fundamental rules of democracy. However, there are notable outliers to this pattern. Table 6.1 presents an overview of major electoral system reforms and shows that there have been changes in several European countries. For instance, governments in Italy have successfully and rapidly changed the electoral system several times, driven by a party-political desire for seat maximization and the desire to find a different balance between representation and accountability. Since the early 1990s, Italian voters have voted for parties in national elections under list proportional representation, mixed member proportional system, and a parallel voting system. Frequent electoral reforms also have occurred in eastern Europe, in particular in Bulgaria and Croatia, with both countries switching between majoritarian, mixed systems and proportional representation with closed and flexible lists.

Table 6.1 Major Electoral System Reforms in Europe since 1945

Country	Year	Status quo	Reform
Bulgaria	1991	Closed-list MMM	Closed-list PR
Bulgaria	2009	Closed-list PR	Closed-list MMM
Bulgaria	2011	Closed-list MMM	Flexible-list PR
Croatia	1992	Majoritarian (TRS)	Closed-list MMM
Croatia	1999	Closed-list MMM	Closed-list PR
Croatia	2015	Closed-list PR	Flexible-list PR
Cyprus	1979	Majoritarian	Open-list PR
France	1951	Flexible-list PR	Flexible-list Reinforced proportional
France	1958	Flexible-list Reinforced proportional	Majoritarian (TRS)
France	1985	Majoritarian (TRS)	Closed-list PR
France	1986	Closed-list PR	Majoritarian (TRS)
Hungary	2011	Closed-list MMM/TRS	Closed-list MMM/FPTP
Iceland	1959	Flexible-list MMM	Flexible-list PR
Italy	1993	Flexible-list PR	Closed-list MMP
Italy	2005	Closed-list MMP	Closed-list PR
Italy	2017	Closed-list PR	Closed-list MMM
Romania	2008	Closed-list PR	MMP
Romania	2015	MMP	Closed-list PR

Source: Pilet et al. (2016).

6.6 Direct Democracy in Europe

We conclude our discussion of elections and systems of voting with an examination of the rules governing direct democracy, which has become an increasingly common feature of European democracy. Although voters usually cast ballots for politicians who make policy on their behalf, sometimes they cast votes directly on policy. Just like in parliamentary and presidential elections, where electoral systems determine how voting occurs and the relationship between voters and their representatives, direct democracy is also governed by rules that impact outcomes.

In the great majority of European countries, **referendums** can be triggered to allow citizens to decide directly on some issues. 'Direct democracy' is an umbrella term used for a variety of decision processes by which ordinary citizens can vote directly on policy matters. Often, direct democracy is contrasted with representative democracy in which citizens delegate decision-making to elected representatives. In reality, however, this distinction is artificial since no political system uses direct democracy as their main mode of policy-making. European countries vary considerably in the degree to which they give citizens the right to vote directly on policy matters, with Switzerland, at one extreme, where citizens regularly vote on policies in referendums and initiatives and Germany, at the other extreme, where referendums are prohibited at the federal level.

What all referendums have in common is that they allow the mass electorate to vote directly on some public issue, but they vary on four important dimensions: whether the referendum is constitutionally required or not, which actors (such as the government or citizens)

Table 6.2 Types of Referendums

	Mandatory constitutional referendum	Abrogative referendum	Consultative referendum	Citizen initiated referendum (Initiative)
Also known as	Compulsory referendum	Popular referendum; Popular veto	Plebiscite; Optional referendum; Advisory referendum	Citizens' initiative; direct initiative; popular initiative
Format	A referendum required to effect a change in the constitution	A procedure to force a popular vote on a law that has been passed by the legislature. In some context triggered by citizens, in others by a minority of the legislature	A referendum on any subject, usually initiated by government or legislature	A referendum on any subject brought about by a petition of citizens
Result binding/ non-binding	Binding	Generally binding	Generally non-binding	Generally binding
Question formulated by	Government	Citizens or Parliament	Government or Parliament	Citizens
Example	Ratification of the Lisbon Treaty (Ireland, 2008)	Approval of replacing the mixed-member proportional electoral system (Italy, 1999)	EU membership (UK, 2016)	Political reform (Slovakia, 2010)
Common in	Denmark, Ireland, Lithuania, Switzerland	Austria, Italy, Switzerland	France, Finland, Hungary, Italy, Switzerland, UK	Lithuania, Slovakia, Switzerland

can initiative a referendum, what types of issues are decided by the referendum, and whether the outcome is binding on the government. On the basis of these dimensions, we can distinguish between four common types of referendums (and initiatives) in Table 6.2.

The first type is referendums that are mandated in the constitution (mandatory constitutional referendum). Ireland, for instance, always requires a referendum if policy authority is transferred to the supranational level. The results are binding, even though the government can hold the referendum again, as happened when voters were asked twice to ratify the Treaty of Nice and Treaty of Lisbon.

The second type is an abrogative referendum, also known as a popular referendum or veto, which constitutes an ex-post opportunity for voters to veto a law or constitutional amendment passed by parliament. This can be triggered by a certain minimum number of registered voters or by a minority of members of parliament. Unlike a citizens' initiative that allows voters to suggest new legislation, an abrogative referendum allows them to suggest repealing existing legislation. In Italy, abrogative referendums are commonly used. The Italian constitution allows for 500,000 voters, or five regional councils, to trigger an abrogative referendum to repeal, in whole or in a part, any law, with the exception of tax, budget, amnesty and pardon laws, and international treaties. For example, in 2011, Italian voters repealed several laws regarding the reintroduction of nuclear energy, the privatization of water services, and a criminal code provision exempting the cabinet from appearing in court.

Third, many European executives can initiate consultative referendums, the results of which are generally non-binding. Such referendums can be called by presidents (e.g. in France) or prime ministers (e.g. in the UK). For example, the 2016 Brexit referendum in the UK was called by Prime Minister David Cameron as a consultative referendum. Thus, technically, the British government could have ignored the outcome of the public vote and put the question back to the House of Commons. However, by taking the decision to hold such a referendum, governments risk a major credibility crisis if they ignore the outcome. Thus, governments usually accept the outcome of the referendum despite its legally non-binding nature. This was also the case for the consultative referendums on the EU's Constitutional Treaty in France and the Netherlands. The results were accepted by the governments and led to the abandoning of the ratification process of the EU constitution. One noteworthy exception to this is the 1955 Swedish consultative referendum on the introduction of right-hand traffic in 1955, which was rejected by 83 per cent of voters. Nonetheless, the Swedish Parliament approved the change and eventually switched to right-hand driving in 1967.

The fourth type is citizen-initiated referendums, also known as citizens' initiatives or popular initiatives. Compared to the first three types, popular initiatives are the only variant in direct democracy that allows citizens to put a legal question up for a popular vote, subject to certain minimum support that initiatives have to gain in order for them to qualify. For instance, Swiss popular initiatives require the collection of 100,000 signatures over the course of eighteen months. Other European constitutions also provide provisions for citizens' initiative, although these are more restrictive and rarely used. In Latvia, for example, a minimum of one-tenth of eligible voters has the right to initiate a national referendum regarding recalling of parliament, and the Hungarian constitution allows 200,000 eligible voters to initiate a binding 'national referendum' on political questions.

Figure 6.5 shows the use of both citizens' initiatives and (elite-initiated) referendums since 1945 in Europe. The top row figures reflect the increasing use of initiatives and referendums in Europe, excluding Switzerland. They show that referendums called by governments or parliaments are more common than initiatives and that the latter were only introduced outside Switzerland in the late 1980s. The figure also indicates a clear rise in the use of referendums from the 1990s onwards. The increases are not surprising given that most of the constitutions adopted in the post-communist EU member states contain provisions for referendums and initiatives. Moreover, countries that have not had a tradition of direct democracy, such as Britain and the Netherlands, have resorted to this device in recent decades. The bottom row figures display the number of referendums in Switzerland. It is clear that Switzerland is an outlier when it comes to the use of direct democracy in Europe, both in terms of the high frequency and the large volume of citizen-initiated referendums. There are no referendums at the EU level. However, the Treaty of Lisbon introduced a new democratic instrument for citizen involvement, the European Citizens' Initiative, described in Box 6.4.

Despite the increase in referendums and initiatives across Europe, direct democracy remains contested. Some argue that the direct influence of citizens in law-making should be minimized, while others favour greater direct involvement of citizens in decision-making. The main arguments in favour of direct democracy relate to procedural legitimacy. Proponents

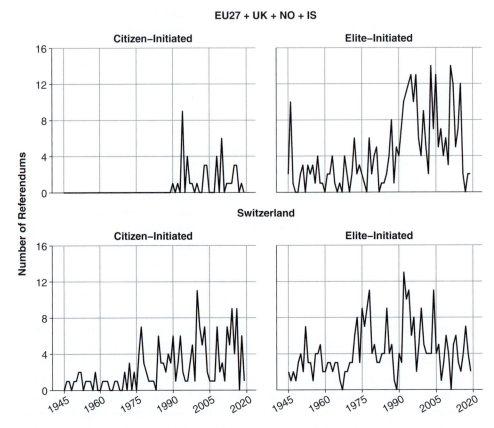

Figure 6.5 Initiatives and Referendums in Europe

Data source: C2D (Serdült et al., 2018)

of referendums suggest that they enhance democracy by enabling people to become directly involved in policy-making. By allowing citizens a say on specific policies, direct democracy can enhance the popular legitimacy underpinning key political decisions. This is also why some constitutions, such as the Irish and the Danish, require referendums on significant policy reforms, such as constitutional amendments and the surrender of sovereignty to international institutions. The argument is that, unlike elections, where voters are influenced by many considerations, referendums can confer legitimacy upon a particularly significant policy choice, such as joining the European Union or secession (e.g. Scottish or Catalan independence). The threat of direct democracy can also encourage elected representatives to be more responsive to the electorate and their preferences. Citizen initiatives and abrogative referendums can pull elite decisions that are out of line with public opinion back into line and foster greater representation (Leemann and Wasserfallen, 2016). Moreover, it is argued that participation in referendums can help educate voters about issues, as they are exposed to arguments on either side of the issue. By allowing people to participate directly in policy-making, citizens also feel more empowered and engaged in democratic processes, which is inherently a good thing.

Box 6.4 CASE STUDY: The European Citizens' Initiative

The European Citizens' Initiative (ECI) was launched on 1 April 2012, and it allows citizens to ask the Commission to draft a proposal for a legal act on an issue which falls within the authority of EU institutions. It must receive one million signatures to be valid. An ECI is a direct call for a specific legal instrument, must abide by specific rules, and it is addressed to the European Commission. It is different from a petition. EU citizens have a right to submit a petition on matters that fall within an area of EU authority and affect the petitioner directly. Petitions can be addressed to European Parliament. Unlike the citizen initiated referendums described in Table 6.2, the ECI does not give citizens the opportunity to vote directly on a policy issue. Instead, the ECI enables EU citizens to ask the Commission to bring forward a European legislative proposal if the supporters number at least one million (signatures need to be collected within twelve months) and come from at least one quarter of EU member states. In other words, the Commission maintains its legislative agenda-setting powers, but it needs to provide a justification if it does not put forward a proposal following such an initiative.

In the first eight years of the ECI, five initiatives were successfully submitted to the Commission, on a range of issues such as human right to water, research on embryos, vivisection, toxic pesticides, and linguistic minorities. In order to make the procedures more accessible and less bureaucratic, new rules came into force in January 2020. To give organizers more time to prepare their campaigns, they can set the signature collection start date anytime within six months of the registration of their initiative. Moreover, to simplify the collection of signatures, the European Commission has introduced a centralized online collection system.

Of the ECIs that have thus far acquired enough signatures, none has led to the adoption of a legal act. In some cases the Commission, which is not legally required to propose a new legislative proposal argued that the EU's legislative framework was satisfactory; in other cases it suggested that soft law measures and new consultation were sufficient. Thus, this new mechanism in theory is meant to foster more democratic responsiveness, but it has not had much impact in practice.

The main arguments against referendums relate to their majoritarian nature and questions around the quality of decision-making by voters. Since referendums are often binary choices where a simply majority decides the outcome, there is a concern that they may be insensitive to or prejudiced against minorities. Opponents of referendums argue that the use of direct democracy allows majorities to discriminate against minority rights. The scholarly evidence on whether minority rights are undermined more by direct democracy than representative legislatures is mixed, however (Matsusaka, 2005). In one study, Hainmüller and Hangartner (2019) consider the effect of direct democracy on the naturalization rates of immigrant minorities in Switzerland. Eligible immigrants that seek Swiss citizenship have to apply with the municipality in which they reside, and decisions on the naturalization applications are taken either by (1) direct democracy where citizens vote on the applications using referendums or by (2) representative democracy in municipality councils. The study finds that naturalization rates surged by about 60 per cent once politicians rather than citizens began deciding on naturalization applications. This suggests that direct democracy, at least on issues such as citizenship applications, may lead to greater discrimination against more marginalized immigrant groups.

Another set of concerns about direct democracy lies in the quality of decision-making and policy outcomes. While the ideal scenario is that well-informed voters cast their votes on the basis of their views on the issue at hand, studies have suggested that many people decide how to vote on the basis of a range of extraneous factors, including their views on the government of the day (Hobolt, 2009). Referendums can also be exploited by populist politicians to stir anti-establishment feelings and bypass, rather than complement, the work of the legislature. Moreover, some fear that well-organized interest groups or lobbyists, who have specific interests, will bankroll direct democracy initiatives and exert undue influence on voters (Broder, 2000; Gerber, 1999). Critics of referendums thus argue that the quality of policy-making is worse in direct democratic contests than in the legislative arena, since elected politicians have broad policy expertise and can understand difficult trade-offs, whereas referendums are likely to lead to more incoherent and less balanced policy outcomes. This debate on whether direct democracy enhances or undermines the quality of democratic decision-making also pertains to referendums on European integration, which we turn to next.

6.7 Referendums on European Integration

Among the most consequential and salient referendums in Europe are the votes related to the European Union. The 2016 referendum on UK membership of the EU, which led to Brexit, might have been the most visible referendum related to European integration, but it certainly is not the only one. There have been over fifty EU-related referendums (Hobolt, 2009). In the early stages of the European integration process, as discussed in Chapter 4, policy-makers believed a **permissive consensus** existed among citizens. Elites assumed citizens generally supported steps that furthered integration, but direct democracy played no role and citizens had limited input. Since the early 1970s, though, referendums on aspects of European integration have become increasingly common. The first EU referendum was held in France in 1972, concerning the entry into the EU (then known as the EEC) of Denmark, Ireland, Norway, and the UK. This was followed by three accession referendums the same year: in Denmark and Ireland citizens voted to join, whereas Norwegian voters rejected membership.

EU-related referendums can be classified as either membership referendums, treaty ratification referendums, or single-issue referendums. The most common type of EU referendum is a membership referendum. Most countries that have joined the EU since the 'founding six' (Belgium, France, Germany, Italy, Luxembourg, and Netherlands) have held popular referendums where voters were asked to decide whether or not to join. Some of these referendums have been mandatory, in accordance with national constitutions, whereas others have been consultative. In either case, national governments have followed the wishes of the people. With the exception of negative votes in Norway and Switzerland, all referendums have endorsed the accession decision and led to the enlargement of the European Union. Moreover, two national referendums have been held on whether to stay in the EU, both in the UK. In 1975, British 67 per cent of voters endorsed continued membership of the EEC. In 2016, 52 per cent of British voters voted to leave the EU, and the UK left the EU in January 2020. The only other example of such a referendum on continued membership is the 1982 referendum in Greenland, an autonomous territory of Denmark, where 53 per cent of voters decided that Greenland would leave the European Communities. Greenland formally left the EC in 1985, but continues to be considered an Overseas Countries and Territory of the EU, giving it a special relationship with the Union.

The second most common type of EU referendum involves treaty ratification. All member states need to ratify EU treaty revisions, such as the most recent Lisbon Treaty. Most countries do so by a simple majority in their national parliaments, however, in some countries this ratification process has involved an element of direct democracy, where citizens are given a say on the treaty. Such treaty ratification referendums are sometimes mandatory, when constitutional provisions are in place that require referendums before signing up to international treaties that require surrender of national sovereignty. Mandatory constitutional referendums have taken place in both Denmark and Ireland. In other cases, such as the referendums on the Constitutional Treaty in 2005 in France, the Netherlands, Luxembourg, and Spain, such referendums are consultative, as governments decided to consult the public even though they could have decided to ratify the treaty in their respective legislatures. The Constitutional Treaty was never ratified due to the negative votes in referendums in France and the Netherlands.

This raises a question about why governments choose to hold consultative referendums on EU treaties, despite the risks associated with it. Studies have shown that the most compelling reasons for governments to hold referendums are rooted in domestic politics (Prosser, 2016). By allowing voters a vote on an EU issue, governments facing a Eurosceptic public seek to ensure that the EU issue does not overshadow the subsequent elections. This is a particular concern when governments have to ratify a treaty close to an election. Referendums may also be used as an attempt to resolve internal divisions within the governing party or coalition of parties. British Prime Minister David Cameron's pledge to hold an EU membership referendum in 2015 is an example of the impact of such domestic concerns (see Chapter 14).

The final, and least common, type of EU referendums are single-issue referendums. Whereas all referendums are essentially issue-specific, the membership and treaty ratification referendums touch upon a number of interconnected economic and political issues relating membership and the integration process. In contrast, in referendums on specific issues national elites often have more control over the ballot proposal and the timing. Examples include the first French referendum on enlargement in 1972 and the 2015 Danish referendum to reform Denmark's Justice and Home Affairs opt-out to allow for closer cooperation in this area. Other examples include the two Scandinavian referendums on joining the Euro in 2000 (Denmark) and 2003 (Sweden), which both failed at the hands of the electorate.

These examples illustrate that all types of EU referendums possess the potential to have 'elite-defying', or non-cooperative, consequences. While European governments, mainstream parties, businesses, and media have usually been fairly united in favouring EU membership and the integration process, and advocating a pro-integration (cooperative) vote in these referendums, a significant number of proposals have been rejected by voters. This is illustrated in Figure 6.6, which depicts the cooperative (pro-integration) and non-cooperative (anti-integration) outcomes across countries. Given the constitutional provisions for mandatory referendums in Denmark, Ireland, and Switzerland, we also see the most non-cooperative votes in these countries, but even consultative referendums in the Netherlands, France, and the UK have ended in ways not anticipated, or desired, by the national governments. This has had serious consequences for the European integration process.

The direct implications are evident. It is due to referendums that Norway, Switzerland, and the United Kingdom are not members of the EU. Referendums have also led to differentiated integration for other countries, not least Denmark and Sweden, that remain outside the Eurozone. Referendums have led to delay in the ratification of the Maastricht, Nice, and

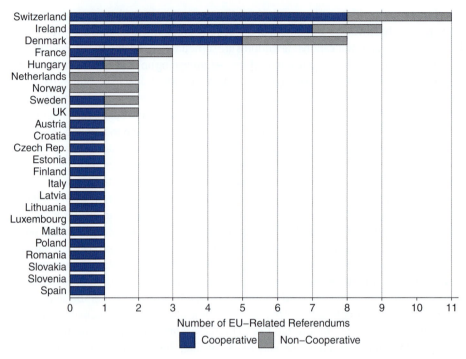

Figure 6.6 Referendums on European Integration

Note: Cooperative outcomes favour integration; Non-cooperative outcomes oppose integration

Data source: C2D (Serdült et al., 2018) and own coding

Lisbon Treaties, due to No votes in Denmark (1992) and Ireland (2001, 2008), which were later overturned in subsequent treaty ratification referendums. The carefully negotiated Constitutional Treaty was abandoned due to the No votes in 2005 in France and the Netherlands. EU referendums have also had tangible consequences in the domestic political arena, in some countries leading to the division of established parties, to the formations of new parties and alliances and the resignation of governments and prime ministers.

The indirect consequences of national EU referendums are more difficult to establish. Proponents of referendums would argue that the anticipation of a referendum might make governments more responsive to the preferences of citizens. Referendums, such as the rejection of the Maastricht Treaty in Denmark in 1992, have certainly served to highlight the concerns about European integration shared by many citizens, and have encouraged politicians to listen more carefully to their electorates. Referendums have also contributed to greater knowledge and engagement among citizens. However, it remains a contested question whether national referendums are an appropriate mode of decision-making in an international organization and the best way of securing citizen involvement. Some have argued against the use of an institutional device that allows citizens to undercut their elected representatives. The multilevel structure of the EU brings about an additional complication with the use of direct democracy. While decisions are taken by institutions and governments at the EU level, EU referendums are conducted at the national level, and national electorates are asked to decide on a treaty that is a political compromise made by the EU member states collectively. This raises the question of whether it is fair that a small majority of voters in one or more countries can determine the future of the European project for all. For this reason, even a failed referendum on treaty ratification in one or more member states (for example, after the Nice Treaty, the Constitutional Treaty, and the Lisbon Treaty) has not led to an abandonment of the European integration project, but rather to a slowing down of the process of ratification. In fact, at least up until now, no negative treaty ratification referendum has led to a reversion to a status quo that existed before the treaty that was subject to ratification.

6.8 Summary

Electoral systems are the central democratic political institution connecting voters to representatives. They determine the way in which politicians gain office and how they are removed from their posts. They both help shape and are shaped by the number of parties competing for seats. In short, they have significant ramifications for party systems, representation, and government accountability. Moreover, we have shown that there is a great diversity in electoral rules used across Europe. There is no one single democratic way to elect representatives or to allow voters to participate in the policy process. But the different systems do lead to trade-offs and compromises with regard to different aspects of democracy. Finally, we have discussed various instruments of direct democracy in Europe, which are also governed by a variety of rules. These rules dictate how votes get turned into policy, bypassing the process of delegation, the roots of which are electoral systems. Referendums and direct democracy have played a particularly important role in the development of European integration.

Online Data Exercise: The Parliaments and governments database (ParlGov)

The interactive online exercise explores how electoral systems are connected to the party system on the national and the EU level. Using the ParlGov dataset, you can compare outcomes across electoral systems. Furthermore, the connection with the EU level provides insights into how different electoral systems influence disproportionality within the same country.

 Take your learning further with this interactive data exercise, available at **www.foundationsofeuropeanpolitics.com**

 For additional material and resources, including multiple-choice questions, web links, and more, please visit the online resources: **www.oup.com/he/devries1e**

7 Representation

This chapter discusses different concepts of political representation—substantive, descriptive and symbolic—and examines which institutions foster different types of representation. It presents two visions of democracy, proportional versus majoritarian, and considers what they imply for congruence and responsiveness. When examining descriptive representation, it looks in detail at the representation of women across legislatures. It discusses symbolic representation with respect to actions taken by members of parliament.

To what extent, and in what ways, does a political system represent its citizens? Whenever citizens delegate power to representatives, we can assess the extent to which this delegation results in **political representation**. In other words, when, how, and to what extent do voters feel that the political representatives reflect their views, and more generally, speak for people like them? When citizens feel that the system reflects them and their interests, they have greater trust in the political system, become more likely to participate in politics, and are more supportive of democracy. Political representation is therefore one of the ways in which we can assess democratic quality.

But just what constitutes good political representation? And how do we know when it exists within a political system? There are different ways we can conceive of political representation and assess the success of a political system in achieving it. People may want their political system to accomplish different things, and they may measure the achievements of democracy in different ways. In this chapter, we discuss the different forms that political representation can take and how we can measure them. We also consider different visions of democracy, proportional versus majoritarian, and how they influence representation. We present evidence on the representation of women in European politics, and we discuss how actions taken by elected members of parliaments impact representation.

7.1 Types of Representation

We can think of the relationship between citizens and the politicians they elect as either a form of trusteeship or as a form of delegation. If representation is marked by a trusteeship, voters elect representatives who take decisions on the behalf of the voters that they, the representatives, think are best. In contrast, if representation occurs through delegation, politicians may be expected to represent ideas and views held by the electorate, or at least some part of it, regardless of their own views. When determining the proper course of action, delegate conceptions of representation require representatives to follow their constituents' preferences, while trustee conceptions require representatives to follow their own judgement.

The distinction between the **trustee** and the **delegate models of representation** was put forward in the late eighteenth century by the Irish MP and philosopher Edmund Burke, who favoured the trustee model of politicians following their own conscience and judgement in the best interest of the public.

In the twentieth century, political theorist Hanna Pitkin (1967) described political representatives as either *acting for* or *standing for* the citizens who elect them. Politicians who act for their citizens have some formal authority to do so, and democratic political systems task them with making substantive policy decisions on citizens' behalf. **Substantive representation** focuses on the inputs and outcomes of the policy-making process. Representatives may propose and decide policy in either the capacity of a trustee—suggesting policy that they feel is best—or a delegate—suggesting policy that they feel best reflects the wishes of their voters. If voters feel that politicians have failed in their representative task, they can hold politicians to account through elections. No matter how they develop policy positions, either as trustees or delegates, politicians may be seen as having a mandate from voters to support some policies and not others, depending on the policies they supported during the election campaign. If voters disagree with what the politicians have done, they can retrospectively remove them from office. Mansbridge (2003) has referred to this as **promissory representation**, as politicians make promises to voters at election time that voters expect them to fulfil.

But substantive representation of policy interests is not the only type of representation that politicians can provide. Pitkin also thought of politicians as *standing for* the voters. This type of representation does not require direct action on the part of politicians, but rather can be descriptive or symbolic. Politicians may represent voters simply by reflecting particular characteristics of voters. For example, politicians may belong to the same social class as the voters they represent, they may speak the same language, or have the same skin colour or other physical features. Pitkin referred to sharing such characteristics as **descriptive representation**. It may matter a great deal to voters to have representatives to whom they can relate because they share similar features, especially for voters from groups that have been traditionally under-represented in politics, including women and racial or ethnic minorities. They may trust politicians who look, sound, or act like them to make better decisions on their behalf. The quality of descriptive representation is judged by the resemblance between the representatives and the electorate as a whole.

Similarly, irrespective of policy content, Pitkin suggested that politicians can offer voters **symbolic representation**. Citizens may feel that the political system better reflects them when an elected official tasked with representing their region, or belonging to a party that they support, takes part in the activities of parliament, for example. When voters see or hear about politicians participating in political acts on a national stage, perhaps by asking questions during a parliamentary question period, actively participating in a committee hearing, giving a speech, or drafting an amendment to a bill, they may take this as a symbol of a government working for them.

Substantive representation approaches ask how well the policies that governments develop reflect public opinion. High levels of substantive representation can emerge both when elected politicians act as delegates and as trustees; however, when politicians view themselves as trustees, substantive representation arises only when the politicians and voters happen to share the same position. If they view themselves as delegates, in contrast, politicians may actively change positions to align with voters. Even descriptive and symbolic representation may relate to substantive representation. Representatives from particular groups may be more likely to advocate for policies that support and are supported by the groups to which they belong. Likewise, largely symbolic acts, like giving a speech on the floor of parliament, may be better received by voters if the representative's stated position matches with the voters' own policy stance. Substantive representation is assessed by the extent to which policy positions, or policy outcomes, advanced by representatives align with the interests and preferences of citizens.

The focus on policy has raised many interesting questions about whether some types of electoral institutions create better incentives to produce policy that reflects the electorate than others; or whether coalition governments offer better or worse policy representation than single party governments. It has led to research on how to measure policy representation, which requires researchers to both assess the policy content of particular legislation and compare it to what voters want, often using public opinion data. This is no easy task.

To help us understand these different types of representation, we examine two dimensions of representation. The first is a temporal dimension. We can either treat representation as static or dynamic. Studies that conceive of representation as static focus on particular snapshots in time and ask whether the elected representatives match the electorate on key characteristics. Studies that focus on dynamic aspects of representation examine whether the nature and position of representatives change in line with changes that occur in the electorate. The second dimension distinguishes between policy representation and non-policy representation. While policy representation is substantive in nature, non-policy representation can refer to descriptive representation and symbolic acts. Table 7.1 presents four types of representation as the intersection of these dimensions.

Parties and representatives may offer a static level of non-policy, symbolic responsiveness through constituency service, making themselves available to voters through constituency offices. We can also conceive of descriptive representation as a form of static, non-policy representation. For example, we can examine whether the characteristics of representatives, such as gender and ethnicity, are reflective of the population they are meant to represent. Of course, there may also be dynamic changes in descriptive representation if underlying populations change, for example, to be more ethnically diverse, and this change is also reflected in the composition of the legislature over time.

We can think about forms of symbolic representation that can change quickly and in very dynamic ways in response to different demands from voters. Members of parliament, for example, may seek to give more speeches in parliament when an issue affecting their local area requires specific attention. Likewise, they may seek to change their behaviour in hopes of maximizing their re-election chances as elections approach.

Most research on representation, however, focuses on policy, or **substantive representation**. Studies of representation that fall into the upper-left quadrant of Table 7.1,

Table 7.1 Two Dimensions of Representation

	Policy	Non-policy
Static	Congruence	Descriptive Representation
Dynamic	Responsiveness	Rhetoric & Signalling

policy **congruence**, examine whether there is a match, or significant overlap, between the policy positions of voters (usually the median voter) and representatives. For example, they may examine whether voters are more left-wing than the average (median) parliamentarian. Congruence could occur either because representatives view their role as that of a delegate and try to match the position of their voters, or because the relationship between voters and representatives is that of a trusteeship where the representatives happen to hold the same position as voters.

Congruence is most often measured as ideological congruence on the left–right scale. This can be measured as the distance between the average (mean) voter and the position of the government or the average party in parliament. The smaller the distance, the higher the level of congruence. Applying the **spatial model** that we introduced in Chapter 2, Figure 7.1 illustrates congruence using the Italian political system during 2018–20. There were two governments in this period, both led by Prime Minister Giuseppe Conte: the Conte I cabinet and the Conte II cabinet. After the 2018 general election in Italy, the populist Five Star Movement (M5S), which had come first in the election, and the radical right-wing League (Lega) agreed to form a coalition government led by Conte (the Conte I cabinet). In August 2019, Matteo Salvini, Deputy Prime Minister and leader of the League, announced a motion of no confidence against the government, after growing tensions within the majority. This resulted in a new coalition government (Conte II cabinet), without the League, between the Five Star Movement (M5S) and the centre-left Democratic Party (PD). Using this figure, we can explore ideological congruence between the mean voter and the parties and government in Italy. We see that there are high levels of congruence between the average voter and the median legislative party, the Five Star Movement, although the average voter is slightly to the left of the median legislative party. The figure also reveals, however, that the first Conte I government was considerably to the right of the median voter and that voter–government congruence was low. However, after the change in government where the radical right-wing League was replaced by the

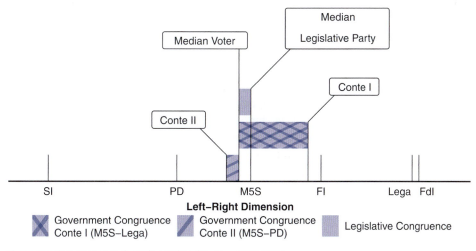

Figure 7.1 Congruence in the Italian Political System: 2018–2020

Data source: Party positions are calculated from CHES (Polk et al., 2017) and voter positions from CSES (2020)

centre-left Democratic Party, the level of congruence became much higher, as the government moved just slightly to the left of the average voter.

This figure displays a static picture of representation with fixed voter and party positions, where greater congruence is achieved through a change in government composition. But congruence, or lack thereof, might also come about through changes in the positions, as voters shift their preferences and parties move to be closer to voters.

To explore this, we need to move beyond static congruence to examine dynamic **policy responsiveness**. In other words, we must examine whether representatives change policy positions when voters change their preferences. If representatives move in the same direction as public opinion, for example, adopt more measures to tackle climate change when the public is more concerned about the environment, this may indicate responsiveness. This is also sometimes referred to as **dynamic representation**. There are two key pathways of policy responsiveness. The first is 'electoral turnover'. Put simply, elections are a mechanism for ensuring that changes in public opinion are reflected in policy through replacement as some politicians who refuse to change are replaced with others who better reflect current public opinion. The second pathway is 'rational anticipation' as representatives shift their policy positions in line with public preferences in between elections, in anticipation that, if they don't, they may lose their seat or office at the next election. Mansbridge (2003) has referred to this as **anticipatory representation**, as representatives, or at least those who view themselves as delegates, focus on what they think their constituents will approve at the next election, not on what they promised to do at the last election.

Using a spatial model, Figure 7.2 illustrates an example of responsiveness between elections. The figure shows the median voter shifting from a position on the centre-right to a more centrist position. Such a shift of the preferences of voters presents a challenge to parties, as they may fear that being positioned too far away from the median voter they will be punished in the next election. The bottom panel of Figure 7.2 illustrates how each of the parties responds to this shift in voter preferences. In this example, Party B is a centre-right party in a governing coalition with a radical right-wing Party C. In response to the shift of voters, Party B also shifts to the centre, so its position is congruent with that of the median voter. Due to the shift of Party B, the mean position of the governing coalition also moves to the left, closer to the preferences of the (new) median voter. This is an example of policy responsiveness. In contrast, Party C does not adjust its position in line with the public mood, but retains its position on the far right of the political spectrum. Research by Adams et al. (2006) has shown that, whereas mainstream parties (such as Party B) are generally responsive to the median voter, niche parties (such as Party C) are often responsive to their own supporters. In this scenario, the supporters of Party C may be located further to the right. However, we see that Party A, a left-wing party, has moved further to the centre, perhaps in response to the move of Party B, to be more competitive in the centre-ground of politics. Overall, Figure 7.2 shows that policy representation happens not only at election day, but also in between elections as parties seek to respond to changing voter preferences.

When examining this dynamic relationship empirically, some researchers have uncovered a lag between public opinion and position change among politicians, leading researchers to suggest that the link between public opinion and policy (and dynamic substantive

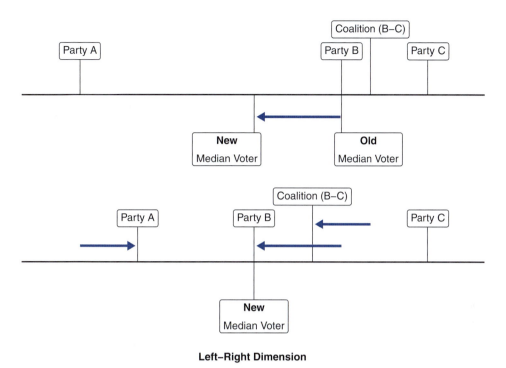

Figure 7.2 Spatial Model of Policy Responsiveness

representation) is **thermostatic** (Wlezien, 1995; Soroka and Wlezien, 2010). Much like a thermostat regulating temperature in a building, when policy-making moves in one direction, public opinion tends to slowly move back in the opposite direction. In the example in Figure 7.2, we can see that the public has responded to the policies of a right-wing government, shown in the top panel, by shifting its position further to the left, as shown in the bottom panel. Policy-making may then track public mood back in the other direction, possibly pushing public mood back in the other direction. This thermostatic model would suggest that representation is responsive, but rarely perfectly congruent.

Political institutions, and specifically electoral rules, can have a significant impact on how political representation manifests itself. Electoral rules can impact both what policy positions parties and politicians take, and also which candidates parties put forward as candidates for office. And as discussed in the previous chapter, direct democratic institutions can also have an effect on congruence. In particular, when the positions of elites and the public diverge, a citizen-initiated or abrogative referendum may serve as a corrective and produce policy outcomes that are closer to the median voter's position. This may be particularly relevant on policy issues which parties do not primarily campaign on, and on which there may be a representational gap (Leemann and Wasserfallen, 2016). The remainder of the chapter examines different aspects of political representation and how institutions shape the connection between voters, their representatives, and the actions that those representatives take while participating in acts of governance.

Box 7.1 CONTROVERSIES AND DEBATES: Do Parties Respond to Shifts in Public Opinion?

In line with classic spatial theories of party competition, we would expect parties to be responsive to changes in public opinion to appeal to voters in elections. According to the theory of **dynamic representation** by Stimson, MacKuen, and Erikson (1995), politicians calculate the future electoral implications of their current policy positions and act accordingly (rational anticipation). In two-party systems at least, this should lead to a continuous convergence around the median voter's preferences. A large number of empirical studies have demonstrated that political parties react to shifts in public opinion (Stimson et al., 1995; Erikson et al., 2002; Adams et al., 2004; Hakhverdian, 2010; Wlezien and Soroka, 2012). For example, as the 'public mood' shifts to the left, parties will move their policy positions in the same direction.

Yet, some studies have challenged the view that parties respond to changes in median voter preferences by changing their own positions. One strand of literature has focused on the difference between different types of parties (see Chapter 8) and have argued that mainstream parties' responses differ from those of niche parties (Adams et al., 2006; Bischof and Wagner, 2017). These studies have argued that, in comparison to mainstream parties, niche parties are penalized electorally for moderating their policy programmes. As a consequence, it is often not electorally feasible for niche parties to adjust their policies in response to changes in public opinion, while such policy adjustments are electorally feasible for mainstream parties.

Another set of studies has focused on how parties do not necessarily respond to the median voter, but to different segments of the electorate. For example, parties have been shown to be highly responsive to the views of opinion leaders, i.e. citizens who regularly engage in political discussions and persuasion, but less responsive to 'ordinary voters' (Adams and Ezrow, 2009), and to be more responsive to the preference shifts among men than among women (Homola, 2019). However, O'Grady and Abou-Chadi (2019) analyse Europeans' ideological positions across four different issue dimensions and find very little evidence that European political parties respond to public opinion on any issue dimension. The authors argue that the lack of evidence for responsiveness could be due to poor measures of party positions, a lack of nuance in theories of responsiveness, or the current attention to policy platforms rather than actual policy outcomes.

Taken together, these studies show that the classic dynamic representation model cannot be straightforwardly applied to European multiparty systems. Indeed, different types of parties may adopt different strategies. Moreover, focusing on a single dimension of responsiveness is unlikely to capture the many ways in which parties can respond to voters. Responsiveness may result from changes in voters' issue priorities rather than their issue opinions (Hobolt and Klemmensen, 2008; Klüver and Spoon, 2016). Or perhaps parties respond not to the electorate in general, but to sub-groups such as citizens who are more politically engaged or wealthy, swing voters, groups with higher turnout, or their own party supporters. Finally, much of the literature on party responsiveness does not take into account that parties can also strategically *influence* public opinion through their policy positions and campaigning, and not merely respond to it.

7.2 Substantive Representation in Proportional and Majoritarian Systems

A long-standing debate in the discussion of representation is the tension between two competing visions of the democratic ideal: a majoritarian vision and a proportional (or consensus) vision. The majoritarian principle emphasizes that democracy is equal to majority rule and based on a concentration of power. **Majoritarian democratic institutions** tend to create sharp divisions between those who hold power (political winners) and those who do not (political losers), but also provide for strong and accountable governments (Powell, 2000). In contrast, **proportional democratic institutions**, or the consensus principle, promote the idea that democracy should represent as many citizens as possible. Consensus democracy disperses power so that there are multiple decision-makers, actors with veto power, and checks and balances, thus limiting the power of the central government while providing for the representation of a broader array of interests. While most European countries are closer to the proportional than the majoritarian ideal, we observe a continuum between the ideal types. The clearest example of a majoritarian system in Europe is the United Kingdom with its first-past-the-post electoral system, while the Netherlands is an example of a highly proportional system. France is an example of a hybrid model, with its semi-presidentialism and its majoritarian two-round electoral system (see Chapter 6).

In political science, much of the debate has focused on the effect of electoral institutions on democratic practices, in particular the distinction between majoritarian and proportional electoral systems. Powell (2000) has argued that two constitutional features determine whether a democracy tilts more toward a majoritarian or proportional principle. The first is the electoral system: a low district magnitude favours a majoritarian design, increasing the likelihood of a single-party majority government; proportional electoral systems with large district magnitudes, in contrast, promote multiparty systems and proportional democracy (see Chapter 6). The second is legislative rules, which in majoritarian democracies give the parliamentary majority a more or less unconstrained capacity to implement policies, while rules in proportional democracies favour the dispersion of power and enhance the opposition's influence. Table 7.2 summarizes the main features of the ideal type majoritarian and proportional (consensus) visions of democracy.

These two ideal types of democracy also have different implications for representation and responsiveness. For policy congruence, proportional systems ensure a stronger link between vote and seat distributions in legislatures (see Chapter 6), and therefore such legislatures may more accurately reflect the range of preferences in the population, whereas majoritarian

Table 7.2 Majoritarian and Proportional Visions of Democracy

	Majoritarian	Proportional
Electoral system	Majoritarian—Low district magnitude	Proportional—Large district magnitude
Party system	Two-party	Multiparty
Government	Single-party	Coalition
Legislative-executive relations	Executive dominance	Opposition influence
Congruence	Median voter represented by majority party and government	Median voter represented by median legislative party and range of voter preferences reflected in legislature
Responsiveness	Single-party majority governments can more effectively respond to changing voter preferences	Broad-based coalitions may be responsive to a wider range of policy preferences
Accountability	Greater clarity of responsibility enhances electoral accountability	Low clarity of responsibility but greater checks and balances on executive

Box 7.2 **CONTROVERSIES AND DEBATES:** Is the European Union Responsive to Voters?

The European Union has been traditionally regarded as relatively unresponsiveness to voters. Historically, governments in the Council have been been able to negotiate and legislate away from the glare of public scrutiny and their actions in the EU have little impact on their chances of re-election domestically (Bailer et al., 2015). Without public attention, there are few incentives for politicians to respond to public opinion. According to this view, public opinion plays a limited role in shaping the positions of governments and politicians in EU policy-making, which is driven instead by economic, partisan, and geo-strategic interests.

Moreover, as multiple institutions are involved in decision-making at the European level—the Council, the Commission, and the European Parliament as well as the member state—it is also characterized by low clarity of responsibility, making more difficult for voters to hold their representatives to account in national and European Parliament elections. Studies have shown that voters in European Parliament elections do not punish or reward parties on the basis of economic performance, as retrospective models of voting would suggest (Hobolt and Tilley, 2014). One reason is the lack of clarity about who is 'in government' in the European Union, which makes it difficult for voters to know whom to hold to account. In addition, citizens have perceptual biases in attributing responsibility to the EU. Eurosceptic citizens tend to blame the EU when conditions deteriorate, even when member states may formally share some policy responsibility. Conversely, EU supporters are more likely to attribute responsibility to the EU when conditions are improving, even when responsibility lies almost exclusively with the member states. This accountability deficit has fuelled broader concerns about a **democratic deficit** in the EU, where policy-making is largely insulated from public preferences.

Recent studies, however, have questioned this received wisdom of an 'unresponsive union' and argued that, as the EU policy-making has become more transparent and more politicized domestically, there are also greater incentives for legislators to respond to the public mood. For example, Wratil (2018) has shown that that governments do respond to the 'public mood' on Europe when legislating in the Council in the run-up to national elections. Moreover, Hagemann et al. (2017) have demonstrated that governments engage in **signal responsiveness** in the EU Council, i.e. they use their opposition to legislative proposals in the Council to signal to their Eurosceptic domestic electorates that they are responsive to their concerns, especially when the issue of European integration is salient in domestic party politics. In her book titled *The Responsive Union*, Schneider (2019) also challenges the assumption that European-level issues are not salient enough to warrant significant domestic contestation. She demonstrates that governments signal responsiveness to their publics by taking positions that are in the interests of politically relevant voters at the national level.

These studies thus provide evidence that governments in the Council, and other politicians involved in EU decision-making, take domestic public opinion into account, but not at all times and not necessarily in ways that ensure congruence. Instead the evidence suggests that responsiveness occurs when electoral sanctioning is more likely, namely when the issues are salient domestically and elections are approaching.

---

systems favour the larger parties and make it more difficult for smaller parties to gain representation. There is no doubt that proportional systems allow for greater congruence at the party level, i.e. between individual voters and the party of their choice. When it comes to ideological congruence between the median voter and the government, the consensus in the literature has also been that proportional systems tend to produce greater congruence; specifically, the general ideological disposition of the government that emerges after an election and the ideological bent of the electorate tends to match up better in proportional systems

(Powell, 2000). Yet, later studies have shown that the difference in congruence levels between proportional and majoritarian systems has declined in recent decades, primarily due to convergence toward the median of plurality parties in majoritarian systems (Powell, 2009), or have found no evidence that proportional representation leads to better congruence (Blais and Bodet, 2006; Golder and Lloyd, 2014; Ferland, 2016).

When it comes to responsiveness, there is also a debate as to which system provides greatest incentives and opportunities for governments to react to the changing public mood. Governments in majoritarian systems may be more responsive to changes in voter preferences in between elections. Single member district plurality systems create a direct link between the voter and the elected representative through the representation of constituencies through a single member of parliament. Moreover, single-party majority governments may also respond more effectively to a changing public mood than broad-based coalition governments (Soroka and Wlezien, 2010). However, others argue that responsiveness depends on the competitiveness of the race, since politicians are more likely to be responsive if they fear that they will lose the next election. Since no 'safe' seats exist in proportional systems, unlike in majoritarian systems, representatives have greater incentives to engage in 'anticipatory representation' in be responsive to the changing public mood. More proportionality also means that a wider range of policy preferences can be represented in parliament and in government.

7.3 Descriptive Representation and Gender Equality in Politics

Both congruence and responsiveness, discussed in the previous two sections, are strictly about substantive policy representation. But as discussed in the first part of this chapter, that is only one aspect of representation. Voters might also care that their representatives reflect them in other ways.

Descriptive representation, or the reflection of the electorate in their representatives in terms of language, race, ethnicity, gender, class, and other characteristics, is important for a variety of reasons. First, it may impact substantive representation. There is a debate in the literature about the degree to which representatives must reflect voters descriptively in order to represent them substantively. Some scholars have argued that there is not an automatic, direct relationship between descriptive representation and substantive representation (e.g. Phillips, 1995; Mansbridge, 1999). They argue that voters might associate the sharing of descriptive characteristics with the sharing of substantive policy positions, when, in fact, they may not do so. However, much scholarship also suggests that people from under-represented groups place different emphasis on policy issues and problems (e.g. Schwindt-Bayer and Mishler, 2005) and that their presence increases perceptions of democratic legitimacy (Clayton et al., 2019). Unless people from these different, under-represented groups are reflected in politics, their views and the issues that they care about will not get addressed.

Recent work on British politics, in particular, has demonstrated that members of parliament belonging to the working class, and who have held working-class careers, talk about politics in a fundamentally different way compared with careerist MPs, typically drawn from the middle class (O'Grady, 2019). Other studies have shown that ethnic minority parliamentarians in the UK ask more questions related to minority interests (Bird et al., 2010). Similarly, studies have demonstrated that female identifying politicians and voters focus on different issues than male identifying politicans and voters (Wängnerud, 2006; Campbell, 2004) and that having women in leadership roles within parliament can shape parliamentary debate (Blumenau, 2019). This research all suggests that descriptive characteristics of politicians have real consequences for both policy and non-policy representation.

Despite the fact that Europe has become a multicultural and multi-ethnic continent, there has been relatively little research on the political representation of **ethnic minorities**. Ethnicity refers to social groups that share a real, or assumed, common origin and cultural legacy that collectively ties members of the group and is transmitted across generations, rooted in, for example, race, religion, culture, geography, immigration status, or a combination of these. The diversity of ethnic minority groups creates a challenge for the study of representation. Yet, the research that exists suggests that the representation of ethnic minorities in legislature and government can be beneficial not only to increase trust among those groups in the political system, but also to provide substantive representation, especially in 'low-cost' activities like asking parliamentary questions (Ruedin, 2020).

Much of the research on descriptive representation in Europe has focused instead on women in politics and the fact that they are generally under-represented. Some countries have been more successful than others in electing women to parliament and having them serve in higher office. However, no country in Europe has achieved gender parity. Different features of countries and parties may help to explain the extent to which gender parity is achieved. For example, more ideologically left-wing parties have tended to elect more women to parliament, in part because they have been more willing to take active measures to ensure that women are represented within the party, parliament and government. Other research has focused on the importance of electoral institutions and gender quotas.

Figure 7.3 shows the development of the share of women in European parliaments. Parliaments with a high share include all Scandinavian countries as well as Iceland, the Netherlands, and Spain. The European Parliament also belongs to the set of parliaments with a higher than average share of representation. Countries in which the representation of women is still low include Cyprus, Greece, Hungary, Ireland, Malta, and Romania.

Early research on the success of women in parliament focused on the role of electoral institutions in fostering women's representation, uncovering a correlation between closed list PR systems and greater numbers of women in parliament (Norris, 1985; Matland and Studlar, 1996). Researchers posited that central party organizations could and would place women higher on a closed list because they need not worry that voters would be turned off from voting for a woman candidate. However, whether parties actually put women higher on a list depends greatly on the internal culture within the party. While some parties, those on the ideological left in particular, may make promoting gender equality a priority, other parties may not. Moreover, there are mechanisms for ensuring greater representation of women even in majoritarian systems, for example, by running woman candidates in safe, easy-to-win electoral constituencies.

Gender quotas are a set of institutional mechanisms that has been used to ensure that women are represented in politics (see Krook, 2009; Krook et al., 2009). Indeed, according to the IDEA Gender Quotas Database, almost every country covered in this book uses some form of gender quota, either at the party or country level. Quotas can take on a variety of different forms, one of the most common being voluntary party-level quotas. Even without being mandated by

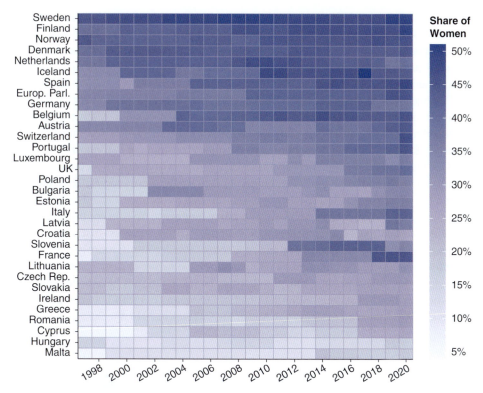

Figure 7.3 Development of Female Representation in European Parliaments

Data source: European Parliament (2019) and Inter-Parliamentary Union (2020)

law to do so, parties may commit that a certain percentage of the candidates will be women. How they accomplish this depends on the electoral system that they use. In list PR systems, parties may dedicate a certain number of spots on the party list to women or alternate between a woman and a man, while in single-member district systems parties can ensure that women are selected as candidates in a certain number of districts. The effectiveness of these quotas can vary depending on party rules, such as whether women candidates are given list spots or compete in constituencies that are likely to result in electoral victory, i.e. safe seats. In the 1990s, the British Labour Party wished to increase the share of women in the parliamentary party. At the 1993 party conference, it was decided that at the next election female Labour candidates should compete for at least half of the seats held by retiring Labour men, along with half of the seats that the party deemed to be competitive. This policy resulted in 101 Labour women being elected to parliament in 1997, constituting around a quarter of the Labour Party group in parliament.

Legislative quotas, written into law and applied to all parties, are becoming more common. In Belgium, for example, electoral law states that the difference in the number of men and women candidates on an electoral list cannot exceed one, and that the top two candidates on each list must not be of the same gender. As of 2019, Greek law mandates that at least 40 per cent of candidates on lists for any office must be women. And in France, electoral laws state that the difference in the number of men and women candidates within a party for single member constituencies cannot exceed 2 per cent. This rule ensures gender parity among candidates, but gender differ-ences could still arise depending on the constituencies in which women run. Importantly, legal requirements are not necessary for women to be elected to parliament. Finland has never had any formal quotas with respect to electoral politics, but the country has always ranked at or near the top when looking at the number of women in parliament. Moreover, in 2019, the Finnish Social Democrat Sanna Marin became the youngest woman to head a government worldwide.

The introduction of quotas raises the question under what conditions are such quotas introduced by political parties that have been largely dominated by men (see Valdini, 2019). Weeks (2018) offers a party-competition based explanation, arguing that quotas are intro-duced for reasons of both interparty and intraparty competition. With respect to interparty competition, they tend to be passed when parties face a new, more progressive challenger party on the left of the political spectrum, as was the case in Portugal. Regarding intraparty competition, the introduction of quotas allows **party leaders** to (re)gain control over a de-centralized candidate selection process inside their own parties, a process that has occurred in Belgium. In short, quotas not only reflect an ideological shift towards more gender equal-ity, but their introduction is oftentimes contingent upon the nature of party competition.

Turning to the highest political offices in Europe, female politicians have been a head of government or head of state in more than half of European countries between 2015 and 2020, as shown on the map in Figure 7.4. And at the EU level, in 2019, the European Council

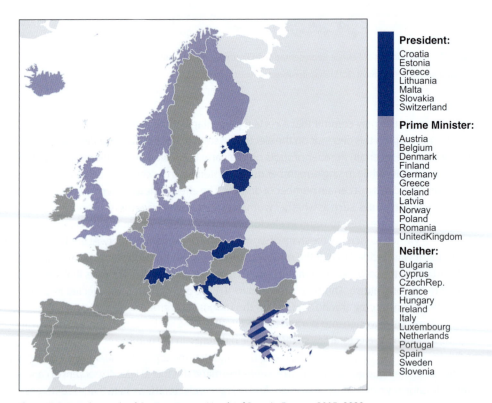

Figure 7.4 Female Heads of Government or Heads of State in Europe, 2015–2020

nominated and the European Parliament elected for the first time in the EU's history a women, Ursula von der Leyen, as Commission President.

Interestingly, some of the most prominent female leaders have headed centre-right governments. Germany's Angela Merkel has been Chancellor of a Christian-Democratic led government since November 2005, serving as head of government longer than any other Chancellor except Helmut Kohl. And Theresa May became the second woman to serve as both Prime Minister of the United Kingdom and leader of the Conservative Party (the first being Margaret Thatcher) after David Cameron stepped down in 2016. Commission President Ursula von der Leyen is a member of the German Christian Democrats and had previously served as cabinet minister in Germany under Angela Merkel continuously for fourteen years. Central and eastern European states have also had a fair number of women leaders. All three Baltic states, for example, have had women in either the prime ministerial or presidential positions. In Lithuania, Dalia Grybauskaité moved from being a highly respected European Commissioner for financial programming and the budget to being elected for two five-year terms as President of Lithuania, 2009–2019, remaining very popular throughout.

The number of women in cabinets has increased significantly over time, as shown in Figure 7.5. Whereas the average share of women in ministerial positions was below 10 per cent up until the 1980s, nowadays around one-third of all ministers are women.

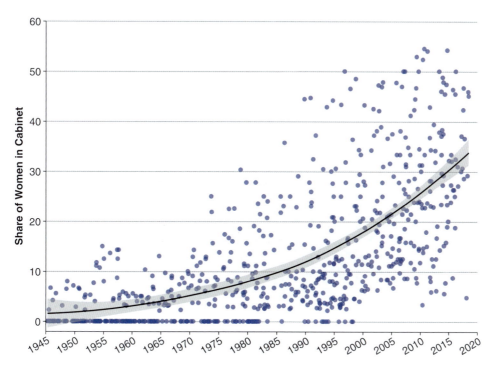

Figure 7.5 Female Ministers in Cabinets in Europe

Data source: Krauss and Kroeber (2020)

In a few instances, cabinets have included more women than men, as was the case in governments in Finland, Iceland, and Sweden.

When women are elected to parliaments in greater numbers, they are also more likely to hold higher level government offices and cabinet positions (see Krook and O'Brien, 2012). In government, women have even greater opportunities to shape substantive policy outcomes, affecting representation. The number of women holding top positions within politics, although still relatively small, has been growing. Figure 7.6 shows the relationship between female representation in parliament and in government. The plot shows cabinets that were formed between 1997 and 2018, and the share of women in parliament refers to the share in January of the year of government formation.

More women in cabinet positions has likely had an impact on policy and governments. There is evidence that a greater number of women in cabinet can lead to longer serving governments (Krauss and Kroeber, 2020), thus increasing government stability. The presence of female leaders may not only influence policy and government, but also the way that voters think about politicians. Another study has demonstrated that voters view parties led by women as more moderate, even if parties have not altered their positions (O'Brien, 2019). Of course, this has significant implications for representation, as the policy offerings of these parties have not actually changed, only voters' perceptions. In sum, descriptive representation can matter a great deal to voters, but also has consequences for policy and political stability.

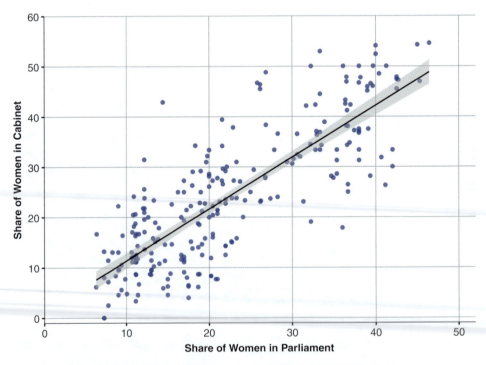

Figure 7.6 Relationship between Female Representation in Parliament and in Cabinet

Data sources: Krauss and Kroeber (2020); Inter-Parliamentary Union (2020)

7.4 Political Rhetoric and Signalling

An alternative way to examine representation is by directly analysing the various activities of members of parliament, presumably undertaken on behalf of their voters. Scholarship has long examined how electoral institutions and policy disagreements affect interactions inside legislatures. From a bird's eye perspective, legislative patterns in parliamentary systems are driven by the conflict between political parties that are in government and those that are in parliamentary opposition, rather than on the ideological left–right dimension that dominates the conflict during election campaigns (Hix and Noury, 2016). Similarly, analyses of the texts of legislative speeches have revealed that government parties speak in a more positive tone than opposition parties during debates (Proksch et al., 2019) and that governing parties alter their speech in response to public opinion (Hager and Hilbig, 2020). These patterns reflect the fact that governments set the legislative agenda and control—in most cases—legislative majorities. In contrast, the opposition's main tool for communicating their disagreement with the government is to vote (unsuccessfully) against government bills and to criticize them during the debates.

The systemic government–opposition divide, however, cannot tell us much about how individual MPs decide to act in a particular context, and how those decisions relate to representation. For example, MPs may decide to vote and speak against the position of their own party if they disagree with party policy or feel that it does not match the views of a particular constituency they seek to represent. Such behaviour may often look symbolic; rarely do 'rebellious' votes or speeches affect the ultimate policy outcome. However, even such symbolic behaviour may have electoral consequences. Intraparty conflicts, which rise to the surface when MPs vote or speak against their own party policy, can reduce the appeal of a party and cost it votes (Kam, 2009). On the other hand, voters sometimes view politicians who rebel against their party positively and feel better represented by such MPs (Campbell et al., 2019). We can think of numerous such situations when the goals of the party leadership and a member of parliament collide.

To understand how individual legislative behaviour relates to representation, we must understand the role of electoral institutions in creating personal vote incentives for MPs and the dynamics inside parliamentary parties. Electoral rules may either create incentives for parties to allow their MPs significant freedom in the actions they take within parliament, or they may create incentives for parties to exercise strict control over their members. In other words, electoral systems create electoral connections between individual MPs and voters of different strength. Political scientists have long examined the role of a **personal vote** both with respect to how voters cast their votes, and how MPs seek to gain voters' support (Cain et al., 1987). The personal vote refers to the amount of support a particular candidate for office receives due to their own personal characteristics, rather than the characteristics of the party to which they belong. In political systems where the personal vote is important, an individual MP's own electoral fate is less tied to that of their party.

In the British system with single member plurality elections where candidates' names appear prominently on the ballot, the personal vote has, at times, been important. British MPs are expected to interact directly with their voters. They spend time in their constituency and perform constituency service, addressing the problems of constituents in their local surgery and attending local events. In contrast, in proportional systems with closed lists it makes little sense to talk of a personal vote. Candidates' names (with the exception of the top candidates on each list) do not appear on the ballot and electoral districts tend to be large, meaning that local connections are weaker and voters do not perceive themselves as having an MP of their own to represent them in parliament. Instead, they expect political parties, rather than individuals, to act on their behalf. MPs, meanwhile, are dependent on their party to advance their career in politics, and have little incentive to create an individual name for themselves. The party determines their place on the party list and thus determines their hopes of getting into parliament and rising through the party ranks.

Carey and Shugart (1995) theorize about the relationship between electoral systems and the incentives of MPs to cultivate a personal vote. They argue the personal vote incentive is a function of intraparty competition created by electoral systems. When competition between individuals within a party is strong, individuals need to create a name for themselves because their party identity cannot distinguish them from their fellow partisans. When competition within the party is low, and when MPs are dependent on their party leadership for their individual success, then the incentive to create a personal vote is low. Carey and Shugart argue that these incentives are created by an interaction between district magnitude and the open versus closed nature of the party list. When party lists are open, meaning that candidates must seek votes to climb up the party list, higher district magnitudes increase intraparty competition and create greater incentives for candidates to seek to generate a personal vote. In contrast, when lists are closed, meaning parties determine the list ordering, increasing the district magnitude decreases incentives for MPs to seek personal votes. After the district magnitude is larger than a few seats, voters are unlikely to know who any individuals running in a district are, and they will focus on the party. In this framework, single member districts represent a middle ground between high district magnitude open lists, and high intraparty competition for votes, and high district magnitude closed lists and very low intraparty competition for votes.

The second aspect of individual legislative behaviour is the intraparty dynamics in parliament, in particular between **party leaders** and **backbencher MPs** (those without leadership positions). While both leaders and backbenchers care about policy, office, and electoral votes (Müller and Strøm, 1999), electoral institutions affect how much leaders care about protecting the party label and how much backbenchers need to care about their own electoral fate. The need to generate a personal vote can thus have an impact on how MPs behave in parliament and how loyal they need to be to their party. One way for individual MPs to generate name recognition and to gain the attention of voters is by acting against the wishes of their own party on issues in parliament. They may take a stance either in voting or in legislative debate that runs contrary to the position taken by the party leadership or the majority of their party. Having done so, they may generate some news coverage for themselves, especially if the issue that they rebel on is sufficiently high profile. But even if they do not generate much coverage for themselves, they can report back to constituents that they have taken a position at odds with the party, which they may cast as an act of standing up for constituents or as a marker of their own free-thinking independence. For instance, the British Conservative Party has been one of the most internally divided parties on the issue of European integration, and in many instances Conservative MPs who disagreed with the party leadership with respect to its position on membership in the EU gave dissenting speeches on the floor of parliament and voted against their party. In 2019, when the Conservative British government led by Theresa May attempted to get approval for the withdrawal agreement to leave the EU, several Conservative Party rebels repeatedly voted against the deal, eventually leading to Theresa May's resignation as prime minister.

In countries where the electoral system means that MPs can benefit from creating a name for themselves, party leaders may be more willing to tolerate some degree of rebelliousness, at least among certain MPs who stand to benefit most from it. The party is best served by getting as many members elected as possible, and therefore may not sanction some disobedience to accomplish this goal. Additionally, some political scientists have argued that parties may benefit electorally from blurring their positions to appear to represent a wider range of views, appealing to a wider range of voters (Rovny, 2012; Somer-Topcu, 2015). Allowing dissent might be a strategy that creates such blurring. A party may ensure that there are particular times in the legislative agenda when ideological dissidents can express themselves in ways that are relatively harmless to the party as a whole. However, parties face a problem in that blurring may be too costly. Ultimately, they benefit from presenting a unified message that signals a meaningful position to voters (Cox and McCubbins, 1993). Party leaders do not want to appear internally divided or in disarray, which could cost them at election time. They must therefore manage internal rebellion to the extent that it is possible for them to do so. They have to balance the possible electoral benefits of allowing some members to express opinions at odds with the party leadership with the potential costs of appearing divided and in disarray.

In sum, we can expect different behavioural patterns between party leaders and backbenchers in parliament depending on the level of intraparty disagreement. If MPs disagree with some aspects of party policy set by leaders, then electoral institutions mediate the way in which such disagreements are displayed in parliament. Table 7.3 shows the expected patterns of behaviour for candidate- and party-centred electoral systems. **Candidate-centred systems** are those in which personal vote seeking incentives exist, such as plurality systems or open-list proportional systems, whereas **party-centred systems** are those in which party labels matter more, such as closed-list proportional representation systems. The differences between candidate- and party-centred systems result in differences in legislative behaviour in particular when the disagreement inside parties is high. When everyone in the party agrees, the goals of leaders and backbenchers align, but they clash if there are conflicts over policy.

Proksch and Slapin (2012, 2015) examine how these dynamics play out within parliamentary debate, arguing that debate makes a good venue for examining how parties control members most likely to deviate from the party. Debate gives MPs the opportunity to express

Table 7.3 Legislators' Behavioural Incentives in Parliament

	Candidate-centred electoral systems	Party-centred electoral systems
Party leaders	Tolerate low party discipline if it helps MPs in re-election	Protect party message and unity in parliament
Backbencher MPs	Rebel against party if it helps attract personal votes	Follow party line to not endanger re-selection by party

opinions and explanations in more nuanced ways than they could in yes or no vote on a legislative bill. Moreover, MPs can point out to voters that they have stood up for their views on the floor of parliament and can quote from their floor speeches in other materials, such as press releases, social media statements, and campaign materials. Proksch and Slapin develop a model in which a party leader has the ability to delegate floor time to an MP to give a speech on behalf of the party, or alternatively the leader can give the speech themselves. The leader prefers to delegate the task of speech-making to the MP, who is likely more knowledgeable about the subject under debate, and has more time to prepare the speech. But the leader is also worried that the MP may stray too far from the party position. This means that a leader ought to be more likely to grant floor to an MP who generally has positions close to that of the leadership.

But importantly, Proksch and Slapin also argue that the degree of freedom that party leaders grant to MPs is a function of incentives created by the electoral system. Where electoral systems create incentives for a personal vote and reward party unity to a lesser extent, party leaders are more willing to grant floor time to MPs who may not toe the party line. In contrast, when MPs have fewer electoral incentives to deviate from the party, party leaders have little reason to grant floor time to anyone who might deviate. The party brand, rather than the features of any individual MP matter most for the party's electoral success. Proksch and Slapin test their theoretical argument in the United Kingdom and Germany, and they find that British MPs who hold ideological positions further away from their party leadership are more likely to give speeches on the floor, while ideologically distant German MPs are less likely to give speeches. Studies focusing on gender representation have also looked at speech-making and find that women are less likely to participate in debate, even in countries, such as Sweden, where women are well-represented in parliament (Bäck et al., 2014; Bäck and Debus, 2019). According to these studies, such patterns may exist as a result of gender stereotypes or, possibly, male obstruction of women in parliament.

We can examine intraparty interactions in the European Parliament, as well. Although we lack a government–opposition divide in the European Parliament, legislators clearly care about policy and about re-election. What makes the European Parliament interesting from a representational perspective is the fact that voters do not cast votes for the transnational political groups that organize parliamentary activities in the EP, but for national parties. Elected members from national parties join together with other similarly minded parties from other EU countries within the EP to form the transnational European political groups after the election has taken place. Thus, there are two party entities that control different resources: while the political groups (and their leaders) can control the speaking time allocations, the national parties control candidate selection for the next EP election. This is not a problem as long as the national parties share the same policy views as the political group to which they belong. But when there are policy disagreements between them, MEPs are likely to side with their national party on legislative votes. The leaders of the political groups can tolerate these rebellions because they do not need to protect the group brand in European elections. As a consequence, MEPs need to signal to their national parties that they are loyal when disagreements exist, and are more likely to take the floor to express this disagreement in speeches (Slapin and Proksch, 2010).

MEPs sometimes wish to return to national politics, creating another interesting dynamic within the EP. Høyland et al. (2017) demonstrate that the candidate- versus party-centred nature of the electoral system can impact MEPs' behaviour in this regard. They show that MEPs who express an interest in returning to politics in their home country spend less time engaging in activities at the European Parliament, such as voting and participating in debate. However, the difference between those MEPs with career ambitions at home and those who prefer to stay in European politics is much starker amongst MEPs who come from countries using candidate-centred electoral systems than those using party-centred systems.

7.5 Summary

Political representation is a complex and multifaceted concept. It is absolutely critical to democracy, but at the same time, it is both hard to measure and hard to know when it exists in adequate amounts. This chapter has argued that substantive policy representation—a link between voters' attitudes on particular policies and the policy positions that politicians take and ultimately pass into law—is of fundamental importance. Evaluating policy congruence and responsiveness is essential to understanding how democracy works. But it is certainly not the only type of representation. Descriptive representation, as well as symbolic acts of standing up for voters in parliament, also matters. The nature of representation across all these various dimensions is shaped by political institutions and the incentives that they create for elected politicians.

Online Data Exercise: CSES Comparative Studies of Electoral Systems

The interactive online exercise explores the Comparative Study of Electoral Systems (CSES) data to study the congruence between political parties and voters. The CSES surveys include left–right placements both for respondents and political parties, as well as election results and electoral system variables. You will investigate which electoral systems have higher congruence between voters and parliaments. In addition, you will be able to study which possible coalitions between parties are more congruent with voters' positions.

Take your learning further with this interactive data exercise, available at **www.foundationsofeuropeanpolitics.com**

For additional material and resources, including multiple-choice questions, web links, and more, please visit the online resources: **www.oup.com/he/devries1e**

8 Political Parties

This chapter considers the nature and evolution of political parties in European democracies. It discusses the important functions of political parties and how they have developed over time. Starting with the social cleavage approach, the chapter examines the origins and transformation of European party families and party systems, both nationally and in the EU. It presents evidence of the 'unfreezing' of European party systems and discusses whether we are witnessing not only a dealignment of traditional cleavage patterns, but also a realignment along a new 'cultural' dimension of politics. Finally, it considers the evolution of party types from cadre over catch-all to modern entrepreneurial challenger parties.

Many European constitutions do not mention political parties, yet they are among the most central institutions of modern democracy. But what is a political party? A **political party** is an institutionalized coalition of people organized to gain control of public office by winning elections. Political parties usually share a core objective of being in government (office-seeking) to implement their policy programme (policy-seeking), and they achieve this through electoral support (vote-seeking). Thus, parties differ from other political pressure groups, such as interest groups, in that they seek not only political influence, but do so by standing for office in competitive elections (see Chapter 11.5).

What is the role of parties in democracies? First, parties help structure politics by aggregating interests for both voters and elites. For voters, they structure politics by offering a set of choices through clear, coherent, and comprehensive policy platforms that governments can implement. For policy-makers, they help elected officials find agreement and govern. If hundreds of representatives in parliament were not organized into clearly defined political groups, with a shared ideology, policy programme, internal hierarchies, and discipline, governing would be almost impossible.

Second, political parties provide a crucial link between voters and their representatives. Party names, or labels, provide informational shortcuts about candidates' values, ideology, and policies that voters can use. When political parties do not fulfil their policy promises in office, voters are able to hold them to account by switching their support to other parties. Political parties thus allow voters to better select candidates that share their viewpoints and to sanction representatives in office. They also mobilize citizens to participate in politics, as members of parties and as voters in elections (see the discussion of voting behaviour in Chapter 5).

Thirdly, political parties play an important role in recruiting and training political elites. To become a representative in parliament, candidates are first vetted, socialized, and selected by political parties. Equally, membership in a political party is often a requirement for becoming a minister and a leader of a country. Parties act as educators and gatekeepers for the political elite. In short, parties play a crucial role in democratic governance.

In addition to exploring individual parties and the roles they play in democracies, we can also discuss groups of parties—e.g. party families and party systems. **Party families** are cross-national groupings of like-minded parties, often sharing a similar ideology, voter base, and similar origins. Classification by party families helps us to compare parties across different countries. A **party system**, in contrast, is a description of all the parties within a country, for example, the number of parties that compete in elections and their ideological leanings. We can also compare party systems across countries, something we will do in greater detail in Chapter 9.

In this chapter, we examine the origins of political parties, party families, and party systems, looking at their sociological roots, as well as how political entrepreneurs shape parties. We examine both the stability of parties as well as how they change over time. And finally, we examine different types of organizational structures that we find within parties.

8.1 The Origins of Parties: Stasis and Change

Where do political parties and party systems come from? There are two main views of how parties, and the systems they operate within, develop. The first is sociological and demand-driven. It focuses on the formation of parties in response to societal demands for representation of particular set of interests. A second approach is supply-driven and strategic. It focuses on the interests of political entrepreneurs in forming a party to achieve a set of objectives, be they office, votes, or policies. From this perspective, parties are not merely a response to societal divisions, but they also play a role in shaping the political agenda. These two perspectives are not mutually exclusive. The study of the origins and evolution of political parties is an account of the interplay between demand and supply factors.

We start from the demand-driven perspective. Lipset and Rokkan (1967) developed the most influential account of the origins of party and party systems from this perspective. As previously discussed in Chapter 5, they highlight the role of four major societal cleavages in shaping parties and party systems; these cleavages are centre–periphery, church–state, rural–urban, and the capital owners–workers. Although the class cleavage (capital owners versus workers) has been by far the most powerful in structuring European politics, each of these cleavages has left a lasting imprint on the party systems in European democracies.

The centre–periphery cleavage gave rise to political parties that resisted the centralizing force of the nation-state. Many of these parties have advocated secession from the state, and some still do. Regionalist parties are prevalent in the the United Kingdom with regionalist (and some separatist) parties in Scotland, Wales, and Northern Ireland. In Scotland, the Scottish National Party called a referendum on Scottish independence in 2014, which was defeated by 55 to 45 per cent of the vote. Belgian parties are split along linguistic and regional lines, with Flemish parties operating in Flanders and Brussels and Francophone parties in Wallonia and Brussels, but only some of these regionalist parties are also seperatist (e.g. Flemish Interest). Spain also has strong regionalist parties, particularly in Catalonia and the Basque Country, with some calling for independence for their regions (see the case study of Catalan independence in Chapter 3). A number of other countries have parties that represent regional and linguistic minorities without calling for secession; these include the South Tyrolean Party People's Party in Italy, which represents German speakers in the South Tyrolean region of northern Italy; and the South Schleswig Voters' Association in Germany, which represents Danish minorities in Schleswig-Holstein in northern Germany.

The church–state cleavage, the result of eighteenth- and nineteenth-century conflicts between state-builders and the church, has also shaped party systems. In countries with large Catholic populations—e.g. Austria, Belgium, Germany, Italy, Ireland, the Netherlands, Portugal, Spain, as well as several former Communist countries, notably Poland—the **Christian Democratic** party family became a powerful electoral force. These parties have evolved into large centre-right **catch-all parties**. In the Protestant north, the Christian-based families have been less influential. But religiosity also has influenced vote choice in these countries, generally favouring the centre-right conservative parties. In more recent years, the question of religion has become salient again, as radical right-wing parties—such as the Party for Freedom in the Netherlands and the Danish People's Party in Denmark—have politicized the issue of the role of Islam and Muslim immigrants, calling for bans on religious symbols, such as the Burqa and minarets.

The Industrial Revolution in the nineteenth century gave rise to two additional cleavages: the rural–urban cleavage and, most importantly, the class cleavage. In most European countries, the urban–rural cleavage divide has not left a lasting imprint on the party system. However, in Scandinavia, agrarian parties were formed in opposition to the urban elites. Agrarian parties such as Venstre (Liberal Party) in Denmark have since become more traditional centre-right parties, but often retained their electoral strongholds in more rural areas. The urban–rural divide has also remained relevant in other ways, as parties on the radical right consistently do better in more rural areas and towns whereas new left and liberal parties tend to attract more voters in metropolitan cities.

The most defining cleavage for European party systems is no doubt the class cleavage. Parties in the Social Democratic party family advanced workers' rights through parliamentary means, while Communist parties advocated the need for radical societal change through the means of a revolution of the working class, the proletariat (Przeworski and Sprague, 1986; Benedetto et al., 2020). Countries that were more accommodating of workers' demands, such as the Scandinavians and British, often saw stronger Social Democratic families and weaker Communist parties. In other countries, such as France and Italy, more radical Communist parties remained electorally powerful for several decades. The class cleavage has remained dominant in most European party systems, pitting Socialist parties on the 'left' against Conservative and Liberal parties on the 'right'. Socialist parties forged close alliances with labour unions and emphasized workers' rights and economic redistribution by the state in their policy platforms. Conservative parties, on the other hand, maintained strong ties to capital owners and tended to advocate less redistribution and conditions favourable to businesses and capital investment.

Today, the left–right dimension is less explicitly concerned with 'class', although working-class voters are still more likely to vote for socialist parties and business owners are more likely to vote for conservative and Christian democratic parties in most European countries (see Chapter 5). Rather the left–right dimension has evolved into a 'super-dimension' that structures much of European party politics—with parties that did not emerge from the struggle between workers and owners still identifying themselves as belonging to the 'left' and the 'right' (see also Chapter 4). For example, most Christian, liberal, and agrarian parties are generally located on the centre-right of this dimension, whereas some regionalist parties are centre-left (e.g. the Scottish National Party in the UK) while others are on the right (e.g. the League in Italy and the Flemish Bloc/Flemish Interest in Belgium).

Cleavage theory is generally considered more instructive for understanding party politics in western Europe than in post-Communist Central and Eastern Europe (CEE), where democratic politics was disrupted for almost five decades by Communist regimes. As a consequence, we also observe far less stability in CEE party systems, with new parties entering the system and other parties ceasing to exist. Likewise, voters show lower levels of loyalty to parties. While the social cleavages have not been firmly embedded in CEE party systems in a similar manner as we have seen in western Europe, that does not imply that social divisions are not significant factors in explaining the structure of parties and party competition. In Catholic countries, such as Poland, the church–state divide is clearly apparent, with some parties such as the Law and Justice party more clearly identifying with the stances of the Catholic Church. Similarly, urban–rural divisions are also pronounced in a number of CEE countries and agrarian parties have proved to be significant political forces. Evans and Whitefield have shown evidence of a social basis for ideology and, in turn, party support in CEE (Evans and Whitefield, 1993). They demonstrate that almost all post-Communist countries have some element of ideological division over distributional (left–right) issues, and social class. urban–rural location, age, and education are social predictors on this dimension. Religiosity and ethnicity also matter in some CEE countries, notably in Catholic and ethnically divided states (see Whitefield, 2002).

Not surprisingly, the process of transition from communism to democracy created a divide in post-Communist party systems, pitting parties favouring more radical liberal democratic reforms against those who were more opposed to rapid marketization. As a result of this transition experience the left–right dimension has also been seen to operate differently in central and eastern Europe. Tavits and Letki (2009) have argued that in the context of the dual transition to democracy and to a market economy, left-wing parties have had stronger incentives and better opportunities to enact tighter budgets, whereas rightist parties were compelled to spend more in order to alleviate economic hardships. Consequently, parties on the left have been more likely to pursue rightist policies of fiscal responsibility and economic reform than the rightist parties themselves (see Box 8.1).

Lipset and Rokkan noted that west European party systems in the 1960s, with only few exceptions, reflected the cleavage structures of the 1920s. This has been referred to as the **freezing-hypothesis**, but it was not so much a hypothesis as an empirical observation about the unchanging nature of the main conflict dimensions in European party systems at the time. There are a number of reasons why cleavages might persist. First, the cleavages reflect real and enduring divisions in societies, such as the clash between workers and owners. Second, voters are attached and mobilized to existing parties, so even when the underlying social structures change, voters remain loyal to the established parties. Thirdly, some electoral laws make it difficult for new parties to enter the system, such as a high **electoral threshold** and **first-past-the-post** electoral system that benefits established parties (see also Chapter 6). Finally, established parties can also strategically use their position within the system to remain dominant, for example, by shaping the political agenda, adopting positions that appeal to larger segments of the electorate, and emphasizing their experience in office (De Vries and Hobolt, 2020).

Box 8.1 **CASE STUDY:** Left-Wing Parties in Poland and Hungary

Across central and eastern Europe, the left-wing successor parties of former Communist parties faced a similar problem after the collapse of Communism. They had to distinguish themselves from their past and demonstrate their commitment to democracy and to a market economy. At the same time, they wished to maintain their traditional base of support. By and large, they succeeded (see Grzymala-Busse, 2002).

According to Tavits and Letki (2009), the Hungarian and Polish socialist parties—the MSZP and the SdRP, respectively—were able to do this by adopting right-wing economic policies while in government in the 1990s. The Hungarian MSZP even formed a governing coalition with the liberals in 1994–8 and again in 2002–8, signaling a commitment to free markets. While in government in the mid-1990s, the MSZP initiated a series of economic reforms involving privatization and government spending cuts. The Polish SdRP enacted similar economic reforms when in government to prove that they, too, had shed their communist past. Despite enacting policies that likely caused their core voters economic pain, both these Hungarian and Polish parties retained support, at least in the short term, possibly because there were no other major left-wing parties to challenge them.

Parties on the right in both of Hungary and Poland were free to adopt economic policies more traditionally associated with left-wing parties as they did not have to burnish their anti-communist credentials. The right was also more fragmented and lacked a traditional voter base as a result of the communist legacy. As a result, they were less willing to enact policies that could hurt the pocketbooks of voters.

Tavits and Letki (2009) analyse government spending across all of post-Communist central and eastern Europe from 1989 to 2004, and find that governments with more left-leaning election platforms actually spend less than parties with more right-leaning platforms, both overall and in the policy areas of health and education. However, in a more recent article, Coman (2019) argues that their general finding may be a result of measurement error in the way that government ideology is measured from election manifestos. He argues that there is no general relationship between ideology and spending in these countries. But even this finding is different from findings in western Europe, where there is a clear relationship between right-wing governments and lower spending (see e.g. Bawn and Rosenbluth, 2006).

While there are thus structural reasons for the relative stability of European party systems, the decline of the historical cleavages was already evident at the time when Lipset and Rokkan wrote their study in the late 1960s. This decline has affected party systems. The post-industrial era has weakened the class divide. The proportion of the workforce in blue-collar manual jobs has fallen with the rise of service and professional employment. Moreover, the decline of church attendance and organized religion has reduced the salience of the church–state cleavage. This, combined with the diversification of working life and greater mobility, has weakened the social ties that bind individuals to traditional social groupings. Citizens' responses to rapidly changing social and economic conditions have led to a changing demand for political offerings.

While there is a general consensus that this 'unfreezing' of traditional cleavages has been occurring for several decades, there are two different perspectives on the consequences for European party systems. The first is to see the decline of cleavages as a part of an ongoing process of dealignment. **Dealignment** is a process whereby voters abandon their loyalties to parties without developing new partisan attachments to replace them. This perspective suggests that voters have become like critical consumers that vote for parties with the best offer in each election and parties no longer seek to appeal to particular social groups. The second perspective is one of **realignment**, according to which a new set of divides have emerged that structure political competition and voting behaviour.

There are several indications that the ties between voters and parties have weakened, as suggested by the dealignment perspective. One piece of evidence is the decline in formal party membership. Figure 8.1 clearly shows a steep and consistent decline in the absolute numbers of party members across western Europe, following a peak in the mid-1950s.

Voters are not only less likely to be members of parties; they are also less emotionally attached to specific parties, that is, they have a weaker partisan identity. As a consequence they are more likely to switch party allegiances between elections, creating greater voter volatility. Figure 8.2 shows the over-time trend in party identification by measuring the proportion of citizens who say that they are 'very close' or 'fairly closer' to a party in western Europe countries since the mid-1970s. The general trend is one of a decline from two-thirds of people feeling close to a party in the mid-1970s to around 55 per cent four decades later.

There is, however, considerable variation across countries in western Europe. Some countries, notably the Scandinavian countries and the Netherlands, generally have higher levels of party attachment, reaching as high as over 70 per cent of the electorate feeling attached to a party. Identification with a party is much lower in other countries, such as Ireland and Spain. According to the dealignment view, the decline in party members and party attachments heralds a new era of democratic politics where voter groups are no longer tied to specific parties.

Figure 8.1 Party Membership in Western Europe, 1945–2015

Data source: MAPP (Van Haute et al., 2018)

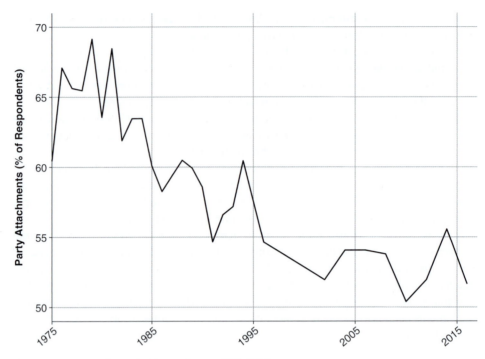

Figure 8.2 Party Attachment in Western Europe, 1975–2016

Data sources: Eurobarometer and European Social Survey

But realignment may also be occurring. While traditional cleavages are weakening, a new divide (or set of divides) has become more salient and provides structure to the political system and to voting behaviour. A prominent example of the realignment argument has been put forward by Inglehart (1977). As already discussed in Chapter 4, Inglehart argued that political conflict was shifting from a class-based to a value-based pattern of political polarization as early as the 1970s. He referred to the 'silent revolution' to describe the gradual value change along the materialist/post-materialist dimension. In response to the rising demand for a new form of politics, a new set of green and new left parties emerged in the 1970s and 1980s across western Europe. These parties campaigned on **post-materialism**, or 'new politics' issues, and rallied against the political establishment. These messages were popular among the younger and better educated segments of the electorate.

While green parties may have represented the silent revolution, the rise of the populist radical right in the 1980s and 1990s, and more significantly since the 2010s, has been described as the 'silent counter revolution'. Rather than embracing the internationalist, tolerant, and progressive agenda of 'new politics', the recent wave of populist radical right-wing parties have defined themselves in opposition to these developments. This has also been linked to socio-economic changes associated with the changing class structure. Increasing globalization has created a new set of 'winners' and 'losers' which in turn is closely tied to the rise and success of radical right parties (see Kriesi et al., 2008). Since the 1980s, a new crop of radical right-wing parties have emerged that embody this cultural backlash. The French National

Rally (previously National Front), the Belgian Flemish Interest, the Austrian Freedom Party, the Italian League, and the Danish People's Party, among several others, have established themselves as a significant force in west European countries.

Regardless of whether the increased importance of cultural issues represents a complete realignment or not, there is little doubt that their emergence has had a profound impact on parties and party systems across Europe. This has been reflected in the debate over whether to call this new divide a cleavage (see Hooghe and Marks, 2018). In other words, to what extent does the **cultural dimension** have a basis in a distinct social structure? Research suggests that the parties that align themselves along the cultural dimensions have distinct electoral groupings with recognizable social characteristics (Stubager, 2010; Hooghe and Marks, 2018; Ford and Jennings, 2020). Notably, education discriminates powerfully between supporters of culturally liberal parties (green, new left etc.), who are generally highly educated, and supporters of culturally conservative parties, who are generally less well educated. Other socio-economic predictors include gender (radical right-wing parties more popular with men) and location (new left parties more popular in large cities whereas radical right-wing parties perform better in towns and rural areas). Education and gender are social characteristics largely distinct from those that define the four main cleavages, although education may be related to class. But the final characteristic clearly maps onto the urban–rural cleavage. Table 8.1 summarizes the main cleavages and their translation into European party families, including the new, disputed, cultural cleavage.

While many of the social changes over the past decades have been quite uniform across Europe, party systems have evolved in somewhat different ways. There is considerable variation in how these social divides translate into party systems. This suggests that the evolution of European party systems is not only determined by the demand structure, but also by the strategic decisions of political parties, i.e. the supply. Other theories of party system change have therefore focused on the supply-side.

A supply-driven strategic approach to political parties and party system changes suggests that, although a change in demand might be a necessary condition for political change, it is not sufficient. Party system change crucially depends on the activities and agency of political parties. In part because political parties themselves are able to generate and maintain political

Table 8.1 Summary of Main Cleavages

Cleavage	Historic era	Voting groups	Party families
Class	Industrial Revolution	Middle class; Working class	Conservative, Liberal, Social Democratic, Communist
Centre–Periphery	National Revolutions	Regions	Regional, Separatist
Church–State	The Reformation	Religion; Denomination	Christian Democratic
Rural–Urban	Industrial Revolution	Urban; Rural	Agrarian
Material–Postmaterial/Cultural	Post-Industrial Revolution/Globalization	Generations; Education	Green, New Left, Radical Right

demand for their programmatic appeals. De Vries and Hobolt have coined the term 'issue entrepreneurship' to describe the strategy of mobilizing new or previously ignored issues to appeal to voters (Hobolt and De Vries, 2015; De Vries and Hobolt, 2020). This strategy is used mostly by **challenger parties**, which are defined by their lack of previous government experience. These parties seek to mobilize issues that drive a wedge within the support for mainstream parties. As an example, green parties have been able to raise the awareness of environmental issues through their activism, and populist radical right-wing parties have increased the salience of anti-immigration concerns. The strategic approach starts from the assumption that politics is a competitive struggle among political parties about which issues come to dominate the political agenda. Political parties are not understood, as in sociological explanations, to be passive vessels for carrying societal divisions, but rather they are seen to actively structure and determine the content of societal conflict. As a result, the content of political competition varies from election to election as new issues or positions are identified and mobilized by one party or another. Political parties politicize a previously non-salient event, policy issue, or societal conflict and attempt to encourage public attention to this controversy. Of course, they have to carefully choose which issues to mobilize and position to take in order to ensure that it resonates with people's interests. Nevertheless, within the strategic perspective, an issue is likely to structure the political debate only when a political party or candidate gives it political expression.

To understand the nature and evolution of European party systems, we should thus consider both the transformations of voter preferences and the ways in which parties seek to mobilize these voters. Section 8.2 considers how parties can be categorized according to the party families they belong to and shows evidence of how the support for party families varies over time and between countries.

8.2 Party Families

Most European parties can be classified in groups, or party families. There are three types of (often overlapping) characteristics normally used to classify parties into party families: origins, cooperation, and ideological similarity. First, parties can be classified according to their shared origins, as outlined in the cleavage theory. As such the traditional Christian democratic, conservative, social democratic, liberal, and communist party family arose from specific historical junctures, while more recent party families, the green, 'new left', and radical right grew out of the post-industrial revolution. Second, party families may be defined by the parties themselves, as they build transnational cooperation, such as the cooperation between social democratic parties in the Socialist International, a worldwide organization of political parties which seeks to establish democratic socialism that has antecedents in the late nineteenth century. Finally, party families may be identified on the basis of the similar policy stances that parties adopt.

On the basis of these approaches, most parties can be classified as belonging to a small number of party families: the Christian democratic, the social democratic, liberal, the radical left, the regionalist, the green, and the radical right. As already discussed, the **Christian democratic party family** is rooted in the church–state cleavage. Parties locate themselves on the centre-right on the left–right dimension while adopting more traditionalist value policies. The **liberal party family** is on the centre-right economically as well, but adopts a more progressive stance on the cultural dimensions. The **social democratic party family**, on the left, is rooted in the class cleavage, as are the **radical left** parties. In contrast, **green parties** and **radical right-wing parties** take more distinct positions on either extreme of the cultural dimensions. **Regionalist parties** arose out of the centre–periphery cleavage and advocate more devolved powers to their regions or even secession.

While every European country has a distinct blend of party families, there are also striking similarities between party systems. One similarity is that in most countries the mainstream party families, including Christian democratic, conservative, liberal, and social democratic parties, have dominated politics over the last 100 years and continue to do so. Figure 8.3 shows the evolution of west European party systems over the last century and demonstrate the dominance of the major centre-right and centre-left party families. Another similarity, however, is the increasing fragmentation of party politics that is taking place across Europe. In the last few decades, and in particularly in the aftermath of the financial crisis, more voters are turning to challenger parties, often those on radical right, the radical left, or green parties.

We can also look at the more recent development of party families in post-Communist central and eastern European countries since their transition to democracy in the early 1990s. The pattern is generally very similar to western Europe with the centre-right and centre-left

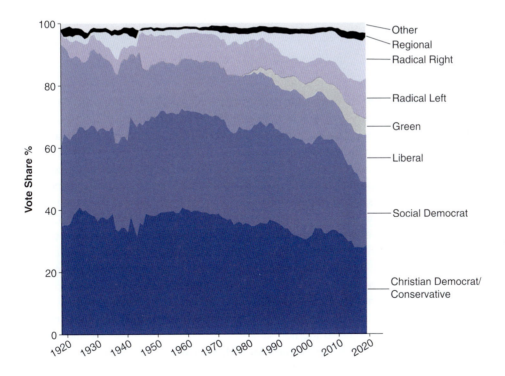

Figure 8.3 Party Family Vote Shares in Western Europe, 1919–2019

Data source: Hix et al. (2020)

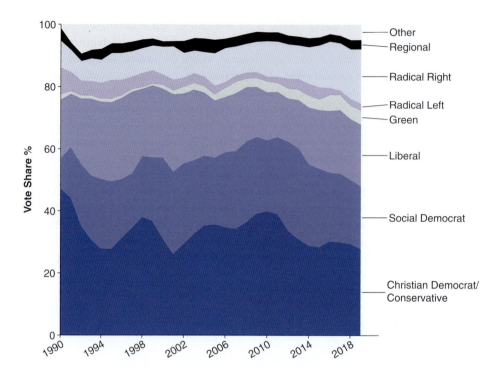

Figure 8.4 Party Family Vote Shares in Post-Communist European Countries, 1990–2019

Data source: Hix et al. (2020)

families still dominating, but a sizeable radical right-wing party family also exists. The green party and radical left party families remain weaker in the post-Communist countries, though.

Figures 8.3 and 8.4 show considerable stability over time, with some increased fragmentation over the last couple of years. Yet they also conceal much of the country-specific nature of party systems. To illustrate the diverse nature of party competition in Europe, we outline the party systems in four large European countries by plotting parties according to their ideological positions in a two-dimensional space consisting of the economic left–right dimension and the cultural libertarian–authoritarian dimension. We rely on the Chapel Hill Party Expert Survey (CHES) to locate the parties on the two dimensions. On the horizontal axis, parties are located on the basis of their ideological stance on economic issues. Parties on the economic left want government to play an active role in the economy. Parties on the economic right emphasize a reduced economic role for government: privatization, lower taxes, less regulation, less government spending, and a leaner welfare state. On the vertical axis, parties are located on the basis of their views on cultural (or postmaterial) issues. 'Libertarian' or 'postmaterialist' parties favour expanded personal freedoms, for example, access to abortion, same-sex marriage, or greater democratic participation. 'Authoritarian' parties often reject these ideas; they value order, tradition, and stability, and believe that the government should be a firm moral authority on social and cultural issues. A higher score indicates a more right-wing/authoritarian position. The size of the bubbles indicates the relative vote share of the parties.

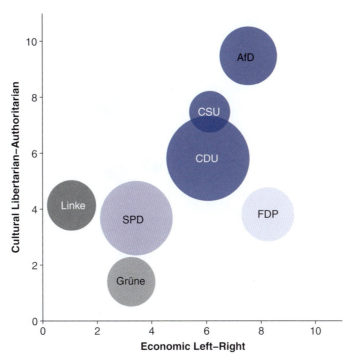

Figure 8.5 Political Parties in Germany.

Data source: CHES (2019)

Note: Size of bubble indicates the relative vote share of the parties.

Starting with the largest country in the EU, Germany, Figure 8.5 plots the parties in the German Parliament, Bundestag, on two dimensions. All of the main party families are represented in the German party system, with the exception of some small regionalist parties. The party with largest vote share is the Christian democratic CDU and its sister party in Bavaria, the CSU. Figure 8.5 shows that the CDU is positioned ideologically only slightly to the right of centre (5) on both dimensions. The main opposition party in post-war Germany has been the social democratic SPD, which is located slightly to the left of centre on both dimensions. But the two major parties are not that far apart ideologically, and they were serving together in a coalition government at the time of the expert survey (2019). Two parties are further to the left of the SPD: the radical left-wing Die Linke, which is to the left on the economic dimension, but not on the cultural dimension; and the Green Party, which is very similar to the social democrats on the economic dimension, but more libertarian on the cultural dimension. On the right, we also find two parties to the right of the CDU: the liberal Free Democratic Party (FDP), which is more economically on the right, but also more libertarian, and the radical right-wing Alternative for Germany (AfD), which competes primarily on the second cultural dimension by adopting more anti-immigration and Eurosceptic stances than the other parties. Germany has also followed the path of other European countries with the emergence of Green parties in the 1980s and challenger parties on the radical left and the radical right fringes in the last couple of decades. This indicates that a two-dimensional space is needed to capture party

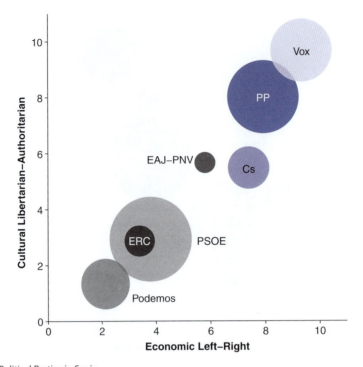

Figure 8.6 Political Parties in Spain

Data source: CHES (2019)

Note: Size of bubble indicates the relative vote share of the parties. Only parties with vote share >1.5% included.

competition in Germany today, as challengers have emerged to compete on the cultural dimension with the Greens at the socially progressive end of that spectrum and the AfD at the socially conservative end. Meanwhile, in the centre, the social democratic party and the liberals have been losing electoral support.

Spain's party system emerged in the late 1970s after the death of the fascist dictator Franco in 1975 and the country's transition to democracy. Just like Germany, Spain is a multiparty system dominated by a large right-wing party, the conservative People's Party (PP), and a centre-left social democratic Spanish Socialist Workers' Party (PSOE). Looking at Figure 8.6, it is noteworthy that Spanish politics appears more polarized than German politics. In particular, the conservative PP is both more economically and culturally to the right than the more centrist German Christian Democrats. Spain also differs from Germany in that regionalist parties, such as the Republican Left of Catalonia (ERC) from Catalonia and the Basque Nationalist Party (EAJ-PNV) from the Basque Country, are represented in parliament. Despite being relatively small at the national level, the regionalist parties play a key role in Spanish politics, not least since minority governments—those lacking formal majority support in parliament—led by either PP or PSOE have often relied on their votes in parliament. In Spain, the centre–periphery cleavage thus remains highly salient. A relatively new development in Spanish politics is the arrival of smaller challenger parties, such as the radical left Podemos, the liberal Ciudadanos (Cs), and more recently the radical right-wing Vox. Spain thus follows the European pattern of greater fragmentation as well as competition on both the economic left–right and on the cultural dimension.

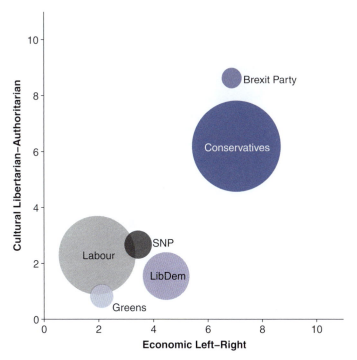

Figure 8.7 Political Parties in the UK

Data source: CHES 2019

Note: Size of bubble indicates the relative vote share of the parties.

Looking at the UK in Figure 8.7, we can observe the clear dominance of two-party politics. This is not surprising given the UK's majoritarian first-past-the-post electoral system that favours larger parties (see Chapter 6). Since the 1920s, the two main parties have been the centre-right Conservative Party and the social democratic Labour Party. Before the Labour Party became a dominant force in British politics, the Liberal Party was the other major political party, along with the Conservatives. The Liberal Democrats is the successor of the once dominant Liberal Party, and remains an economically centrist, but culturally progressive party. Traditionally, the class cleavage has been the dominant cleavage in British politics, with the Labour Party representing the interests of the working class and the Conservative Party representing the interests of landowners and employers. Today, social class plays a much diminished role in structuring politics in the UK, and the cultural dimension has become more important, not least with the arrival of challenger parties such as the UK Independence Party (UKIP), and subsequently the Brexit Party, advocating anti-immigration, Eurosceptic positions. At the other end of the cultural dimension are the Greens and the Liberal Democrats that adopt more post-materialist stances. Another important dimension in British party politics is the centre–periphery cleavage, which is particularly salient outside England, for example in Scotland where the Scottish National Party (SNP) is very popular (note that this figure does not display all the minor regional parties represented in the British House of Commons).

The most recent of the national party systems discussed here is the Polish, which emerged as a multiparty system during the transition from the one-party Communist regime to democracy in

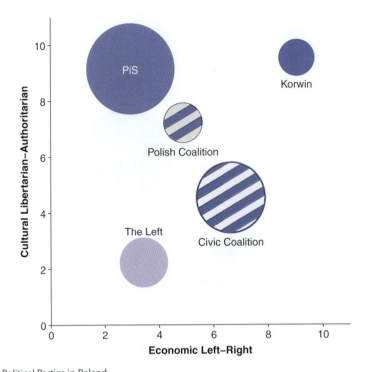

Figure 8.8 Political Parties in Poland

Data source: CHES 2019

Note: Size of bubble indicates the relative vote share of the parties. Hatched circles represent coalitions of two or more parties.

the early 1990s. What is particularly noteworthy in Figure 8.8 is that right-wing parties dominate Polish politics. After transition to democracy, the centre-left Communist successor party was one of the dominant parties. But the main political battleground is no longer between ex-Communists and those who opposed the regime. Instead, the division is on the second cultural dimension between the national conservative Law and Justice party (PiS) and the economically conservative, but more socially liberal Civic Coalition (KO)—shown as a hatched circle in the figure as it is an electoral coalition of parties with Civic Platform (PO) as the major party. The left–right dimension is also seen to operate differently in post-Communist countries such as Poland, and often socially conservative parties, such as PiS are relatively left-wing on the economic dimension, as we see on in Figure 8.8, as they favour more expansionary fiscal policies combined with traditional conservative and even authoritarian values. The urban–rural cleavage is also evident in Poland with the representation of agrarian interests by the centre–right Polish People's Party (PSL), standing in recent elections as a part of the Polish Coalition. Moreover, Poland is a multiparty system with a relatively high turnover of smaller parties. In 2019, the coalition of left-wing, pro-European parties, The Left, and a populist right-wing coalition with Korwin as the main party, were also represented in the Polish parliament, Sejm.

These four large European countries show considerable variation in their party systems, not only with respect to the societal divisions that are mobilized, but also in the stances adopted by social democratic and conservative/Christian democratic parties. Despite these differences, political parties do work together across national boundaries in Europe-wide parties and in political groups at the EU level.

Box 8.2 METHODS AND MEASUREMENT: How to Measure Party Positions

Measures of party positions are frequently used by political scientists to explore party systems and party competition. Researchers use several methods to systematically measure these positions: they include mass surveys of voters, elite surveys of representatives, dimensional analysis of roll call votes in legislatures, expert surveys of national party experts, and content analysis of parties' electoral manifestos or speeches (for an overview see Laver, 2014).

Manual Coding of Party Manifestos: The most widely used measure of party positions is the hand-coded estimates of party manifestos provided by the Manifesto Project, which includes position estimates of the main political parties in a wide range of democracies going back to the Second World War (Budge et al., 2001; Klingemann et al., 2006; Volkens et al., 2019). Unlike other measures of position placements, the manifesto project data provide cross-national, time-series data on party placements. The content analysis process involves several steps.

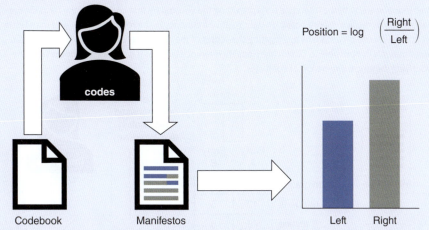

$$\text{Position} = \log\left(\frac{\text{Right}}{\text{Left}}\right)$$

codes

Codebook   Manifestos   Left   Right

A master codebook contains descriptions of all fifty-six categories and how sentences should be identified and coded, in case of multiple coding possibilities. Based on these coding instructions, trained expert coders classify sentences of each manifesto into one of 56 policy categories. The provided estimates for each category are the percentages of sentences in that category out of all sentences in the manifesto. This coding scheme captures the relative emphasis a party places on any one policy category over the other categories. For the purposes of investigating how changes over time in party polarization affect vote choices in most countries, manifesto data are often the only readily available data source. Recently, however, researchers have begun to debate the reliability and validity of the manifesto measures of party positions and its 'one-size-fits-all' left–right scale. A common critique is that a coding scheme created in the 1980s (before the end of the Cold War) can only partially reflect policy conflicts in Europe more than several decades later. Nevertheless, scholars do use data both as dependent variables (e.g. explaining party position change) and as independent variables (e.g. explaining policy outcomes) in their research. The data allow the construction of policy scales. The commonly used scale is the left–right (RILE) scale, which is constructed by subtracting the sum of 13 'left' policy categories from the sum of thirteen 'right' categories and dividing by the total number of sentences in the manifesto. While being a straightforward measure, it has the undesirable property of measuring left–right ideology of parties by considering non-ideological content in the denominator. Lowe and co-authors have therefore proposed an alternative transformation through the logit scale, which divides the total number of sentences in the right category by those in the left category (Lowe et al., 2011), as shown in the figure. The transformation can be used on any policy categories to produce policy position scales from the hand-coded manifesto data.

(continued...)

Automated Text Analysis of Manifestos and Speeches: With the advance in automated text analysis, some researchers apply quantitative content analysis on manifestos and speeches in order to extract policy positions. With the continued development of text-as-data methods, this field promises to yield new measures of party positions and related concepts, such as populism. There are two basic approaches available to researchers: supervised and unsupervised text scaling. The workflow in both is similar. First, electronic versions of manifestos or speeches are processed and transformed into a term-document matrix. This bag-of-words transformation preserves words and their frequencies, but does away with syntax. One possible way to scale manifestos and speeches is to use a dictionary-based approach. For instance, researchers may be interested in measuring the sentiment of legislators vis-á-vis a bill proposal. A sentiment dictionary that counts positive and negative words in speech can then be used to construct a sentiment score, for instance through a subtraction or a ratio of the counts. This approach can capture legislative conflict between government and opposition parties quite well (Laver et al., 2003). It is supervised because researchers need to select a reference text to anchor a one-dimensional scale, with the reference texts providing the vocabulary that constitutes the basis for the analysis. Words receive a score based on their relative frequency in the reference texts, and manifestos can then be placed on a scale by aggregating the scores of the reference text words that they contain. Sometimes it is not possible to obtain high-quality reference texts, or it is, in fact, unknown what the underlying rhetorical dimension of conflict is.

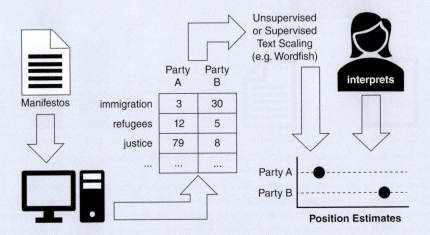

In such a case, an unsupervised procedure such as Wordfish (Slapin and Proksch, 2008) may be a useful alternative. This text scaling procedure relies on a parametric statistical word model, with the assumption that ideology is a latent concept and word counts reflect ideological differences. Like Wordscores, this procedure yields estimates of party positions in a one-dimensional space and is useful to discover the latent conflict in political debates. In any automated procedure, whether supervised or unsupervised, the researcher needs to use great care in validating and interpreting the resulting estimates. While the estimation has high reliability (the computer will always produce the same result), validation is of great concern given that the analysis can be scaled up easily to allow for a large quantitative analysis (which may get prohibitively expensive with traditional manual coding procedures).

Expert and Voter Survey Data: Finally, as an alternative to manifesto data, researchers can also rely on comparative party expert surveys. The idea behind these surveys is to measure party positions by asking informed experts, usually academics, to place parties on pre-defined policy scales. Scholars then use the average placement of experts as an estimate of a party policy position. The longest-running party expert survey in Europe is the Chapel Hill Expert Survey (CHES), which has run since 1999, covering western Europe and now all central and eastern Europe (Bakker et al., 2015; Polk et al., 2017; Bakker et al., 2020). Positions can also be found by using the perceptions of citizens. The proliferation of comparative election surveys has continued in recent years under the auspices of international collaborative projects, such as the Comparative Study of Electoral Systems (CSES) and the European Election Studies (EES), and many of these surveys contain items on party and voter positions on one or more dimensions.

Party families do not only operate at the national level. Legislative political parties in the European Parliament are organized into political groups that look very similar to the party families we are familiar with domestically. These groups are made up of national delegations of parties and bring together Members of the European Parliament (MEPs) from different member states. MEPs thus vote along partisan rather than national lines. To achieve the formal status of a political group it must consist of at least twenty-five MEPs, elected in at least one-quarter of the member states (i.e. at least seven). MEPs may only belong to one political group. Following the 2019 elections, there were seven political groups in the European Parliament (see Figure 8.9). These political groups are rooted in one or more European political parties, or Europarties, which are party organizations operating transnationally in Europe and

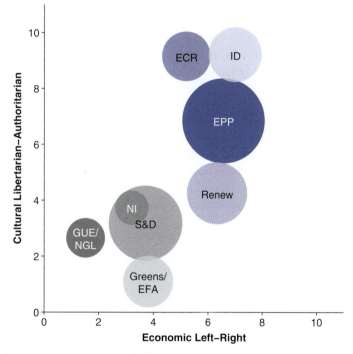

Figure 8.9 Political Groups in the European Parliament, 2019

Data source: CHES

Notes: Size of bubble indicates the relative vote share of the parties. EPP (European People's Party); S&D (Progressive Alliance of Socialists and Democrats); Renew Europe (Renew Europe/ALDE); Greens/EFA (Group of the Greens/European Free Alliance); ID (Identity and Democracy Group); ECR (European Conservatives and Reformists Group); GUE/NGl (European United Left-Nordic Green Left); NI (non-attached).

within the European Union institutions. Take for example the Progressive Alliance of Socialists and Democrats (S&D). This is the political group in the European Parliament of the Europarty, Party of European Socialists (PES), and consists of national delegations of social democratic MEPs, such as representatives of the Spanish PSOE and the German SPD.

The European Parliament has traditionally been dominated by two large political groups, the centre-right European People's Party (EPP), which consists mainly of Christian democratic national party delegations, and the centre-left S&D, which consists mainly of social democratic/ socialist national party delegations. In each successive election, the European Parliament has become more fragmented. The effective number of parties (ENP) in parliament—the number of political parties weighted by their relative strength (see Chapter 9)—in 1979 was 2.5 and this had increased to 6.5 following the European Parliament elections in 2019. The other party groups include Renew Europe (previously ALDE), consisting of centrist and liberal parties, the Greens/European Free Alliance, made up mainly by Green parties, and the radical left-wing European United Left-Nordic Green Left. To the right of the EPP, there is also a fluctuating number of Eurosceptic radical-right-wing political groups that have grown stronger over the years. This picture thus reflects the success of parties in domestic parliaments, although smaller opposition parties tend to perform better in European than in national parliament elections.

8.3 Party Types and Organization

Parties are categorized not only on the basis of their origins in societal divisions, but also on the basis of party types. This categorization is centred on the organizational structure of parties and the nature and role of their membership. At one extreme, we can think of parties with a large and homogeneous membership base that funds the party and formulates the policy programme and an organizational structure where elected party representatives are accountable to the membership base. At the other extreme, some parties are merely the product of a political entrepreneur, who with private resources (e.g. from corporations) sets the policy agenda independently, and where the party membership is either non-existent or irrelevant. These distinctions can be useful devices for examining the ways in which parties have changed over time as well as differences between parties currently in the party system.

Duverger (1951) discussed the evolution of the modern party in his book *Political Parties*. He distinguished between the old **cadre parties** and the newer mass parties. The earliest 'modern' type of parties were cadre parties that had emerged with the rise of parliamentary government and were loosely structured and elite-centred parties with minimal organization outside parliament. They are also referred to as elite parties. With mass suffrage and an expanding electorate, some of these parties developed local organizations with caucuses of prominent individuals that would mobilize resources and support. However, the parties remained centred around members of parliament, and were funded from their personal wealth and connections.

In the second half of the nineteenth century, the **mass party** developed. In contrast to the cadre party that was rooted in parliament, mass parties have highly developed organizations outside parliament and large party memberships. The party membership was large and relatively homogeneous, typically based on the social ties described by cleavage theory, such as for example social democratic parties with a large working-class memberships and strong links with trade unions. Such a large membership required a complex organizational structured with local branches. Mass parties were also funded by membership fees and fundraising as well as support from ancillary organizations, such as trade unions and churches. The membership of mass parties was given considerable influence through the nomination of party representatives and contributed to decision-making at policy programmes in national congresses. Most mass parties have a hierarchical structure with decisions taken centrally, but the leadership remains ultimately accountable to its members,

Mass parties, however, were forced to change as the nature of their electoral base became more diffuse and the pressures on a party in public office called for increasing professionalization. Kirchheimer (1966) argued that most mass parties transformed themselves into **catch-all parties**, abandoning their distinct ideological brand and narrow group appeals, and seeking support among the wider electorate with an emphasis on competence and professionalism. Similarly, Panebianco (1988) coined the term 'electoral-professional party' to refer to parties that are centrally organized and professionally run, seeking to maximize electoral support. As mass parties became catch-all parties they retained their membership, but the membership was often more diffuse and less influential in decision-making.

A later iteration of the catch-all party is what Katz and Mair (1995) have called the **cartel party**. Cartel parties moved further away from the membership-centred version of parties towards a professionalized organization dominated by the party in office. The key difference, however, between the catch-all parties and the cartel parties is that cartel parties are defined by their relation to the state. Cartel parties have ceased to operate as true brokers between civil society and the state and have become instead agents of the state.

Figure 8.10 shows an overview of different types of parties on two dimensions: their membership base and their organization structure.

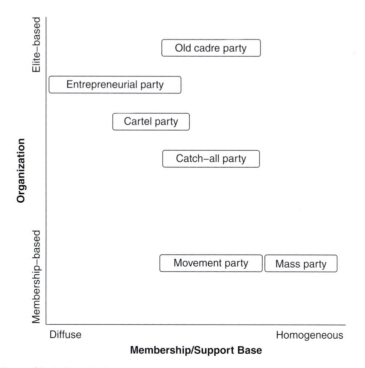

Figure 8.10 Types of Party Organizations

While catch-all and cartel parties can be seen as evolving from the original mass-based parties, such as the large social democratic, Christian democratic, and liberal party families, we have in recent decades also witnessed the emergence of new parties with no firm roots in mass-based membership. On the one hand, **movement parties** have grown out of a social movement organized around a single issue or a set of issues, such as the environmental movement that led to the rise of green parties in a number of countries. Such movement, or new politics, parties often have very flat organizational structures and tend to expect a much deeper commitment from their members and give their membership considerable influence on the policy direction and election of party representatives. In this way, they are similar to mass parties. However, they are organized around a set of shared ideas rather than a social group.

At the other extreme of new party types are **entrepreneurial parties**, founded by a single or a group of political entrepreneurs, without a membership base or a social movement behind them, but often with corporate resources. One such entrepreneurial type of party is what Hopkin and Paolucci (1999) identified as the business-firm parties, such as Forza Italia, which was created by businessman Silvio Berlusconi and was linked to an existing corporate empire. However, entrepreneurial parties need not be founded by business people. Other political entrepreneurs can also set up parties with the primary function of mobilizing electoral support at election time and with a very limited organizational structure and power organized around the party leadership. Nigel Farage's Brexit Party in the UK provides an example. What the entrepreneurial parties have in common is that they are founded with minimal formal organization and hierarchical control of the leadership, as well as a non-existent or irrelevant membership. There are thus clear similarities with the old cadre parties, although the entrepreneurial parties often originate outside parliament. While entrepreneurial parties and movement parties are very different in terms of their internal organization, both can generally be classified as a type of challenger party (De Vries and Hobolt, 2020). Developments in digital communication and social media have offered opportunities for these new parties to communicate more directly with potential supporters without the organizational structure and resources available to mainstream parties. And they have often been more savvy in their usage of digital media. The Italian populist Five Star Movement provides an example of a challenger party that has used such technological advances effectively. It has mobilized its supporters through an online platform called Rousseau, which has allowed registered members to vote in primaries and discuss, approve, or reject legislative proposals.

8.4 Niche, Populist, and Challenger Parties

There is a growing literature on the type of parties that challenge the established mainstream parties. Breaking from the traditional typologies, these parties are not classified on the basis of their internal organizational structure, but rather by the way in which they disrupt mainstream politics. Numerous labels have been used to describe these parties, such as niche parties, populist parties, 'new politics' parties, and challenger parties. They are often contrasted with 'mainstream', 'established', or 'dominant' parties. While there is considerable overlap between the different typologies of parties, these labels nonetheless refer to different features of parties.

Scholars who refer to **niche parties** take as a starting point the concept of a party family, discussed above, and argue that parties originating in the traditional party families, based on class, religion, territory, etc. are 'mainstream', whereas those that do not are 'niche' (see Adams et al., 2006). New niche parties arise as a result of changes in the electorate's composition and preferences, and are not based on traditional cleavages. Instead such parties may campaign on issues such as the environment, anti-immigration, or Euroscepticism. Others focus on the the programmatic strategies of niche parties, that is to say, the types of issues they mobilize, namely 'non-centrist' or 'new issues'. Meguid (2008), classifies niche parties as those parties that reject the traditional class-based orientation of politics, mobilize issues that do not coincide with existing lines of political division, and limit their issue appeals. On the basis of this classification, most green, radical right, and single issue parties are considered niche.

A second approach focuses on the distinction between 'populist' and 'non-populist' parties (for a discussion of **populism** as an ideology see Chapter 4). The literature on populism has been burgeoning over the last two decades as populist parties have gained in electoral strength. There is no firm consensus on how to define populist parties. However, the most influential conceptualization of populist parties has been put forward by Canovan (1999) and Mudde (2004) and rests on the understanding of populism as a thin-centred ideology that separates society into two homogeneous and antagonistic groups, 'the pure people' and 'the corrupt elite', and that holds that politics should be an expression of 'the general will' of the people. Since populism is a thin-centred ideology it is extremely malleable and can be easily integrated into any other more complex host ideology, such as socialism or liberalism. This means that populist parties can be found both on the left and the right (or indeed the centre) of the political spectrum.

The final approach classifies parties on the basis of whether they have served in government. While some niche and populist parties may have participated in government, a challenger party is defined by its lack of government experience (De Vries and Hobolt, 2020). De Vries and Hobolt contrast challenger parties with dominant parties, which have previously served in government or are currently in office. This definition thus focuses on parties' structural position in the political marketplace, rather than their ideological and programmatic commonalities. Due to their position in the system, challenger parties are able to mobilize new issues as issue entrepreneurs and adopt anti-establishment strategies to win over voters.

There is thus overlap between the parties classified as niche, populist, and challenger, but they are not identical lists of parties. Whether researchers focus on niche, populist, or challenger parties often depends on the questions they wish to answer.

8.5 Summary

This chapter has looked at what parties are, how they are formed, how we classify them, and how they interact with each other. It has revealed some remarkable stability in European party politics over time. Major party families that have existed for a century and are rooted in national and Industrial Revolutions still hold considerable sway over democratic politics in Europe today. Yet, we have also highlighted change in party politics. Parties themselves have changed from mass parties to catch-all parties. And now we witness the emergence of entrepreneurial challenger parties. These changes have partly been in response to societal changes resulting from the post-industrial globalized era, with the rise of 'new politics' and the counter-movement of the populist radical right. The chapter has also shown that party politics is not only reactive to changing societal structures, but that parties themselves can help shape the political landscape as challenger parties mobilizing new dimensions and issues in politics. In Chapter 9, we look more closely at how parties compete with each other to appeal to voters.

Online Data Exercise: The CHES Dataset

The interactive online exercise introduces the party position dataset of the Chapel Hill Expert Surveys (CHES). The CHES dataset provides expert perceptions of the positions of European political parties on a general left–right scale, an economy policy dimension, a cultural libertarian–authoritarian dimension, a European integration dimension, and many more. You will visualize the relationship between these dimensions and explore the composite parts of common ideological scales in the European political sphere.

Take your learning further with this interactive data exercise, available at **www.foundationsofeuropeanpolitics.com**

For additional material and resources, including multiple-choice questions, web links, and more, please visit the online resources: **www.oup.com/he/devries1e**

9 Party Competition

This chapter looks at the competition between parties. First, we outline the ways in party systems are described and categorized in terms of the number of parties (fragmentation) and their ideological positions (polarization). Second, we turn to the theoretical models that seek to explain how parties compete with one another. We start with the simple spatial model that predicts that parties position themselves close to the centre of politics to appeal to the median voter. Then we move to issue competition models that expect parties to champion issues they 'own' and valence models focused on competence, leadership traits, and other non-policy characteristics of parties and candidates. Finally, we discuss how mainstream parties seek to respond to the rise of challenger parties using insights from all of these theoretical approaches.

Chapter 8 focused on individual parties—their origins, characteristics, and organization—but parties do not exist in a vacuum; rather they interact with one another. This chapter is interested in the connections between parties: what constellations do we find in party systems? How do parties position themselves relative to one another? What policies and other attributes do parties offer to appeal to voters and ultimately win seats in parliament?

A liberal democracy requires that two or more parties, representing a range of views, are able to freely appeal to voters and compete for office. The nature of this competition between parties determines the shape and size of a **party system**. Party systems are often classified on the basis of the number and the size of parties (fractionalization) and the ideological distance between them (polarization). These classifications are rooted in the dominant spatial approach to party competition, where parties compete by adopting different policy positions. Yet parties can also compete for electoral support in other ways: by raising different issues (issue competition) or highlighting non-policy characteristics, such as competence, integrity, or charisma (valence competition). While simple spatial models predict that parties converge, that is, that they adopt similarly centrist policy positions, the reality of European politics is often one of greater fragmentation and often polarization, as challenger parties seek to disrupt mainstream dominance by mobilizing new issues. This chapter therefore proceeds to discuss the options available to mainstream parties when competing amongst themselves and with challengers. But first we discuss the format of party interactions, namely the party system.

9.1 Party Systems

How do we best describe the nature of party competition? One starting point is to look at the shape of the party system, namely which parties exist within a country, as discussed in the previous chapter. This includes the number and size of **political parties** and the interaction between them. Early classifications of party systems focused on a simple distinction between two-party systems and multiparty systems, focusing on just the number of parties competing (Duverger, 1951). As we discussed in Chapter 6, electoral systems play a central role in shaping the number of parties in a party system, with majoritarian systems making two-party systems more likely, while multiparty systems are the norm in proportional systems. If we account for both the number and the size (dominance) of parties in a system, we arrive at a four-fold typology:

- **Single-party system:** In these systems, only one political party is allowed to hold power. This type of one-party state is not a democracy, but this was the dominant party system model in central and eastern Europe under Communism, for example.

- **Dominant party systems:** A system with one large party with a more than absolute majority of votes and seats and limited alternation of government. This type of party system is very rare in modern democratic European states.

- **Two-party system:** Two parties with a combined vote share of around 80 per cent. Alternation between parties in government, normally single-party government. Examples in Europe include the UK and Malta.

- **Multiparty system:** Several parties in parliament, with none approaching 50 per cent. Alternation of government between parties, high frequency of coalition government. This is by far the most common type of party system in Europe. Many European countries have **bipolar party systems** where parties are divided into ideological blocs that form relatively stable coalitions.

More complex classifications of party systems have been developed to take into account not simply the number of parties and their size, but also the ideological positions of those parties. Using this approach, party systems can be summarized focusing on two main elements:

1. **Fragmentation:** The number and size of the competing parties. How many parties are there and how strong are they? Strength can be measured either in terms of the votes parties get or in terms of their seats in parliament. Party system fragmentation thus captures not only the number of parties, but also the dominance of those parties within the system (see Box 9.1)

2. **Polarization:** The ideological distribution of parties in the party system, i.e. the polarization in the party system. Polarization reflects the distribution of parties along a single ideological dimension. In Europe, this is generally conceptualized along a single left–right dimension (see Box 9.1).

Figure 9.1 provides an illustration of a system with low fragmentation (just three parties) but high polarization, as the parties are distributed across the ideological spectrum, rather than converging in the ideological centre.

Sartori (1976) developed a typology that incorporated both fragmentation and polarization. He argued that, rather than focusing on just fragmentation, the starting point should be the ideological distance between the parties competing, arguing that there were both

Box 9.1 **METHODS AND MEASUREMENT:** Party System Fragmentation and Polarization

The most frequently used measure of party fragmentation is **Effective Number of Parties (ENP)**, introduced by Laakso and Taagepera (1979) to present an adjusted number of political parties in a country's party system, weighted by their relative strength (votes or seats). According to Laakso and Taagepera (1979) the effective number of parties is computed by the following formula:

$$N = \frac{1}{\sum_{i=1}^{n} p_i^2} \tag{9.1}$$

where n is the number of parties with at least one vote/seat and p_i^2 the square of each party's proportion of all votes or seats. The proportions need to be normalized such that, for example, 50 per cent is 0.5 and 1 per cent is 0.01. The number of parties equals the effective number of parties only when all parties have equal strength. In any other case, the effective number of parties is lower than the actual number of parties. The relative strength can refer to either their vote share (effective number of electoral parties, ENEP) or seat share in the parliament (effective number of parliament parties, ENPP). This is a far more useful way of describing a party system than simply counting the number of parties represented. Take for example the UK. Following the 2019 general election, nine parties took seats in parliament, which suggests a true multiparty system. However, the effective number of legislative parties was 2.4, which more accurately describes the nature of the British party system, with two very dominant parties (Labour and Conservatives) and a number of much smaller parties.

Measuring party polarization is a little more complicated. A general assumption is that polarization reflects the distribution of parties along a single ideological dimension—in a European context, this is usually assumed to be the left–right dimension. A stylized example of this is shown in Figure 9.1, which shows the distribution of three parties in a system on the left–right dimension, as well as the location of the mean (average) party. This party system appears to have low fragmentation (only three parties) and high polarization (ideological positions of parties across the entire ideological spectrum). To measure party system polarization more systematically, we need a measure of the ideological position of each of the parties. There are different ways of obtaining this—through manifesto codings, party expert surveys, or mass surveys, as described in the previous chapter. When we have measures of each of the positions of the parties, we can then measure the distribution of the parties along the left–right scale to arrive at a polarization measure. Two commonly used measures of party polarization capture this distribution as a measure of the standard deviation of party positions from the party mean, either giving all parties equal weight (9.2) or weighted by party size (9.3) (see Ezrow, 2007):

$$\text{Unweighted Party Polarization} = \sqrt{\frac{\sum_{j=1} (P_{jk} - \bar{P}_k)^2}{n}} \tag{9.2}$$

$$\text{Weighted Party Polarization} = \sqrt{\sum_{j=1} VS_j (P_{jk} - \bar{P}_k)^2} \tag{9.3}$$

where P_k is the weighted mean of all the parties' left–right ideological positions in country k, P_{jk} is the ideological position of party j in country k, n is the number of parties included in the analysis for country k, and VS_j is the vote share for party j.

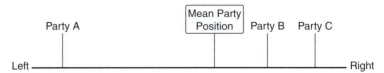

Figure 9.1 Polarized Party System

centripetal and **centrifugal** forces that influenced parties' location on the ideological spectrum. Centripetal forces would encourage parties to concentrate in the centre, creating **moderate pluralism**, whereas centrifugal forces led parties to adopt more extreme positions in systems of **polarized pluralism**. Whereas moderate pluralism is more common in Europe, examples of polarized pluralism include the Italian party system before the 1990s and France between 1946 and 1958. Recent scholarship, though, focuses less on debating typologies of party system and more on developing nuanced measures of the degree of fragmentation and polarization of party systems. This is discussed in Box 9.1.

Researchers use measures of fragmentation and polarization not only to classify party system, but importantly to measure the effect on feelings of citizen representation, on turnout as well as systemic factors such as government and regime stability. For example, it has been argued that high levels of polarization contributed to the demise of the Weimar Republic and the French Fourth Republic.

But why do parties adopt a particular policy position? Why are some party systems polarized while in others parties converge on the centre-ground? Spatial models of party competition address these questions.

9.2 Spatial Models of Party Competition

The discussion of party system polarization rests on the basic assumptions of the spatial model of party competition introduced in Chapter 2. In its simplest form, parties and voters are located along a line, a uni-dimensional policy space, as depicted in Figure 9.2 as a left–right dimension. In addition to the political parties, the figure also depicts the median voter. In this model we will assume that political parties seek to maximize their electoral support in order to win office. If we assume that voters vote for the parties with the preferences most similar to their own, i.e. the most proximate party on the left–right scale, then as Downs (1957) argued (see Chapter 4), the parties ought to converge on the position of the median voter (often, but not necessarily always, located near the centre of the space). The position of the **median voter** is the position that will defeat all other positions in pair-wise majority-rule contests. Thus, the party holding that position will win the election.

In a two-party contest as shown in Figure 9.2, parties should adopt the position of the median voter to win office. Downsian logic would mean that Party A would win the contest against Party B, since Party A's ideology is more aligned with the median voter and the party is more likely to implement policies in line with the voters' preferences, if elected. This would give a strong incentive for Party B to move closer to the position of the median voter in order to win back some of Party A's voters. Ultimately, taken to its logical conclusion, the argument means that parties ought to stack right on top of the median voter. However, if

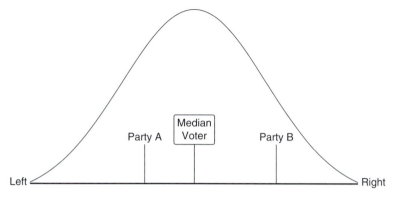

Figure 9.2 Downsian Model of Party Competition

some voters on the extremes decide to abstain from voting, parties might have incentives to diverge from the median to entice these disenchanted extremists to vote again. Downs also argued that it would not be sensible for Party B to 'leapfrog' Party A to chase voters on the opposite side of the median voter, since such radical shifts in position would be unlikely to be seen as credible by voters.

The spatial model provides important insights into party competition and helps us understand the strategies that parties often adopt in order to increase their electoral support. However, it also makes a number of strict assumptions about the nature of party systems that generally do not apply well in European politics. These assumptions also lead to an expectation that party competition is essentially centripetal, leading to parties' **convergence** on the centre. However, the reality of most European party systems is one where parties diverge ideologically. To understand why the simply spatial model may not explain the reality of European party competition all that well, we need to look at the key assumptions of the Downsian model, which have been challenged by scholars of European party competition:

1. Two-party system (rather than multiparty system)

2. Uni-dimensionality of electoral competition (rather than multidimension competition)

3. Voter preferences as exogenous to party strategies (rather than influenced by party strategies)

4. Primacy of policy preferences over non-policy preferences (rather than emphasis on valence issues)

We have already demonstrated in the previous chapters that the first two assumptions are unlikely to hold in most European countries. The Downsian model assumes a two-party system, however, with the exception of perhaps Malta and the UK, all European party systems are multiparty systems. This also has consequences for the strategies of parties. If we assume that both Party A and Party B converge close to the median voter in Figure 9.2, then it might be rational for a third party, Party C, to take a position to, say, the left of Party A and appeal to voters with more left-wing positions. In multiparty systems, we may expect parties to be spread along the left–right dimension, rather than all parties converging on the median voter. Indeed, if we look at the positions of parties in most European party systems, then we find the large mainstream social democratic and Christian democratic parties adopting centre-left and centre-right positions, whereas radical left and radical right-wing parties adopt more extreme positions on the left–right dimension. In Chapter 8, we showed that almost all European party systems are polarized ideologically, either because there is considerable divergence between the major centre-left and centre-right parties (e.g. in the UK and Spain) or because challenger parties on the ideological fringes adopt more extreme positions (e.g. in Germany and Poland),

Moreover, the simple Downsian model assumes that political competition is one-dimensional rather than multidimensional. However, as our discussion in Chapter 8 of the origins of European parties has shown, there are often multiple conflict dimensions at play. To the extent that these conflicts and issues are aligned with a single overarching left–right dimension, the uni-dimensional model is still meaningful. Yet, if these conflict dimensions are **cross-cutting**, rather than overlapping, this also affects competition between parties (see Chapter 4). Cross-cutting issues are ones that are not aligned with the dominant left–right dimension, and thus tend to divide parties and their supporters.

These challenges to the assumptions of the Downsian model have led scholars to develop alternative theories of party competition as well as extensions to the simple spatial model. In sections 9.3–9.5, we discuss issue competition as well as valence theories of party competition. In addition to relaxing the first two assumptions of the Downsian model, these theories relax the third and fourth assumptions as well.

9.3 Issue Competition and Issue Entrepreneurship

According to the spatial model, parties are simply trying to adopt positions close to the median voter to maximize their vote share and thus chances of getting into office. But if voters care about multiple issues in an election, a party can also try to strategically shape which issues voters care about in the ballot box in the hope that they vote based on issues where parties have an advantage. The literature on **issue competition** has argued that parties seek to influence what issues voters think about when making electoral choices to gain an electoral advantage. This is in line with thinking of Schattschneider (1960) who argued that politics is essentially about which political conflicts come to dominate the political agenda. According to Schattschneider, societies produce a number of diverse conflicts over public policy and the outcome of party competition depends on which of these conflicts gains the dominant position. Similarly Riker (1986) argued that political actors seek to structure the debate in ways that would allow them to win. He coined the term **heresthetics**, which is the art of strategic manipulation of political situations by political actors pursuing their objectives. Losers in a political system will seek to mobilize an issue in order to divide the majority with a new alternative conflict that is expected to give them an advantage. Hence, the purpose of campaign messages is not to engage the opposition in debate or dialogue but to increase the salience of issues over which the party is perceived to be credible. This is also the starting point for the issue approach to party competition, which argues that parties campaign on issues that might benefit them while ignoring issues of other parties that will benefit the competition.

For example, the party closest to the median voter on economic issues would emphasize economic issues rather than cultural issues, while the party closest to the median voter on cultural issues would emphasize those issues. In a European context, Budge and Farlie (1983) have developed a saliency theory, arguing that most political parties engage in selective emphasis of issues on which they have a competence and avoid issues where they have no such advantage. Similarly, Petrocik (1996) **issue ownership** theory has highlighted that parties tend to campaign on issues that they 'own', i.e. where voters consider them competent. Examples of this would include centre-right parties emphasizing issues related to crime and economic management, because they have a reputation among voters as parties that can deliver on law and order and the economy, while centre-left parties are more likely to talk about healthcare, social care, and education, since they are seen by voters as caring more about public services.

Parties thus compete to influence which issues voters care more about at the ballot box; if they are primarily worried about crime, they will vote for the right-wing choice, whereas if they are concerned with healthcare provision, they will opt for a left-wing choice. Green-Pedersen (2019) has proposed an issue incentive model of party competition where parties consider not only issue ownership, but also the characteristics of policy issues (solubility and scope) and coalition consideration (issue positions need to be compatible with potential coalition partners). Taken together, these issue competition approaches all assume that parties strategically choose a set of issues to emphasize to influence the salience of different issues to voters and thus increase their appeal to voters and their chances of forming government.

If parties can influence what issues voters care about, this can also be exploited by **issue entrepreneurs** that seek to appeal to voters by mobilizing new issues. De Vries and Hobolt (Hobolt and De Vries, 2015; De Vries and Hobolt, 2020) have shown that in European multi-party systems, it is **challenger parties** (rather than simply opposition parties) that are more likely to mobilize new, or previously ignored issues, in order to increase the importance of an issue that is most likely to split the majority coalition and thus sway voters in their favour. They refer to this strategy as issue entrepreneurship. Examples of issue entrepreneurship include green parties across Europe mobilizing environmental issues and radical right-wing parties mobilizing immigration concerns and Euroscepticism. These issues are all cross-cutting issues that can divide existing coalitions or even parties. Once an issue has been mobilized by a challenger party, they are likely capable of maintaining an advantage, or a degree of ownership over the issue, at least in the short to medium term. In the next section, we look closer at one example of such a cross-cutting issue that has been mobilized by challenger parties at both the national and European level, namely European integration.

9.4 Mobilizing the EU Issue

European integration is one of the clearest examples of a cross-cutting issue that challenger parties on both the left and the right of the political spectrum have mobilized (Hobolt and De Vries, 2015). As mainstream parties are on the whole pro-European, challenger parties on the fringes have had an opportunity to mobilize **Euroscepticism** in the population. The EU issue has been described as a major 'touchstone of dissent' with a clear potential to divide governing parties and coalitions (Taggart, 1998). As the power of the EU's supranational institutions has increased and the scope of EU jurisdictional authority has widened, European integration has become ever more contested within domestic politics in Europe, especially when politicized by challenger parties.

This has also led to tensions within parties on both the left and the right. For example, most centre-right parties, such as the People's Party for Freedom and Democracy (VVD) in the Netherlands, tend to favour market integration in Europe, but some are more reluctant to support the transfer of authority to supranational actors in other policy areas. For the Dutch Liberals, these internal divisions prompted Geert Wilders's successful split from the VVD and the creation of the Eurosceptic populist Party for Freedom (PVV). The rise of the PVV in the Netherlands in the mid-2000s illustrates how effective issue entrepreneurship can change the shape of party competition in a country (De Vries and Hobolt, 2020).

The issue of European integration had been largely ignored in Dutch politics until the early 2000s, but Wilders, a charismatic populist politician, changed this. He left the VVD party in 2004 over its position favouring Turkish accession to the EU, something which Wilders fiercely opposed. In 2006, he founded his own party, the Party for Freedom, on the back of a successful referendum campaign, *tourNEE* (a tour for NO) against the European Constitutional Treaty referendum the previous year. During the campaign, Wilders mobilized issues of sovereignty, national identity, and Turkish accession to the EU in order to drive a wedge within the constituencies of mainstream parties. The Constitutional Treaty was defeated by a sizeable majority of the Dutch electorate in a referendum in June 2005 (see Chapter 12), and Wilders's PVV went on to win 9 out of the 150 parliamentary seats in the subsequent parliamentary elections.

In many ways, the issue entrepreneurship of the PVV helped to reshape party competition in the Netherlands. It mobilized a new issue, European integration, making it salient to voters. Wilders's successful anti-European campaign combined with his anti-Islam and anti-immigration rhetoric would ultimately make the PVV the second largest force in Dutch parliament by 2017. Moreover, his Eurosceptic mobilization has caused rifts in the two largest mainstream parties, the liberal and social democratic parties, who tried to downplay the issue. Right-wing challenger parties, like the PVV and the Forum for Democracy, and the left-wing Socialist Party (SP) have changed Dutch politics by mainstreaming Eurosceptic sentiment and increasing the importance of European integration concerns in Dutch party politics and among Dutch voters. We can find similar examples across Europe where challenger parties have changed the nature of the political agenda and party competition by mobilizing a Eurosceptic message that has appealed to a segment of the electorate.

The mobilization of a Eurosceptic agenda by challenger parties happens not only at a national level, but also at a European level. In fact, studies have shown that European Parliament elections offer good opportunities for challenger parties to mobilize new or previously ignored issues and attract attention nationally (Hobolt and De Vries, 2016b; Schulte-Cloos, 2018). Since the European elections are **second order national elections** that do not lead to the formation of a national government, voters are often more willing to vote on the basis of specific issues that they feel strongly about. The EU issue in particular is ripe for mobilization in these elections where the question of further European integration is on the agenda. Consequently, voters are more likely to vote on the basis of their EU attitudes in European elections, and Eurosceptic challenger parties can use this to appeal to voters and to gain momentum nationally.

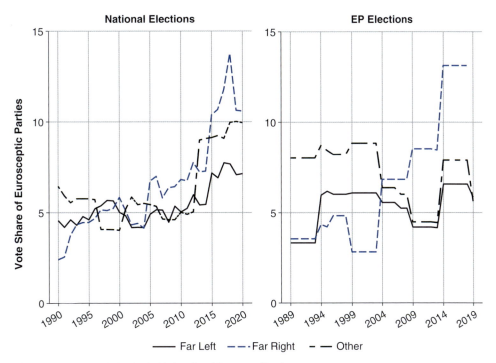

Figure 9.3 Eurosceptic Parties in National and European Elections

Data sources: The PopuList (Rooduijn et al., 2019) and ParlGov (Döring and Manow, 2019)

Figure 9.3 illustrates the rise of Eurosceptic parties in both national and European Parliament (EP) elections. This figure also demonstrates that Eurosceptic parties are primarily, but not exclusively, found on the fringes of the ideological spectrum. In the early 1990s, Eurosceptic parties attracted less than 15 per cent of the vote share in national and European parliament elections. By the end of the 2010s more than a quarter of voters would cast their ballot for a Eurosceptic party, and the rise of far-right parties that are opposed to European integration has been particularly pronounced at both the national and the European level.

In Chapter 1, the successes of Nigel Farage's UKIP (and the Brexit Party) and Le Pen's National Front in European elections were discussed as prominent examples. But many challenger parties have translated their successes in European Parliament elections into higher national voter shares. On the far right, the Alternative for Germany (AfD) and the Sweden Democrats have gained momentum from their successes in European Parliament elections to increase their vote share in subsequent national elections. Challenger parties on the left can also benefit from mobilizing a more Eurosceptic message in European elections, as illustrated by the Spanish left-wing populist Podemos that attracted attention nationally after winning seats in European elections on a platform critical of the EU's handling of the Euro crisis and its austerity agenda (Hobolt and Tilley, 2016). Pro-European mainstream parties have struggled to respond to challengers' success on the European integration issue. This has created space for pro-European challenger parties, such as Green parties, to successfully appeal to the pro-European electorate.

These examples of the mobilization of the EU issue demonstrate that a one-dimensional spatial model cannot fully capture party competition in Europe. Issue entrepreneurship, such as that which mobilizes Eurosceptic voters, can explain why parties on the fringes of the left–right dimension can attract more voters when the EU issue is salient to the electorate. Issue competition theory thus challenges three assumptions of the spatial model: that party competition can be reduced to a single dimension, that voter preferences and priorities are entirely exogenous to party strategies, and that voting behaviour is driven by policy preferences alone. The last of these assumptions—the primacy of policy preferences over non-policy preferences—is also the focus of **valence models** of party competition, to which we now turn our attention.

9.5 Valence Models of Party Competition

Much of the work on party competition has focused on the **spatial competition** between parties on matters of policy position. Yet, as we discussed in Chapter 5 on vote choices, policy preferences are not the only thing about parties that voters care about. In his critique of spatial models of party competition, Stokes (1963) argued that voters care as much about **valence issues** as they care about positional issues. Whereas positional issues involve ideological competition along the left–right dimension, valence issues are those about which a broad consensus exists and where the question thus becomes 'which party is best to deliver?' Such issues thus include voters' evaluation of policy management, leadership quality, delivery, and competence. To account for observation that both policy and non-policy characteristics matter to voters, Adams et al. (2005) have proposed a unified model of party competition that incorporates non-policy characteristics into the spatial modelling framework. Their model shows that when non-policy-characteristics—such as party loyalty and leadership evaluations—are incorporated into the spatial model, parties are not necessarily incentivized to converge ideologically, as they may seek to appeal on policy grounds to voters who are biased against them for non-policy reasons.

To give an example of the difference between spatial and **valence competition**, a voter may choose Party A because the party has promised to raise taxes to spend more on healthcare, whereas Party B wishes to cut taxes and reduce spending on healthcare. That is a choice that can be thought of in spatial terms with Party A to the left of Party B. Yet, the same voter may not be concerned with different positions on the healthcare and taxation issue, but rather which party is seen as more competent in delivering public services. In the second scenario, voter evaluations may be based on an evaluation of past performance (retrospective voting, see Chapter 5), leadership evaluations, and perceptions of competence, rather than an ideological choice between different policy options.

Numerous studies of elections have shown that valence issues are highly important to party competition and to political choice. Political debate often centres on consensual issues on which there is agreement across politics, such as lower crime, better schools, or economic growth. When such issues are debated, valence attributes such as perceived competence and leadership qualities can matter greatly (Green and Jennings, 2017). Particularly when the major parties converge ideologically, valence issues have been shown to matter more, as voters will care more about who is the most competent manager of the economy, of social

welfare provision, education, etc., when there are few differences between their policy positions on these issues (Green and Hobolt, 2008). Studies have also shown that leadership
characteristics and evaluations are an important driver of voter choice. For example, Bittner
(2011) has demonstrated that leaders' traits matter to voters, but that not all traits are equally
important and not all leaders are evaluated according to the same criteria. In particular, her
findings suggest that voter evaluations of leaders' character seem more important than those
of leaders' competence.

Parties therefore compete not only by offering policy platforms that are most closely
aligned with the voters' policy preferences, but also by presenting themselves as the most
competent and trustworthy. While established mainstream parties often have a distinct advantage when it comes to presenting themselves as competent and experienced, an alternative electoral strategy is to appeal to voters using populist anti-establishment rhetoric. Such
a strategy is more likely to be adopted by challenger parties, outside government, as parties
that have been in office can more easily be blamed for problems and grievances and it is far
easier to paint them as dishonest or even corrupt than parties that have never held office.
Studies of party competition have shown that anti-establishment political rhetoric can be an
effective way to attract voters, not by offering alternative policy positions to dominant parties, but by questioning the integrity and competence of the political establishment to serve
the interests of the people they are meant to serve. Such a strategy is more likely to succeed
if voters already harbour doubts about the ability of mainstream parties to deliver on their
promises, and if voter attachments to such parties have already weakened (De Vries and
Hobolt, 2020). Yet, it is more difficult for parties that are in government or that have recently
governed to credibly present themselves as anti-establishment. This raises questions about
what options are available to mainstream parties in Europe as they come under attack from
challenger parties on the left and the right. This is discussed in the next section.

9.6 Responses of Mainstream Parties to Challengers

This chapter has discussed that challenger parties can mobilize the European integration issue. In Chapter 8, we furthermore explored the rise of non-mainstream parties,
such as populist, radical right, green, radical left, and other challenger parties in recent
decades. As the dominance of mainstream parties has been tested by challenger parties
across Europe, there is a growing literature not only on the strategies of challenger parties,
but also on how mainstream parties should best respond. In interacting with challengers,
mainstream parties are faced with a strategic decision: should they ignore these parties
and their demands, coopt the parties' positions, or take a completely opposing position?
In her important work on **niche parties**, Meguid (2008) has referred to the three available
strategies for mainstream parties to respond to niche parties which can be easily applied
to challenger parties as well:

1. **Accommodative strategy**: involves mainstream parties adopting a similar strategy to
   the challenger parties in a hope to draw voters away from a threatening competitor.
2. **Adversarial strategy**: involves mainstream parties competing with the challenger parties
   by adopting an opposing position on an issue mobilized by challenger parties.

3. **Dismissive strategy**: involves mainstream parties seeking to ignore the issue mobilized
   by the challenger party. By not taking a position, the mainstream party signals to voters
   that the issue lacks merit.

The accommodative strategy is in line with the simple Downsian model: if the challenger
party position is preferred by the median voter, this model would tell us that mainstream parties should move towards that position to recapture lost voters. An example of this strategy
might be how the success of radical right-wing parties has encouraged some mainstream
parties, on the left and on the right, to shift their positions to the right along the socially conservative axis, e.g. by adopting more anti-immigration positions. Based on a proximity-voting
perspective, it may be argued that, if the median voter is immigration-sceptical, the best way
to win back voters from the radical right is to adopt similar positions.

Yet, there are reasons why the accommodative strategy may not succeed. First, when party
competition is multidimensional, little may be gained from highlighting the issues where
challengers have gained an advantage by raising the issue first, and hence gaining issue ownership in the short to medium run (De Vries and Hobolt, 2020). From the perspective of issue
ownership, the recommendation would therefore be to downplay the issue and highlight
issues that are 'owned' by the mainstream parties, e.g. issues more aligned with economic
left–right positions. If voters are persuaded that the challenger party's issue is not highly salient, this will matter less in the ballot box, even if voters agree with the position adopted
by challenger parties. Hence, even though a dismissive strategy does not challenge the dis-
tinctiveness or ownership of the niche party's issue position, its salience-reducing effect will
allow mainstream parties to win back voters from challenger parties.

Secondly, even when radical right-wing parties, and other challengers, become successful, that does not imply that their issue positions are shared by a majority of the electorate.
Hence, if mainstream parties shift to the right on, say, immigration to win back radical right-
wing voters, they may lose other traditional supporters who do not agree with the new culturally conservative positions. For example, studies have shown that social democratic parties
seeking to win back their traditional working-class worker base by moving to the right on immigration, may lose part of their more socially progressive supporter based of more educated
professionals (Abou-Chadi and Wagner, 2019, 2020). Hence, an accommodative strategy can
be risky for mainstream parties. If the dismissive strategy is not an option, because the issue
remains high on the political agenda, mainstream parties may therefore also compete by
adopting an adversarial strategy, competing with challenger parties by adopting the opposite
position. This can be a risky strategy if the median voter is close to the position of a challenger
party. However, where the public is more polarized, mainstream parties may win some voters
while losing others. Moreover, many studies of public opinion formation have shown that
voter preferences can be shaped by the position taken by parties. This is sometimes referred
to as **cue-taking**. If voters trust mainstream parties, they may shift their own position in the
direction of that of the mainstream party if the mainstream party adopts a clear adversarial
strategy. In our immigration example, the strategy would be to persuade voters who were
immigration-sceptical about the benefits of immigration by taking a clear pro-immigration
stance. While this goes against the basic assumption of the spatial model that voter preferences cannot be shifted by party positions, there is evidence to suggest that political elites can
influence the positions of voters (e.g. Brader et al., 2020). Nonetheless, an adversarial strategy

is obviously particularly precarious if party leaders go against most of their own supporters. Taken together, the theoretical models of party competition—spatial, issue ownership, and other valence models—do not suggest a clear pathway for mainstream parties responding to challenger parties. However, the insights from both spatial, issue, and other valence models of party competition clearly highlight the dilemmas faced by European mainstream parties as they navigate challenges from niche parties on the left and on the right.

9.7 Summary

Party systems are often described in terms of the number of parties and their size (fragmentation) as well as the ideological polarization on a single dimension. But this information only offers a cursory glance at the interaction between parties as they compete for votes and office. A uni-dimensional spatial model offers a starting point for understanding party competition, but this chapter has shown that the dynamics of party competition in Europe often differ from the expectations of spatial models in important ways. In almost all European party systems, multiple parties compete on multiple dimensions. And voters care about party and politician attributes that go beyond simple policy positions. The appeal of populist rhetoric and charismatic leaders underlines that party competition is not only about diverging policy positions, but also about non-policy characteristics such as competence and leaderships traits. Moreover, parties can shape the issues that voters care about by highlighting them and raising their importance for electoral competition. Both challenger parties as well as external events can raise the salience of new issues, such as immigration and Euroscepticism. Relaxing some of the strict assumptions of the spatial model makes it more difficult to precisely predict and explain party strategies and electoral behaviour; however, incorporating insights from valence and issue competition models also provides a more nuanced and often more accurate picture of party competition in Europe.

Online Data Exercise: The Parliamentary Speech Dataset (ParlSpeech) Dataset

The interactive online exercise introduces a text corpus of translated parliamentary speeches in selected European parliaments. You will perform your own automated text analysis by creating a dictionary in order to estimate party positions according to the word usage of politically opposed categories, e.g. environmental protection versus economic growth. By designing your own dictionaries, you can explore which words make up the substantial policy dimension underlying political conflict.

Take your learning further with this interactive data exercise, available at
 www.foundationsofeuropeanpolitics.com

For additional material and resources, including multiple-choice questions, web links, and more, please visit the online resources: **www.oup.com/he/devries1e**

Part 4

Governments and Policy

10 Political Systems and Government Formation

This chapter examines executive branch politics in European democracies. It explores the nature of parliamentary democracy and compares it with other forms of democracy such as separation-of-powers systems using the principal–agent framework discussed in Chapter 2. The chapter looks closely at the link between parties and institutions to understand the processes of both government formation and collapse. It provides an important foundation for understanding the process of law-making, which is explored in much greater depth in Chapter 11.

Citizens in Europe cast votes for political parties, but in most instances those votes do not immediately translate into choosing executives. Most governments in Europe are formed in post-election bargaining between parliamentary parties, and how votes translate into executive power for elected politicians varies significantly across political systems. These relationships are governed by national constitutions and electoral laws, and are mediated by parties. In this chapter, we examine the differences between the national systems of European democracies as well as the political system of the European Union. In the second part of the chapter, we examine the process of building governments and choosing executives in Europe, both at the national level and at the EU level.

10.1 Institutional Variation of Democracy in Europe

Representative democracy varies across different types of political systems. At the most basic level, we can distinguish systems according to a) whom voters elect, and b) what the relationship is between the parliament and the government. We can classify democracies into three basic regime types: parliamentary systems, presidential systems, and semi-presidential systems. Cheibub et al. (2010) provide clear instructions for distinguishing between these three types using two questions: 1) is the government responsible to parliament? and 2) is there a head of state who is popularly elected for a fixed term? A negative answer to the first question leads to a classification of democracy as a presidential system. If the answer is positive, then the answer to the second question determines whether a system is considered semi-presidential (if the answer is yes) or parliamentary (if the answer is no). We will discuss these three types in more detail.

Parliamentary systems are political systems where the formation of governments (the executive branch) occurs within parliament. The head of government (chief executive) in a parliamentary system, called the prime minister or chancellor, needs the support of a parliamentary majority. Once elected by voters, the parliament either formally elects the prime minister in what is known as an **investiture vote**, or the head of state appoints a prime minister who needs (at least the implicit) support of a parliamentary majority. The prime minister and the ministers responsible for specific policy portfolios, such as finance, foreign affairs, or the environment, make up the **cabinet**. If parliament is unhappy with the cabinet's performance, the parliament can recall the government through a **vote of no confidence**. If a government loses a vote of no confidence, it resigns and a new government that can command a parliamentary majority may form, or, sometimes if no new government is possible, new elections are called. In some countries, the constitution requires that parliament nominate a prospective replacement candidate for prime minister when calling a vote of no confidence. Such a **constructive vote of no confidence** was originally introduced in the German constitution following the Second World War, after the negative experiences of government instability during the Weimar Republic—the period immediately following the First World War prior to the Nazi regime taking power. During this period, polarized parliamentary majorities could agree to vote down the government using a vote of no confidence, but were unable to agree on a successor for chancellor. The requirement to nominate a successor thus increases government stability in parliamentary democracies. Today, this variant of the vote of no confidence also exists in Belgium, Hungary, Poland, Slovenia, and Spain.

The head of government can also ask the parliament to express its confidence in the government through a **vote of confidence**. A prime minister can use this tool to discipline a parliamentary majority that is threatening not to vote in line with the government, and such votes can sometimes be tied to a particular legislative bill. If, however, a parliamentary majority does not express confidence in the prime minister, the government resigns. In such instances, the constitution often determines whether early elections are called or whether and how a new government may form. Sometimes, a prime minister can also force an early election or ask the head of state to dissolve parliament. Parliamentary systems are thus characterized by a mutual dependence (Stepan and Skach, 1993, 3) between parliament and the government. Sixteen countries in Europe are parliamentary systems. In these countries, voters participate in parliamentary elections, but are unable to vote directly for the chief executive.

Parliamentary systems in Europe are either **republics** or **constitutional monarchies**. The difference relates to the choice of the head of state. The head of state in a parliamentary system is not the chief executive: instead, the head of state holds a largely ceremonial position, representing the country as a whole without getting involved in daily political decisions. In parliamentary systems that are republics, the head of state is indirectly elected (as in Germany) by parliament and called president. Most parliamentary systems in Europe are such republics. In constitutional monarchies, the head of state is a hereditary monarch, as in Belgium, Denmark, Luxembourg, Netherlands, Norway, Spain, Sweden, and the United Kingdom. The role of the head of state (president or monarch) becomes political only in rare instances that are constitutionally well-defined. For instance, the head of government (prime minister or chancellor) oftentimes requires the consent of the head of state in a parliamentary system to dissolve parliament and force new elections. As we will demonstrate later, the head of state in parliamentary systems also may play a political role when new governments are formed.

Presidential systems offer an alternative form of democratic governance, characterized by a 'mutual independence' (Stepan and Skach, 1993) between parliament and the executive (the president). Citizens participate in two elections: the parliamentary election which determines which candidates and parties represent the country in the legislature, and the presidential election which determines the chief executive. The parliament and the president thus have two separate electoral mandates and their own legitimacy. They are independent from one another: neither can the president dissolve parliament, nor can the parliament recall the president—at least not for purely political reasons. The most well-known presidential democracy is the United States of America. In Europe, Cyprus has adopted a presidential political system. And according to the classification scheme by Cheibub et al. (2010), Switzerland also should be considered a presidential system. However, Switzerland differs from the other countries in the sense that parliament delegates executive power to a collective government, composed of representatives of several parliamentary parties, for a fixed term in office. Parliament elects this government, composed of seven individuals representing different parties, regions, and linguistic backgrounds, at the start of a parliamentary term. But once elected, the government is not responsible to parliament and cannot be recalled. Nor can the government dissolve the parliament and call for new elections.

Finally, several political systems in Europe are **semi-presidential**. As the term suggests, these systems combine elements of parliamentarism and presidentialism. Whereas earlier definitions of semi-presidentialism emphasized the power of the presidency vis-à-vis parliament (Duverger, 1970), there is nowadays a scholarly consensus that such systems are characterized by a popularly elected president with a fixed term who exists alongside a prime minister and cabinet who are responsible to a legislative majority in parliament (Elgie, 1999; Cheibub et al., 2010). Using this purely constitutional definition, thirteen countries in the EU can be considered semi-presidential: Austria, Bulgaria, Croatia, Czech Republic, Finland, France, Ireland, Lithuania, Poland, Portugal, Romania, Slovakia, and Slovenia. Mixed systems thus have two institutions with popular legitimacy: the presidency and the parliament. There is less consensus over the extent to which such systems, however, actually embolden a president over parliament. Instead, the powers of presidents over the executive vary significantly (Schleiter and Morgan-Jones, 2010). Some countries, for example, combine a rather weak president with a strong prime minister; these include Austria, Ireland, and Slovenia. In these countries, the president has limited input into the legislative process and cannot block bills. France has experienced phases in which the president and the prime ministers come from opposing political parties, and in these instances power has shifted from the president to the prime minister. Some research suggests that heads of state in parliamentary systems can sometimes be more powerful than directly elected presidents in mixed systems (Tavits, 2009). Other scholars, however, have pointed out that semi-presidentialism may affect the way in which political parties operate. If the pursuit of the popularly elected presidency is important for political parties, they may become 'presidentialized'. This means that parties delegate more discretion to party leaders so that these leaders can campaign for, and possibly win, presidential elections. If a party leader wins the presidency, the party may have even fewer levers of control over the leader because they now have a fixed term in office, making it very difficult to remove them as president or party leader during the course of their term (Samuels and Shugart, 2010). This may set semi-presidential parties apart from parties in parliamentary systems, where prime ministers, and thus party leaders, can be recalled by the legislative majority at any time during the legislative term. Table 10.1 shows which countries in Europe are parliamentary, presidential, or semi-presidential, as well as whether they are a republic or a constitutional monarchy.

A natural question emerging from the classification of democratic political systems is whether any one system can be considered 'better' than the others. This debate was prominent in the 1990s following the fall of communism in which newly independent states in central and eastern Europe had to choose between democratic regime types. For some scholars like Linz (1990), parliamentary systems are less prone to instability than presidential systems. He argued that they emphasize the representation of a wide array of interests

Table 10.1 Political Systems in Europe

Country	Monarchy or republic	Head of state	Head of government
Parliamentary Systems			
Belgium	Constitutional monarchy	Monarch	Prime Minister
Denmark	Constitutional monarchy	Monarch	Minister of State
Estonia	Republic	President	Head Minister
Germany	Republic	Federal President	Federal Chancellor
Greece	Republic	President	Prime Minister
Hungary	Republic	President of the Republic	Minister-President
Italy	Republic	President	President of the Council of Ministers
Latvia	Republic	President	Minister-President
Luxembourg	Constitutional monarchy	Grand Duke	Prime Minister
Malta	Republic	President	Prime Minister
Netherlands	Constitutional monarchy	Monarch	Minister-President
Norway	Constitutional monarchy	Monarch	Prime Minister
Spain	Constitutional monarchy	Monarch	President of the Government
Sweden	Constitutional monarchy	Monarch	Minister of the State
United Kingdom	Constitutional monarchy	Monarch	Prime Minister
Presidential Systems			
Cyprus	Republic	President	
Switzerland	Republic	Federal Council	
Semi-Presidential Systems			
Austria	Republic	Federal President	Federal Chancellor
Bulgaria	Republic	President	Minister-Chairman
Croatia	Republic	President of the Republic	President of the Government
Czech Republic	Republic	President	Chairman of the Government
Finland	Republic	President	Head Minister
France	Republic	President	Prime Minister
Iceland	Republic	President	Prime Minister
Ireland	Republic	President	Taoiseach
Lithuania	Republic	President	Minister-President
Poland	Republic	President	President of the Council of Ministers
Portugal	Republic	President	Prime Minister
Romania	Republic	President	Prime Minister
Slovakia	Republic	President	Chairman of the Government
Slovenia	Republic	President	President of the Government

in parliament over a winner-takes-all approach to power. Moreover, because governments form within the parliament and are responsible to it, it is possible to get rid of poorly performing governments quickly: governments fall if they no longer possess the confidence of a parliamentary majority. Such fusion of power between government and parliament may lead to less instability of the political system as a whole, because conflict between parliament and the government can be resolved in a constitutional manner. In contrast, Linz identified the two separate fixed-term electoral mandates of parliament and the president in a presidential system as the main cause for instability, as there is no constitutional mechanism (other than impeachment, which is a legal procedure, or resignation) in place to resolve conflicts between the two branches when both can claim to represent the will of the people. A resolution may only be possible through extra-constitutional processes, such as a coup.

Critics of Linz's argument, such as Horowitz (1990), have pointed out that winner-takes-all politics is more a function of the electoral system rather than just the regime type, thus the relationship is at a minimum a conditional one. Similarly, other scholars such as Shugart and Carey (1992) and Mainwaring (1993) made important contributions to this debate, pointing out that the institutional variation within each regime type is high and it is of utmost importance to consider the particular arrangements to understand whether they lead to instability. For instance, strong legislative powers granted by the constitution to the president, such as veto powers or the right to make amendments to legislation, may reinforce the conflict between the parliament and the president.

Finally, another important variable in this debate is the role of political parties. Parties are strengthened in a system that emphasizes coalitions and consensus, something we return to later in this chapter when talking about government formation. Presidential systems, on the other hand, focus on a separation of powers. They emphasize institutionalized checks and balances of the parliament and the presidency, with both being able to monitor the other. Election results are usually clear, as the chief executive is an individual who has received a popular majority. Presidential systems thus foster more personalization of politics (Linz, 1990).

10.2 The Political System of the EU: A Mixed System

While using the typology from Cheibub et al. (2010) to classify regime types of countries is straightforward, scholars have struggled to do the same with the political system of the EU. In contrast to a national political system, the EU has a dual executive: executive authority is shared between a supranational executive in the form of the European Commission and the national governments of EU member states represented in the European Council. The reason for this dual executive is that, while member states have delegated policy-making authority to the EU, they have only done so in specific policy areas. For instance, while the European Commission is responsible for all EU trade negotiations on behalf of the member states, the European Commission does not have sole authority to set the foreign policy of the EU. The dual executive means that there is no single individual who functions as the equivalent of a prime minister or president. Instead there is one President of the European Commission and another President of the European Council. The former is chosen by the member state governments, but must also have the support of the European Parliament whose members are directly elected by European voters in European-wide elections held once every five years. The latter is simply chosen by the heads of government.

Figure 10.1 shows the chain of delegation in the EU as well as its shared executive. Voters in each EU member state elect (at least) two parliaments: they cast votes for national parties in national parliamentary elections and European Parliament elections. In parliamentary systems, parties in the national parliament form the government, and the prime minister as head of government automatically becomes a member of the European Council. In some semi-presidential systems (such as in France, Lithuania, and Romania) and in presidential systems (Cyprus), the directly elected president joins the meetings of the European Council. In both cases, national governments are furthermore represented in the Council of the EU via cabinet ministers responsible for the particular policy jurisdiction under consideration. The European Council (heads of government) and Council of the EU (ministers) jointly represent member state interests. The selection of the Commission presidency is then an interplay between the European Council and the European Parliament. The European Council proposes a candidate by qualified majority who needs to gain majority support in the European Parliament before taking office. This is comparable to a prime ministerial appointment procedure in parliamentary system, but with the involvement of two legislative chambers. In sum, while voters remain the ultimate principals, some EU institutions are more directly responsible to member state governments (e.g. the Council of the European Union) while others have a shorter chain of delegation leading directly to voters (the European Parliament).

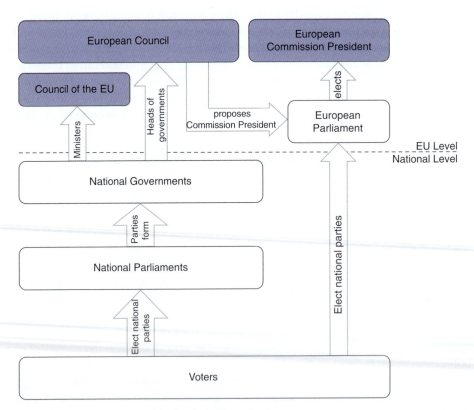

Figure 10.1 The Political System of the EU: Shared Executive Power

Although there is no directly elected president in the EU, several aspects of the EU system nevertheless suggest that the EU is structured along elements of a separation-of-powers system. The European Parliament cannot elect a Commission President on its own, but it formally requires the support of the national governments who propose a candidate to the parliament. Importantly, just like in a presidential system, the President of the Commission cannot ask for a confidence vote and dissolve parliament. The electoral mandates of the Commission and the Parliament are thus more independent than they are in a parliamentary system. At the same time, the EU does have features of parliamentary democracy: the supra-national executive in the form of the President of the Commission is not directly elected, but rather elected by an absolute majority in the European Parliament together with a qualified majority in the European Council. Moreover, the European Parliament can express its lack of confidence in the Commission through a so-called motion of censure, which is adopted if it secures a two-thirds majority of the votes cast, representing a majority of the members of the European Parliament. In short, the mixed political system of the EU puts a strong emphasis on consensus-seeking within and across chambers (European Council, Council, and Parliament).

10.3 Government Formation at the National Level

National governments play an important role in European politics: both domestically as well as at the EU level. It is thus important to understand how they form and how they work. This section deals with government formation in parliamentary democracies, the most common regime type in Europe, whereas the next chapter provides analytical tools for understanding how governments make policy.

Consider the parliamentary election in the Netherlands in 2017. On 15 March 2017, Dutch voters went to the polls to elect a new Tweede Kamer der Staten-Generaal, the House of Representatives. A more fragmented party system in combination with a highly proportional electoral system meant that thirteen parties gained seats in parliament, bringing the effective number of parties in parliament to a record-breaking 8.1 parties. Once the votes were counted, it became apparent that voters had punished the People's Party for Freedom and Democracy (VVD), the party of Prime Minister Mark Rutte. However, with just above 21 per cent of the votes, his party was able to remain the largest party in parliament in 2017. The election result meant that any future government would have to rely on at least four parties to form a coalition government that would obtain a majority in parliament. Negotiations were difficult and various options were explored. Eventually, 225 days after the election, the liberal VVD together with the Christian Democratic Appeal (CDA), the Democrats 66 (D66), and the Christian Union (CU) agreed to form a centre-right coalition government. These coalition negotiations set a new record for the longest government formation in Dutch history.

Drawn out and difficult government coalition negotiations are not unheard of elsewhere in Europe. In fact, lengthy talks are the norm in Belgium, where a highly fragmented party system—a function of linguistic, geographic, and ideological differences—makes negotiations over forming governments particularly fraught. For instance, after the elections in 2010, it took Belgian parties more than one year and half to form a government, setting the overall record for coalition bargaining in a parliamentary democracy. The United Kingdom, in contrast, has often represented the other extreme. With one party typically winning a majority of seats, the nature of the next British government is typically known within hours of the polls closing. However, even the UK is not immune to negotiations over who joins government. Following both the 2010 and 2017 elections, the Conservatives became the largest party, but failed to win a majority of seats in parliament. They had to negotiate deals with other parties in order to effectively govern. In 2010, they entered a coalition with the Liberal Democrats, and in 2017 they formed a **minority government**—a government controlling less than a majority of seats—supported by a small Northern Irish party, the Democratic Unionist Party (DUP).

These tales of post-election bargaining illuminate a basic truth of multiparty politics in Europe. When more than two parties win seats in parliament following an election (generally the case in parliaments across Europe), there is no guarantee that one party will win a majority of seats in parliament. And when no party controls a majority of seats, a party that wishes to govern must strike a deal of some sort with other parties so together they command a majority of votes, at least implicitly, and can pass a policy programme.

All European countries eventually need to form governments that can command a majority in parliament to pass policies. This may include governments that do not rely on a stable majority on their own, but need to seek the support from opposition parties to legislate. Moreover, no European parliament in the post-war period has ever had only two parliamentary parties holding seats. Even the UK in the immediate post-war years, with its strong two-party system dominated by the Conservatives and Labour Party, a third party often won a handful of seats, namely the small Liberal Party, which later merged into the Liberal Democrats. In more recent years, regionalist parties (the Scottish Nationalists, the Welsh Plaid Cymru, and several Northern Irish parties) along with the Greens and the United Kingdom Independence Party (UKIP) have also held seats.

In an assembly with only two parties and an odd number of legislators (like the United States House of Representatives), a majority for one party is guaranteed to exist, but once there are more than two parties, the possibility always exists that no party gains an outright majority of seats in parliament, requiring bargaining amongst parties to create a government, possibly consisting of a coalition of parties. In some countries, such bargaining is the norm (e.g. Belgium) while in others it is the exception (e.g. the UK), but as the British elections of 2010 and 2017 demonstrated, it is possible everywhere.

There are two questions we must examine with respect to coalition negotiation and government formation. The first is which parties enter government, and the second is, conditional upon entering government, what are the responsibilities of each governing partner? The first question is more about the overall composition of government—how many parties join the government and which parties are they? The second question is more about what each of those parties gets out of the deal. Which government ministries does each party control? We will discuss the set of questions about the overall composition of government first.

10.4 Types of Government Coalitions

After a parliamentary election, the party receiving the largest number of votes is often touted in the press as the winner of the campaign. But to enter government parties do not necessarily need to win more votes than any other party, although being the biggest party certainly helps. Parties need to place themselves in a good position to form a coalition with multiple parties. In addition to the size of each party, ideology matters (Martin and Stevenson, 2001). Parties with ideological platforms that allow them to coalesce and cooperate with multiple other parties are more likely to be included in a coalition government. The formation of government is a process that starts with an election, but does not end there. It involves a series of negotiations among parties that can involve a number of formal and informal rules and processes that vary across countries. We first discuss the role of party size and ideology and then take a closer look at the role of institutions.

To examine the relative importance of size and ideological positioning, consider the German Christian Democrats (CDU/CSU) and the Free Democratic Party (FDP). The German Christian Democrats have been the largest party in the German Bundestag for the vast majority of time since the first election in 1949. And for much of that period, the German chancellor was a Christian Democrat, as well. Because there are no term limits, chancellors can have long-lasting terms as chief executive: Chancellor Helmut Kohl was in power from 1982 until 1998, more than sixteen years and twice as long as a single US president can be in office. Angela Merkel, the first female chancellor of Germany and also a member of the CDU, has been in power for more than fifteen years. In the first seventy years since the adoption of the German constitution (1949–2019), the Christian Democrats were in government for an astonishing fifty years.

Compare this history to the small Free Democratic Party. The FDP has never won more than 15 per cent of the vote in any election since 1949, and over those elections it has averaged only roughly 9 per cent of the vote. However, even though it is much smaller than the CDU/CSU, the party has served in government for forty-five of the first seventy years, longer than any party except for the CDU/CSU. In fact, the FDP has participated in government with its own cabinet ministers for significantly longer than the much larger Social Democratic Party (SPD), which was in government for thirty-three of those seventy years. So how did the small FDP manage to hold such an influential position in German politics for so long, despite its small size? The answer lies in its ideological position relative to the other parties. It is known as a liberal party, espousing small government, free market views with regard to the economy, and supporting civil liberties and personal freedoms on social issues. Its support of free markets and lower taxes has made it an attractive partner to the centre-right Christian Democrats, and its socially progressive politics has made it a viable partner for the Social Democrats, as well.

If both party size (measured by the number of seats a party controls in parliament) and ideology matter for who gets into government, then the next question is when and why do they matter. To answer this question, we need to think more systematically about coalition formation and consider what drives parties to enter government, and whether there might even be times when parties prefer to stay out of government.

Researchers who study coalition formation have tended to argue that there are two considerations that politicians make when deciding whether their party should enter government. We will term the first consideration the 'benefits of office' and the second we will call 'policy' (Müller and Strøm, 1999). When politicians enter political office, they receive certain material benefits, often related to prestige of holding office. Cabinet positions are among the best paid political offices in Europe, and parties can give such positions to party members, rewarding them for their contributions to the electoral success of the party. In addition to the regular trappings—chauffeurs, nice offices, and the opportunity to allocate other positions to fellow party members—office benefits may also include greater access to the press and appearances on the world stage. Politicians may seek office to acquire these benefits and the prestige associated with holding office. We call this sort of motivation 'office-seeking'. For office-seeking politicians and parties, the drive to hold office comes first. Politics is viewed as a zero-sum game in which the fixed payoffs (office) have to be shared. Office-seeking parties are willing to sacrifice policy goals to win more seats and occupy more offices.

The story typically goes that office-seeking politicians do not wish to share the spoils of office, and certainly not with politicians from other parties. Thus, if we assume that politicians are primarily office-seeking, we can hypothesize that a party with a majority of seats will form a 'single-party majority' government. If no party controls a majority in parliament, the governing coalitions that form from an office-seeking perspective should include the smallest number of parties possible to secure a majority of seats, and no additional parties. Political scientists have termed this type of coalition as **minimal winning**, meaning that if any one of the parties in the coalition were to drop out, the parties in the coalition would no longer control a majority of seats in the parliament. There is no guarantee that an election would produce only one minimal winning coalition, and in multiparty systems, there are often several potential coalitions that would be minimal winning. Out of all minimal winning coalitions, the one that has the lowest number of surplus seats is known as the minimum winning coalition.

When we look at what governments actually form in Europe, then single-party majority governments and minimal winning coalitions only constitute around half of all governments since 1945. What are the remaining types of government? First, there are coalitions that include more parties than necessary, so-called **surplus majority** governments or oversized coalitions. These governments are oversized in the sense that, even if one of the coalition parties were to withdraw support, the coalition would still be able to muster a majority. These make up roughly 23 per cent of all European governments since 1945. Finally, almost 30 per cent of governments are so-called **minority governments**. These are either single-party or coalition governments that do not possess a parliamentary majority. They govern by forming ad-hoc coalitions with parties outside of government or by gaining the support of one or more opposition parties on key legislative votes. Figure 10.2 shows the frequency by which

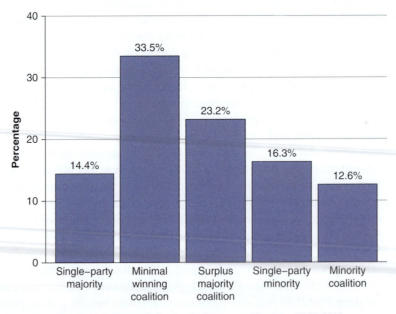

Figure 10.2 Government Types in Europe Following Parliamentary Elections, 1945–2019

Data source: ParlGov (Döring and Manow, 2019)

all of these different types of governments occur in Europe. Minimal winning coalitions are by far the most common government type, followed by surplus majority coalitions. Minority governments have occurred after about every third election. Single-party majority governments are the least common type in Europe.

10.5 Coalition Formation with Policy-Seeking Parties

Given that only one in three governments is a formal minimal winning coalition, office-seeking explanations do not seem to capture the whole story of government formation. We know that politicians care about more than just the spoils of office. The notion of minimum winning coalitions suggests that seat shares in parliament are the only thing that matters. This is not the case; politicians also care about policy. In fact, policy concerns and interests are often what drive people to participate in politics in the first place. Parties and the politicians in them likely seek office to implement policies that they think will make the country (or at least their voters) better off. We can assume that these politicians are 'policy-seeking'. If we view parties as primarily policy-seeking, it would be hard to envision a radical right party forming a government with strident communists, even if seat shares meant that they could form a minimal winning coalition. They would never be able to agree on what their government should do. If we want to understand, or even predict, which coalitions form, we need to take ideology into account. We need to think about where parties lie in an ideological space, as we did back in Chapter 2.

We can line parties up according to their ideological stances from left to right. And having done so, we might predict that only parties that lie next to each other in the space will form a government together. We can look for 'minimal winning connected coalitions'—those minimum winning coalitions that are formed by parties that lie next to each other in the ideological space.

Figure 10.3 presents a simplified one-dimensional left–right space of the Dutch party system following the 2017 elections. Thirteen parties received representation in the parliament. Below the position of each party is the seat share of the party in parliament. The actual government coalition that formed was composed of the VVD, CDA, D66, and CU. This government formed only after an alternative coalition negotiation failed: a coalition between the VVD, CDA, D66 and the Green party Groen Links. This coalition would also have constituted a minimal winning coalition. If we presume that the distances between the parties in the figure are an expression of their ideological differences, then this alternative coalition would have actually included a more diverse set of positions, as the distance between the most extreme parties in the coalition, the VVD and the Groen Links, is larger than that between the VVD and the CU in the actual coalition that formed. Additionally, the figure indicates which majority coalition could have been formed as a centre-left alternative without the largest party, the VVD, and without the two populist radical right parties, the PVV led by Geert Wilders and the FvD led by Thierry Baudet. Only an eight-party coalition ranging from the far left to the centre could have mustered sufficient votes in parliament to do so. However, having so many parties in a coalition would have been a novelty in Dutch parliamentary history. Also, it would have been less clear under which leadership such a coalition would form given that both CDA and D66, were equally strong in parliament.

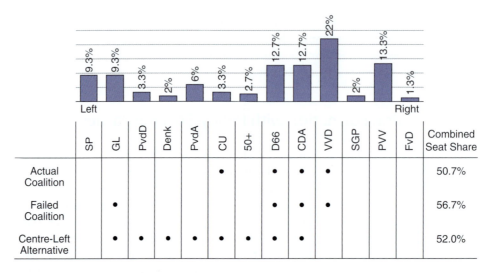

	SP	GL	PvdD	Denk	PvdA	CU	50+	D66	CDA	VVD	SGP	PVV	FvD	Combined Seat Share
Actual Coalition						•		•	•	•				50.7%
Failed Coalition		•						•	•	•				56.7%
Centre-Left Alternative	•	•	•	•	•	•		•	•					52.0%

Figure 10.3 Ideology and Coalition Formation in the Netherlands, 2017

Now imagine a slightly different scenario. The ideological positions shown in the figure make clear that the ideological range of the actual coalition government includes the positions of an opposition party: the seniors' party 50Plus. From a policy-seeking perspective, the parties in the minimal winning coalition have no ideological basis for excluding this party—it should want more or less what all of the other parties in the coalition want. But one could argue that it might be rational to exclude it on the basis of an office-seeking assumption, as the two large parties now would have to give up some ministerial positions to a third party. If the coalition had included 50Plus, the government would now possess a surplus majority—it would have more parties in it than are absolutely necessary to pass legislation. There may be occasions when having an oversized government is beneficial. Imagine that one of the larger parties in our coalition has an internal division on a policy issue—perhaps more centrist and more extreme members cannot always agree (we represent parties on our line as a single point, but we can think about that point as the average position of all the members in that party). If a government cannot always count on the votes of some of its MPs, having an extra party in government as an insurance policy may not be such a bad idea. Alternatively, sometimes the inclusion of an extra party has legislative benefits. For instance, in Hungary, the national conservative ruling party Fidesz (Hungarian Civic Union) has been in a political alliance with the smaller Christian Democratic People's Party (KDNP). Together, the two parties have been able to form a surplus majority government with a two-thirds parliamentary majority for three consecutive parliamentary terms. This supermajority allowed Viktor Orbán, the Fidesz party leader and prime minister, to enact amendments to the Hungarian constitution and pass laws to reduce press freedom and limit opposition rights, a development we discuss in more detail in Chapter 14.

A far more common alternative scenario in European parliaments involves the formation of so-called 'minority governments'. Imagine a scenario, shown in Figure 10.4, where we have a

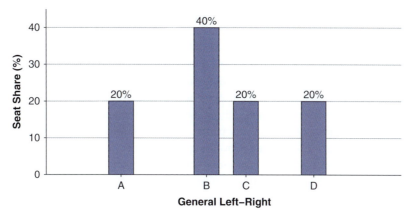

Figure 10.4 Opportunity for Minority Government

large centrist party which could form a parliamentary majority with parties both on its right and its left. Party B holds 40 per cent of the seats and faces three equally sized parties in parliament. Moreover, it is located rather to the centre of the policy space. Due to its size and its position, party B has a particular advantage which we know from the theoretical Chapter 2: it holds the median position in parliament on this policy dimension. This scenario puts party B in a strong bargaining position: it may be able to form a 'minority' government, that is a government which does not control a majority of seats but which can pass policy on the basis of ad-hoc coalitions with different parties depending on the issue. In fact, the term 'minority' is in some sense misleading, as minority governments exist because they have an implicit majority in parliament. In other words, minority governments are stable because a majority in parliament cannot agree to oust it through a vote of no confidence and force new elections. In some instances, a smaller party may even agree to support a government and provide it with votes without actually entering the government. In such instances, we speak of 'support parties'. The agreements between a minority government and support parties can range from a limited deal, in which the support party simply promises to support the government in confidence and budget votes, to a more broad agreement, in which the parties agree to certain policies. An example of such an agreement is the deal made between the British Conservatives and the Northern Irish DUP after the UK elections in 2017. With the Conservative Party having lost its majority, it formed a minority government, but secured an agreement with the DUP to support the government on all votes in the parliament related to confidence, the budget, and legislation related to Brexit. In return, the DUP secured an extra £1 billion of funding for Northern Ireland.

Support parties exist in around a quarter of all minority governments in Europe (Franchino and Wratil, 2019). The question remains, however, why a party would rather support a minority government as an opposition party, while forgoing the benefits of office. It might be that a party could actually perceive there to be costs associated with governing. Voters could be more likely to blame it for failed government policies or for an inability to enact all of its promises. Small parties that have joined government have sometimes faced electoral losses in subsequent elections as they have trouble distinguishing themselves from the larger coalition partners (Klüver and Spoon, 2020). The British Liberal Democrats faced steep losses in 2015 following their participation in government with the Conservatives from 2010 to 2015 after agreeing to support the larger coalition partner's proposal to triple the cap on university tuition fees despite previously pledging to abolish fees altogether (see Fortunato, 2021). Similarly, the FDP in Germany lost after coalition participation with the CDU and CSU and failed to gain enough votes to enter parliament following the 2013 election, having served in government from 2009 to 2013. Again, as the smaller party, the FDP was unable to implement one of its core pledges, major tax reform including tax cuts, and instead had to support many of the CDU/CSU's social spending proposals. Thus, junior parties may be cautious about joining governments in the future if it means jeopardizing their entire existence. Smaller parties moreover may care only about a few issues strongly, but not so much about others. Governing requires policy-making on a range of issues even if the party does not necessarily hold strong positions on them. Thus, a policy-seeking small party may be better off supporting a minority government in return for policy concessions on issues it cares about (Strøm, 1990). Therefore, while minority governments do not hold explicit parliamentary majorities, they do so implicitly in parliament. Figure 10.5 shows the occurrence of minority and majority governments over time at the beginning of each year. In addition, the

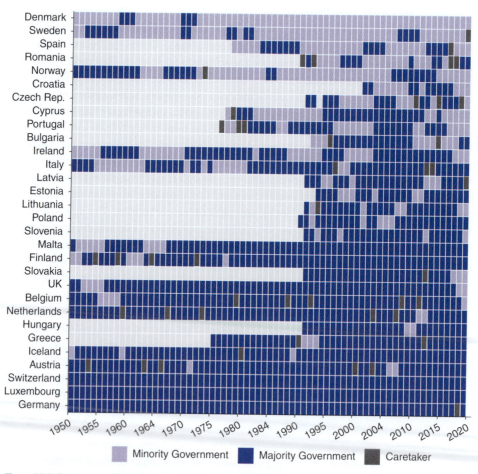

Figure 10.5 Frequency of Majority, Minority, and Caretaker Governments in Europe

Data source. ParlGov (Döring and Manow, 2019)

figure shows caretaker cabinets. These are interim cabinets with a limited mandate (McDonnell and Valbruzzi, 2014) and include technocratic, non-partisan cabinets and so-called continuation cabinets that occur if a prime minister or an entire cabinet resigns, parliament is dissolved, or after an election but before the new cabinet forms. Almost one in ten cabinets in Europe are caretaker governments (Döring and Manow, 2019).

The figure shows that Denmark, Sweden, and Norway are countries for which minority government is the norm. However, almost all countries in Europe have had some experience with minority governments. The only countries where no minority governments have occurred at the national level are Germany, Luxembourg, and Switzerland. It also shows that minority governments are on the rise. In 2019, for instance, almost half of the countries in Europe had minority governments.

Governments end for multiple reasons, but it is important to understand that in parliamentary systems 'the death of an old government and the birth of a new one are always two sides of the same coin' (Laver, 2003, 25). A common definition in the literature of government termination includes the following scenarios: (1) the government may reach its end due to new elections, (2) the prime minister resigns or is replaced by someone else, such as their successor as party leader, or by parliament through a constructive vote of no confidence, (3) the parties that form the coalition change due to the withdrawal or addition of one or more parties, and (4) the prime minister and the cabinet resign, either voluntarily or involuntarily following a lost confidence vote (Browne et al., 1984; Laver, 2003). When governments fall, constitutions always mandate that there be continuity in office. Oftentimes, the old government stays in office as a caretaker government to fulfil essential governmental functions, such as signing bills or keeping government offices open.

So far, we have discussed government formation as if politics is one-dimensional. While a simple conflict dimension is sometimes enough to capture political disagreement, we know from Chapter 2 that often a multidimensional space is required to accurately capture the ideological divisions of parties. Indeed, our description of how the German FDP managed to stay in power for so long in Germany implies two-dimensional politics: an economic dimension and a societal dimension. Rather than thinking about the FDP as a centrist party, it may be more accurate to describe it as an extreme party on both dimensions. The larger parties simply stress different dimensions when deciding how to develop a coalition, with the SPD concentrating on social policy and the CDU focusing on the economic dimension.

In Chapter 8 we displayed party positions in Germany in a two-dimensional policy space in Figure 8.5. The first dimension shows German party positioning on an economic dimension, whereas the second dimension reflects German party positions on a cultural dimension (cosmopolitan versus authoritarian values). We discuss the precise nature of these dimensions in much greater depth in Chapters 4 and 8. We can see why the SPD, CDU, and CSU may coalesce with the FDP for different reasons. Whereas the FDP is the most right-wing party on economic policy, propagating a reduced role for government including privatization, lower taxes, less regulations, a leaner welfare state, the FDP is on the left on a cultural dimension, advocating postmaterialist and libertarian values including expanded personal freedoms, access to abortion, and same-sex marriage. A one-dimensional space does not capture these differences well. We also notice that, once we move out of a one dimensional space to a multi-dimensional one, the notion of what a 'connected coalition' is becomes somewhat difficult. A party may be closer to one partner on one dimension, but to another on a different dimension.

> ### Box 10.1 **CONTROVERSIES AND DEBATES:** Citizens' Perceptions of Coalition Compromise
>
> Scholars increasingly dedicate attention to how voters perceive coalition governments. When some parties repeatedly form governments together, their cooperation may have electoral implications beyond policy-making itself. Fortunato and Stevenson (2013), for instance, show that voters perceive parties that have governed together as ideologically closer on the left–right dimension than they really are compared to parties who do not serve together in a cabinet. These effects are strongest for the least-informed voters, but they also exist in weaker form for well-informed voters who rely less on a cabinet membership heuristic to link parties to policy positions. A similar coalition heuristic result is found by Adams et al. (2016) for the European integration dimension. Citizens perceive the positions of coalition partners shifting in the same direction over time on European integration. Such results reflect that coalitions ultimately need to make compromises which may dilute their policy positions and voters perceive coalition parties either as moving in tandem or as more similar than they are. An additional view has been proposed by Adams et al. (2020) who estimate that citizens perceive parties as more similar when elections approach and when they have exhibited cooperative public relations (as measured by news reports). Thus, the government participation of political parties may not be the only impact on citizen perceptions of coalitions, but also the communications of political parties themselves. Fortunato (2017) explores further how **coalition compromise**, which may be seen as a failure to win concessions from coalition partners, is perceived by voters. Using a retrospective voting approach (see Chapter 5), he finds that cabinet parties that are viewed as compromising are not rewarded for good economic outcomes, but punished for bad ones. Moreover, voters punish parties that are viewed as compromising and that are distant from voters ideologically. The results suggest that coalition parties have incentives to have public disputes over policy in order to avoid being perceived as too compromising, even when there are no major policy disagreements between them.

10.6 The Role of Institutions in Government Formation

Until now we have discussed government formation as if all that mattered were the number of seats that parties hold and their ideological positions (in one or more dimensions). But there are also rules that govern how governments form, and these rules, or institutions, matter. In some instances these rules are formal and may even be enshrined in the constitution and in other instances they may be informal, the result of norms that have developed over many years.

For example, we have to consider who gets the first opportunity to negotiate with other parties to try to form a government, a person often referred to as the **formateur** (a former)—the chief negotiator and potential head of government—in political science literature. In some instances, this may be the leader of the party in power prior to the election (usually the prime minister); in other instances, it may be the leader of the largest party following the election. These rules could matter for the composition of the government that forms.

In the United Kingdom, custom dictates that the outgoing prime minister gets the first opportunity to form the new government. Usually, majoritarian British politics means that this institution is of little consequence. If the prime minister's party wins, it is clear that he or she will continue on in office, and if the PM loses, it is clear that the leader of the opposition will become the next prime minister. However, in 2017 the norm meant that, following the election in which Theresa May lost her majority, she had the opportunity to seek an arrangement with the DUP that allowed her to stay on in government. In Greece, it is also the case that the leader of the largest party has the first opportunity to form a coalition, but here it is the constitution that offers this right to the largest party.

In other instances, there is a political role for a person responsible for appointing a formateur, on the basis of the election outcome, called the **informateur** (informer). This person, perhaps a retired senior statesperson, the speaker of the parliament, or the head of state, is supposed to choose the formateur on the basis of information they gather about which coalitions are most likely to work. For instance, in Sweden the parliamentary speaker was tasked with going around to the various party leaders to determine the most viable coalition opportunities. The German constitution formally gives this role to the federal president, who makes a recommendation to the Bundestag regarding who should be elected chancellor. Unlike in Sweden, though, the role of the German president is rarely of consequence as the chancellor has always come from the largest party following the elections. Informateurs also play a role in the Netherlands. In the cabinet formation process following the 2017 election, a total of three former politicians acted as informateurs trying to facilitate the negotiations between the political parties.

The rules governing who gets to enter negotiations about the composition of government are not the only rules that matter. Some new governments may face a vote known as an investiture vote. This is typically a formal vote in parliament at the beginning of a parliamentary term, not on any particular policy but rather on whether the new government can take office. For instance, the German constitution dictates that the Bundestag must officially elect the new chancellor. In Norway, there is no such requirement, making it easier for a minority government to take office, precisely because no parliamentary majority ever has to explicitly give its backing to the government (Rasch et al., 2015). However, even in Germany, the constitution foresees the possibility of a minority government. If the candidate for chancellor fails to receive a majority in two rounds of voting, and only receives a relative majority in the third round of voting in the Bundestag, then the head of state, the president, can appoint the chancellor or dissolve parliament and call for new elections.

The structure of parliament may affect the types of coalitions that form. The existence of a bicameral parliament may require the government to consider not only the majority in the first but also the second chamber when making policy. Thus, even though most second chambers formally do not take part in the government formation process, governments may have an incentive to consider partisan composition when deciding what kind of coalitions to form (Druckman and Thies, 2002; Druckman et al., 2005; Proksch and Slapin, 2006). Even formally weak upper chambers without a formal veto over legislation may be able to slow down the parliamentary process sufficiently that it may be better to anticipate the situation during government formation (Tsebelis and Money, 1997). Such institutional constraints may therefore lead to surplus majority coalitions or to the selection of a minimal coalition with a majority in the upper house. In Germany, this may have been one reason why in 2005, Angela Merkel's CDU/CSU formed a grand coalition with the SPD even though other minimal winning coalitions or even minority government seemed feasible (Proksch and Slapin, 2006). In 2017, the grand coalition, however, did not muster enough votes on its own in the Bundesrat, the upper chamber, but it was the coalition that had the least policy disagreements among all feasible minimal winning coalitions.

Finally, it is important to keep in mind that the process of coalition formation may begin before election day. As parties are familiar with the policy pledges of their competitors, they can rule out certain coalitions or express explicit preferences for a preferred coalition as part of their campaign strategy. For example, in Sweden the centre-right coalition of the Moderates, the Center Party, the Liberals, and Christian Democrats have cooperated and participated in government together. When these parties win jointly, they may anticipate that they will govern together and they may even make pre-electoral pacts to this effect. Forming a pre-electoral alliance has two potential benefits: first, it may allow parties to receive votes from strategic voters that they might fail to attract if they were to run individually. In fact, coalition signals, i.e. the declared preference during an election campaign for particular coalition partners, has been shown to affect voters' calculus. Even though voters cast votes for parties during the parliamentary elections, the signals raise the importance of coalition considerations and reduce partisan ones when voters decide whom to vote for, possibly leading some voters to change their minds (Gschwend et al., 2017). Parties may receive a second benefit at the time of government formation: even though constituent parties of an alliance may be individually too small to be the largest party in parliament, they may very well achieve the largest party status as a bloc following the pre-electoral alliance. As such, they have an advantage in the coalition formation process, as one of their leaders may be chosen as formateur, thus increasing the chances of government participation (Golder, 2006).

Box 10.2 CONTROVERSIES AND DEBATES: Policy Portfolios and the Spoils of Government

Governments are not only about who is in power, but also what they have power over. Cabinet ministers lead ministries, so-called **cabinet portfolios**, and parties negotiate over both how many and which ministries they get to control. Drawing on the work of Gamson (1961), Browne and Franklin (1973) proposed what has come to be known as Gamson's Law, namely that parties receive cabinet ministries roughly in proportion to the number of parliamentary seats that they bring to the coalition. Empirically, this rule of proportionality offers a rather close approximation of government cabinet portfolio allocation, although smaller parties tend to be somewhat over-represented relative to seat shares. The strong empirical pattern in support of Gamson's Law has generated research as to why this relationship exists in the first place. After all, dividing up ministries 'fairly' according to the seat share of the party does not capture that some parties have more bargaining power than others. In other words, we may expect parties in the coalition to be stronger if they have more outside options to form alternative majority coalitions with other parliamentary parties, and consequently more portfolios. Several explanations for this puzzle have been proposed. Carroll and Cox (2007) have argued that pre-election pacts between parties can favour a fair distribution of portfolios if these parties do end up forming a coalition. An agreement amongst them about a fair share of portfolios makes parties in the pact campaign harder and contribute to the overall success of the potential coalition. More recently, Martin and Vanberg (2020b) propose a model in which the bargaining and proportionality perspective can be reconciled by putting the focus on voters' observability of the division of portfolios. According to this view, parties with more bargaining power accept proportionality in line with Gamson's Law for portfolio allocation, since the number or proportion of portfolios is relatively easily observable to voters. However, they are then compensated by receiving ministries that give them control over the policy dimensions that they care about most, and on which the preferences of the parties significantly diverge. These aspects of coalition bargaining are less easily observable to voters.

These results suggest that it is not just the number of portfolios that matters, but also which ones a party controls. A green party may fight hard to get control of the environmental ministry, while a party popular amongst farmers and rural interests might seek to appoint one of its members as minister of agriculture.

Martin and Vanberg's account is rooted in work by Laver and Shepsle (1996) who have posited that cabinet ministers have some degree of ministerial autonomy over their respective domains. This means that if a socialist party and a green party were to enter government together, the policy proposals made by that government would look different if the socialist party controlled the labour ministry and green party controlled the environmental ministry, compared with a situation where the green party controls the labour ministry and the socialist party controls the environmental ministry. The green party would probably be willing to sacrifice jobs, for example in the coal industry, to protect the environment, whereas the socialist party would probably seek to do the opposite. Because cabinets need to sign off on policies, though, ministers and their parties face constraints in what they can do within their ministries, and in truth, while ministers do have a good deal of power, policy proposals that come out of cabinets are more likely to reflect a bargain among the parties in coalition. Additionally, parties entering a coalition typically write a **coalition agreement** prior to entering government, outlining the types of policies the government would like to put forward, and setting out a list of priorities.

10.7 Choosing the EU Commission President

Coalition politics also come into play at the European level, albeit in a slightly different way than at the national level. As discussed at the beginning of this chapter, unlike most European democracies, the European Union combines elements of a parliamentary and a separation-of-powers system. The European Commission is not directly responsible to either the European Council or the European Parliament, or at least not in the way that governments are responsible to parliaments in parliamentary systems. This means that the parties in the European Parliament and the Council do not need to, and indeed cannot, build formal coalitions to create an executive and to set policy for the European Union. Instead this role is reserved for the Commission and the European Council. Moreover, the makeup of the Commission, at least with respect to nationality, is set out in the EU Treaties. At present the Commission consists of one member from each member state. This limits the ways in which the Commission can become a fully partisan coalition cabinet as in a parliamentary system, since national governments control whom they nominate as their Commissioner (i.e. cabinet member) in Brussels.

The election of the President of the European Commission, however, has been a very salient topic of debate in the EU. The current rules in the Treaty of Lisbon (Article 17(7)) state that the Commission President is subject to approval in two bodies: the European Council and the European Parliament. After the European Parliament elections, the European Council must propose a candidate by qualified majority 'taking into account the elections' and 'after having held the appropriate consultations'. This candidate must then be elected by the European Parliament by a majority. However, the exact meaning of the phrase 'taking into account the elections' remains vague.

The political parties in the European Parliament have taken the phrase to mean an increase in their role in the process. In both 2014 and 2019, European parties nominated individuals to run as candidates for the Commission presidency. They became known by the German phrase *Spitzenkandidaten*, or lead candidates, and the candidates even held candidate debates during the campaign. In 2014, the European People's Party (EPP), the centre-right European party group in the European Parliament, won the most seats, but less than a majority, and claimed the Commission Presidency for themselves. Their lead candidate, Jean-Claude

Junker, the former prime minister of Luxembourg, was quickly supported by the runner-up political group, the Party of European Socialists, and the European Council nominated him for Commission President. For the first time, however, a Commission President was not unanimously supported in the European Council; two member states opposed him—Hungary and the United Kingdom. But under the rules, the two 'no' votes were not sufficient to block the nomination. Once nominated, the European Parliament swiftly elected Jean-Claude Juncker as Commission President for the 2014–2019 term. He received votes from both his party group as well as from the European Socialists. Formally, the Commission President was thus supported by a grand coalition of the centre-right and centre-left in the European Parliament.

The involvement of two institutions, the European Council and the European Parliament, creates an interesting setting for government formation. While at the outset it seems like the European Parliament and the European political party groups were able to impose their lead candidate system on national governments, we could also interpret the approval of Juncker differently. Not only was he the EPP lead candidate in 2014, he was also a former long-serving prime minister of Luxembourg. In this role, he was, himself, a member of the European Council. Thus, the twenty-seven heads of government of the EU were able to nominate 'one of their own'.

Following the European Parliament elections in 2019, the EPP once again won more seats than any other group in the Parliament. Its lead candidate in the campaign was German MEP Manfred Weber, who swiftly claimed the Commission Presidency after the election just as Juncker had in 2014. However, there were two key differences: first, the grand coalition of the centre-left and centre-right no longer held a majority of seats in the EP. Thus, a candidate could only be elected if he or she received the support of an additional political group in the European Parliament. Second, Manfred Weber had made his career primarily in the European Parliament, and lacked previous national government experience. Some heads of government in the European Council, notably French President Emmanuel Macron, stated his inexperience as a reason to oppose him. The lead candidate from the second largest group, the European Socialists, the Dutch Frans Timmermans, was considered as an alternative. However, he received opposition in the European Council from the Hungarian and Polish governments. Timmermans had been a vocal critique of developments related to the decline of the rule of law in Hungary and Poland. Thus, in contrast to 2014, the European Parliament could not set the agenda vis-à-vis the member states by proposing a lead candidate behind which member states could rally in the European Council. Eventually, the European Council nominated a cabinet minister from Germany without any previous EU-specific expertise, Ursula von der Leyen. In December 2019, she became the first female Commission President in the EU's history.

In short, the political groups of the European Parliament do not bargain over the partisan composition of the executive branch in the same way as national parties negotiate over coalition membership in national governments. Because of the EU's mixed system, coalitions must form among parties and countries within and across branches of the EU government. The Council's super-majority rules mean that national governments from across the ideological spectrum must agree to pass policies, even before accounting for cross-institutional differences between the European Parliament and the Council. Indeed, most votes taken in the Council are unanimous. Only occasionally do national governments go on the record as dissenting to an agreed Council position. This does not imply that national governments always agree on EU issues, but only that they rarely disagree publicly, or that issues that face substantial opposition from a minority never proceed forward. In the European Parliament a majority of the main centre-left group, the Socialists and Democrats, votes with a majority of the main centre-right group, the European People's Party, over 70 per cent of the time. Both of these groups vote even more frequently together with the smaller liberal group, the Alliance of Liberals and Democrats for Europe. In 2019, the European elections have reduced the seat share of the centre-right and centre-left to the benefit of smaller groups, including the Liberals (including Macron's party from France), the Greens, and the populist radical right. Coalition negotiations over policy have therefore become more complicated, but possibly also more inclusive than ever before.

10.8 Summary

Drawing on a principal–agent framework, this chapter introduced the major institutional distinctions between parliamentary, presidential, and mixed political systems, all of which are present in Europe at the national level. The supranational political system of the European Union is not a fully parliamentary system, as it shares many elements that suggest more separation of powers between the institutions, similar to those found in presidential systems. The chapter furthermore discussed the process of government formation and highlighted the role of coalition formation in parliaments across Europe. Government coalition-building lies at the heart of executive politics and plays a decisive role in the political process and in determining how policies get made. As parties differ in their office- and policy-seeking motivations, we observe a wide variety of types of governments that form, including coalition majority governments and minority governments. The nature of the executive impacts the policy-making process that will be discussed in the next chapter.

Online Data Exercise: ParlGov Dataset

The interactive online exercise accompanying this chapter allows you to explore different possible coalitions for a set of elections using the ParlGov dataset. You can visualize which coalitions maximize policy, offices, generate majority or minority governments, or which lead to surplus majorities. You can then compare these coalitions to the ones that actually occurred after elections and discuss which coalitions are more or less likely.

 Take your learning further with this interactive data exercise, available at **www.foundationsofeuropeanpolitics.com**

 For additional material and resources, including multiple-choice questions, web links, and more, please visit the online resources: **www.oup.com/he/devries1e**

11 Law-Making in Governments and Parliaments

In this chapter, we discuss how political systems across Europe actually make and change policy by passing laws, examining in greater detail how the coalitions we discussed in the last chapter function. Using the theoretical lens of Veto Players theory, we explore how the nature of governments and the parties in them affect the types of policies that become law, and the ease with which governments can change existing policy. The chapter also discusses the role of informal actors such as interest groups. We examine how processes differ both across different countries and at the level of the EU. It provides an important foundation for understanding variation in the policy outcomes we observe across European countries, which is explored in much greater depth in Chapter 12.

Chapter 10 explained how governments form following elections at the national level and at the European Union level. Notably, a core feature of parliamentary democracy in Europe and the political system in the EU is that there are rarely any clear electoral winners. At the national level, with few exceptions (e.g. in some countries such as the UK, Greece, or Spain), a single party does not control a majority of seats in parliament. Single party governments represent only about 15 per cent of governments in Europe over time. And even in countries where single party governments are the norm, coalitions have recently occurred, such as in the UK from 2010 to 2015, and even more recently in Spain where, beginning in 2020, the main Spanish socialist party formed a minority coalition with a number of smaller leftist parties. The nature of these governing coalitions affects how policy gets made.

The historical record across Europe shows that the most common form of national government is a coalition that includes at least two parties in the **cabinet**. The transition from touting partisan rhetoric during electoral campaigns to being tasked with finding agreement with political opponents is astonishingly fast. Cooperation seems the norm, but coalition governments often place parties in an awkward situation where they are governing together, making policies with partners who will compete against them for votes during the next election. Parties entering a coalition, therefore, often draft an agreement about the policies that their government will pursue, inevitably involving compromise. In western Europe, around two-thirds of coalition cabinets are based on such explicit agreements, and the vast majority of them are available in the public domain (Müller and Strøm, 2008; Strøm et al., 2010). But the instant parties enter an agreement they have an incentive to shirk—that is, to violate that agreement to move closer to policies they would have liked to pursue in the absence of having to form a coalition.

We can think about parties in government as being in a principal–agent relationship with their voters and activists who wish to see their party stay true to their ideals rather than compromise in a coalition. Parties are the agents of their voters, but at the same time, they cannot deviate too far from the **coalition agreement** without risking punishment of some form by their partners. So from whom do they shirk, their voters or their coalition partners? The answer may depend, in part, on where they are in the electoral cycle. At the beginning of the parliamentary term, passing policies that are compromises between several parties may be easier. But as elections near, the pull of the voters may be stronger.

Before we delve deeper into the internal workings of coalition governments and the consequences on law-making, it is useful to consider more generally the capacity of different governments to make and change laws. A useful approach that allows us to compare governments across countries and their effects on policy-making is the Veto Players approach proposed by George Tsebelis (2002).

11.1 Veto Players and Law-Making

In parliamentary democracies, in principle, it is the parliament that makes the laws, but in practice, laws are prepared by the parties in government. Across Europe, the vast majority of legislation is introduced by governments—the executive branch. While individual members of parliament may have some ability to introduce legislation themselves, it is rare that such legislation passes, especially if it does not enjoy the support of the government. An exception are situations in which the cabinet does not enjoy a parliamentary majority, which we will discuss in section 11.4. More generally, parliamentary rules may make it difficult for individual members of parliament to have their bills considered on the floor of parliament as governments often control parliamentary timetables, albeit to varying degrees depending on the country. In short, governments have **agenda control** over the legislative process. The fusion between government and parliament is the main reason that they enjoy such power; governments exist because they enjoy an implicit or explicit majority of seats in parliament. This parliamentary majority delegates the task of proposing legislation to the cabinet. Once introduced to parliament by the government, passage of a bill is virtually guaranteed. Thus, when studying what policies emerge, the focus should lie initially on the cabinet and the government itself, rather than on parliament. This is what Veto Players theory proposes.

Veto Players theory is a framework that focuses on political institutions and actors that can block policy change. As we first discussed in Chapter 2, according to Tsebelis (1995, 2002), **veto players** are political actors whose support is necessary to change a legislative **status quo**, e.g. political parties in government or a directly elected president with the power to block legislation, in other words, any actor who can block legislative change. The focus on veto players allows for useful comparison of political institutions and practices across countries because the phenomenon it seeks to explain is the amount of **policy stability**, i.e. the difficulty with which current legislation or policy (often referred to as the legislative status quo) can be modified.

In a first step, institutional veto players are identified through constitutions. Constitutions will, for example, mandate which parliamentary chambers need to agree to pass laws and with what majorities. Almost half of Europe's legislatures are **bicameral**, meaning they consist of a lower house and an upper house. Such bicameral institutions have historically evolved for different reasons. In their seminal contribution of bicameral parliaments, Tsebelis and Money (1997) argue that a first set of bicameral parliaments emerged to ensure the inclusion of societal groups. The upper house not only served as a check on legislation, but also to guarantee representation for certain parts of society. Legislators in the upper house were selected differently than lower house members, either from different electoral constituencies or through political appointment, often focusing on wisdom, education, wealth, or heredity. The UK House of Lords offers an example of a fully appointed chamber, originally focused on guaranteeing the representation of the upper classes, and now providing a mechanism for input from individuals with various relevant experience. The other major historical development of bicameralism involved territorial representation of subnational constituent units, such as states or provinces.

From a veto players perspective, the crucial distinction is related to the constitutionally guaranteed veto power of parliaments. In many instances, a **unicameral** national parliament may be sufficient (such as in Greece), but in others, constitutions mandate more veto players (such as in Germany or Italy) where the upper chambers represent regions, and both the lower and the upper house of parliament need to agree to change legislation. In Italy, both chambers have equal powers, while in Germany the assent of the upper chamber is only required for certain types of legislation. The European Union treaties, which constitute the de facto constitutional provisions of the EU's political system, provide for clear federal representation. The Council, representing member states through the national governments, and the European Parliament, representing European citizens, need to jointly agree to policy following a proposal that can only originate from the European Commission (the supranational executive).

Most European political systems are unicameral, and most bicameral systems do not have upper chambers with veto power. Table 11.1 shows the different types of parliaments in Europe. It distinguishes four types of parliamentary system: unicameral ones, weak

Table 11.1 Parliaments in Europe

Type	Does upper house have veto power?	Both houses congruent?	Parliaments
Unicameral	–	–	Bulgaria, Croatia, Cyprus, Denmark, Estonia, Finland, Greece, Hungary, Iceland, Latvia, Lithuania, Luxembourg, Malta, Norway, Portugal, Slovakia, Sweden
Weak Bicameralism	No	Yes	Austria, Czech Republic, Ireland, Poland, UK*
Medium strength Bicameralism	No	No	France, Spain, Slovenia
	Yes	Yes	Italy, Netherlands, Belgium, Romania
Strong Bicameralism	Yes	No	Germany, European Union, Switzerland

Sources: Lijphart (2012), Armingeon et al. (2018)

* Lijphart considers the UK in between weak and medium-strength bicameralism.

bicameralism, medium strength bicameralism, and strong bicameralism (Lijphart, 2012). This typology is a function of the formal veto power of the upper house as well as of the ideological congruence (or similarity) between the chambers. Oftentimes the partisan, and therefore ideological, composition in the upper house resembles the one found in the lower house of parliament, meaning that if one house supports passage of a bill, the other chamber is likely to support it, too. Only in Germany, the EU, and Switzerland, do we have two institutional veto players, which are likely to disagree on policy. In medium strong bicameral systems, such as Italy, Netherlands, Belgium, or Romania, the upper houses do have formal veto power, but it is likely to be of less consequence in the law-making process due to the similar ideological composition in the two houses.

It is thus important not only to count institutional veto players, but to take into account the ideological disagreement between them. Veto Players theory therefore breaks up institutional veto players into so-called partisan veto players, and this is the preferred way to think about veto players generally. Thus rather than just counting institutional veto players in the constitution, it is necessary to identify the partisan actors that control the majorities following political competition and elections. For example, in the aftermath of the Italian election in 2018, for the first time in Europe, a coalition of two populist parties formed a majority government: the Five Star Movement (M5S) together with the Lega. These two parties were the partisan veto players in the Italian political system, as each party's support was necessary to change the status quo. Together, the parties also controlled a majority of seats in the Italian upper house, so it is sufficient to consider only these two parties for the veto player analysis.

Once we consider the political preferences of the veto players, it is possible to predict the amount of policy stability in any given government. Policy stability in this context refers to the degree of difficulty politicians would face when seeking to change the legislative status quo, or current policy. Policy is stable when it cannot be changed by the coalition because at least one of the veto players dislikes the proposed change. The set of policies that veto players cannot agree to change is also known as the unanimity **core** of the political system, or the **pareto set**. It is defined by the number of veto players, their policy disagreement, and the voting rules: the larger the ideological policy disagreement among veto players, the larger the number of policies that cannot be changed. Thus, veto player theory does not care about the number of veto players, per se. Instead, the ideological differences between them are more relevant. More veto players likely means more policy stability, but not if the additional veto players agree with others already present in the system.

The core concepts of this theory are best illustrated visually. We show an example of veto players in a single dimension in Figure 11.1. The two parties in the Italian coalition hold different positions on a general left–right dimension. The size of the policy disagreement is the amount of policy stability: the set of policies that cannot be changed (pareto set or unanimity core). Thus, by identifying and analysing preferences of veto players, it is possible to explain why coalitions, despite having multiple governing parties, can oftentimes act quickly (because they have little policy disagreement) or why coalitions with only few governing parties cannot agree on how to change policy (because they have large disagreements). This analysis can easily be extended to multiple dimensions.

A peculiarity of our Italian example is that the veto player distance includes an opposition party, Forza Italia (FI). As the seat shares indicate, the Five Star Movement could have also formed a coalition with Forza Italia, the party of former Prime Minister Silvio Berlusconi,

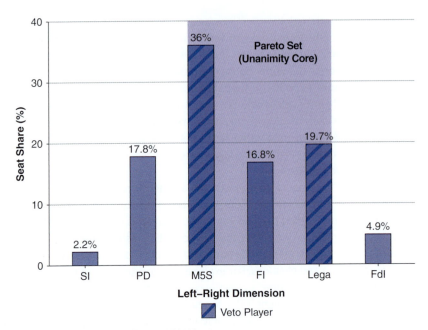

Figure 11.1 Veto Players in Italy Following 2018 Election

which in fact would have had a smaller veto player distance by most measures. However, the party had campaigned strongly against the mainstream political parties during the campaign, with one prominent Five Star politician referring to Berlusconi as the 'absolute evil of our country', thus ruling out any formal arrangement. Such differences are not visible in the policy disagreements if we only take into account the left–right dimension.

Veto players theory is also able to yield predictions about what kind of policy is expected if the current status quo is outside the core. In such instances, all veto players will be better off by moving the policy closer to the policy they would ideally like. Consider the Italian situation after the coalition government formed. The previous government was led by PD, the Democratic Party, that formed a majority coalition with a smaller centrist party. Imagine for simplicity two scenarios. In the first, we assume the PD was able to move the status quo during its tenure close to its ideological position to the left of the Five Star Movement. Thus, the coalition government can, in fact, move the status quo, as such a change would make both parties better off. However, veto players theory is vague with regard to the agenda-setting process— or who gets to make the proposal—among parties in government. While governments can set the agenda in parliaments, how exactly this agenda comes about within the government is not something that the theory aims to capture. Instead, the value of the approach lies in its ability to compare many different government types and institutions in a unified framework. We would expect the new outcome to lie somewhere in the pareto set of the coalition, representing an overall policy change to the right in Italy following the 2018 election. In the second scenario, let us assume that the PD was not able to move the status quo policy to the left of the Five Star Movement, but in fact exactly to where the Five Star Movement places itself on the left–right dimension. Since the status quo would now be inside the pareto set, the new coalition would be unlikely to produce any policy change as the Five Star Movement would veto such a change, and the coalition would fail. In fact, the majority coalition between M5S and Lega failed after a lost vote of no confidence initiated by Lega party leader Matteo Salvini in August 2019. A month later, M5S agreed to form a coalition government with Democratic Party (PD) without a new election. Thus, a single veto player (or multiple veto players all of whom agree) can react nimbly and rapidly change policy, while disagreement among veto players generally means slow or no change.

Another way to look at veto players is to consider the involvement of societal groups in the decision-making process. Some European democracies are often hailed for their consensus-oriented policy-making due to compromise involving many veto players. In these systems it can be hard to make policy, but once agreement among all actors is reached, that policy is 'sticky', meaning that when compromise is struck, it is likely to last for quite a long time. This is because, with numerous veto players, the compromise is likely to lie within the unanimity core for quite some time.

Lijphart (2012) called such systems consociational systems because they include often-times oversized coalitions that are able to take into account a wide array of preferences, eventually leading to a 'kinder, gentler democracy'. This notion contrasts with the traditional parliamentary model from the United Kingdom, the Westminster system, in which a single veto player is not only able to change policy quickly if it wants to, but where electoral losers are more or less shut out of the policy-making process altogether. For a systematic understanding of law-making, it is thus important to dive more into the details of legislative agenda setting and decision-making. We do so by focusing on a large literature that emphasizes the role of cabinet ministers and the compromise they are forging when legislating on new policy.

Box 11.1 CONTROVERSIES AND DEBATES: Is Policy Stability Good or Bad?

The seeming inability of many governments to produce major policy reforms is a topic of recurring discussion in policy-making across Europe. Terms like 'reform backlog' or 'political gridlock' are frequently used to characterize the absence of major legislation at the national and the European level. From an economic perspective, we may argue that rapid policy changes in a political system—or even the mere possibility of such changes—can be bad: policy change can create economic uncertainty and generate costs associated with implementing new policies. For instance, if tax rates were to change frequently, consumers and firms may delay or refrain from investments, given uncertainty about their tax bill. On the other hand, rapid change allows politicians to be responsive, something that may be considered a positive attribute of a political system. Notably, the ability to change policy is a necessary precondition for governments to be responsive to changing public opinion (see discussion in Chapter 7), and fewer veto players or policy disagreements in cabinets make such changes more likely. Ultimately, the normative view on veto players hinges on the location of the status quo. If the status quo policy enjoys widespread support among citizens, and this support is rather stable, it may be desirable to lock this policy in. This can be ensured with many institutional veto players such as strong bicameral systems, qualified majority voting rules inside legislatures, or multiparty coalition governments. If, on the other hand, an unexpected event makes a status quo policy unsustainable, we may prefer institutions that allow politicians to change it quickly.

11.2 Cabinet Ministers: Agenda-Setters for their Party

While Veto Players theory assumes that the government (or cabinet) as a whole is the agenda-setter in the legislative process, able to make a proposal to the parliament which will then be accepted, we can also use policy-making models that investigate the role of ministers and the consequences on law-making more directly. In a famous model of government formation, Laver and Shepsle (1996) assume that **ministerial autonomy** is a price that parties pay for being part of a coalition government. Once portfolios, i.e. formal responsibilities for policy areas, are assigned to ministers, coalition partners have a certain degree of discretion in implementing their own party's position in that particular area. For instance, the party in control of the immigration ministry will have a reasonable degree of leeway to implement the party's immigration policies. Additionally, the minister could engage in gatekeeping (see Chapter 2.1) and decide not to propose new policies. Such ministerial autonomy may also result from an informational advantage provided by expertise present in the ministerial bureaucracy. After all, ministers are supported by hundreds of civil servants that aid in the preparation and implementation of legislation.

Let us consider how such a model can be applied to an actual government. Figure 11.2 uses our illustration of the Italian coalition of 2018 from the previous section. Consider that the parties had to divide up two policy portfolios: the immigration portfolio (under the responsibility of the interior minister) and the social policy portfolio (under the responsibility of the labour and social policy minister). Both parties, M5S and Lega, rose to power on anti-establishment platforms, but took very different positions on policy issues: whereas the M5S tended to support more government spending, advocating for a basic income scheme for everyone, and a less restrictive immigration policy, the Lega campaigned strongly on a more restrictive immigration policy, pledging to expel illegal immigrants, and an economic policy advertising a flat tax rate.

There are two alternatives for allocating the responsibility across these policy issues: either the M5S controls the ministry responsible for labour and social policy and the Lega the ministry responsible for immigration (cabinet A), or vice versa (cabinet B). Because both parties have different policy positions, this allocation of portfolios may incentivize the parties to use the ministries to implement their own preferred partisan preference. If we translate the ministerial autonomy model to one of policy-making, then under the first allocation—which corresponds to the actual allocation among the parties following the 2018 election—the M5S could introduce a bill in parliament with its ideal policy on social policy and the Lega a bill with its ideal policy on immigration. In fact, this is what happened in 2019. The government rolled out a citizens' income scheme, which the M5S party leader Luigi DiMaio and minister of labour and social policy praised as a kept campaign promise. The party leader of Lega and minister of the interior, Matteo Salvini, on the other hand, drafted a legislative initiative that abolished protections for migrants and made it easier for them to be deported.

From a Veto Players perspective, we may additionally consider what the parties in government prefer over the existing policy, or the status quo (SQ). Depending on where this status quo is located, the policy mix emerging from ministerial autonomy may or may not make both parties better off. Let us assume the status quo represents a less restrictive immigration policy and a centre-right economic policy. In Figure 11.2 the indifference curves (see discussion in Chapter 2.4) make it apparent that the M5S actually prefers the hypothetical

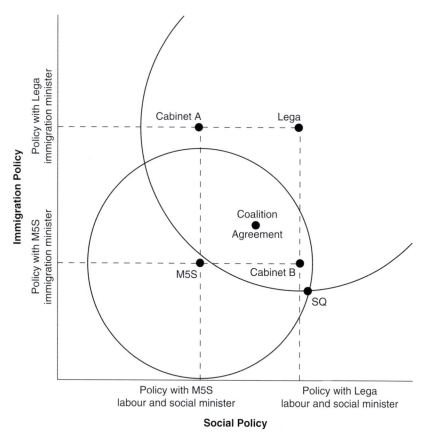

Figure 11.2 Ministerial Autonomy and Compromise Model of Policy-Making

status quo over the policies of cabinet A, whereas the policies of cabinet B make both parties better off. Recall that indifference curves in multidimensional policy spaces represent the set of policies equidistant between the actor and the status quo, so that an actor is indifferent between the policy and the current policy. Thus, they represent the boundary between all positions preferred by the actor to the SQ and those that make the actor worse off. The intersection of the two curves in Figure 11.2 does not include cabinet A, and as both parties are veto players and can block policies that make them worse off, this cabinet would not be able to produce policy and would likely fail. The intersection, meaning the winset of the status quo (see Chapter 2), does include cabinet B, though, making this cabinet configuration more likely. Note, however, that even a portfolio allocation that is preferred over the status quo may not represent the best outcome for both coalition parties. They could strike a better deal through negotiation. The figure depicts the position of hypothetical coalition agreement that both the M5S and the Lega would prefer (see Figure 11.2) over cabinet B. Ministerial autonomy thus is a concept that is at odds with the notion of compromise in policy-making. The party in charge of a ministry may want to use resources for partisan position-taking, whereas the partner party in the cabinet may want to rein in such behaviour to enforce the initial compromise. How can this be done?

11.3 Enforcing Coalition Compromise Inside and Outside Parliament

Veto Players theory helps us to compare policy-making and policy change across governments, but it does not offer much insight into the details of how coalition government works on a daily basis. The analysis of Figure 11.2 makes clear that government parties know that their partners have the opportunity to use the ministries that they control to shirk to please their voters. They could do so by engaging in position-taking to distinguish themselves from their partners, possibly by proposing bills that reflect their party platform rather than a **coalition compromise**. They also know that parties may have an informational advantage about what goes on in the ministries that they control, giving them the ability to shirk without their partners knowing. As such, parties often seek to use various institutional features of governments and parliaments to monitor and rein in opportunistic behaviour of coalition partners.

Parties seeking to form a coalition government often write a coalition agreement as part of the coalition bargaining process. These agreements set out jointly decided policy pledges that coalition government will seek to enact, and serves as a contract for the parties while they cooperate with one another in government. Although they are not legally binding, these political agreements can serve as the basis for monitoring the activities of cabinet ministers. Coalition agreements tend to grow in length when ministers have more autonomy (Indridason and Kristinsson, 2013) and they focus more attention on issues on which the coalition partners are divided (Klüver and Bäck, 2019). Coalition parties can try to enforce the policy bargains they strike in the coalition agreement either inside or outside parliament.

With regard to monitoring outside parliament, Thies (2001) has shown that coalition partners are likely to have the opportunity to appoint junior ministers to shadow the work of the senior minister in the ministries that they do not control. A junior minister is the 'second-in-command' politician in the ministry, operating under the position of the minister, and can act as a **shadowing minister** in order to monitor the activities of the minister who is a member of another coalition party. However, the appointment of junior ministers is a blunt instrument for control, especially for small governing parties, who may not be granted enough junior minister positions to shadow all of the ministries they would like to. And not all countries have partisan junior ministers. Coalition committees are therefore another instrument to enforce compromise. Such committees are usually composed of the party leaders of the government parties and meant to clarify the short-term legislative agenda of the coalition.

But government parties can also resort to parliamentary institutions directly. Such **parliamentary policing** can happen when legislative institutions are strong. This is an aspect worth highlighting, because traditionally the strength of parliament has been seen as something that weakens, rather than strengthens, governments. Martin and Vanberg (2005, 2011, 2020a) have shown that coalition partners can use the legislative amendment process to check their coalition partners. Strong parliaments are defined by several features. A large number of parliamentary committees allow members of parliament to specialize on certain policy issues. Moreover, a correspondence between the committee jurisdiction and that of a ministry means that committee members can more efficiently scruntinize government business. Smaller committees are in this regard more effective than larger ones, and in particular those that have the authority to rewrite bills and propose legislative amendments. Another indicator for strong parliaments and scrutiny of governments are binding plenary debate on government bills,

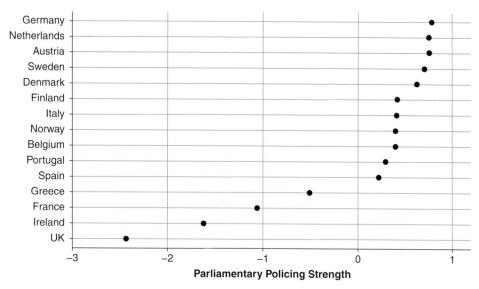

Figure 11.3 Variation of Parliamentary Policing Strength in Europe

Data source: Martin and Vanberg (2020a)

Note: Values represent the average policing strength in each lower house of parliament between 1973 and 2010.

the right to compel witnesses and documents, and guaranteed limits on the government to curtail debate and legislate with urgency procedures (Martin and Vanberg, 2011, 2020a). On the basis of these attributes, Martin and Vanberg construct a parliamentary policing strength score that indicates how lower houses in Europe fare on this scale. Figure 11.3 shows results for fifteen European parliaments, averaged between 1970 and 2010. The strongest parliaments in Europe are found in the north and include Germany, Austria, the Netherlands, Sweden, and Denmark. Parliaments with moderate powers include Finland, Italy, Belgium, Norway, and Portugal. Weak parliaments include those from Spain, Greece, France, Ireland, and—with quite a distance to the other parliaments—the House of Commons in the United Kingdom. These values are not static, and Martin and Vanberg (2020a) demonstrate that some parliaments have become weaker or stronger over the years. Most changes over time are due to modifications to the number and size of parliamentary committees as well as to the degree to which they mirror the policy jurisdiction of ministries. Among the countries with important movement towards more policing strength, Martin and Vanberg highlight France, in which a constitutional amendment granted committees the authority to rewrite draft bills (in 2009), and Ireland, where a permanent committee system was set up in the 1990s. Some parliaments have experienced trends towards weaker policing strength, such as the Netherlands and Belgium, where the number of committees were reduced substantially.

Over time, changes to parliamentary oversight of government business have also occurred at the EU level. As a result of the increasing transfer of policy-making authority to the EU in the 1980s and 1990s, many national parliaments have developed EU-related oversight institutions (Winzen, 2017). Strong parliamentary oversight mechanisms of a government's EU activities include access to legislative and planning documents, government memorandums, the installation of a standing parliamentary committee on EU affairs, and mandating that governments follow the instructions of parliament in the negotiations in Brussels. According to Winzen (2017), Scandinavian and northern European countries tend to have stronger levels of parliamentary control over EU affairs than countries in the south of Europe.

A thought-provoking aspect of Martin and Vanberg's research on parliamentary policing is that the institutional strength of parliaments, often associated with powers for the opposition, may serve governing parties themselves to enforce compromises. Coalition parties can use the institutions to monitor, and rein in if necessary, position-taking activities of coalition partners which result from ministerial autonomy. In strong parliaments, backbenchers from governing parties, for example, can ask parliamentary questions of ministers from coalition partners, pressing them to explain what is going on in their ministry in a public forum and relieving their party leaders from having to engage in an awkward exchange with a government partner. Likewise, members of parliament may have the opportunity to offer amendments to legislation, trying to restore policy to more accurately reflect coalition agreement compromises when deviations occur. Committee chairs from governing parties can table amendments to legislation to enforce compromises. Stronger parliaments make it easier for governments to do so. As it turns out, such corrective mechanisms produce a policy that makes coalition partners overall better off. Where exactly this compromise will be located is a matter of bargaining strength. Models that have predicted an average between positions, weighted by the relative size of the governing parties in terms of their parliamentary seat share, have done well in predicting which policies become law (Martin and Vanberg, 2014). A coalition compromise may furthermore be important for how governments in the Council of the EU negotiate with each other. There is evidence that cabinet ministers, when they represent their member state in Council meetings, defend coalition compromises rather than their own party position (Franchino and Wratil, 2019). However, this seems more likely in cases where executive coordination is strong. Regular exchanges between ministries and dispute resolution mechanisms outside of parliament, such as coalition committees, create such strong coordination. Thus, at least on EU affairs, the enforcement of coalition compromise outside of parliament seems more important than the policing strength of parliaments per se (except for cases of minority governments where they do play a role).

Because coalition government often means parties are trying to please everyone—both their voters and their coalition partners—they may lead to costly outcomes compared with single party governments. Higher spending on coalition partners' priority areas may be one way to paper over differences between coalition partners and help to prevent shirking once in government. Bawn and Rosenbluth (2006), for instance, have shown that budgets have a tendency to increase in size with the number of parties participating in government. In a later study, Martin and Vanberg (2013) have shown that this relationship is conditional on the presence of certain fiscal institutions: where such institutions are present and sufficiently strong, an increase in the number of government parties has no effect on spending.

11.4 Why Minority Governments Work

Minority government is such a regular, yet puzzling, phenomenon in European democracies that it deserves closer investigation when it comes to law-making. There is ample empirical evidence that such governments last shorter, on average, than coalition majority governments.

And yet, governments seem able to make policy, pass legislation, and cope with the lack of a formal majority. How are governments able to legislate in such a situation? Strøm (1990) has provided a rational explanation for the occurrence of minority governments, rooted in a policy-based explanation. Chapter 10 illustrated situations in which a minority government can form. Governments can propose bills and pass them successfully if they have the support of parts of the opposition. To get this support, governments can offer policy concessions. From the government's perspective, this can be either done through ad-hoc coalitions that are formed anew on each policy issue, presumably with the opposition party that shares the most policy positions. Alternatively, a government can try to conclude a support agreement with an opposition party. In such an arrangement, the support party formally remains outside of cabinet but promises to support the government on crucial parliamentary votes, such as budget votes or confidence votes, in exchange for specific policy concessions.

Thus, parties that form minority governments are able to control ministerial portfolios, but need to pay for this privilege by making various policy concessions, possibly confusing voters about what they stand for. In effect, minority governments therefore enjoy implicit majority support. Once this support is withdrawn, new elections are highly likely. Several studies have provided evidence for such a policy-based explanation. Thomson et al. (2017) show that minority governments fulfil electoral pledges just like majority governments, and Klüver and Zubek (2018) focus on the level of policy disagreement between minority governments and the opposition and find that the implementation of policies is more likely as the disagreements are smaller.

So why don't opposition parties just join governments? As we have described in Chapter 10, such parties may primarily care about policy, not office. Moreover, they may fear sanctioning at the next elections and therefore tolerate, rather than enter, a government, even if the party cannot allocate office to its members. Junior partners in coalition governments often get punished electorally by their voters at the next election (Klüver and Spoon, 2020). As the smaller partner in the coalition, they may not be able to pass much of their policy agenda and may need to compromise too much with their partners, at least in the eyes of their supporters. Knowing that they might face such future electoral punishment, they might prefer to try to extract some policy 'wins' while remaining on the sidelines, avoiding blame for anything that might go wrong with the government. Institutions also play a role. Stronger parliaments allow the opposition to modify government legislation.

11.5 Interest Groups and Informal Influences on Policy-Making

Veto players theory focuses attention on the formal actors in the political process, such as the parties in government and other actors with institutional authority to block change. It suggests that the positions that they take on issues are crucial to understanding what policies actually come out of the political process. Because these actors and their positions are so important, there are many other actors in the political process that seek to influence the policies that these veto players advocate for. These actors are often called interest or pressure groups. They are organizations that wish to influence policy outcomes, but do so by pressuring parties and politicians to take on certain positions favourable to them, rather than by running for office themselves. Just like political parties, then, interest groups are policy-seeking organizations, but neither seek office nor votes in elections. Such groups include industry lobby groups, corporations, trade unions, and other groups representing special interests such as environmental organizations or even sporting clubs—any group that organizes to influence policy by seeking to change the position of elected politicians rather than running for office themselves.

Interest groups are organized in different ways across countries and may have a more formal or more informal role. This leads to different **interest group systems**. In many countries, trade unions and business organizations have a more formal role in the policy-making process. This is known as **corporatism**. It grants two sectors of society, business and labour, privileged access to policy-making. Together with the government, these sectors, represented by umbrella organizations that coordinate the activities of all labour unions and business groups, participate in an institutionalized process of negotiations over certain types of economic policy. Additionally, interest groups may have formal or informal links to particular parties (e.g. labour unions to Socialists). One concern about corporatist structures is that employers and labour organizations may have overlapping preferences to the benefit of their sector (e.g. weak car emissions standards for the car industry), and have privileged access to politicians in the policy-making process. This may be to the detriment of broader societal concerns, such as environmental protection or public health.

In other systems, the link between interest groups and politicians is less formal and more competitive, with different groups all competing for the attention of politicians. This is referred to as a pluralist interest group system. One precondition under which pluralist interest group systems work is that there is a level playing field: each group should have the same opportunity for access to policy-makers. Oftentimes, this is difficult to realize in practice. First, some broader interests, such as consumer protection interests or environmental interests, are more difficult to organize than more narrow interests (e.g. chemical industry). Following the logic of collective action (Olson, 1965), more similar (homogeneous) interests are easier to organize due to the incentives that the group can provide. If a group produces a collective good that benefits everyone (e.g. higher consumer protection standards), this means that benefits arise also for those who were not involved in the process. More dispersed (heterogeneous) interests are less likely to form strong interest group organizations.

Agriculture subsidies are an often-cited example of an outcome of narrow interest group success in Europe. Agricultural subsidies have made up a large share of the EU's budget since the early days of European integration. One possible reason for the large subsidies lies in the level of organization of farmers and taxpayers and the type of good. Subsidies benefit farmers, a relatively small group, and they provide them with a large and very perceptible benefit. Meanwhile, the financial burden is spread across many shoulders, the large and diverse body of taxpayers, who do not know exactly how much of their tax bill is going to support farmers. Moreover, even if they did know, it would only be a relatively small amount per person—hardly worth the cost of organizing. Farmers, in short, are much more capable at organizing than taxpayers.

Beyond mere organizational strength, it is useful to think about the actual role of interest groups in policy-making. While it is clear what interest groups want (to move policy closer to their group's interests), it is less clear what they have to offer. One possible way of rationalizing interest groups is that they are engaging in a resource exchange with politicians: interests groups may provide them with information that would otherwise be difficult or impossible to acquire, for instance with regard to the consequences of policy alternatives on various industrial sectors, the environment, or societal groups. In exchange for this expertise, they gain access to the agenda-setters and veto players of the legislative process. For instance, interest groups may meet directly with decision-makers and suggest wording that may make it into legislative bills or amendments. This strategy is known as **inside lobbying**, and it is usually available to better funded and organized interest groups, such as business or corporate organizations. Culpepper (2010) shows that, in particular, for issues with low public salience, such as corporate control regulations, corporations and their executives can exercise influence over the design of regulations. However, as the political salience increases, e.g. through scandals, corporations are less likely to shape the process. Alternatively, interest groups may try to adopt a strategy of **outside lobbying**, circumventing the decision-makers but running public campaigns for particular causes, including demonstrations and street protests.

11.6 Law-Making in the European Union

Our discussion so far has concentrated on policy-making in the national context, but some crucial policies are no longer decided at the national level alone. In the EU, policy-making authority on many issues has been transferred from the national to the supranational level. Over time, member states through revisions of the EU Treaties have revised the way in which law-making in the EU occurs. The standard procedure for passing laws in the EU is the so-called ordinary legislative procedure (formerly known as the co-decision procedure, in which the European Parliament decides together with the Council), a simplified version of which is shown in Figure 11.4. It involves three institutional actors: the European Commission, as the supranational agenda-setter, and the Council and Parliament as the two legislative chambers that have to approve the proposal. The supranational Commission is part of the executive branch of the European Union. It is composed of a political leadership, i.e. the President and the Commissioners in the so-called College of Commissioners, and of a bureaucracy of European civil servants. For policy-making purposes, the main task of the Commission in the EU Treaties is the initiation of legislation. Only the Commission can formally introduce legislation, and it is supposed to promote the European Union interest as a whole. Just like many national legislatures in Europe, the EU's legislature is set up as a bicameral system made up of

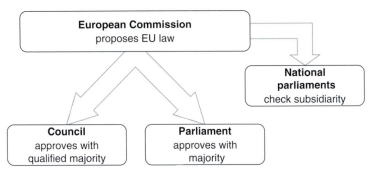

Figure 11.4 The Ordinary Legislative Procedure in the EU

the Council of the EU and Parliament. The Council of the European Union represents member states through national governments at the ministerial level. From a comparative perspective, it can be considered an upper house, as it represents the interests of the constituent units of the EU's federal political system.

Member states also meet at the level of the heads of states and governments in the European Council, which may provide guidance and reach general political agreement on controversial issues, but it is at the ministerial (or lower level) where actual legislative decisions and votes are taken. As a body representing member state governments, the Council is not directly elected; it is simply the representation of the governments that have formed in each EU member state. Therefore, the composition of the Council changes when there is a national government change, for example following a national parliamentary election or a government composition change. The European Parliament represents European citizens and can be considered the lower house of the EU's legislature. It is the only directly elected body of the EU. European elections take place every five years at the same time in each member state on the basis of national party lists. The elected representative from national parties join so-called (transnational) political groups in the EP, which are party groups that include ideologically similar parties across the member states.

Once the political leadership of the Commission decides to go ahead with a formal legislative proposal, it is transmitted to all national parliaments in the EU. This is done to give all national parliaments the opportunity to check the subsidiarity principle, which states that policy should be made by the level of government closest to the citizens as is reasonably feasible. The national parliaments cannot veto the proposal, but they can force the Commission to issue clearer reasons why EU action is necessary or give the Council and the Parliament the task to decide whether the legislative proceedings should continue. Once the legislative proposal reaches the Council and the Parliament, it is up to both bodies to find agreement on a common version. Both Parliament and Council can propose amendments, but ultimately the (amended) version must find the support of a qualified majority of member states in the Council and a majority inside the European Parliament.

As with national legislation, the Commission's proposal typically follows extensive consultations with interest groups. In doing so, the EU has adopted a pluralist interest group system. There are more than 10,000 officially registered interest group organizations in Brussels alone, ranging from firms, employer associations, to government organizations, NGOs, and non-profit associations. Many of these organizations try to persuade actors inside the Commission, the Council, or the Parliament directly (inside lobbying). This strategy works for well-organized interests with large numbers of lobbyists in Brussels. Alternatively, an interest group can also try to create public attention by organizing demonstrations or protests (outside lobbying), see section 11.5. Transparency organizations, such as Transparency International, attempt to make inside lobbying strategies known to the wider public. Figure 11.5 shows the number of meetings of different interest group types with European Commission officials. It shows that the most active interest groups using inside lobbying are indeed corporations (such as Google) or business umbrella organizations (such as BusinessEurope). Civil society organizations and NGOs (e.g. European Consumer Organization) have only half the number of meetings with Commission officials as companies.

Consider one of the most significant, but also controversial, pieces of recent European Union legislation: the general data protection regulation (GDPR). In force since 2018, the EU

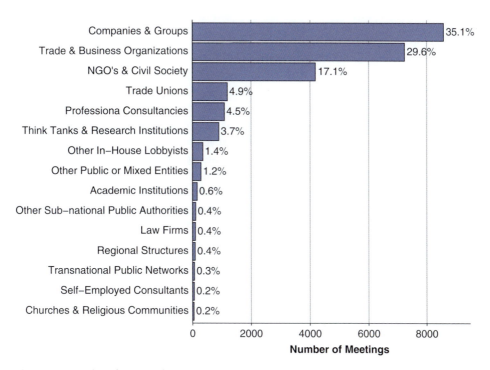

Figure 11.5 Number of Meetings between Interest Groups and the European Commission (2014–2020)

Data source: EU Integrity Watch (2020)

regulation provides strong data protection rules applicable to all companies operating in the EU (independent of their base of origin). The scope of this legislation is far-reaching: it allows EU citizens to have more control over the use of their personal data, in particular online, and it benefits businesses to have a single set of rules applicable across the EU. Moreover, it provides a global template for how to deal with personal data protection in the digital world. So how did this major EU law come about?

First, we need to consider what policy authority the member states have delegated to the supranational level. Up until the most recent change of the EU treaties, the EU's quasi constitution, data protection laws in the EU have been based on Treaty rules allowing the EU to legislate to facilitate the functioning of the EU's single market. Through the Treaty of Lisbon, member states chose to delegate the authority to set single data protection rules to the EU. In fact, the right to protection of personal data is enshrined in both the EU's charter of fundamental rights as well as the Treaties. On this new legal basis, the European Commission was able to propose a legislative initiative as the agenda-setter. The Commission proposal was presented to the European Parliament and the Council in 2012. With regard to the subsidiarity check by national parliaments, four parliaments voiced concerns over the necessity to adopt an EU-wide regulation, but that was insufficient to trigger further scrutiny (see Chapter 12.1 for a discussion of yellow and orange card processes). The Council met more than twenty times to discuss the proposal for the regulation, and it was not until 2016 that the regulation was approved, following the passage of several amendments, by the Council and the European Parliament.

It is useful to consider how the legislative procedure in the EU, involving veto powers of the Council and the European Parliament, has come about and its implications on the policy stability in the EU. Table 11.2 divides the legislative decision-making history of the EU into four phases and allows an analysis from a Veto Players perspective. The first phase lasted from the foundation of the EU until the passage of the Single European Act. During this time, the EU treaties provided for a legislative procedure with only one legislative chamber, the Council of the European Union, as the representation of the national governments. This procedure was known as the consultation procedure, as the Parliament (at the time indirectly appointed by national parliaments) was only consulted, and did not have any amendment or veto rights. Even more important was the fact that legislative decisions inside the Council could only be taken unanimously, thus giving each member state a veto right over EU policy. This voting rule was meant to change to qualified majority voting, but instead it was effectively retained in the 1960s through the 'Luxembourg Compromise' after a conflict in the Council, the so-called 'empty chair' crisis (see Box 3.2 in Chapter 3), led to the continued use of national vetoes. The consequence was legislative gridlock in the Council.

The initial goal, formulated in the Treaty of Rome, of achieving the single European market could not be achieved through the adoption of European legislation providing for a common regulatory framework, as every country could claim that support was not feasible due to vital national interests. Veto players theory predicts in such instances increased discretionary power to bureaucracies and courts, which can issue rulings of political significance without fear of being overruled by the member states in the Council. Indeed, the European Court of Justice was able to push forward European economic integration through a range of landmark judicial rulings, an aspect we will address in the next chapter.

The second phase of the EU's legislative decision-making rules began with the adoption of a new Treaty, the Single European Act. Faced with increased global economic competition, member states decided to switch to qualified majority voting in the Council on matters

Table 11.2 History of EU Decision-Making Rules from a Veto Players Perspective

	'Luxembourg Compromise'	SEA/Common Market setup	Post-Maastricht	Post-Lisbon
Period	1958–1987	1988–1992	1993–2014	As of 2014
Legislative Procedure	Consultation	Mainly Consultation	Mainly Co-Decision	Ordinary Legislative Procedure
Veto Players	Council	Council	Council + EP	Council + EP
Council Voting Rule	Unanimity	QMV	QMV	Lower QMV threshold (double majority)
Main Characteristic	Legislative gridlock, large policy discretion to Court	Council more effective, Commission agenda-setting	Parliament a co-equal legislator (bicameral system)	Bicameralism, decisions in Council facilitated

related to the single market. This allowed the European Commission to propose a range of common rules that eventually led to the completion of the internal market in the early 1990s. The third phase began with the Treaty of Maastricht, which for the first time turned the EU into a bicameral legislature. In addition to the Council, the European Parliament was able to veto legislation through the newly established co-decision procedure, albeit in the beginning only in some limited policy areas. Over the course of subsequent treaty revisions in the 1990s and 2000s, however, the application of the co-decision procedure was expanded to other areas. The Treaty of Lisbon marks the start of the fourth phase, which lowered the threshold necessary to achieve a qualified majority in the Council and expanded the veto power of the European Parliament to almost all policy areas. The co-decision procedure was renamed the ordinary legislative procedure, since it is now the standard way of adopting EU legislation.

Two institutional veto players thus structure EU legislative decision-making: the Council of the EU, representing national governments, and the European Parliament, representing EU citizens. Relating this back to the institutional structure of national legislatures found in Europe, this bicameral configuration is very similar to the one found in Germany. One controversy surrounding the EU's legislative system is that the ordinary legislative procedure only provides the European Commission with the sole right of legislative initiative. In practice, however, both the national governments and the European Parliament can call upon the Commission to propose legislation. However, the final decision, including the exact timing and the scope of the initial proposal is still up to the Commission. In addition, since the Treaty of Lisbon, European citizens can call on the European Commission to propose legislation through the Citizens' Initiative (see Box 6.4). Some researchers have pointed out that while the treaties confer the Commission a formal agenda-setting role, the ability of the Commission to set the policy agenda is limited and its success rate of getting its policy proposals adopted is lower than the success rates of governments in EU member states (Kreppel and Oztas, 2017). There is evidence that the overall legislative output of the EU is actually declining. Both the number of EU directives and EU regulations have decreased since the early 2000s (Toshkov, 2020). While there are notable and significant EU laws, such data suggest that the EU has adopted policies that tend to be rather stable, perhaps due to its relatively high number of veto players.

Finally, researchers have examined the role of interest groups in EU policy-making. On the one hand, there is strong evidence that business interest groups rely more on inside lobbying than other groups, such as citizen groups, and have better access to decision-makers (Dür and Mateo, 2016). On the other hand, the empirical evidence on the impact of business groups is mixed. Business groups appear no more likely influence the European Commission's legislative proposals than other types of organizations (Klüver, 2013). One reason may be that business interest groups need to increasingly defend the status quo, rather than work towards changing it. Dür et al. (2019) argue that, after the single market was more or less completed, the European Commission, supported by the European Parliament, has tended to introduce proposals that aim to increase environmental protection or advance the interests of consumers. These are areas in which it can strengthen its regulatory role. Citizen interest groups can therefore often work with the Commission and Parliament towards policy change, leaving business interest groups on the defensive and with only national governments in the Council to influence the negotiations on their behalf.

11.7 **Summary**

This chapter introduced law-making in Europe as a process characterized by agenda-setting rights and veto power. On the basis of the Veto Players theory, it is possible to analyse the potential for a legislative change across different systems by taking into account the number of veto players but also their policy disagreements. Delegation to cabinet ministers in parliamentary systems creates the opportunity for partisan position-taking and the need for coalition partners to monitor, and rein in, ministerial action in parliament. Beyond these formal actors, other actors influence the policy process through more informal routes, such as interest or pressure groups. The formal strength of these actors and the way that they access the policy process varies across countries.

The chapter furthermore discussed law-making in the EU, in which a supranational agenda-setter, the Commission, proposes legislation to national governments and the European Parliament. The EU has evolved towards a strong bicameral system, where national governments share ultimate policy-making authority with the directly elected Parliament. Although its institutional structure differs from that of national political systems in Europe, we can use the same principles of veto players theory to understand how politics works at the European level.

Online Data Exercise: WhoGov Dataset

This chapter's interactive online exercise focuses on two key concepts in coalition politics: Gamson's Law and portfolio allocation. Using the WhoGov dataset on cabinet compositions in government, you will examine whether governing parties receive their fair share of ministerial positions and whether they receive their preferred policy portfolios.

 Take your learning further with this interactive data exercise, available at **www.foundationsofeuropeanpolitics.com**

 For additional material and resources, including multiple-choice questions, web links, and more, please visit the online resources: **www.oup.com/he/devries1e**

Policy Outcomes in Europe

This chapter explores policy outcomes across European countries. We look at a number of particularly salient policy areas, ranging from those that are decided primarily at the national level (e.g health) to policies that are determined at the EU level (e.g. trade), and those where decision-making is shared across different levels of government (e.g. environment and immigration). The chapter focuses on the role of position-taking by political parties and other groups, such as interest groups and social movements, in explaining variation in policy outcomes.

Why do policy outcomes change over time and why do they differ across countries? In Chapter 11, we introduced law-making in Europe as a process characterized by agenda-setting rights and veto power. **Veto Players** theory allows us to understand differences in the extent of legislative change across systems by taking into account the number of veto players and also their policy disagreements. Yet, Veto Players theory provides less insight into the content of that policy change. For example, why do some countries spend more on healthcare than others? And, why have some countries adopted more restrictive immigration policies over the years? In this chapter, we provide some insight to these questions by focusing on two specific factors: the position-taking of political parties and other groups, such as interest groups and social movements, as well as the degree of sharing policy authority across different levels of government. As we have highlighted in Chapter 3, European politics is characterized by a multilevel governance structure in which responsibility for policy-making is shared across several territorial levels. Although it may seem reasonable to expect that policy outcomes of EU member states would be more similar as a result of cooperation, this is not necessarily the case. Policy outcomes ranging from economic growth, to inequality, to air pollution, and renewable energy differ tremendously across the EU.

An important source of cross-country variation stems from the way in which power is institutionalized domestically. Throughout virtually all the chapters of this book, we have highlighted important institutional differences across European countries. In some countries power is highly concentrated among a small set of political institutions and actors, while in other countries power is much more dispersed. Research suggests that these institutional differences affect the policy outcomes we observe (e.g. Lijphart, 1992). The relationship between the EU and national institutions in specific areas of policy-making offers another source of variation in policy outcomes. The extent to which the EU and national institutions actually share power in policy-making differs tremendously across policy areas. In some policy areas, like trade or competition policy, EU institutions dominate policy-making. Yet, in other policy areas, like immigration or the environment, EU institutions share policy-making authority with member state institutions. In still other policy areas, like health and taxation, EU institutions have little policy influence. The way in which responsibility to make policy, known as

policy competence, is shared with the EU or not shared affects the degree of variation in policy outcomes we observe. Of course, decision-making in the EU involves member state governments through their participation in the Council of the EU. And even if EU institutions are more dominant in policy-making vis-à-vis national institutions, EU institutions often have to rely on member states to implement those policies. The different national bureaucratic institutions and traditions may again have an important bearing on the kind of policy outcomes we observe (e.g. Knill and Lenschow, 2005; Mbaye, 2001).

The degree to which national institutions share policy authority with the EU has also become a hot topic of political debate. Eurosceptic political parties, especially those on the extreme left and right of the political spectrum, have politicized the growing influence of EU institutions on domestic policy-making. The reasons for the politicization of EU competences differ for parties on the left and right. Extreme right parties, such as the National Rally in France or Party for Freedom in the Netherlands, often criticize the influence of supranational institutions on domestic politics or the free movement of people in the context of the Single Market, while parties on the extreme left, such as the Left Party in Germany or Podemos in in Spain, criticize the market-orientated focus of EU policy-making and the lack of shared social policy (Hooghe et al., 2002). In addition to national political parties, other domestic institutions, such as national constitutional courts, for example, have contributed to the politicization of EU policy competences (see also Chapter 13).

In this chapter, we provide an overview of the complexities of policy-making in Europe. The first part of the chapter outlines how the mix of national and EU authority varies across policy areas. We introduce the distinction between policy areas based on the exclusive competence, shared competence, or supporting competence of EU institutions. The second part of the chapter focuses on the policy-making process and policy outcomes in four policy domains: health, immigration, environmental, and trade policy. These areas have been characterized by considerable politicization in domestic politics recently.

12.1 Policy Authority in a Multilevel Europe

Who should decide on policy? This a crucial question to be answered in any political system, but especially within the multilevel governance structure of the EU. In fact, when it comes to the EU, the question of who decides on what has, itself, become a salient topic in political debate. According to some politicians the EU decides too much. For example, the British Conservative politician Boris Johnson, while acting as British foreign minister, stated that the EU wanted to create an 'overarching European state' and centralize policy-making in Brussels (BBC, 2018). Yet, other politicians claim that the EU does not do enough when it comes to policy-making. French President Emmanuel Macron has repeatedly called on the EU 'to do more and sooner' to meet policy challenges like climate change or growing inequality (Macron, 2019). The relationship between EU and national institutions when it comes to policy-making are laid down in European Treaties (see Chapter 3). The Treaties define the scope of the powers of each institution within the EU and the relationships to member states.

Article 5(2) of the Treaty of the European Union explicitly states that the EU only has the competences that are conferred on it by the Treaties. The exercise of competences by EU institutions is subject to two fundamental principles: the **principles of proportionality** and **subsidiarity**.

Proportionality refers to the notion that the content and scope of action by EU institutions should go no further than what is necessary to achieve the objectives as laid down within the Treaties, while subsidiarity is the idea that EU institutions only take action when EU-level action would be more effective than actions at a lower level (national, regional, or local) (see also Chapter 3). The Court of Justice of the European Union checks and reviews the exercise of powers by EU institutions (see also Chapter 13).

Member states have agreed to transfer policy-making power to the EU to achieve certain goals only in some policy areas. It is important not to confuse increasing competences with a general transfer of power by the member states to the EU. The degree to which the EU has policy authority depends on the type of conferral that has taken place. Broadly, we can distinguish between three different types of competences: (1) **exclusive competences**, i.e. areas in which policy can only be decided at the EU level, and not at the national level, (2) **shared competences**, i.e. areas in which member states can act, but only if the EU has chosen not to, and (3) **competences to support**, coordinate, or supplement national actions, i.e. the EU may not adopt laws that lead to a EU-wide harmonisation of national laws or regulations. These are areas that remain the remit of member states. Figure 12.1 illustrates provides examples of policy areas that fall under the different type of competences. The degree of EU authority is the highest in the case of exclusive competences and the lowest when it comes to supporting competences, EU authority in policy areas characterized by shared competences falls in between.

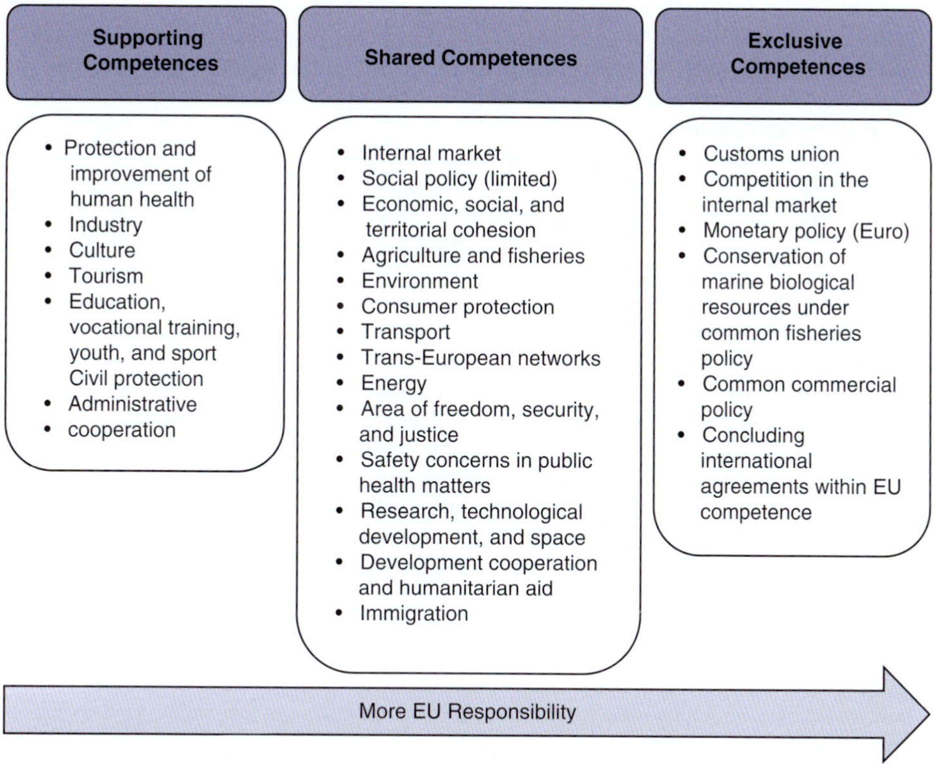

Supporting Competences	Shared Competences	Exclusive Competences
• Protection and improvement of human health • Industry • Culture • Tourism • Education, vocational training, youth, and sport Civil protection • Administrative • cooperation	• Internal market • Social policy (limited) • Economic, social, and territorial cohesion • Agriculture and fisheries • Environment • Consumer protection • Transport • Trans-European networks • Energy • Area of freedom, security, and justice • Safety concerns in public health matters • Research, technological development, and space • Development cooperation and humanitarian aid • Immigration	• Customs union • Competition in the internal market • Monetary policy (Euro) • Conservation of marine biological resources under common fisheries policy • Common commercial policy • Concluding international agreements within EU competence

More EU Responsibility →

Figure 12.1 Policy-Making Powers of the European Union

EU member states have decided to give the EU the sole authority to make policy regarding the customs union, EU trade policy, and policing competition in the internal market. This means that the EU sets the external tariff rates for bringing goods into the EU from the rest of the world for all its member states. The EU, specifically the Commission, also negotiates trade deals with other countries, such as the EU's bilateral trade deal with Japan, and represents all EU member states in the World Trade Organization. Lastly, the Commission alone can fine firms for violating antitrust regulations and attempting to create monopolies, as it has done previously with major multinational corporations such as Microsoft and Google. In other areas, both the EU and the member states can make policy, such as in the area of the

Box 12.1 CASE STUDY: Monetary Policy in the EU

In 1993, the EU paved the way for the creation of the Economic and Monetary Union (EMU) through the Treaty of Maastricht. The EMU is a combination of monetary and fiscal policy, and EU institutions have exclusive competence in the case of monetary policy for member states which are part of the Euro, the Eurozone. The Eurozone, established in 1999, is the group of nineteen EU member states that use the Euro as their currency. While Denmark and the United Kingdom (before it left the EU) were permanently exempted from joining the Eurozone, all other member states are legally required to join at some point. Whether they will, though, remains an open question.

An independent central bank, the **European Central Bank** (ECB), issues the Euro currency, thereby controlling money supply for the entire Eurozone. While monetary policy is a competence of EU institutions, fiscal policy in the form of taxation and government expenditure remains under the control of national governments, even for Eurozone members, albeit within some limits. EU institutions can use some softer instruments of coordination through annual cycles of economic policy discussions or the formulation of broad economic policy guidelines. When it comes to the Eurozone, the EU is a monetary union, but not a fiscal union.

Monetary policy for the Eurozone is managed through the ECB and a European system of national central banks. The ECB is an independent body that can make monetary policy free from political influence of EU or national institutions. According to the Treaty, its primary mission is to ensure price stability by keeping price inflation in the Eurozone below 2 per cent. Decisions on monetary policy in the Eurozone are taken by the ECB's governing council which is made up by the members of the ECB's executive board and the governors of the national central banks of Eurozone countries. EU member states outside the Eurozone coordinate their monetary policy with the ECB within the European system of central banks.

Members of the EMU are expected to comply with the Stability and Growth Pact (SGP) which provides a set of rules for coordination of fiscal policy. Under the SGP member states are expected to keep their national debt and budget deficits and low, with debt not to exceed 60 per cent of GDP, and deficits below 3 per cent of GDP. There exists the potential for fines for countries that violate the rules. However, the credibility of the SGP was undermined by both Germany and France in 2003 when they ran a yearly deficit of more than 3 per cent of GDP and were not fined. Other countries then widely broke the government budget deficit criteria. The SGP was reinforced in the aftermath of the financial crisis in 2008, with the addition of new penalties.

During the Eurozone crisis, the ECB also sparked controversy by undertaking a range of unorthodox monetary policies. The effectiveness and legality of some of these policies, especially the buying of struggling Eurozone countries' bonds in unlimited amounts on secondary markets, has divided policy-makers and constitutional lawyers, best illustrated by legal challenges to the ECB's mandate in cases before the German Constitutional Court. The struggle between national courts and European constitutional court over the primacy of EU law is a topic we will address Chapter 13.

environment or developing laws to protect consumers. Finally, some areas are considered too sensitive to allow for much EU involvement, beyond coordination agreed to by member state governments. These areas include policing, education, and health. But even in these areas, the EU facilitates cooperation between members. In short, the involvement of the European Union in policy-making across Europe depends heavily on the type of policy under consideration.

In areas of shared competences, EU and national institutions are both able to legislate and adopt legally binding acts. National institutions exercise their own competence only when the EU does not already have related laws in place. EU legislation not only replaces the content of national law, but it also removes the national right to legislate in the covered area. When EU and national institutions share competence, EU law has primacy over any adopted national law (see also Chapter 13). Shared competences apply to the single market—which includes the free movement of goods, services, persons, and capital—agriculture, transportation, immigration, and environmental protection, for example.

With shared competences, the dividing line between EU and national competences is not always so clear, and the principle of subsidiarity comes into play. Indeed, political disagreements may exist about whether policy should actually be decided jointly with EU institutions or not. Subsidiarity is a political principle rather than a source of clear legal guidance, and is subject to interpretation. For example, does the burden of proof to legitimize EU action lie with national or EU institutions? Over the years the role of national parliaments in EU policy-making has been strengthened in keeping with the principle of subsidiarity. Specifically, an **early warning mechanism on subsidiarity**, also referred to as the **yellow card mechanism**, has been created. Through this mechanism any national parliament or any chamber of a national parliament has the right to object to draft EU legislation if it considers it not to be in compliance with the principle of subsidiarity. If one-third of national parliaments consider that a legislative proposal by the European Commission violates the principle, the Commission receives a so-called 'yellow card': the Commission must then decide whether to go ahead with the proposal, whether to amend it, or whether to withdraw it altogether. It must also indicate reasons for its decisions. If more than half of national parliaments consider the principle of subsidiarity to be violated, then they issue an 'orange card': it is then up to the Council or the European Parliament to decide whether to withdraw the proposal. The procedure thus does not allow national parliaments to veto an EU proposal. Instead, it forces the political actors, the Commission, Council, and the Parliament, to take an explicit decision on subsidiarity and indicate reasons for pursuing the policy. However, under the orange card procedure, the Council could stop the legislative procedure unilaterally with a 55 per cent majority. Thus, the national governments retain the ultimate power to stop an EU legislative procedure on grounds of a violation of the subsidiarity principle when following the opinions of their national parliaments (in which they presumably control at least an implicit majority). The orange card procedure has never been invoked, possibly because the Commission refrains from initiating proposals that are likely to trigger an orange card.

In other areas, policy-making power is exclusively in the hands of national institutions. EU institutions only have **supporting competences** to coordinate or complement the action of national institutions. Income taxation and healthcare are examples of policy areas in which there is primarily national level competence. In these areas EU institutions have no power to pass laws and cannot interfere with the policy-making of national institutions. As we explained in Chapter 3, there has been much more sharing of policy authority with EU institutions in the economic realm compared to other policy areas, such as social policy, taxation, or defence. Social policy, taxation, and defence are part of what political scientists coin **core state powers**. Core state powers generally refer to two aspects of policy. First, they refer to power over policy related to a state's monopoly on the legitimate use of coercion and taxation, e.g. policies related to coercive capacity (military, police, border patrol), fiscal capacity (money, taxes, debt), and the administrative capacity needed to manage coercive and fiscal capacity and to implement and enforce public laws and policies (Weber, 1978). Second, they refer to how important policy areas are for defining a state as a sovereign entity, such as the political notion of 'high politics' (Hoffmann, 1966), which generally refers to policy areas central to state survival and national security.

Next to the three types of competences outlined in Figure 12.1, the EU has also **special competences** in some policy areas. For example, it can take measures to ensure that member states coordinate their economic, social, and employment policies at EU level. Additionally, Common Foreign and Security Policy (CFSP), as the EU's foreign policy is known, deals with diplomacy, security, and defence cooperation. This is an area of 'high politics'. CFSP is formally an intergovernmental policy area where the national governments are the key actors and decisions are taken unanimously. European direction is given through the European Council and the Council of Ministers. Yet, the European Commission is responsible for the implementation of the CFSP, which is carried out by the High Representative of the Union for Foreign Affairs and Security Policy. This position was created in 2008 as a way to strengthen the EU's diplomacy. The various forms of the EU's external relations constitute a mixture of different competencies and actors.

Thus, while some coordination exists, member states essentially decide foreign policy on their own. This has led to criticisms that the EU's ability to take a common stance is undermined by divisions between member states, something that became apparent during the invasion of Iraq by allied forces in 2003 which created deep divisions between EU member states. France and Germany opposed the war, while the United Kingdom, Italy, Spain, and the Netherlands supported the invasion of Iraq led by the United States. Another example of tensions in foreign policy coordination is Russia. While the EU has maintained sanctions on Russia since 2014 after the annexation of Crimea, member states remain divided over how closely to work with Moscow on energy and other areas. The EU has also witnessed areas of concerted diplomatic effort, for example, when playing a leading role in negotiating international agreements including the Paris climate accord and the Iranian nuclear deal finalized in 2015.

12.2 Trade Policy

The EU is active in many policy areas, and the relationship between EU and national institutions differs tremendously across these areas. In this section and the following ones, we will discuss policy-making and outcomes in four areas—trade, immigration, environment, and health—to illustrate how the different relationships between EU and national institutions matter for the policy outcomes we observe. While EU institutions have exclusive competences in trade policy, they share competences with national institutions in the areas of immigration and the environment, and only have supporting competences in the area of health policy.

As European countries are major players in world trade, it should come as no surprise that removing barriers to trade has been one of the core areas of policy-making within the EU. In the early days of integration, internal trade liberalization was accompanied by external trade barriers. In recent years, the EU has intensified its efforts to negotiate international trade agreements. The EU needs a unified trade policy because of its customs union, which sets a single external tariff for the entire bloc, and its single market, which treats all goods and services that enter the EU the same. The EU's trade policy is of enormous importance not only within Europe but across the globe. In 2019, EU exports represented 15.9 per cent of global exports and EU imports 15.4 per cent, making it one of the world's biggest trade players alongside the US and China. In 2019, the top exporter nations among current EU member states were Germany, France, Netherlands, Italy, and Spain.

Because trade outside the EU is an exclusive responsibility of the EU, the EU institutions make laws on trade matters and negotiate and conclude international trade agreements. By acting as one at the World Trade Organization and when negotiating trade deals, EU countries benefit from increased negotiating power. Trade agreements help European businesses with supply chains, as they can access raw materials or necessities more easily and at lower prices, and gain better market access for their goods and services. This should make companies more competitive and help secure growth and employment within the EU. Trade agreements also give consumers a wider choice of products at lower prices. Yet, trade agreements may also have adverse effects on working conditions and the environment, especially within economically developing nations. Increasingly, EU institutions seek to ensure that trade agreements foster human rights, working conditions, and environmental protection.

To complete a trade agreement many institutions are involved. First, national governments, through the European Council and the Council of Ministers, must agree to give the European Commission a mandate to negotiate with a specific partner. The European commissioner for trade then takes the lead and negotiates a deal. Before any deal can be signed, it must be approved by the European Parliament and the Council of Ministers, just like any other piece of legislation. Finally, if a trade deal is particularly broad, it may also require the individual approval of each EU member state.

The European Commission helps put EU trade policy into effect. This sometimes involves updating the EU's existing trade laws. Between signing and ratifying the deal, parts of the agreement can be 'provisionally applied'—put into effect before ratification—if the Council decides to do so. Provisional application usually only takes effect once the European Parliament has given its consent. The EU–Canada Comprehensive Economic and Trade Agreement (CETA) offers one such example. Although signed in 2016 and given consent by the European Parliament in 2017, CETA is currently applied on a provisional basis and has yet to take full effect because only not all member states have been able to ratify the agreement. Canada has already completed its ratification process.

In recent years, the EU's efforts to sign trade agreements with non-EU countries, like Canada, or other international organizations, like MERCOSUR, have generated unprecedented controversy. The Transatlantic Trade and Investment Partnership (TTIP) is perhaps the best example of this development (Sojka et al., 2020). TTIP is a proposed trade and investment treaty between the EU and the US. Negotiations were launched in 2013, but ended without conclusion after the election of Republican Donald Trump as US President in 2016. The EU and the US have the largest and deepest bilateral trade and investment relationship in the world and have highly integrated economies (Hamilton, 2014). TTIP was designed to solidify the trading relationship. The negotiations focused on lifting trade barriers to allow free international trade between the EU and US. They dealt, among other things, with the abolition of customs tariffs, government procurement, sustainability, and various regulations, standards, and procedures for product and firms.

There has been strong resistance to TTIP especially among political parties on the left of the political spectrum and some unions, charities, NGOs, and environmentalists in Europe. The main concerns included the agreement's potentially adverse effects on environmental and food-safety standards, the erosion of sovereignty under the proposed procedures for investment arbitration, and the overall lack of transparency in the negotiations. In July 2014 a committee of citizens and organizations asked the European Commission to register a proposal for a European Citizens' Initiative (ECI) called 'Stop TTIP' with the intention of blocking the TTIP (later also CETA) and delivered over 3 million signatures against the agreement. In September 2014, the European Commission denied the committee's request on legal grounds, but the Court of Justice of the EU (CJEU) annulled that decision in May 2017. On 10 July 2017 the ECI 'Stop TTIP' was formally registered and started a one-year process of collection of signatures (European Commission, 2017).

Opposition towards TTIP was strong in many member states, but particularly in Germany and Italy (Caiani and Graziano, 2018). The Italian opposition was organized through Slow Europe, an organization that supported several other ECIs. Slow Europe is part of a broader social movement called Slow Food founded in 1989 with the objective of defending small-scale traditional food producers and raising awareness among consumers at the grassroots level. Slow Europe's opposition concentrated on the fact that TTIP would align the EU's food and environmental safety regulations with the US's less strict laws with respect to genetically modified crops and the use of growth hormones in livestock. In Germany, TTIP became a focal point for parts of the public to create a protest movement against free trade. The movement included ordinary citizens, trade unions, nature conservation movements, and Christian organizations. It generated enormous public pressure and ultimately changed the opinions of many Germans on TTIP negotiations (Chan and Crawdford, 2017). An analysis of anti–TTIP mobilization in Austria, France, Germany, Italy, Spain, and the United Kingdom, shows that while the movements in different countries varied in terms of activities and actors, a Europeanized approach could be found in terms of similarity in the topics and targets addressed as well as organizational features (Caiani and Graziano, 2018).

Concluding EU trade agreements has not only become more politicized in national politics; it is also complicated by the fact that some trade agreements require ratification by national parliaments. While some EU trade agreements cover only policy areas that are within the exclusive competence of the EU institutions, other agreements involve areas of shared competence. In the case of these mixed trade agreements, national parliaments have to ratify the agreement, thus adding a potential veto player to the decision-making process. While for a long time the role of national parliaments consisted of 'rubber-stamping' an agreement that had been signed by their government, in recent years parliamentary ratification has become more difficult. The role of national parliaments has been topic of heated discussion at the EU level.

In 2014, the European Commission asked the CJEU to rule if the EU–Singapore trade agreement could be approved by EU governments in the Council or if national parliaments must also be included in the ratification process. In a ruling from 2017, the CJEU reaffirmed that national parliaments across the EU should have a say on ratifying the Singapore trade agreement. The Court ruled that the provisions relating to non-direct foreign investment and dispute settlement do not fall within the exclusive competence of the EU. This ruling set an important precedent for other trade agreements that are currently being negotiated or ratified.

12.3 Immigration Policy

Competence over immigration policy is shared between EU and national institutions. According to the Treaties, on the basis of a principle of solidarity, immigration policies are to be governed by the fair sharing of responsibility, including its financial implications, between the member states. When it comes to regular migration, EU institutions have the authority to lay down the conditions governing entry into and legal residence in a member state, including for the purposes of family reunification, for third-country nationals. National institutions retain the right to determine volumes of admission for people coming from third countries to seek work. When it comes to irregular migration, EU institutions are required to prevent and reduce irregular immigration, in particular by means of an effective return policy, in a manner consistent with fundamental rights. Finally, when it comes to integration of migrants and refugees, EU institutions can provide incentives and support for measures taken by national institutions to promote the integration of legally resident migrants and refugees, yet EU law makes no provision for the harmonization of national laws and regulations.

Immigration policy has become one of the most salient and divisive policy issues in Europe. While in the area of trade, EU institutions have pushed for liberalization and openness, external immigration policy has focused on border fortification policies and the creation of a system of border patrols and detention centres to prevent irregular immigration—activities that have led to the coining of the phrase 'Fortress Europe' in public debate. EU and national leaders face a dilemma when it comes to immigration policy. While significant parts of the public are increasingly sceptical of immigration, labour and skill shortages as well as an ageing population make immigration necessary. Moreover, within the EU, free movement of people is one of the founding principles of the single market. Yet, even internal EU migration has become a touchstone of dissent within national politics. Especially radical right Eurosceptic parties attempt to increase their vote shares by mobilizing discontent towards EU migrants, in addition to other forms of migration (De Vries, 2018). Figure 12.2 shows the importance different party families in Europe attach to the immigration issue across four time points, 2006, 2010, 2017, and 2019, based on a party expert survey (Bakker et al., 2015; Polk et al., 2017; Bakker et al., 2020). A score of 10 indicates that a party family attaches high importance to the issue, while 0 indicates it attaches no importance at all. The figure indicates that party families associated with the right of the political spectrum, such as the radical right and conservative, place the highest importance on immigration. Yet, the importance of the immigration issue has also increased somewhat for liberal and social democratic parties.

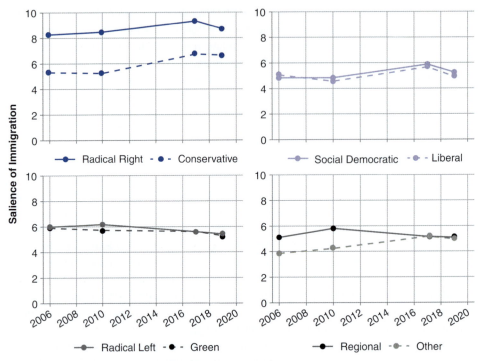

Figure 12.2 Importance of the Immigration Issue for Party Families in Europe

Data source: CHES (Bakker et al., 2015; Polk et al., 2017; Bakker et al., 2020)

Part of the recent increase in the importance parties attach to the immigration issue can be explained by the refugee crisis which reached a peak in 2015. In that year, more than a million migrants and refugees crossed into Europe, sparking a crisis about what role EU institutions should have in deciding how to resettle them. The majority of refugees and migrants fled the civil war in Syria, but other conflicts, most notably in Afghanistan and Iraq, also sparked refugee flows. Many of those fleeing violent conflicts and arriving in Europe claimed asylum. In 2015, Germany received the highest number of new asylum applications, almost half a million, followed by Hungary, Sweden, Austria, Italy, and France. Many migrants and refugees tried, and continue to try, to cross the Mediterranean from Turkey to Greece or from Libya to Italy. These sea journeys are very dangerous, and many refugees and migrants die in the crossing according to data from the International Migration Outlook (OECD, 2016).

The refugee crisis renewed concerns about European border control, in particular. Indeed, one of the most prominent examples of cooperation on border control has been the European Border and Coast Guard Agency, also known as Frontex. Established in 2004, Frontex is an EU agency headquartered in Warsaw, Poland, and tasked with border control of the European Schengen Area, in coordination with the border and coast guards of Schengen Area member states. In response to the refugee crisis, Frontex's mandate was transformed into a European Border and Coast Guard agency. This allowed it to have a permanent funding structure and staff, rather than relying solely on the voluntary contributions by member states. It has since taken up more operational duties using its own aircraft and boats to patrol the Mediterranean. The activities of Frontex have faced strong criticism from human right organizations in recent years. These criticisms focus on Frontex's role in helping national coast guards to block and push back refugees and migrants who have reached member states' territorial waters instead of rescuing them, which is their obligation under EU regulations.

The plight of refugees in 2015–16, as well as the EU's role in the crisis, quickly became politicized. Tension grew, in part, because of the disproportionate burden faced by some countries where the majority of migrants were arriving, most notably Greece, Hungary, and Italy. The escalation led European leaders to reconsider their policies on migrant processing. The European Commission proposed a ten-point plan that included the European Asylum Support Office deploying teams in Greece and Italy to process asylum applications. Many Syrian refugees eventually took refuge in Germany, whose Chancellor Angela Merkel had taken a liberal stance on entry. Her approach was severely criticized by the radical right party, Alternative for Germany (AfD) (Arzheimer and Berning, 2019). The party stoked anti-immigrant fears by linking several terrorist attacks on German soil to the arrival of Syrian refugees.

In some central and east European countries—the Czech Republic, Hungary, Poland, and Slovakia, in particular—opposition grew to a new EU system of quotas to distribute non-EU asylum seekers across the member states. Political parties in these countries had taken increasingly anti-immigrant positions (Rovny, 2014). In Hungary, the ruling party of Prime Minister Viktor Orbán mobilized the issue against the EU, going so far as to hold a referendum on the quota system in October 2016. While an overwhelming majority of voters rejected the EU's migrant quotas, voter turnout was below 50 per cent, rendering the vote invalid. The Hungarian government nonetheless refused to agree with the quota system, a decision that was condemned by the European Commission. In 2020, the CJEU ruled that Hungary, together with the Czech Republic and Poland, violated EU law by refusing to accept asylum seekers under the 2015 migrant redistribution scheme. The Czech, Hungarian, and Polish governments opposed the quota system arguing that accepting refugees would have posed a security threat. The CJEU rejected these claims in their ruling and argued that the three governments should have conducted a case-by-case investigation for each applicant to prove they posed a security threat. Despite this ruling, the fact that EU institutions share policy authority with national governments in the area of immigration makes it difficult to enforce compliance.

One of the key reasons why member states seek to cooperate in the areas of immigration, refugee, and asylum policy is the fact that the Schengen agreement secures free movement of people within the borders of many European countries, and also makes it easier for migrants and refugees to move from one member state to another. The Schengen area, which includes all EU member states (except for Bulgaria, Croatia, and Romania) as well as Norway, Iceland, Liechtenstein, and Switzerland, allows citizens and legal residents to move around without needing to show a passport. The entry into Schengen of some central and eastern European member states was a major concern for some. For example in the Netherlands, radical right political entrepreneur Geert Wilders and his Party for Freedom stirred opposition against labour migration, especially from Poland. Labour migration is, of course, allowed and guaranteed by free movement within the single market, but is made even easier in the absence of borders. In 2013, the Party for Freedom launched a website where people could report complaints arising from Polish migrants living or working in their neighbourhood, leading Polish migrants to report an increase in feelings of discrimination.

Even in non-Schengen countries, like the United Kingdom, labour migration from central and eastern European member states became a salient political issue. The British government under Prime Minister Tony Blair decided, unlike most other EU member states, not to impose restrictions on workers from the central and eastern European member states after accession (Ireland and Sweden also immediately allowed workers from these countries). The inflow of migrant workers was politicized by tabloid newspapers and political parties, in particular the *Daily Mail* and the UK Independence Party. Notwithstanding the positive economic impact of migration on the British economy, the influx of migrant workers from other EU member

---

Box 12.2 **CONTROVERSIES AND DEBATES:** Is the EU a Regulatory State?

Over the years, an academic debate has arisen about the nature of policy-making in the EU. While some, like Giandomenico Majone (1998), suggest that the EU is a **regulatory state**, others like Andreas Føllesdal and Simon Hix (2006), argue policy-making at the EU level has clear redistributive consequences. A regulatory state is one that pursues economic policy objectives through regulatory and deregulatory means, rather than direct intervention and redistribution. The delegation of regulatory powers to supranational institutions is a means for member states to credibly commit to integration and the implementation of EU policies. Majone, compares delegation to the Commission with national forms of delegation such as to an independent central bank.

As a regulatory institution, Majone argues that the European Commission can develop policies that are efficient in the long term for member states, as it does not face electoral pressures. Member state governments, in order to be re-elected, might be motivated to increase spending or implement tax cuts even if this is not the optimal policy in the long term. Political accountability of the EU's regulatory institutions is secured, according to Majone, by a variety of substantive and procedural controls, among which judicial review is especially important.

Majone's notion of the EU as a regulatory state has been most prominently criticized by Føllesdal and Hix (2006). They argue that EU policy-making has clear redistributive consequences. Many aspects of EU policy-making, such as the common agricultural policy or structural funds, involve the allocation and redistribution of the EU's budgetary resources. While regulation in Majone's thinking is about addressing market failures and producing policy outcomes that are efficient, Føllesdal and Hix suggest that many policies create both winners and losers. Føllesdal and Hix suggest that who gains from these redistributive policies depends on the interests of member states, the power of organized interests, and the institutional rules of budgetary decision-making. Hence, redistributive policies require democratic, responsive, and accountable decision-makers.

For Føllesdal and Hix, another reason why the EU may go beyond a simple a regulatory state is because member state governments are able to undertake policies at the EU level that they cannot pursue at the domestic level, where they are constrained by parliaments, courts, and corporatist interest group structures. These policy outcomes include a market-driven regulatory framework for the single market, a monetarist framework for EMU and massive subsidies to farmers through the common agricultural policy. These policies may lead to policy drift so that they no longer reflect the policy preferences of European voters. Føllesdal and Hix therefore plead for more democratic contestation over policy and leadership at the EU level to legitimize the distributional choices made. While this may lead to a loss of efficiency the benefits of democratic contestation outweigh the costs according to the authors.

states would become one of the major themes in Eurosceptic mobilization in the United Kingdom as well as in the 2016 Brexit vote (Hobolt, 2016).

12.4 Environmental Policy

Environmental policy has gravitated from being a marginal aspect of the European integration process to the centre stage of EU policy-making. Citizens in Europe view environmental protection as a key priority for the EU. When European citizens were asked what they thought the priorities for the European Commission should be in 2019, 40 per cent of them stated that the environment should be its key priority for the future, followed by protecting jobs, 34 per cent, and social security, 23 per cent (De Vries and Hoffmann, 2019). The EU's environmental policy is also one of the few areas that consistently generates a high level of support among European citizens (Eurobarometer, 2020). As EU and national institutions implement more policies to combat climate change, through renewable energy policy for example, public opinion shifts towards prioritizing the environment (Anderson et al., 2017).

The EU's environment policy dates back to the environmental action programmes adopted by the Commission after Europe's heads of governments declared the need for a joint environment policy flanking economic expansion at a European Council held in Paris in 1972. The Single European Act provided a more secure legal basis for a common environmental policy by introducing a specific 'Environment Title' with the aims of preserving the quality of the environment, protecting human health, and ensuring rational use of natural resources. Subsequent treaty revisions strengthened the EU's commitment to environmental protection. The Treaties of Maastricht and Amsterdam established the duty to integrate environmental protection into all EU sectoral policies to promote sustainable development. 'Combating climate change' became a specific goal with the Treaty of Lisbon, as did sustainable development in relations with third countries. EU institutions could now conclude international agreements on behalf of its member states. In 2020, the European Commission launched a set of policy initiatives, also known as the European Green Deal, with the overarching aim of making Europe climate neutral in 2050 if they are adopted into law.

Since the 1970s, the EU's environment policy has evolved from a set of single measures to a system of multilevel environmental governance. The legislative output, that was rather limited in the 1970s, sky-rocketed in the 1980s and 1990s, only to tail off again in the 2000s (Benson Gravey, and Jordan et al., 2016). Key directives involved regulation concerning air quality, water, chemicals, and maritime issues. The CJEU played a crucial role in establishing and safeguarding the EU's environmental policy through rulings on the **direct effect** of directives (for more information on direct effect, see also Chapter 13). The development, implementation, and evaluation of environment policy is supported by the European Environment Agency based in Copenhagen. This EU agency, which is also open to non-EU members, is responsible for providing sound and independent information on the state of and outlook for the environment.

The Commission's plans for a European Green Deal aims to transform the EU from a high- to a low-carbon economy. It will work through a framework of regulation and legislation which sets out clear overarching targets. Through the European Green Deal, the EU wishes to achieve the goal of net zero carbon emissions by 2050, and a 50–55 per cent cut in emissions by 2030 compared with 1990 levels. It 'aims to protect, conserve and enhance the EU's natural capital, and protect the health and well-being of citizens from environment-related risks and impacts' (European Commission, 2019b). The European Green Deal will require a myriad of policy changes and detailed measures. These will have to pass through the EU policy-making processes and require the approval of all member state parliaments.

Despite the relatively high level of policy coordination through and regulation by EU institutions, environmental policy outcomes are very different across member states. Figure 12.3 shows the level of greenhouse gas emissions per capita and the share of recycled and composted municipal waste in 2017 across EU member states. When it comes to greenhouse gas emissions per capita we see that southern European and some eastern European member states pollute less than their northern counterparts, the only exception being Sweden. When it comes to the share of recycled waste, we observe less clear patterns. Germany leads in terms of the share of recycled waste followed by Austria and Slovenia, while the share is lowest in Romania and Greece. While some aspects of environmental policy have become similar across EU member states, there is no apparent long-term convergence towards a European model of environmental protection (Jordan and Liefferink, 2004).

Interest groups and political parties have played a crucial role in getting environmental protection on the political agenda, both at the EU and national level. Environmental policy involves regulation and standard setting, and EU institutions have been quite open to input from interest groups. This is in part because EU institutions have a relatively small civil service

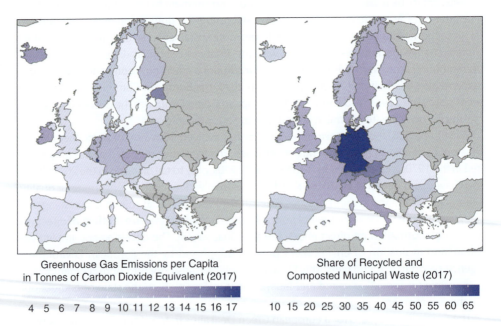

Greenhouse Gas Emissions per Capita in Tonnes of Carbon Dioxide Equivalent (2017)	Share of Recycled and Composted Municipal Waste (2017)
4 5 6 7 8 9 10 11 12 13 14 15 16 17	10 15 20 25 30 35 40 45 50 55 60 65

Figure 12.3 Environmental Outcomes in EU Member States

Data sources: European Environment Agency (2018, 2019). Please note that as of 31 January 2020, the UK was no longer considered an EU Member State

compared to national governments, and are heavily reliant on outside technical expertise for policy-making. EU institutions have an incentive to keep communication flows with interest groups open, and interests groups benefit from cooperation with and funding by EU institutions. The resource endowment and organizational structures of interest groups play a crucial role for effective lobbying at the EU level (Klüver, 2012).

Green parties have undoubtedly played a crucial role in getting and keeping environmental protection on the political agenda. One of the first and most electorally successful green parties originated in Germany. In the 1983 West German elections, the Green Party became the first new party since 1953 to successfully pass the 5 per cent electoral threshold to enter the German parliament. Since the 1980s the Green Party has also performed well in several state-level elections, but only in the western part of Germany. The pinnacle of the electoral success of the German Green Party came in 1998 when it entered a coalition government with the Social Democrats at the federal level in Germany for the first time.

The German Greens were seen as the first successful 'postmaterialist' party in Europe. Their success was rooted in a changing social structure and the emergence of the materialist–postmaterialist conflict dimension (Inglehart, 1977). As West Germany became more prosperous in the 1960s and 1970s, a segment of German voters, especially younger ones in urban areas, started to prioritize the environment over material concerns. In other European countries green parties also became more successful. Greens have established a presence in many national parliaments from Austria to Malta and from Ireland to Portugal.

The rise of green parties has also affected the content of the political agenda. Research suggests that the environmental issue mobilization of green parties can lead other political parties to raise the importance of the environment as well (Spoon, 2011). The extent to which other parties respond depends on several factors. For example, it is easier for green parties to shape the political agenda when the electoral system is more open to new and smaller parties, as is the case in proportional electoral systems. What is more, other parties are more likely to raise the salience of the environment when the green party poses an electoral threat to a specific party and when the economic context makes the green issue a potential vote winner (Spoon et al., 2013). When economic conditions worsen, economic growth and redistribution gain in prominence in the political debate and may crowd out environmental issues.

12.5 Health Policy

While EU institutions aim to improve the efficiency of Europe's health systems and facilitate coordination in health policies, EU countries retain primary responsibility for organizing and delivering health services and medical care. EU health policy therefore serves to complement national policies, and to ensure health protection in all EU policies. The European Commission supports the efforts of member states in protecting and improving the health of their citizens and to ensure the accessibility, effectiveness, and resilience of their health systems. This for example includes securing patients' rights in cross-border healthcare. One way in which this is achieved is through the European Health Insurance Card scheme.

Through this scheme all EU member states offer their citizens insurance for emergency medical treatment and insurance when visiting other participating European countries on a reciprocal basis.

Most European countries have a tightly regulated healthcare system with government subsidies available for citizens who cannot afford insurance coverage or care. Yet, the provision of healthcare varies substantially across countries. Many healthcare systems are two-tiered systems in which a government-provided healthcare system provides basic care, and a secondary private tier of care exists for those who can pay for additional care or faster access. Countries differ in the way the two systems are managed, funded, and regulated. To illustrate these differences, we take a closer look at how several countries—Italy, Lithuania, Sweden, and the United Kingdom—organize their healthcare systems. We have selected countries based on their geographic diversity and the different types of systems they represent (for more information, see Lynch, 2020).

The healthcare system in Italy, the Servizio Sanitario Nazionale (SSN), is organized under the government's Ministry of Health, but delivered at the regional level. It provides universal coverage for all residents financed through taxation collected by the central government which is then distributed to the regional governments. Residents receive mostly free primary care and inpatient care. Patients make co-payments for specialty visits and outpatient care. Exempt from cost-sharing are pregnant women, patients with HIV or other chronic diseases, and young children and older adults in lower-income households. State health interactions are managed through a national electronic healthcare card which is used to monitor and manage each phase of the public health expenditure cycle and contains medical as well as European health insurance information. Private health care also exists, but has only a limited role in Italy's health coverage system. It is mainly reserved for those who are willing to pay for extra services or services not offered within the public system, such as dentistry or psychology.

The Lithuanian health system is funded through a state-run insurance fund that is compulsory for all Lithuanian residents. Residents who are in employment pay health insurance contributions from their salaries, while the government subsidizes the costs for the unemployed and economically inactive. The government's Ministry for Health oversees and regulates the provision of healthcare and runs major public health centres across the country, but municipalities are responsible for running networks of primary care providers. These general practitioners (GP) act as gatekeepers into the system. Pharmaceuticals can be expensive and are not always covered by insurance. They account for a high percentage of out-of-pocket healthcare expenses. Private insurance is not common, but more people are paying out-of-pocket for private services not covered by the state system or to avoid wait times.

Sweden has a fully government-funded and highly de-centralized healthcare system. It is primarily funded through local taxes, with the Ministry of Health and Social Affairs establishing principles and guidelines for care at a national level. But regionally, it is the countries' twenty-one councils that effectively control the healthcare system. The councils, known as municipalities, are responsible for healthcare provision particularly when community care and psychiatric services are involved. Not all treatment is free at the point of care, although 97 per cent is government-funded. Patients pay a nominal fee and the service is centred around a GP. Drug treatments are nominally charged subject to a capped amount. GP visits and hospital outpatient visits are paid upfront, but reimbursed. If patients register, they can also qualify for a reduced capped rate for GP and hospital healthcare.

The United Kingdom has a publicly funded health care system called the National Health Service (NHS) which is funded through general taxation. It was established in 1948 and is made up of the four separate systems of the four nations of the United Kingdom: the National Health Service in England, NHS Scotland, NHS Wales, and Health and Social Care in Northern Ireland. The founding principles are that healthcare services, except for dental treatment and optical care, should be comprehensive, universal, and free at the point of delivery for residents. In England, NHS patients have to pay prescription charges with a range of exemptions from these charges. When purchasing drugs, the NHS has significant market power that can keep prices lower. Private healthcare has continued parallel to the NHS and is paid for largely by private insurance, which is seen as offering an add-on to NHS services and is often provided through employer-funded schemes. The private healthcare sector also sells its surplus capacity to the NHS, sometimes as a way to reduce waiting times.

There are many more ways in which healthcare is organized in Europe. Indeed, every EU member state has its own system of organization, regulation, and funding. These differences in national healthcare systems, and the limited coordination of EU institutions, became evident in the early days of the Covid-19 pandemic. Covid-19 is an infectious disease that can cause severe respiratory infections, pneumonia, but can also affect the entire body, and in severe circumstances can lead to death. The virus originated in late 2019 in Wuhan, China, but rapidly spread across the globe, bringing economic activity to a standstill, shutting borders between countries, leading countries to implement lock-downs, and restricting personal freedom in democracies to an extent that people, only weeks earlier, had probably not thought possible. The coronavirus, and the Covid-19 disease that it causes, unleashed a public health crisis that, in turn, caused an economic crisis. As the pandemic moved across the European continent, national institutions dealt with the emergency response such as the increase in intensive care unit (ICU) beds, protective equipment, or testing capabilities.

While some member states provided assistance to other member states through donations of protective equipment such as masks, cross-border treatments of ill patients, or bringing stranded citizens home, the activities of EU institutions were limited. A joint European policy response was hampered by the fact that the responsibility for making health policy lies with member state institutions, not the EU. The European Commission could only offer help in coordinating national responses through a coronavirus response team, providing objective information about the spread of the virus, financial support for research into vaccines, treatments, diagnostic tests, and coordinating the distribution of vaccines.

The pandemic also highlighted different policies and spending on healthcare in member states. In order to treat the acute respiratory distress syndrome, patients needed to be moved to ICU units in hospitals to receive mechanical ventilation. As a result, the ICU beds available in a country became an important way to treat the disease and deal with the pandemic. The left panel in Figure 12.4 shows the huge variety in the number of available ICU beds per 100,000 inhabitants. While Germany had close to 600 in 2017, Sweden had less than 200. This in part reflects differences in public spending priorities by member state governments.

The different demographic structures that countries face are a key reason why health policy and spending differ across Europe. Germany or Italy for example have a much older age structure compared to countries like the Netherlands and Sweden. This affects spending priorities of member states when it comes to health or social policy more generally. Yet, veto players are also important. While in some countries, like Italy, France, or the Netherlands, central

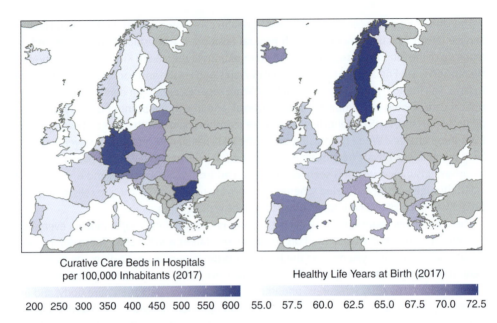

Curative Care Beds in Hospitals
per 100,000 Inhabitants (2017)

Healthy Life Years at Birth (2017)

200 250 300 350 400 450 500 550 600   55.0   57.5   60.0   62.5   65.0   67.5   70.0   72.5

Figure 12.4 Health Outcomes in Europe

Data sources: Eurostat (2020a,b)

Box 12.3 CASE STUDY: European Responses to the Covid-19 Outbreak in 2020

The devastation of Covid-19, beginning in Spring 2020, proved an existential threat to shared ways of life across the European continent, and across the globe. Deaths mounted, economies shut down, jobs evaporated, and social isolation became the new norm. National governments struggled to address the pandemic, and their efforts varied widely in effectiveness. At the initial time of the outbreak, the EU proved particularly challenged in its capacity to respond. A pandemic that does not stop at the border begged for a collective response across a highly interdependent Europe. Yet, the first responses were primarily national. From nationwide lockdowns in Italy, France, and Spain to partial shutdowns in the Czech Republic, Germany, Netherlands, Poland, and Slovakia to only partial school closures in Sweden, member state governments decided on very different measures to stop or slow down the spread of the virus. National governments went as far as to erect barriers to each other through the reintroduction of border controls. The fact that member states brought in border checks initially created some problems in terms of the movement of pharmaceuticals and food within the single market.

What explains the EU's lack of coming together to work through the Covid-19 crisis? For its first fifty years of existence, the EU excelled at the technocratic governance, rooted in law and involving coordination by European and national officials across multiple areas of regulations. Over the past decade and beyond, however, there has been a stark increase in the overt politicization of the issues around European level political authority, as the EU has deepened and extended its influence in everyday life. The Eurozone crisis, which saw countries such as Greece, Ireland, Italy, and Spain suffer economic devastation, made visible divisions across Europe. The Eurozone crisis motivated many citizens to debate the role of the EU in their lives.

On first glance, the science-based challenges of the pandemic might seem to match the EU's strengths as a beacon of expertise and technocracy. However, in the area of healthcare, the EU has little legal authority to act. This lack of political capacity led to criticism of the EU at the start of the health crisis. While the EU cannot close schools or create more ICU beds, it could have carved out a greater coordination role for itself to ensure that medical supplies made in the EU could not be exported, and to call out member states for not sharing them. When it came to the response to the economic downturn resulting from lockdown measures, the EU was more active and had more authority to act. The EU supported national efforts to cushion the economic impact. It temporally relaxed state aid rules and created the SURE programme, a new instrument to help people stay in work. It also proposed a recovery instrument, called Next Generation EU, within the EU's multi-annual financial framework—the EU's long-term budget plan. It amounts to 750 billion Euros of grants and loans to support member state efforts to recover from the crisis, to make the single market more resilient, and accelerate the green and digital transitions.

governments could introduce measures to slow down the spread of Covid-19 with the support of parliament, in other countries, like Germany or Spain, the central government had to rely on and coordinate with regional governments, who could otherwise block policy change.

The Spanish case offers an opportunity to illustrate how veto players shaped central governments' responses to the crisis. As we have outlined in Chapter 3, Spain is a country where policy authority is highly decentralized. The highly decentralized nature of policy-making proved quite a challenge during the early Covid-19 outbreak. In order for the Spanish government to implement lockdown measures to slow the spread of the virus it had to declare a state of emergency based on Article 116 of the Spanish Constitution. These emergency

Box 12.4 CONTROVERSIES AND DEBATES: How to Classify Welfare States in Europe?

A country's healthcare system is part of a larger set of social policies which are referred to as the **welfare state**. The welfare state is a social system in which the state undertakes some responsibility for providing basic social and economic welfare for its citizens. This is usually done via a combination of different social policies and public good provisions, such as pensions, healthcare, unemployment benefits, sick leave, child care, or schooling subsidies. Large shares of national state expenditure and activities are devoted to servicing the welfare needs of citizens. The nature of these expenditures and activities differ across European countries and provide a more or less universalistic and institutionalized commitment to the distribution of welfare.

Esping-Andersen (1990) classified different welfare systems in Europe and beyond based on their degree of decommodification. Decommodification refers to the extent to which individuals can maintain a livelihood without reliance on the market. In pre-capitalist society, workers were commodities in the sense that their survival was contingent on the sale of their labour power. The introduction of social rights implied the loosening of the pure commodity status of workers. The granting of social rights implies a degree of decommodification, because social rights can be viewed as entitlements rather than as commodities that must be paid for or traded on the market. The way in which social rights are given and the extent to which decommodification happens differs greatly among

(continued...)

European countries. Social rights can provide benefits to individuals either through entitlements or means-testing. Entitlement benefits are those to which certain qualified people are entitled to by law regardless of need. Means-tested benefits are those that certain people are entitled to based on their need—below a certain income threshold for example.

On the basis of the degree of decommodification, welfare states can be divided into several types: liberal, conservative, and social-democratic. The liberal welfare state is based on the notion that the majority of citizens can obtain welfare from market, so only a minimal public safety net is required. The state offers only constrained social rights in the form of means-tested benefits and modest universal transfers targeted at low income groups. As a result of this policy mix, decommodification is minimal and inequality tends to be comparatively high. The United States is one of the clearest examples of a liberal welfare state, while in Europe, the United Kingdom comes closest. Yet, unlike the United States, the United Kingdom provides basic universal healthcare.

The conservative welfare state grants social rights, but is based on the notion that the role of the state is only to intervene when the capacity of other societal organizations, such as the church or the family, is exhausted. A conservative welfare state is usually based on mandatory social insurance and occupational distinctions. Entitlement to social benefits is usually based on life-long employment. The conservative welfare state provides more decommodification and social rights compared to a liberal welfare state, but preserves status differentials between people and through the fact that it favours of life-long employment has traditionally benefited men more than women. Germany is one of the best examples of a conservative welfare state in Europe.

A social democratic welfare state is based on the notion that social rights are entitlements that should benefit all and that the state ought to compensate for market inefficiencies and inequalities. It is a system based on entitlement benefits that universally apply and are funded through high taxation. The social-democratic welfare state provides the highest level of decommodification of the three types of welfare states. Sweden is the clearest example of a social-democratic welfare state in the European context.

Typologies, like the three types of welfare states, often rely on ideal types and therefore cannot encompass every country. This often leads to criticism. For example, southern European countries, like Italy or Spain, do not fit nicely into the three types of welfare systems as defined by Esping-Andersen (Ferrera, 1996), due mainly to their strong reliance on family-based welfare. This critique has led to the inclusion of a fourth type, the family-based welfare state, built on the notion that the extent to which welfare is provided by the state is family dependent. In other words, the level of defamilization, rather decommodification, crucially shapes the kind of social and economic welfare a state provides for its citizens. That said, countries in central and eastern Europe still do not fit the typology well.

measures allowed the Spanish government to centralize control to deal with the pandemic. Such a centralization of powers is only allowed in extraordinary circumstances, like a pandemic. Since Spain became a democracy in the late 1970s, a state of emergency had only been implemented once before. In the case of the Covid-19 pandemic, the Spanish government received support in parliament for a time-limited state of emergency. It had to come back to parliament to ask for political backing to extend it several times. Political dynamics became more intense every time as the state of emergency was extended, with opposition parties on the right, the conservative People's Party and the far-right Vox, wanting to restart the economy. The final extension during the initial outbreak of Covid-19 in the first half of 2020, was granted until 21 June 2020. It only received a narrow margin of approval with 177 members of parliament from the 350-seat lower house voting in favour. The conservative

People's Party and the far-right Vox tried to rally enough opposition to the extension. The Spanish example illustrates how veto players are crucial for understanding variation in health outcomes as they can shape what governments are able to do during a health crisis.

12.6 Summary

This chapter has explored policy-making and policy outcomes in Europe's multilevel governance structure. We have highlighted that the extent to which EU and national institutions share competences varies tremendously across policy areas. EU institutions have exclusive competences in trade policy and national institutions exclusive competences in health, while EU and national institutions share policy-making competences in environmental and immigration policy. The relationship between EU and national institutions is most complex when competences are shared, as they often are. While the principle of subsidiarity should provide a tool for deciding who does what, this is often a political rather than a legal question.

While analysing policy outcomes in four salient issues—health, immigration, environmental, and trade policy—we have highlighted the importance of agenda control and position-taking by political parties, interest groups, and social movements. This chapter has also pointed towards possible tensions between EU and national institutions when it comes to policy-making, which often play out in constitutional courts. These political and legal tensions are at the heart of the European integration process itself. As a result, we have witnessed a politicization of the policy authority of the EU over the last years. This is likely to shape policy-making in Europe for years to come.

Online Data Exercise: Environmental Data

The interactive online exercise for this chapter focuses on the case of environmental politics. You will explore key indicators of environmental performance in Europe in relation to the strength of Green political parties, their governing experience, and economic indicators that may explain variation in environmental policy outcomes across European countries.

Take your learning further with this interactive data exercise, available at **www.foundationsofeuropeanpolitics.com**

For additional material and resources, including multiple-choice questions, web links, and more, please visit the online resources: **www.oup.com/he/devries1e**

Part 5

Rule of Law, Democracy, and Backsliding

13 Rule of Law and Judicial Politics

This chapter discusses the importance of law and the rule of law using theoretical models of both why people obey the law and how judges interpret laws. The chapter explores when and why citizens and elected officials follow the law, and the conditions under which this obedience may break down. It then discusses the importance of courts and judges in interpreting the law, and explores the interaction of politics and law to understand how judges come to decisions. It pays particular attention to the interaction between national and EU law.

What is the law? How does law work? And what role does it play in democracy? Governments make laws, bureaucracies make regulations regarding those laws, police and other law enforcement agencies ensure that citizens and governments follow laws, and finally courts interpret law and determine when violations occur. But under what conditions are citizens more likely to violate law, how do courts make decisions, and why are these decisions followed? Rule of law is a necessary feature of democratic government, but how law works varies significantly across Europe.

This chapter explores the nature of law, the 'rule of law', and how courts and the legal system interact with the political system to create and interpret law in European democracies. After a discussion of the nature of law, we discuss the interaction between law and politics, and how judges and courts work within European countries. Lastly, we pay particular attention to the interaction between EU law and national law. Law at the European level and law at the national level have become increasingly intertwined over time to the point that it is impossible to understand national law and courts without also discussing EU law.

13.1 Why Obey the Law? A Theoretical Discussion

Before talking about the judicial systems and courts of European democracies, we discuss why and how law exerts influence over individuals. Why does law matter and how does it act as a constraint on people's behaviour? An understanding of why people obey the law becomes particularly important when discussing the 'rule of law' and its role in shaping democracy. People may obey the law for different reasons: they may obey for fear that disobedience will lead the authorities to catch and punish them (fear of punishment); they may obey because they agree with the intent of the law (policy agreement); they may obey because they feel that obeying the law, regardless of what it says, is the right thing to do, perhaps because they believe that the system that has created the law is legitimate (the law has moral authority or legitimacy); or they may obey because they feel that obedience is what society expects of them (they wish to conform to society's wishes).

Consider, for the moment, situations where breaking the law is very unlikely to lead to the perpetrator being caught and punished. Imagine small offences for which the punishment is minimal and violations are difficult to monitor. These might include failing to clean up after your dog when going for a walk in the park, or walking across the street when the pedestrian light is red. Police are not hiding behind lamp posts in the middle of the night to catch people crossing the street in the wrong place, nor are they waiting to jump out from behind a bush to fine negligent dog owners. The likelihood of facing punishment for these types of offences is exceedingly small.

But we see a great deal of variation in how people respond to such laws across countries. Many Londoners might be shocked when they first travel to Berlin to find Germans patiently waiting for pedestrian lights to change before they cross the street, even late at night with no car in sight. Berliners and Londoners, alike, may be shocked at the attitude of Parisians towards cleaning up after the dogs, despite signs advertising fines for failing to do so. While there may be a small number of people who are genuinely concerned about getting caught and fined, compliance with these laws is probably more related to the latter explanations—people may agree with the content of the law, they may believe that one should always follow the law, or they think that their neighbours expect certain law-abiding behaviour from them. In other words, **social norms** and beliefs about the legitimacy of the system matter. Let us assume for the moment that the last explanation is the most plausible. In this scenario, individuals are willing to accept the inconveniences associated with obeying the law (e.g. stooping over to pick up after your dog or waiting the extra minute for the light to change) if they feel that their neighbours would do likewise and the same neighbours expect this type of activity from them. But individuals may not actually get to observe their neighbours' behaviour. Dogs do not all go out for walks simultaneously, after all, and sometimes the street you are crossing is empty.

In these instances, the law may serve to create a **focal point**—or an outcome on which individuals can coordinate in the absence of communication. Schelling (1960) first talked about the importance of focal points in game theory and their use in solving coordination problems. Thinking back to the simple games in Chapter 3, we could imagine solving a coordination game by flipping a coin. If the coin comes up 'heads' the actors take one action, and if it comes up 'tails', they take the other action. The coin provides a mechanism to help players coordinate on an outcome in the presence of multiple equilibria. Law can aid coordination in the same way. It helps to inform people whether a societal consensus (or agreement) around a particular norm or behaviour exists. Indeed, many leading law scholars view law as functioning through the creation of focal points. Weingast (1997), for example, views constitutional law and other symbols of the state (e.g. flags and national anthems) as things that can create focal points to help citizens coordinate on reining in sovereigns who might otherwise trample on citizens' rights, helping to establish the 'rule of law' and democracy.

If people walk their dog in a park and notice that the park is clean, and they also see a sign that says that the law requires them to pick up after their dog, they can infer that all other dog owners follow the law and clean up after their dogs. Thus, dog owners may infer that a social norm exists—everyone values a clean park and will take costly action necessary to keep it that way. Everyone expects everyone else to pick up after their dog, and the posting of the law advertises this fact. The presence of the sign, coupled with the reality of a clean park, informs everyone that the law works and that society, as a whole, seems to think that clean parks are worth it.

But now imagine that something within society changes—maybe a whole new group of people (let's call them the dirty dog-owners) moves in. Quickly, the park goes from being quite clean to becoming a minefield. The sign making everyone aware of the law now seems to be advertising to everyone that societal consensus around picking up after one's dog has disappeared, and in fact, there is no consequence for not doing it. Clearly no one is picking up after their dog and they are unlikely to face any meaningful consequences. The sign advertising the law now creates a focal point in the opposite direction; it actually points out the meaninglessness of the law. Perhaps this could lead to people taking other similar laws less seriously if they think that societal consensus might also be lacking in other areas, for example, picking up litter or even caring for the environment.

This brief, fictional tale simply highlights one way that law can work—by advertising to all that society agrees on certain norms and standards, even if complying with those standards might involve some costs. It may help to create societal pressures to conform. But it works best when an underlying societal consensus around some norm already exists. Law has to engage in less coercion when society is already relatively cohesive and supportive of the notion that a particular law should exist. The same tale also cautions that law may not work in the absence of societal consensus or agreement. Trying to impose new law in the absence of such consensus could backfire or may even be detrimental as it signals to everyone that society does not support the basic ideas and values that underpin the law. Society often needs to agree on basic norms in order for law to function properly. Indeed, this simple tale relates directly to how Weingast (1997) sees the development of 'rule of law' and democracy. When society agrees on basic norms and standards, the simple presence of focal points—namely written law publicly advertised—can lead people to conform to particular behavioural norms and standards.

This model of the law—namely that obedience results from knowledge of, and compliance with, broad underlying social norms—is particularly pertinent in Europe where European integration has created new laws and regulation for all member states of the European Union. Creating new regulations and laws that are meant to apply across an entire continent, spanning different languages, cultures, and levels of economic and democratic development, may be tricky to say the least. Societal consensus may exist and support law in some parts of the EU, but not others. Moreover, symbolic cues that remind people that they are part of one community, that may give the law greater moral weight, and that Weingast saw a potential focal points (e.g. recognized flags, national anthems, revered constitutions written on parchment) are largely absent at the European level, or not held in as high regard, despite the best efforts of some European politicians to create and publicize such symbols.

It is a puzzle, then, why nation-states would submit to the jurisdiction of a supranational court, such as the European Court of Justice. When norms differ between Spain and Poland, or Bulgaria and France, creating law that works across these different countries may be difficult. These differing dynamics can have implications for how the 'rule of law' develops and changes in different parts of Europe, something we will discuss in greater detail when we examine democratization and democratic backsliding in Chapter 14. If law does function, at least in part, by alerting citizens to a set of norms that society generally supports, it implies that law (and the 'rule of law') and political representation are intricately linked. The law that politicians draft is likely to function best when crafted to fit the society that the politicians represent.

13.2 Politics, Law, and the Legal System

We have considered why law works and how it functions; people may have different reasons for obeying the law, and obedience is not simply about fear of punishment. For law to truly work, citizens must care about what their fellow citizens believe and they should also generally support the notion of law and the right of government to make it. We have also mentioned that law and politics must be linked. Political systems—namely governments and parliaments—make law when they draft and pass legislation through the political process (as discussed in the previous chapters), while the judicial system then interprets the law that the politicians have written and bureaucrats have implemented. We now turn to the question of the nature of the relationship between politicians and the legal system. First, we need to understand why we need a legal system at all. Why is it not enough to simply have politicians make all the decisions?

Politicians write laws, but for several reasons, they cannot draft legislation that covers all contingencies. It is often not feasible, or even desirable, for politicians to draft law that can cover all possible ramifications of the law. Moreover, drafting legislation often involves compromise among different political actors, either within a party or across parties. One way to achieve compromise might be to remain vague on controversial matters. Lastly, law can be difficult to change once in place. But the world moves on. New events might alter the way that the law functions. For example, privacy laws written in a pre-internet age take on new and different meanings with the advent of social media and digital sharing platforms (e.g. Facebook, Instagram, Twitter).

For all of these reasons, laws may be vague and open to interpretation by the actors (citizens, corporations, government bodies, etc.) that they affect and by the bureaucrats that implement them. Someone needs to interpret the law, apply the law in specific cases, and settle disputes about the law when they arise. This is the role of the legal system. The legal system settles disputes between and among individuals, organizations, and the government. It can determine whether a particular action taken by individuals, corporations, or government agencies, is legal or illegal based on existing law.

Returning to our theoretical model of democracy, we can usefully view the relationship between the political system and the judicial or legal system as a principal–agent relationship where the political system delegates authority to the courts to interpret the law. Why would democratically elected politicians delegate authority to unelected judges to oversee the law that they have written? For the reasons that we have already mentioned, politicians cannot foresee all of the ways that the legislation they write may impact citizens into the future and the law may have unintended consequences in the present (see Box 13.1 for an example). Politicians may think that their legislative act allows for certain contingencies, when other actors see many other, different ways to apply the law. Moreover, the government cannot act as an independent arbiter over law that it has, itself, written.

Box 13.1 **CASE STUDY:** Cyber-Bullying in the UK

The legal environment surrounding internet bullying in the United Kingdom provides an example of how the purpose and use of law can change over time. In recent years, with the increasing popularity of social media, the problem of bullying on the internet has grown significantly, but the law has not kept up with the rapid changes in online behaviour. There is no law in the UK specifically related to bullying on the internet. Instead, people seeking protection from online harassment rely on legislation that largely predates the internet and social media age, namely the 1984 Telecommunications Act and the 1997 Harassment Act, among others. These laws were meant to prevent harassing telephone calls and stalking behaviour. While related to internet bullying, clearly the kind of harassment that takes place online is rather different from a harassing telephone call that might have taken place in the late 1980s. With the changing technology, the legal system has had to reinterpret old legislation to fit the new reality as the political system has been slow to produce new law.

As such, the political system delegates powers to the judiciary, giving judges the power to interpret law. However, judges may not be perfect agents of the political system. As we have discussed, all agents have the ability to shirk (to varying degrees). They may have their own views of what the law says or should say. They may offer interpretations of the law that make it much narrower than what politicians originally envisioned, or they may reinterpret it to apply in a much broader range of settings. These judicial rulings may leave politicians feeling that the legal system has upended the political system. But they may be able to rewrite legislation to prevent the judiciary from making 'rogue' interpretations of the law. Judges, if they do not wish to see their rulings overturned, may not press interpretations of the law too far to begin with.

As discussed in earlier chapters, we can draw on Veto Players theory to understand when judges are likely to have more flexibility (Tsebelis, 2002). Veto Players theory would suggest that, when it is more difficult for the political system to agree on how to overturn judicial rulings through the political process, the judiciary will have greater power and leeway to interpret the law, and the political system will, to the extent that it is able, try to draft more concrete legislation, less open to interpretation. This type of argument suggests that judges should have more political power (or independence) in countries like Germany, where federalism, multiparty governments, and bicameralism mean that political change often happens slowly and incrementally, compared with the United Kingdom, where single party majority governments have meant the politics can move much more quickly and nimbly (see also Shapiro, 1981). It also suggests that the German political system may write much more detailed legislation, giving judges less leeway for interpretation in their judgements, compared with British politicians, who can be more confident that they can 'fix' any judicial misinterpretations later. Politicians know that they are vulnerable to 'agency drift' and attempt to prevent it. Indeed, Huber and Shipan (2000) have found evidence for this type of behaviour among governments. This leads to significant differences across countries in the roles that judges and courts play in politics and the law.

In some countries, the highest court can determine that a law is inconsistent with other, higher law, such as the constitution. If the highest court finds that a law contradicts the constitution, they can actually negate the law, declaring it unconstitutional. This is called judicial review or, alternatively, **constitutional review**.

To understand constitutional review, we must first define just what a constitution is and what it does. According to Stone Sweet (2000) constitutions are collections of meta-norms, or higher order norms, that lay out how governments function. Specifically, Stone Sweet writes, 'A constitution is a body of rules that specifies how all other legal rules are to be produced, applied, and interpreted. Constitutional norms are not only higher order rules; they are prior, organic rules: they constitute a given political community' (2000, 20). Most commonly, constitutions are written down in a document, but not necessarily. The constitutional order of the United Kingdom has developed gradually over time and has never been written down in its entirety in one document. Instead, it consists of parliamentary norms and laws that are subject to change by parliament. In contrast, the West German constitution, called the German Basic Law, was drafted after the Second World War in a constitutional convention. It was meant to be a temporary document that would be replaced with a permanent constitution once all of Germany—East and West—reunited. As it turned out, that took quite a long time—over forty years. When Communist East Germany fell and joined with West Germany, the Basic Law was maintained and only slightly amended.

Constitutions also differ in their levels of entrenchment, or the ease with which they can be changed. Some parts of a constitution—for example, those parts protecting the democratic nature of the state, or basic rights—may be unamendable, and therefore highly entrenched. Making changes to the text of constitutions may require supermajorities in parliament or public referendums. The United Kingdom is rather unique in that its constitution is not entrenched. All aspects of British law are subject to a majoritarian principle, and can be altered by a simple majority in the House of Commons.

Difficult-to-amend constitutions, when coupled with the ability of constitutional judges to engage in judicial review, gives judges a great deal of power. However, constitutions often contain rules that limit potential 'shirking' among judges a priori through the appointment process or by restricting who can become a constitutional court judge. Ensuring that judges have certain qualifications, or that they must be acceptable to a wide variety of actors, reduces the likelihood of an extremist judiciary. Returning to the language of Veto Players theory, appointment processes can help to ensure that judges' preferences are centrist and lie within the core of the political system. The key is that procedures prevent a situation where one government or parliamentary majority can appoint all the judges on a high court. For instance, temporal staggering is crucial as it ensures independence from politicians currently in power.

In both France and Italy, the constitution gives different branches of government responsibility for appointments. In Italy, one-third of judges are chosen by the president, one-third by the parliament, and one-third by judges serving on lower courts. In France, the nine members of the Constitutional Council are chosen by the President of the Republic, the President of the National Assembly (the lower house of the legislature), and the President of the Senate (the upper house), with each choosing one new member every three years. In Germany, half of the judges are elected by the Bundestag (the lower house) and half by the Bundesrat (the upper house) by supermajorities in each case. By giving responsibility for appointments to different branches of government, using staggered terms, and requiring supermajorities, the constitutions of these countries make it unlikely that any one particular ideological viewpoint will come to dominate the supreme court, ensuring balance and centrism.

Additionally, constitutions may require (or norms may develop) that judges hold certain qualifications to serve. Most supreme court judges have one of three backgrounds—law professor, appellate court judge, or experienced lawyer working in government. Typically, this means that the views of potential judges are well-known before appointment, allowing those responsible for appointment to weed out extremists. Indeed, the importance of the appointment process for maintaining an independent judiciary and upholding the rule of law has been on display in Poland over the last few years, where the right-wing government of the PiS party (Law and Justice) has attempted to change the appointment process, giving itself more control over who serves on the top courts. These changes are seen by the European Union as undermining the rule of law and democracy and it has staunchly opposed them, even if it has failed to prevent them.

13.3 Power of Courts

Depending on the nature of the political system, courts may have significant power to shape both the law and political outcomes. But the fact that courts have power at all is somewhat of a puzzle for political science. Alexander Hamilton, one of the American 'founding fathers', famously wrote in Federalist Paper no. 78, describing judiciary in the new American constitution, that 'the judiciary . . . has no influence over either the sword or the purse', meaning that courts do not control the police nor do they have the ability to raise money. They cannot enforce their decisions by force or by coercion through funding. Instead, the judiciary is reliant on governments to enforce the decisions that it makes. Politicians can ignore court decisions with relatively few direct consequences. Many political scientists have therefore questioned why politicians permit judges to overrule decisions that they make. There are several potential answers. One is that the public generally holds courts and judges in high esteem and views them as trustworthy.

Figure 13.1 shows cross-country averages of the percentage of respondents who report that they trust an institution or organization—namely the judiciary, the government, the parliament, political parties, and the European Union—across different regions of Europe. Due to the process of leaving the EU, the UK does not fit cleanly into any of the other categories, and therefore forms a category on its own. Within the remaining regions, cross-national differences are small enough that grouping countries is sensible and makes it easier to visualize patterns. In every region, the judiciary is the most trusted national institution. In southern and eastern Europe, the European Union is more trusted than the judiciary, but not in northern Europe. Levels of trust in all types of government institutions, though, are higher in northern Europe than in southern and eastern Europe. Lower levels of trust in the judiciary in eastern and southern Europe may be due to corruption scandals. This is particularly true in Bulgaria, where the judiciary has recently faced high-level charges of nepotism, and Malta, where individuals in the upper echelons of government, including the former prime minister, have been accused of plotting and carrying out the murder of a journalist, who had been investigating government corruption when she was killed in a car bomb in 2017. Many Maltese feared that fair trials for the murder would be impossible because the prime minister had stacked the judiciary with partisan supporters. With the exception of these instances of scandal, though, citizens generally hold the judiciary in very high regard, and place more trust in it than in other political institutions. Politicians attempting to undermine a court decision may pay a political cost for opposing such a valued institution.

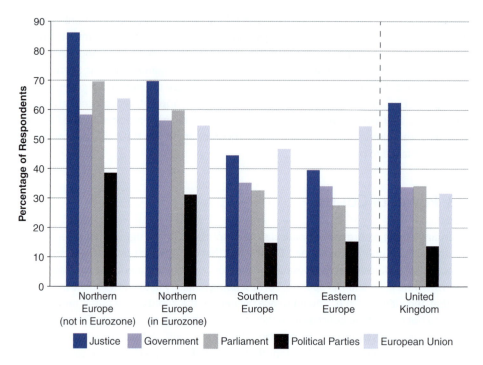

Figure 13.1 Trust in the Judiciary and Other Political Actors

Data source: European Commission (2019*a*)

Second, courts may shape their decisions in such a way that the immediate political conse-quences of a decision are politically advantageous for the government, while the long-term consequences increase the power of the court. Third, politicians may be willing to accept the power of the courts, even when decisions go against them, because they see them as benefi-cial on average over the long term. For example, powerful courts may also be able to rein in decisions of political opponents should they come to power in the future. Lastly, courts may act strategically and politically. They may shy away from making unpopular decisions that they know that the political system will have a hard time implementing, or at least make the decision in the most politically palatable way. Courts do not want to lose the public trust and do not want to appear weak by having their decisions ignored or overturned by the political system. Thus, when able they may carefully choose the cases they wish to hear (not all courts are able to choose their cases, but some are) and make decisions in such a way that they are likely to be obeyed by the political system.

Even if judges are weak in terms of the tools that they have to enforce their decisions, political systems do vary significantly in how much power they bestow on courts to change or overturn law. Some courts across Europe, for example the German Constitutional Court, possess a great deal of power, and have made important and controversial constitutional decisions, while courts elsewhere remain relatively weak. As discussed, at least some of the variation in power can be attributed to the nature of political institutions—judges in systems with multiple veto players are likely to have more leeway to interpret law.

But there are also other legal explanations that differ somewhat from the political explanations. Legal scholars often make a distinction between systems that rely on common law and those that use civil law. The core concept of **common law** is that judges can create law through their rulings by setting **precedent**. Judges making subsequent rulings are expected to use and rely on legal precedent created by earlier rulings and they are expected to cite case law when making rulings to justify their decision. Judges are bound by previous rulings—a principle known by the Latin term **Stare Decisis**, which literally translates to 'let the decision stand' or 'stand by things decided'. In contrast, in **civil law** countries, law is underpinned by a series of codes (such as civil code, criminal code, and administrative code) that judges are meant to rely on when making decisions. These legal traditions date back to Roman law, although different codes, usually based on Roman code, have arisen over time (e.g. Napoleonic code, Germanic code). Judicial decisions in civil law countries do not set precedent, but rather it is the code that is treated similarly to statutory law. Legal scholars have argued that judges in common law systems have much more discretion to make legal rulings than judges in civil law countries, and are therefore more powerful. After all, common law judges can make law through their rulings while civil law judges are merely code interpreters. However, the code mostly consists of general descriptions rather than concrete steps of actions to take in particular settings. Thus, in practice, civil law judges may still have wide latitude to make decisions. Finally, an important distinction between the systems is the different pattern of judicial recruitment. In civil law countries, it is possible to enter a branch of the judiciary as a junior judge right out of law school, and as such the judiciary is more integrated into the state apparatus, almost like a part of the civil service. In contrast, in common law countries such as the UK, for instance, candidates need to have several years experience in law-related work before they can be appointed as a judge.

Most countries in Europe use a form of civil law, with only the United Kingdom and Ireland using common law. But it is hardly the case the British and Irish judges possess greater powers to interpret the law than their counterparts on the continent. Traditionally, British judges have been viewed as quite weak with regard to their powers of judicial review. After all, there is no written constitution for judges to compare law to. Irish supreme court judges, in contrast, do have the power to find laws unconstitutional. Meanwhile, in a civil law system, German constitutional judges have made numerous important, and sometimes controversial, decisions about the constitutionality of specific laws.

13.4 Constitutions, Parliaments, and Judicial Review

In addition to the legal system, the varying nature of constitutions may also impact the interaction between law and politics. We need to consider the role and importance of constitutions, and what it means for judges and courts to be able to interpret them. Constitutions are 'higher order' law that set out the basic framework of governance within a country; they both set up a country's institutional structure and guarantee citizens' basic rights. They vary greatly in their length, level of detail, and the ease with which they can be amended. Often following a period of instability—a major crisis, civil war, or revolution—conventions that draft constitutional documents seek to represent all major segments of society and a wide diversity of views. The idea is to create a political system that can represent all parts of society for many years to come. A significant number of constitutions across western Europe, including the Austrian, French (4th Republic), German, and Italian were drafted in the aftermath of the Second World War, while eastern European countries drafted new constitutions following the collapse of communism. The Spanish constitution, meanwhile, was rewritten after the death of long-ruling Spanish dictator Francisco Franco in 1975, following a special election of the Spanish Parliament in 1977. The parliament selected a small panel of seven individuals to represent all elements of Spain's highly ideological and divided political society. The constitution they drafted came into effect in 1978, ushering in a new period of democratic governance.

When we talk about 'higher order' constitutional law, we mean law that takes precedence over other law, and against which other law can be compared. Law embedded into a constitution, for example, is 'higher order' compared with law generated through regular legislation. If lower order law conflicts with higher order law, the higher order law prevails. Even within constitutions, some law is seen as above all other law. Several constitutions throughout Europe have 'entrenched' or unamendable articles that serve to protect basic features of democracy. The German Basic Law does not allow for amendments that would alter the federal structure of government or the principles of democracy and human rights, while the French constitution has an unamendable article stipulating that France must be a republic, ruling out a (constitutional) return to monarchy or empire.

But there are always tensions between the ease with which a constitution can be amended (its level of entrenchment), its ability to provide political stability into the future, and the role of judges in interpreting constitutional law. When a constitution is set up to be difficult to change, the influence of the drafters over politics can last long after those drafters have died. There may be tensions between what is written in the document and the changing nature of society. In this instance, judges with powers of judicial review may have the ability to reinterpret the document in light of societal changes. Or they may opt for an 'originalist' interpretation, trying to divine what the drafters of the constitution would have done in a similar situation. Regardless, constitutional judges can have a good deal of authority to interpret what is meant by the constitution, and it difficult for the politicians to overturn their rulings through constitutional amendments. The exact mechanisms by which judges exercise these powers, though, vary from country to country.

In most European countries, there is a single constitutional court that, alone, is responsible for handling any matters that touch on constitutional law and which may engage in judicial review. All other matters pertaining to regular legislation are handled by the regular courts system, with a supreme court at its head. This type of system, with a separate court for constitutional matters, is known as the **Kelsenian Court** model, named for Austrian legal scholar Hans Kelsen, who initially favoured it. It contrasts with American model, where there is only one federal courts system that makes both constitutional and non-constitutional decisions. Lower courts can also make both constitutional and non-constitutional decisions, both of which can be referred up to the Supreme Court.

In practice, though, there is never a perfectly clear distinction between what counts as constitutional and what does not, and many countries do allow for some crossover. Kelsen's initial idea, as exemplified by the 1920 Austrian constitution, was that, to preserve the distinction between constitutional and non-constitutional matters, constitutional courts would only engage in abstract review before legislation became law. **Abstract review** refers to ruling on the constitutionality of a law without any reference to a particular case or how the law is applied in practice. Usually it is possible for politicians to bring such a case before the court either before a bill becomes law or for a short period afterwards. Typically, only a limited set of actors (e.g. members of parliament, the head of state, the cabinet) has standing to bring a case before the court, asserting that a piece of legislation runs contrary to the constitution.

However, even within Austria, the possibility for incidental or **concrete review** quickly emerged. Within a decade of the creation of abstract review, a procedure was developed for incidental review, e.g. the review of constitutional matters that arise incidentally as the result of an issue in a specific case. If non-constitutional courts were deciding a particular case that they felt touched on constitutional matters, they could refer it to the constitutional court to make a decision. In these cases, constitutional matters typically arise with respect to a concrete, specific case (hence the term, concrete review). While some systems allow for only abstract review (e.g. France), most others provide opportunities for both abstract and concrete review.

In many European countries, judicial review of any type has been traditionally weak. In the UK and Netherlands, for example, where the notion of parliamentary sovereignty continues to hold sway, parliaments directly represent the 'will of the people' and reign supreme. Unelected judges are not seen to have the authority to overturn law passed by the political system that derives its legitimacy from the citizens through electoral democracy. Judges are merely to act as referees—to interpret how people engage with the law, settle disputes, and call out violations. They are not supposed to change political outcomes. This notion of democracy also requires more flexibility in constitutions, so they can change to reflect changes in society. The UK's constitution is so flexible that it does not even exist, at least not in written form. There is no possibility of judicial review in the Netherlands, where the constitution explicitly forbids it on the grounds that parliament, elected by the citizens, is sovereign and supreme. Indeed, there is no constitutional court in the Netherlands, only a supreme court. Likewise, judicial review is weak or non-existent throughout much of Scandinavia. In other systems, however, judicial review is stronger. For instance, in Germany and Italy, unchecked parliamentary power was discredited by fascism and authoritarianism. After all, Adolf Hitler was elected and his National Socialist party obtained a parliamentary majority. This experience of the dangers of the tyranny of the majority led to stronger constitutional checks through more powerful courts.

We can conceive of judicial independence as encompassing both de jure independence (how independence works according to the law) and de facto independence (how independence works in practice) (Feld and Voigt, 2003). An indicator of de jure independence would be longer terms of judicial appointments, e.g. judges appointed for life are likely more insulated from the political process than those appointed to renewable terms. De facto indicators of independence include items such as how long judges actually tend to serve in practice, with longer terms indicating more independence, and whether court decisions require action of other branches of government in order to actually take effect, meaning that the court is reliant on politics for its ruling to come into practice.

Judicial independence then ultimately refers to the ability of judges to make decisions independent of the political system and political interference. Table 13.1 summarizes the strength of judicial (or legislative) review using data from Vatter and Bernauer (2009). The countries are classified according to the ability of a constitutional court to overturn legislation passed by parliament on the grounds that it is unconstitutional.

Table 13.1 Constitutional Court's Ability to Review Laws

Absent	Low	Medium	High
Finland, Luxembourg, Netherlands, United Kingdom	Belgium, Denmark, Greece, Ireland, Portugal, Romania, Spain, Sweden	Austria, Bulgaria, Czech Rep., Estonia, France, Italy, Latvia, Lithuania, Slovakia, Slovenia	Germany, Hungary, Poland

Sources: Lundell and Karvonen (2003); Roberts (2006); Vatter and Bernauer (2009)

The courts of countries that have high de facto (and de jure) independence, as well as the power to review legislation, can be considered the strongest, most independent courts in Europe. Courts with lower levels of independence and less authority to review laws are weaker. Many of the established democracies in western Europe have relatively high judicial independence, but are weak in their ability to conduct judicial review of legislation. Such countries include Belgium, the Netherlands, and Sweden. In these countries judges overruling the wishes of elected politicians may be viewed as undemocratic. In contrast, judges in Germany, Italy, and Austria have both more judicial independence and stronger powers of judicial review. It is important to note that low levels of independence and weak judicial review do not mean that the courts are corrupt or unable to fulfil their role as a neutral arbiter, or that the courts are unable to adjudicate proceedings fairly. Rather, it means that political and legislative process trumps the legal process when making law. Judges can rarely overturn the policy decisions of elected politicians.

There are, however, cases where a reduction in judicial independence has called into question the ability of courts to uphold the rule of law. Poland and Hungary were both reported to have strong judicial review and high degrees of judicial independence, at least until recently. Governments in both countries, led by the Law and Justice Party (PiS) in Poland and Fidesz in Hungary, have worked to undermine the independence of the judiciary, which the governments viewed as antithetical to their political goals. In 2020, a prominent sitting judge in Poland was threatened with criminal proceedings for taking positions at odds with the government and for asking for the opinion of the EU's legal system on cases involving EU law—a standard legal practice across the EU. The actions of the Polish government against its own judiciary have led the European Commission to start several infringement proceedings against Poland; the Commission believed the measures undermined the judicial independence of the judges and were incompatible with the primacy of EU law. The Hungarian government led by Viktor Orbán of the Fidesz party also has taken several measures to establish political control over the judiciary. As in Poland, the rule of law and judicial independence continue to be a significant problem in Hungary. The low scores for judicial independence highlight the difficulty of setting up an independent judiciary following a transition to democracy.

13.5 European Law and a Changing European Judiciary

Both the nature and strength of courts and judges have been changing across Europe, with the powers of judicial review increasing everywhere. These changes derive from the increasing importance of EU law. Even in countries where the constitution guarantees that parliament reigns supreme, there is now higher order, EU law that national judges can use to review national law. By signing the treaties that govern the EU, EU member states have implicitly agreed that European law takes precedence over national law. This is referred to as **supremacy of EU law** because EU law is supreme to national law. The Court of Justice of the European Union (CJEU)—the 'constitutional court' of the European Union—can rule that national law is incompatible with a member state's obligations under EU law, effectively ruling that national laws are 'unconstitutional' and establishing the principle of judicial review everywhere. Before the Treaty of Lisbon entered into force in 2009, the CJEU was known as the European Court of Justice (ECJ), and we use the time-period appropriate names.

Surprisingly, the original member states of the EU may not have realized that this would come to be the case when they drafted the EU Treaties. Supremacy of EU law is actually derived from case law, rather than a specific provision of the Treaties that founded the EU. The ECJ asserted the supremacy of EU law over national law in a famous court case: Costa v. ENEL [1964] (see Box 13.2 for summaries of several important ECJ/CJEU rulings including Costa). The legal reasoning as to how and under what circumstances EU law supersedes national law varies somewhat from member state to member state. The most open challenge to the CJEU's authority comes from the German Constitutional Court. In a famous ruling of the German Constitutional Court known as the *solange* or the 'so long as' decision, the court ruled that it would effectively allow for the supremacy of European law so long as the European Court ensured the protection of fundamental rights in a manner substantially similar to protections guaranteed by the German constitution. Moreover, the German Constitutional Court openly dismissed a ruling of the CJEU on the member state bonds purchasing programme launched by the European Central Bank in 2015 to stabilize the Euro. The decision provoked strong reactions from the CJEU, which clarified that its ruling is binding upon national courts, as well as from the European Commission, which emphasized that EU law is supreme to national law. The looming conflict between the two courts revolves around the question of which court can rule on the limits of policy authority of the EU.

Box 13.2 **CASE STUDY:** Important European Court Cases in Establishing the EU Legal System

Here we briefly summarize four of the most important court cases that have shaped European integration. These cases are important not only because they have played a role in the development of economic and political ties across Europe, but also because they established an inextricable link between national legal systems and the European legal system.

Establishing Direct Effect: Van Gend en Loos (1963)

Officially known as Van Gend en Loos v. Nederlandse Administratie der Belastingen, this case pitted a Dutch distribution company (now a part of the global logistics firm DHL) against the Dutch tax authorities. In this case, the ECJ established that natural and legal persons (i.e. individual people as well as firms and organizations) had rights under European laws, and not just member state governments. This represented a big leap in how courts view international treaties and law. Usually international agreements do not confer any rights on individual citizens, only on member state governments. Thus, individuals and organizations could not rely on the texts of international agreements when making arguments in court. In this particular case, the Dutch firm Van Gend en Loos sought to import

(continued...)

formaldehyde from West Germany and the Dutch tax authority charged them an import tariff. The firm objected on the grounds that this was a clear violation of the Treaty of Rome, but the tax authority argued that the Treaty of Rome was an agreement between states, and that firms and individuals could not rely on any rights contained within it in a national court. The national court handling the case asked for a ruling from the ECJ using the preliminary ruling procedure. In its ruling the Court clearly sided with Van Gend, stating that the European treaties do confer legal rights directly on individuals and organizations, not just member state governments. Individuals can rely on rights in the Treaty of Rome in national courts. This principle, that European law confer rights directly on individuals, and not only through national governments, has come to be known as Direct Effect.

Establishing supremacy of EU over national law: Costa v. Enel (1964)

This case helped to establish the supremacy of EU law over national law. The ECJ sided with the Italian government, but used legal reasoning that greatly strengthened the importance of EU law in the future. The details of the case are that an Italian citizen, Mr Costa, owned shares in the Italian electric company Edisonvolta, which was then nationalized and became part of state-run Italian energy company, ENEL. Mr Costa opposed nationalization and in an Italian court, he argued that nationalization of the electricity sector violated the Treaty of Rome. Rather than pay his (rather small) electricity bill to ENEL, he argued in court that he should pay Edisonvolta instead. A court in Milan, using the preliminary ruling procedure, asked the European Court of Justice for an opinion, as Mr Costa was relying on the Treaty of Rome to make his case. Meanwhile, the Italian Constitutional Court (to which the case had also been referred) ruled that European law in the Treaty of Rome could not take precedence over the law allowing for nationalization because the signing of the Treaty of Rome preceded the law allowing for the nationalization of the energy sector. Law written later takes precedence over law written earlier. The ECJ, meanwhile, ruled that Mr Costa had no legal right to challenge the Italian government on this particular aspect of EU law, thus supporting the Italian government. It stated that the Treaty of Rome only gave the Commission the authority to decide if the Italian government had engaged in illegal nationalization of the energy sector, not individual citizens. However, it also ruled that, in principle, EU law could take supremacy over national law in the event that they conflict, even when the national law was written after the signing of the Treaty.

Driving European economic integration: Rewe-Zentral v. Bundesmonopolverwaltung für Branntwein (1979)

More commonly referred to as Cassis de Dijon after the French liqueur at the heart of the dispute, this case was integral to the creation of the European single market. A German supermarket group, Rewe, wished to import the French fruit liqueur creme de cassis (a.k.a. Cassis de Dijon), which contains 15–20 per cent alcohol by volume (ABV), and market it as liqueur in its shops. However, the German government informed Rewe that it would not be allowed to sell cassis as a fruit liqueur in Germany because German law required that a liqueur must contain at least 25 per cent ABV. The German government based its argument, at least partially, on public health grounds, presumably because German consumers would be encouraged to drink more alcohol compared to highly alcoholic beverages. But the plaintiffs argued that the German law was effectively a protectionist measure and barrier to trade aimed at keeping products from other European countries off German supermarket shelves, or at least forcing these products to be marketed differently. Like Van Gend and Costa, this case also arrived at the Court of Justice via the preliminary ruling procedure. The Court ruled the German law violated the Treaty of Rome and helped to establish the principle of **mutual recognition**, meaning that products manufactured and marketed legally in one member state must be allowed for sale on the same basis in all other member states. In other words, if Cassis de Dijon is produced and sold as a fruit liqueur in France, Germany must also allow it to be sold as such in Germany.

Freedom of movement: Union Royale Belge des Sociétés de Football Association ASBL v. Jean-Marc Bosman (1995)

This case, commonly referred to simply as the Bosman ruling, had a profound effect on both the freedom of movement across the European Union—the right of EU citizens to move and work freely across member states—and on European football. Jean-Marc Bosman was a footballer who had played for RFC Liège, a club in the Belgian first division. At the end of his contract, unhappy with how he was being treated at Liège, he requested a transfer to the French club, Dunkirk. However, as was the practice at the time, Liège requested that Dunkirk pay a rather high transfer fee—based on Belgium's player evaluation system—which Dunkirk refused to pay. Such fees were common when players moved across national borders, despite the fact that Bosman's contract at Liège had come to an end. Bosman went on to play for lower level teams in Belgium at much reduced wages and took his case to court. The ECJ ruled that requesting transfer fees to cross borders, even after a contract has come to an end, was an illegal barrier to free movement as it prevented EU citizens from pursuing economic activity in another member state. The Bosman ruling also struck down the practice of domestic leagues placing quotas on foreign players when these quotas negatively impacted EU nationals. Much as the Cassis ruling had done for goods, the Bosman ruling made clear that member states and organizations could not create rules that acted as a barrier to the movement of EU citizens seeking to pursue economic activity in another member state. It also helped to change the face of European football, greatly increasing the bargaining leverage of players and internationalizing the game. The world's top leagues, including the English Premier League, would look very different without the Bosman ruling.

While national constitution court judges may have ceded some powers (depending on the country and the initial powers of judicial review), all national court judges can now argue that a national law is incompatible with EU law, and use EU law to back up their decision. National courts also have the power to ask the CJEU for its opinion on how European law impacts a particular case through a process known as the EU's **preliminary ruling procedure**. Some political scientists, such as Karen Alter, have argued that the ability of national court judges to request what is in effect a constitutional decision, from the CJEU, has shaped the constitutionalization of Europe. Kelemen (2011) argued that it has led to an increasingly litigious legal environment, more similar to law in the United States than in most EU member states. The use of the preliminary ruling procedure by national court judges has increased substantially over time, but also varies by member state. Figure 13.2 shows the total number of preliminary ruling referrals by national judges over time and also the number of preliminary ruling referrals by member state in 2018. The figure shows a steady increase in the number of referrals of cases to the CJEU over time, but clearly judges in some countries are more willing to make referrals than others. German, Italian, and Spanish judges make the most referrals. These are, of course, all large countries with many judges, but some other large countries, most notably the UK, make far fewer referrals. Returning to the theoretical discussion at the beginning of the chapter, it may also be the case that countries where citizens view EU law as more legitimate or see the EU as having greater authority may make more use of preliminary rulings. Judges, lawyers, and citizens may be more likely to cite and rely on EU law when making arguments. The preliminary ruling procedure is also the answer to the puzzle why the CJEU could establish its authority: rather than having to rely on the willingness of national governments to implement CJEU rulings, the CJEU could count on

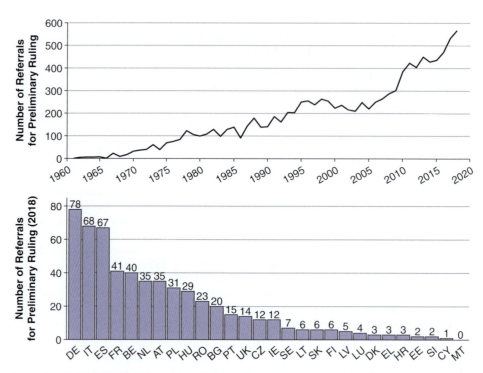

Figure 13.2 Preliminary Ruling Procedure Referrals over Time and by Member State

Data source: Court of Justice of the European Union (2018)

national governments to implement the rulings of national courts who in turn followed a preliminary ruling by the CJEU!

There are also other ways that international law creeps in to increase the power of judicial review. The European Convention of Human Rights has also created a set of international law that national judges can rely on to argue that national law may be incompatible with higher order international commitments. Because all states of the EU (as well as other European states) have adopted the European Convention on Human Rights (ECHR), courts can draw on human rights law to rule that other laws are incompatible with the principles in the ECHR.

Even the United Kingdom, where parliament has always held ultimate authority and where judges can only interpret law, now has a Supreme Court, founded in 2009. Before 2009, the Law Lords—full-time judges and members of the House of Lords—made all final legal decisions, making the House of Lords the highest appeals court in the land. According to the UK Supreme Court's own website, it 'concentrates on cases of the greatest public and constitutional importance'. It has even made important and controversial constitutional rulings regarding the UK leaving the European Union, one of the most politically charged issues relating to Europe in recent times. Gina Miller, a UK businesswoman, brought a legal case against the British government, arguing that the government could not invoke Article 50 (the Article of the EU treaties that allows a member state to trigger the process for leaving the EU) without an act of parliament. The government lost the case in the high court, and then appealed to the Supreme Court, which ruled, once again, that a vote of parliament was required for the government to start the process of leaving the EU. The internationalization of law has made such legal action possible and the need for a Supreme Court greater.

13.6 Rule of Law in the EU: Infringements and Compliance

The increased importance of international obligations raises the question of why national governments accept the fact that European law applies in their country at all. Why do decisions by the CJEU hold sway in EU member states? Why don't governments simply ignore EU law and EU court decisions? The answers to these questions relate to the theoretical discussion from earlier in the chapter, but the reasons for failing to obey law at the national level are likely different from reasons that individual people obey or fail to obey law. Politicians in national governments may not feel much moral compunction to comply with EU law, and if elected politicians feel that EU law contradicts the platform on which they were elected, they might even feel that they are obliged to ignore EU law and follow their voters. However, if citizens (and government officials) tend to support or agree with EU policy or support the right of the EU to make law in a particular area, EU law has the potential to shape behaviour and may lead to greater levels of compliance with (or adherence to) EU law. EU law could create a focal point, leading people to change their behaviour.

To understand the multilevel process of EU law implementation and compliance, it is useful to consider the legal instruments available to the EU. The EU has two basic types of laws: regulations and directives. Regulations set out common binding rules, replacing or complementing all pre-existing national rules on the subject of the regulation. Directives, on the other hand, set common goals to be achieved by a certain time, but leave it to member states to adopt their own rules and legislation to implement the directive. In the past, directives have been the primary instrument of EU legislative politics because they allow a certain degree of flexibility when trying to harmonize pre-existing national legislation on an issue. EU directives thus need to be transposed, or written into national law, meaning action is needed on the part of member state governments. There are two ways in which member states can fail to transpose a directive. First, member states may simply miss the deadline. Directives set out due dates by which the Commission needs to be notified of the national implementing measure. Second, member states may notify the Commission of a measure, but the Commission may decide that the national law or regulation is insufficient, as it does not implement the EU directive or does it incorrectly.

In its role as guardian of the treaties, the Commission is responsible for ensuring consistent application of EU law across member states, and it monitors the implementation of all EU law. The Commission may detect non-compliance following investigations of its own civil service or may take action after hearing about potential problems from other actors, for instance members of the EP, who point out potential violations in their own country. When the Commission suspects that a member state may have breached EU law, it can initiate a infringement procedure. This procedure is summarized in Figure 13.3.

An **infringement proceeding** starts with a letter of formal notice from the Commission to the member state concerned explaining the potential violation. The member state then has a chance to respond. If the response has not clarified the issue to the satisfaction of the

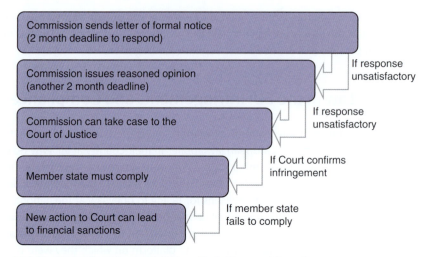

Figure 13.3 Monitoring Compliance with EU Law: The Infringement Procedure

Commission, the Commission can issue a reasoned opinion. If, after another short deadline, the member state still does not comply with EU law, the Commission can take the member state to the CJEU. The Court may then confirm an infringement of EU law, in which case the member state must comply. If compliance still does not occur, the Commission can call on the Court to impose daily financial penalties that the member state must pay until the member state complies. To put this procedure in perspective, the Commission launched 644 new infringement procedures in 2018, sent 157 reasoned opinions, and referred thirteen cases to the Court of Justice. These numbers suggest a substantial and non-trivial level of noncompliance by member states. In the same year, the CJEU imposed financial penalties on four member states.

Before discussing reasons for compliance, we start with the empirical observation that some member states are simply better at complying with EU law than others. Member states vary in their levels of compliance with EU law and how quickly they resolve issues once identified by the Commission. The top panel of Figure 13.4 shows the total number of infringement cases (separated out by the final stage that they reached) by member state from 2002–18. The bottom panel shows the number of infringement proceedings by stage over time from 2002–18. The graphs show that most cases are resolved at the stage of 'formal notice' and that there are very few court cases. The overall number of infringement cases at all stages has been declining over time. It is difficult to know, though, whether the decline is because states are becoming better at complying, or if the Commission is more reluctant to bring action against states for whatever reason.

Notably, there is no immediately clear relationship between Euroscepticism and the number of open infringement cases. The number of cases involving the United Kingdom, formerly the most Eurosceptic member state, is very similar to that of Germany and Belgium, both countries with much higher levels of support for European integration. Spain and Italy have very high numbers of cases despite traditionally high levels of citizen support for European integration. Newer member states in central and eastern Europe have also had relatively few cases brought against them by the Commission. Certainly larger states tend to find themselves

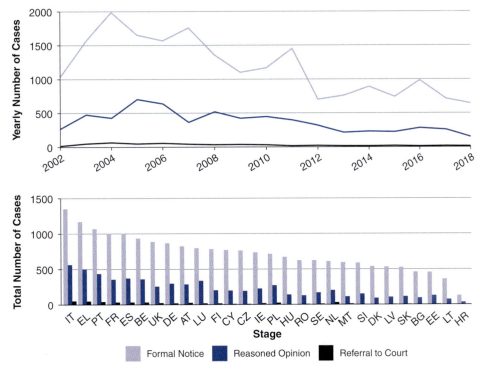

Figure 13.4 Infringement Cases in the EU, 2002–2018

Data source: European Commission (2019c)

involved in more cases; they have more citizens, lawyers, and courts to uncover violations. These states may also be more on the Commission's radar. But some smaller member states find themselves involved in a surprising number of cases; Austria has had almost the same number of cases as Germany, and tiny Luxembourg is just behind them. Size may not matter in some instances—both large and small members need to implement EU law and they may make mistakes in how they do so.

So what does explain the number of infringement cases and how they get resolved? There are a variety of explanations in the literature for why member states violate EU law, leading to an infringement proceeding, how quickly states resolve problems once they encounter them, and even whether the CJEU rules in a state's favour. These include the size and power of the member state, preferences for European integration, the fit between a state's national regulations and regulatory culture and EU law, a state's institutional capacity for implementing EU law, and the number of veto players that the state has. To understand judicial outcomes we must distinguish between explanations for member state's compliance and explanations for Commission behaviour and court decisions. Of course, these are related—in the absence of politics when a state violates an EU law, the CJEU should rule against the state—but in reality, politics creeps in. Member states find themselves in violation of rules for a variety of reasons, and the CJEU may be more reluctant to rule against some members than others. Like national courts, the CJEU may not wish to find itself in a position where large, powerful member states are blatantly ignoring its rulings.

But why might a member state may find itself in violation of EU law to begin with? Perhaps the most straightforward explanation is policy preference. It could be that the member state government disagrees with an EU policy and, therefore, does not comply with it. But if this were the only explanation, we would probably expect to see more compliance among states more supportive of the EU project, but Figure 13.4 suggests that the relationship is not so simple. Indeed, there are reasons why even governments very supportive of the EU may find it harder to comply with EU policy. Some have argued that lack of compliance often results from policy 'misfit' between the EU and the national level, in other words when existing regulatory structures and cultures at the national level differ significantly from the new regulatory regimes that the EU has legislated (e.g. Böerzel, 2000; Knill and Lenschow, 2000). The capacity of bureaucrats to implement new regulations may also play a role (Mbaye, 2001). Where the capacity of the state and its regulatory agencies is weak, perhaps due to a lack of money or training, it may be harder for the government to properly implement EU law. Another perspective points to the power of member states: more powerful member states may be less sensitive to the costs to reputation for non-compliance. Empirical studies confirm that both arguments seem to matter: large member states, for example Italy and France, are less compliant than small member states, but countries with lower bureaucratic capacity, for instance Portugal or Belgium, also comply less than those with high capacities such as Denmark (Börzel et al., 2010).

Variation in political institutions offers another possible explanation. Countries with more veto players might find compliance difficult if it requires changing existing policy through national legislation. But Jensen (2007) has argued that federal countries and those with multiple veto players are more likely to experience infringement proceedings for a different reason. These countries tend to have less direct oversight mechanisms. When politics takes place at different levels of government (e.g. federal and state) and the implementation of policy is not necessarily overseen by a central government, it is easy for the governments of these countries to simply miss or overlook possible violations. Firms or local agencies may be violating EU policy without the knowledge of the government. However, once alerted to problems, some countries are able to fix them rather quickly and avoid facing a court case at the CJEU.

This discussion has offered insights into why governments may or may not comply with EU law, but we are also interested to know why the Commission may decide to bring a case to begin with, or why the Court may choose to rule against a member state. Of course, the most straightforward explanation is that a member state is violating an EU policy. But the violations are not always so clear. The Commission may be strategic in the cases that it decides to pursue (König and Mäder, 2014) and the Court may be cautious in how it makes its rulings (Garrett et al., 1998; Carrubba et al., 2008). Neither wishes a member state to blatantly ignore a court decision and continue to violate EU law. European-level judges, just like national court judges, want to maintain their authority and wish to see their rulings complied with. This means that the court may shy away from making rulings against powerful member governments and governments that will find it particularly difficult to comply with a ruling. The Commission and the CJEU make strategic, political calculations about the likelihood that a government will comply with an adverse ruling when deciding to bring a case and making a ruling that goes against a member state government.

13.7 **Summary**

Increasing judicial review and the importance of EU law is changing the nature of judiciaries and judicial politics throughout Europe. It means that, even in European countries where judges have historically played little role in politics, they are becoming more important and more powerful. It also means that they have the power to apply European law widely, shaping the legal landscape. Whether this leads to greater levels of 'rule of law' may well depend on how norms develop across Europe. As discussed at the start of the chapter, people often obey law because of its moral and symbolic value, coupled with the notion that it may signal citizens to an existing societal consensus about how they should behave. If people are less likely to believe that EU law carries such moral weight, it could be less effective than law made at the national level.

Online Data Exercise: Infringement Cases

The interactive online exercise presents a dataset on infringement cases in the European Union. You will explore potential reasons for why some member states comply less with EU law than others, including the size of contributions to the EU budget, government left–right positions, and government support for EU integration.

 Take your learning further with this interactive data exercise, available at **www.foundationsofeuropeanpolitics.com**

 For additional material and resources, including multiple-choice questions, web links, and more, please visit the online resources: **www.oup.com/he/devries1e**

14 European Politics into the Future

In this final chapter, we explore recent changes in European politics and the future outlook for democracy in Europe. This chapter discusses ongoing political change both within European countries, at the European Union level and in the interplay between both levels. In doing so, we will highlight four important debates about the state of democracy in Europe: the debates about the rise of political fragmentation and its consequences for democracy, democratic backsliding in central and eastern Europe, the impact of the United Kingdom leaving the EU on democracy, and finally the democratic deficit in EU politics.

European politics finds itself in a state of flux. Recent events, such as the rise of challenger parties, the exit of the UK from the European Union, and the fallout from the coronavirus pandemic, have raised questions about what European politics will look like in the coming years, both at the national and supranational levels. In this final chapter, we examine the state of politics and democracy in Europe today by looking at the interplay between the national and European layers of government, just as we have done throughout the book. We offer some, admittedly speculative, thoughts about how European politics might develop in the years to come. And we invite students to consider what the theories discussed throughout the book imply for the future development of European politics.

We examine four current and ongoing concerns that span national and supranational levels of government. At the national level, we explore recent increases in political fragmentation, electoral volatility, the rise of new parties, and we speculate about the consequences of these changes for governance. We then explore two topics that lie at the intersection of the national and EU levels. First, we examine instances of democratic backsliding in Hungary and Poland and discuss the impact that these changes have on European integration. Second, we explore the case of 'Brexit'—the UK leaving the EU—and its relationship to democratic governance both in the UK and the EU. And finally, we examine a topic primarily at the EU level, namely concerns about the EU's 'democratic deficit'. Of course, these are only four topics from the many that we could have explored. We chose these four because they touch on many of core theoretical and empirical themes covered throughout the book, they represent trends that have been developing over years, and many of the issues these topics raise are likely to be with us well into the future.

14.1 Political Fragmentation and its Impact on Governance

Countries across Europe face considerable internal challenges. As we highlighted in Chapter 8, the ties between voters and parties have weakened in recent decades. As a consequence, voters are more likely to switch parties between elections, creating greater electoral volatility as shown in Chapter 5. Election outcomes have become less predictable. The weakening ties between voters and parties have created opportunities for new parties to make electoral breakthroughs. The rise of green parties in the late 1980s and populist or Eurosceptic parties in the late 1990s and early 2000s are a case-in-point. As a result, party systems in many European countries have fragmented and the dominance of mainstream party families—Christian democrats, liberals, and social democrats—has waned. These developments are likely to have both positive and negative consequences for European politics. The rise of new parties that highlight policy concerns that were previously largely ignored by mainstream parties, such as the environment, European integration, or immigration, has increased responsiveness to voter concerns and feelings of representation. This is good news for European democracy. Yet, at the same time, increased electoral volatility and political fragmentation has complicated government formation and left government coalitions that do form more unstable (De Vries and Hobolt, 2020).

This volatility is evident when we visualize the number of new partisan compositions of governments that have never existed before over time (e.g. the first time parties have formed a coalition together or the first time a single party has formed a majority or minority government). A rise in novel government compositions could be an indication of the difficulty of governing in Europe. The top panel in Figure 14.1 shows the share of such new government compositions in the first cabinet after each parliamentary election from 1945 to 2020. The share is naturally higher at times when new political systems formed (e.g. after the Second World War or after the Cold War in the 1990s). The curve suggests an increasing trend towards more and more new partisan government compositions. On average, more than six out of ten new governments that form in a year after an election in Europe have not existed before in either partisan composition or majority status (Döring and Manow, 2019).

As we pointed out Chapter 10, increasing **fragmentation** is one factor that may explain this pattern. The bottom panel in Figure 14.1 shows how the probability of a new government composition increases as a function of party system fragmentation, measured by the effective number of parliamentary parties. Thus, when new challenger parties enter a country's parliament, the likelihood of a hitherto untested government forming is higher. Such governments do not necessarily perform worse, but government formation and survival do require a certain degree of stability among a set of parties that can agree on a number of core policy issues. Such volatility might also make it more difficult for voters to understand the consequences of their vote choice for government formation. If political systems become too fragmented and if competition is diffused along a number of cross-cutting dimensions, then it may become difficult for parties to form stable coalitions. This in turn could hamper a government's ability to act and may prove to be grist for the mill of those parties that attack the current rules of the game. Political fragmentation may create a tension between enhancing representation on the one hand and enabling strong government that delivers for voters on the other (Mair, 2013).

What does this mean for the future of European politics? This is difficult to predict as there are simply too many unknowns. Yet, what we do know is that the rise of challenger parties has made the formation of governments more difficult and their survival less certain (De Vries and Hobolt, 2020). If governments become more vulnerable and struggle to deliver on their policy promises, it may fuel political discontent and provide fertile breeding ground for political entrepreneurs who are critical of existing political structures. Future scholars of European politics will want to examine these questions in much greater detail.

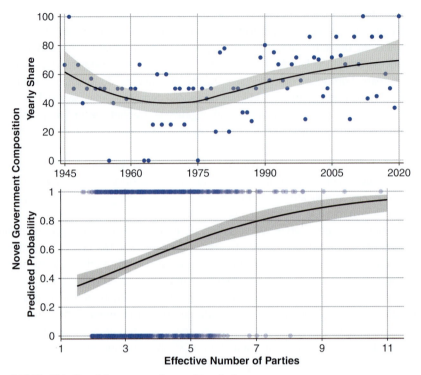

Figure 14.1 The Volatility of Government Compositions in Europe

Data source: ParlGov (Döring and Manow, 2019)

Note: The upper panel shows the share of new government compositions (that have not previously existed) in the first cabinet following a parliamentary election. A new government is defined as one with a novel partisan composition. Moreover, a government is considered new if the majority status of the government is novel (e.g. has never ruled as a coalition or single-party government as a majority or minority before). Each dot represents a year. The line shows a smoothed time-series fit. The lower panel shows the predicted probability of a new government as a function of the effective number of parties including 95% confidence bounds based on a bivariate logistic regression. Each dot represents a cabinet following a parliamentary election.

14.2 Democratic Backsliding in EU Member States

The erosion of democracy represents a second challenge facing some European states, as well as the EU. The EU requires that countries wishing to become EU member states fulfil basic democratic criteria. Its member states are expected to uphold democratic ideals, and, at least theoretically, the EU possesses tools to sanction member states that do not. Nevertheless, there are concerns that **democratic backsliding** has occurred in some member states, primarily in central and eastern Europe, and most notably in Hungary and Poland, although they are not alone in raising concerns.

When communism collapsed, the EU hoped to bring the newly democratic regimes of central and eastern Europe into the EU fold relatively quickly. This, though, would prove to be a much bigger, longer, and more fraught process than what the EU had experienced with the enlargement to the Mediterranean countries of Greece, Portugal, and Spain. The first round of former Communist countries joined the EU in 2004 with two more, Bulgaria and Romania, following in 2007, and Croatia joining in 2013. While much has changed in the intervening years, there remain significant differences between the older EU member states and the newer states, especially with regard to the state of democracy.

Most recently, there have been significant fears of a collapse of democracy in two countries in particular: Hungary and Poland. In both of these countries, parties with authoritarian tendencies were able to win single party majorities in parliament. Viktor Orbán, prime minister of Hungary since 2010 and leader of the Fidesz Party, has embraced a nationalist, anti-foreigner agenda, changing laws to reduce freedom of the press and hamper opposition parties. In Poland, the Law and Justice Party (PiS), since winning the parliamentary election in 2015, has changed the way that the judiciary is appointed to give more power to the ruling party, namely itself. It has also worked to purge the public administration of perceived enemies to the party and has increased its control over the media. In both Poland and Hungary, these anti-democratic parties have come from the right wing of the political spectrum, espousing traditional cultural values, and have frequently used the European Union as a scapegoat, blaming the EU for problems they face.

The data from the V-Dem project (discussed in Chapter 1, Box 1.1) allow us to depict the decline in different aspects of democracy in these two countries. We see that Poland has

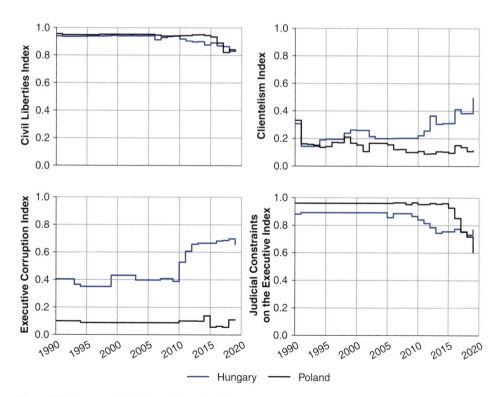

Figure 14.2 Democratic Decline in Poland and Hungary

Data source: V-Dem (Coppedge et al. 2020)

witnessed a sharp decline in judicial constraints on the executive since PiS came to power in 2015, a result of the party chipping away at the independence of the judiciary. There has also been a smaller decline in civil liberties. In Hungary, there has been a similar decline in judicial constraints on the executive and civil liberties, and an even starker rise in corruption and clientelism. According to the V-Dem researchers, as of 2020 'Hungary is no longer a democracy, leaving the EU with its first non-democratic Member State' (Lührmann et al., 2020, 4).

The EU has found it difficult to prevent backsliding for three reasons: intergovernmental structures and the multilevel party system, the financial benefits of EU membership, and free movement. First, due to unanimity voting rules in the European Council, the Polish government can block any attempt to formally sanction Hungary, and Hungary any attempt to punish Poland. But it is also difficult to sanction these anti-democratic parties in the other EU institutions such as the European Parliament. Kelemen (2017, 2020) has argued that the EU has become sufficiently institutionalized that transnational European political parties are politically meaningful and important, and they rely on the support of the national parties that comprise them for coalition building in the Council and in the European Parliament. At the same time, European parties are not sufficiently democratic for voters in western Europe to know or care that the parties they support are coddling anti-democratic forces from elsewhere in Europe. Thus, Christian Democratic and conservative parties from Germany and elsewhere have tolerated the behaviour of Viktor Orbán's Fidesz Party in part because he delivered votes to the EPP group in the European Parliament, and these votes were important for passing legislation and for electing the Commission President. After many years, Fidesz ultimately left the EPP group in early 2021 after the EPP threatened them with expulsion. In general, members of democratic federal political systems may support anti-democratic elements at subnational levels when those subnational elements deliver votes and political support, a phenomenon known as subnational authoritarianism (Gibson, 2005, 2013). According to Kelemen, the critical rhetoric directed towards the Polish PiS party has been somewhat stronger, at least in part because the PiS does not belong to the large European People's Party group in the European Parliament.

The prevention of democratic backsliding has also been hampered by the fact that member states receive subsidies from the EU, and they may use these financial transfers to support clientelist networks. High levels of corruption and allegations of misuse of EU funds contribute to the maintenance of authoritarian power structures. Given the nature of budgetary decision-making in the EU, it has been difficult to cut off funds, even if governments are likely misusing them. Corruption, and the EU's implicit support for it, has been a substantial problem in Hungary, but also in Bulgaria, Romania, Malta, and elsewhere. Finally, the free movement of persons in the EU makes it easier for dissatisfied citizens in those countries to move elsewhere, weakening domestic opposition. In conclusion, Kelemen considers the EU to be in an 'authoritarian trap' or an 'authoritarian equilibrium'. An escape seems difficult and will probably hinge on EU parties expelling national parties that violate fundamental democratic norms and on EU funding being made conditional on the adherence to those norms. To date, the EU parties and institutions have been unwilling or unable to do this.

In sum, the ability of the EU to shape and promote democracy in post-Communist eastern Europe may not be as great as initial optimism suggested it would be (Slapin, 2015). Of course, we cannot know the counterfactual of how democracy would have developed in these countries in the absence of EU enlargement. But European institutions will need to cope with divergent levels of democracy across member states in the coming years. We can

Box 14.1 **CONTROVERSIES AND DEBATES:** EU Enlargement and its Consequences for EU Decision-Making

In the near future, the EU could possibly increase its membership again. As of mid-2020, five countries are officially candidates for EU membership: Albania, the Republic of North Macedonia, Montenegro, Serbia, and Turkey. Bosnia and Herzegovina and Kosovo are considered potential candidates for EU membership, with Bosnia and Herzegovina having submitted its membership application. Turkey has been a candidate country for over twenty years, and the chances of it becoming a member state remain slim. However, further expansion to the Balkan countries is a real possibility.

There has been significant controversy in the EU literature about the impact of enlargement on the EU and its ability to function (Kelemen et al., 2014). Many have argued that a wider EU, i.e. an EU with more member states as the result of enlargement, is necessarily a less deep EU, i.e. an EU hampered in its ability to pursue further, deeper integration. Scholars of EU politics were particularly concerned that the 2004–7 enlargement rounds to include post-communist states from central and eastern Europe would lead to gridlock in EU decision-making processes (e.g. König and Bräuninger, 2004). After enlargement, with no apparent slowdown in EU law-making processes, some scholars including Schimmelfennig et al. (2015) argued that **widening** has not impeded further integration only because the EU has increasingly relied on 'differentiated integration' where various subsets of member states agree to **deepening**, thus more cooperation on particular issues at the European level, leaving other member states behind.

However, Kelemen et al. (2014) argue that expansion could possibly have the opposite effect, leading the EU to explore avenues for deeper integration. Specifically, they argue that while more member states could make reaching agreement in the Council more difficult in the short run, gridlock in the legislative process could empower supranational actors such as the CJEU. They also suggest that the addition of member states, and thus more people, sitting around the table at Council of Minister meetings could lead these meetings to adopt more legislative, and less diplomatic, rules, relying more on formal votes and less on informal 'consensus'. Finally, they argue that potential gridlock could lead the EU to use more majoritarian rules with greater frequency. While there are clearly ways that enlargement could impede deepening in the short term, it never seems to have done so in the long term (Toshkov, 2017). Indeed, the EU could have engaged in deeper cooperation because it has expanded and not in spite of its expansion.

only speculate what this will mean for European-level policy-making. Eventually, parties from countries in northern and western Europe may no longer tolerate anti-democratic parties as part of their coalition and may crack down on them. Or they may continue to tolerate them as they do now, making it difficult or impossible for the EU to pass policy aimed at reducing corruption or enhancing democracy. There is some reason for optimism, though. In July 2020, the opposition candidate and mayor of Warsaw came within a hair's breadth of winning the Polish presidential election, despite the incumbent President Duda and his Law and Justice party effectively controlling state media. These anti-democratic parties are not completely immune to challenges at the ballot box.

14.3 Brexit and the Future of the EU–UK Relationship

The debate over leaving the EU that took place in the UK between 2016 and 2020, and the ongoing debate about the future relationship between the UK and the EU, encapsulates many recent concerns about democratic politics at both the national and EU levels. We may believe that citizens in sovereign, democratic nations should have the ability to choose whether their governments participate in international organizations or a supranational political system such as the EU. And countries should be able to leave these agreements if they wish to do so. The UK's referendum to leave the EU on 23 June 2016 seems to have been just that— a democratic decision by voters in a sovereign country to leave the European Union. But 'Brexit', as the UK's struggle to leave the EU has come to be known, raises many questions about how to implement such changes.

At the most general level, Brexit raises questions about when voters should be involved in decision-making. As we've discussed throughout the book, democracy involves delegation, meaning voters are not directly involved in most political and policy decisions, especially those related to technical or foreign policy matters. Decisions about participation in international organizations, and negotiations with those organizations, are often the prerogative of governments. Viewed through this lens, the decision to give voters a say about leaving the EU may have been unnecessary from the point of view of enhancing democracy.

But voters are often asked to cast votes on decisions that make major constitutional changes. In many countries, a referendum is required to change the constitution (see Chapter 6). The decision to leave the EU clearly has had a major constitutional impact on the UK. Moreover, European integration has become increasingly politicized in recent decades. Thus, it is only right that voters be given a chance to express their views if their government is seriously considering making such a major change. Holding a referendum on the issue, and then carrying out the result of the referendum, is the democratic response to disagreements about participating in the EU.

Arguably, citizens should revisit the relationship between their state and the EU over time as the relationship changes. The UK first joined in 1973, and held a referendum on continued membership in 1975. But the EU changed substantially in the intervening years, becoming much more than an economic organization. These changes made a referendum on the UK's membership a reasonable prospect—citizens should be asked to reflect on whether to participate in an organization that has changed significantly since the last time they reflected on the matter. But they also made a 'leave' decision that much harder to actually implement—integration has left British and continental European politics and markets deeply entwined.

But while we can argue the case for holding a referendum, the referendum also raises questions about how policies get onto the political agenda. Citizens are regularly asked in surveys to reflect on the most important problem facing their country. Figure 14.3 plots what the British public feel to be the country's most important problem over time. Each line in the plot shows the percentage of survey respondents saying that that problem was the most important problem facing the UK at that particular point in time. Prior to the Conservative government taking office in 2015, 'Europe' did not appear as a problem troubling British citizens about their country. Even immigration, which is related to European integration due to free movement of people, was not seen as particularly problematic. Instead, the domestic economy was the issue on the top of people's minds as the country was still recovering from the global financial crisis of 2008. But over the course of the EU referendum campaign and aftermath, Europe quickly became the most important political issue for UK citizens. Interestingly, as the problem of the relationship with Europe increased in importance, the perceived

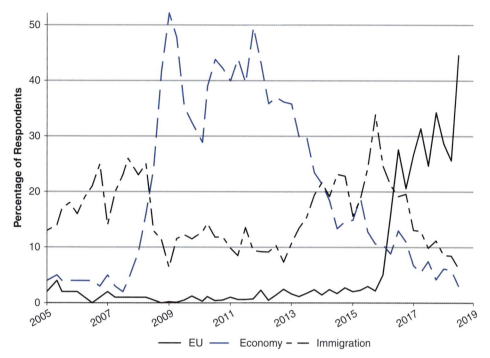

Figure 14.3 Most Important Issue in the UK

Data source: Ipsos-Mori (2020)

importance of immigration as a problem declined. This pattern suggests that salience of the European 'problem' was driven by the referendum, rather than the referendum being a response to a perceived problem among the public.

The structure of the referendum also raises important questions about how democracy works across the UK and its four constituent countries—England, Scotland, Wales and Northern Ireland. The UK is ultimately a unitary state with power residing in Westminster. However, it has devolved powers to regions over the last several decades, with popularly elected assemblies in Wales, Scotland, and Northern Ireland. Majorities in both Scotland and Northern Ireland supported remaining in the EU, but because the referendum did not take the constituent countries into account in its design, the fact that majorities differed across the regions did not matter for the outcome. This is different from how federal units are treated when making constitutional decisions in federal states such as Switzerland, where referendums must pass with a majority of voters in a majority of cantons. Brexit ultimately could increase the prospect of a breakup of the UK with increasing support for independence in Scotland and Northern Ireland.

Furthermore, the referendum was not designed to confirm a decision already made by politicians, but was rather designed to direct politicians to follow a particular path with regard to European relations. This meant that citizens were given the option of voting for Brexit without knowing what the particular arrangement would look like that would enable the UK to leave the EU. Notably, it was clear from the outset that the goals proclaimed by those supporting the Leave campaign were incompatible with each other. These proclaimed goals included that there would be (1) no border between Northern Ireland and Ireland, thereby upholding the Good Friday peace agreement, (2) no border between Northern Ireland and the rest of the UK, and (3) that the UK could leave the EU's single market and the customs union. However, the joint participation of the UK and Ireland in single market and customs union was precisely what allowed there to be open borders. Thus, without knowing how exactly the final withdrawal arrangement would resolve this conflict, it was difficult for voters to make an informed choice.

Lastly, the decision to leave the EU, a policy decision that drastically alters the UK's relationship with its most important neighbours and also has a tremendous impact on the UK's domestic constitution, was arguably the result of an internal struggle within the Conservative Party. It was not really a change that a majority of voters were pressing for, but rather a small, but very vocal minority. The British Conservatives had been one of the most divided parties on matters of European integration in the EU for decades. When David Cameron took over the premiership in 2010 he tried to resolve the issue once and for all. His strategy to overcome the intraparty divisions was twofold. First, he tried to renegotiate the terms of the UK's EU membership to secure more exemptions for the UK from EU policy in controversial policy areas. Second, he planned to hold a referendum on this renegotiated deal, expecting a confirmation of EU membership under the new conditions. Clearly, this strategy backfired. There was a widespread perception that the changes that Cameron had secured were minor. Thus, rather than the deal, EU membership itself became the focal point of the referendum. Intraparty divisions also became evident for the main opposition party, the British Labour Party. In sum, the hope to overcome intraparty divisions through a referendum not only highlighted the disagreements within the major parties, but also created deep division in the country (Hobolt, 2016; Hobolt et al., 2020).

Ironically, the Brexit debate and referendum have underscored that democratic consent lies at the core of EU membership. Even though those supporting Brexit claimed the EU had taken away their sovereignty, the referendum demonstrated that member states are indeed free to leave. This is quite a contrast to other federations which generally do not allow voluntary exit by states (Slapin, 2009). Initially, some were concerned that other countries might try to follow in the UK's footsteps and leave the EU as well. However, as citizens of other member states have watched how Brexit has played out, there has been a general increase in support for the EU in all other member states following the referendum (De Vries, 2018). Fears that Brexit would cause other member states to follow have not yet materialized: support for the EU increased in most member states and some hard Eurosceptic parties abandoned their platform for leaving the EU. As the relationship between the UK and the EU evolves over the coming years through ongoing negotiations regarding trade and access to markets, the fortunes of the EU's first 'emeritus' member state will be watched closely across Europe.

14.4 The Democratic Deficit in the European Union

The EU has had a profound effect on democracy in its member states. It has helped secure peace and economic stability across Europe in the wake of the world wars that devastated the continent in the first half of the twentieth century. And it has allowed states to better respond to the collapse of autocratic and communist governments across the continent in last part of the twentieth century. But many researchers and commentators have argued that we need to be concerned with the '**democratic deficit**'. within the EU itself (Føllesdal and Hix, 2006; Scharpf, 2015).

Indeed, the Brexit debate raised important questions for the EU about its own democratic legitimacy. Is the EU sufficiently responsive to the real and legitimate concerns of EU citizens about supranational overreach? Is it possible for member states to claw back authority? If so, how? If leaving the EU is not a realistic option for many states, then the importance of reducing any democratic deficit at the supranational level becomes even more urgent. The EU has made efforts to address these issues in various ways, but many view them as not going far enough.

The EU's institutions are often said to be too far removed from European citizens and insufficiently responsive, undermining democratic representation across the entirely of the EU. Some see this as leading voters to feel that an unresponsive bureaucracy in Brussels imposes laws upon them without sufficient input into the process, a narrative that is used by populist and Eurosceptic parties across Europe.

The institutional rules of the EU have changed significantly over time, in part to try to respond to concerns of insufficient democracy. As discussed in Chapter 3, the EU has reformed its main governing treaties quite frequently since the founding of the European Communities with the Treaties of Rome. With respect to the level and nature of democracy, the most important changes have come to the European Parliament. Members of European Parliament were originally appointed by member state parliaments. But this changed in 1979 with direct elections to the European Parliament. For the first time citizens of Europe voted for representatives whose sole job was to represent them in a European institution. But the European Parliament had relatively little power at the time. It could amend some types of legislation, subject to the agreement of the national governments, but it could not block the passage of policy. Eventually, it became seen as unacceptable that a directly elected body would have so little power. Over the course of successive treaty revisions and rules changes, the power of the European Parliament has increased. As discussed in Chapter 11, following the most recent major rules change in the 2009 Treaty of Lisbon, the European Parliament has equal legislative powers to those of the Council, at least in areas where it is allowed to legislate.

The Treaty of Lisbon also introduced a mechanism to allow national parliaments to register their objections to proposed EU legislation, the so-called 'early warning system' (also known as the yellow card mechanisms), and if enough parliaments raise an objection, the Commission must revisit the proposal. The goal was to increase **subsidiarity**—the degree to which policy is made at a level closer to the voter. However, the procedure is rarely used. Moreover, it is very unlikely that citizens are sufficiently aware that these mechanisms exist to demand that national parliaments make use of them.

If creating new rules that empower the EP and give greater say to national parliaments is insufficient, then it would seem that increasing the direct involvement of the public would be required. However, when the public are asked about the EU, it is often in public referendums on treaties. Or in the case of Brexit, about whether a country should be a member at all. These questions revolve around integration—should the EU have more or less control over policies, or should institutions be altered to facilitate integration? These are very valid questions and correspond to questions of constitution design in federal states. However, such questions tend to be more abstract, and do not address questions about what policy should actually be.

Voter participation on questions about the direction of policy typically occurs during election campaigns, where voters can vote for parties that will shift policy in their preferred direction, as suggested by the spatial model referenced throughout this book. Although there are European-wide elections to the European Parliament, these are often fought on national (rather than EU) issues and suffer from low turnout (see Chapter 6). Additionally, despite its increased power, some still view the European Parliament as relatively weak. If electoral competition for the European Parliament tapped into a truly European politics that was policy-focused, it would be easier to make the argument that voters hold the EU to account through the usual pathways of representative democracy. But this is not always the case as we have discussed earlier, raising the question of whether and how voters can express their views on integration other than through referendums such as the Brexit vote.

The EU has changed not only with respect to how it makes decisions—empowering the EP and weakening the ability of individual member states to veto proposals—but also by increasing the number of areas in which it makes decisions. It has moved from being an organization that primarily regulates markets to one that has a much stronger regulatory and oversight role covering decision-making on many more policies and issues, as we have highlighted in Chapter 12.

With increased authority and power come increased questions about democratic legitimacy. Increasing the power of the directly elected branch of EU government only goes so far towards reducing the democratic deficit. Føllesdal and Hix (2006) have argued that the EU's democratic deficit lies in the lack of citizen knowledge about the EU and EU politics. Even when citizens vote in European Parliament elections, they often do so on the basis of evaluations of national politics and national leaders, rather than on European issues. There is no European-wide media coverage of the EU or European politics and no European-wide election campaigns. The claim that European elections are just **second order national elections** has been around since the first EP election in 1979 (Reif and Schmitt, 1980), leading many to question the effectiveness of these elections in holding parties to account over European politics. When European elections do focus on European issues, they tend to revolve around whether integration should increase or be rolled back. This leads parties opposed to the European project to seek and win seats in the EP. Such parties, opposed to the very existence of the political entity to which they have been elected, are less common in national politics. A fully functioning democracy at the EU level would require pan-European parties who fight election campaigns on policy issues, and an electorate that is sufficiently informed to vote on the basis of these issues, at least according to some scholars.

Others have argued that concerns about the EU's democratic deficit are overstated, claiming that it is difficult to operationalize in practice or that the yardstick applied to the EU does not correspond to the one applied to national democracies. According to Majone (1998), because the EU is primarily engaged in making regulatory policies, often on topics rather obscure to voters, and because it has only relatively small fiscal authority, relying on member states for money, the EU's existing structure is sufficiently democratic (see also Chapter 12 Box 12.2). Liberal intergovernmentalism as espoused by Moravcsik (see Chapter 3 Box 3.3), suggests that the electoral chain of delegation, through national and European elections, provides enough of a democratic basis for an organization that, after all, does not decide on the issues that most directly affect and concern citizens, such as taxation, education, health policy, and social policy (see Moravcsik, 2002). Member states have full control over the integration process and can change treaties to roll back the EU's authority, if necessary, albeit only by unanimity. But as the EU comes to regulate more and more of European life, these arguments become harder to support. Finally, from an institutionalist perspective, the EU's democratic deficit shrinks when the decision-making capacity of the EU's veto players, the Council and the European Parliament, increases. In particular, the lowering of the voting threshold in the Council has decreased policy stability in the EU and enables more flexible political decision-making (Tsebelis, 2002; Finke et al., 2012).

The debate about the nature and size of the EU's democratic deficit raises important questions about the appropriate yardstick to use when measuring EU democracy. Is it appropriate to compare the EU's supranational structure, and its levels of democracy, to democracy in the member states? Again, a difficult question to answer. But as the EU comes to play an ever more important role in the lives of Europeans, and as citizens become more aware of European integration and its role in national politics, these comparisons are increasingly necessary to consider.

14.5 European Politics into the Future

Politics in Europe today looks different than it did only a few decades or even years ago. If we can be sure of one thing, it is that change will continue into the future. While we certainly cannot predict what the future will bring, the themes we discussed in this book allow us to speculate about how politics may develop within Europe over the coming years and decades.

The coronavirus outbreak in 2020 has been the latest stress test for the EU. In the early months of the outbreak, EU member states were among some of the hardest hit countries globally and many of them put their economies in hibernation to reduce the strain on health services. The extraordinary crisis puts renewed political pressure on the country-bloc to come up with joint approaches to battle the virus and manage the economic fallout. When it comes to shaping Europe's recovery, we have witnessed an EU plagued by deep political divisions over its future. European leaders, like the Italian Prime Minister Giuseppe Conte or French President Emmanuel Macron, even warned that the coronavirus could lead to the break-up of the EU. One of the reasons why it proved so hard to broker a deal to provide EU-level financial support to affected countries was the legacy of both the Eurozone debt and refugee crises on public opinion and party competition. Bruised by these previous crises, trust between member states took a significant blow as stereotypes of northern saints and southern sinners prevailed (Matthijs and McNamara, 2015). Over half a century of integration in Europe has created profound interconnectedness between the fates of member states. At the same time, however, the economic and political fortunes of member states have started to diverge dramatically. The fault lines now cross-cut the European continent from north to south on economic recovery and from west to east on democracy and human rights. A key question for the EU will be how these rifts develop into the future. When they intensify, as a result of growing divergence in public finances or rule of law, the EU might develop into a more loose and differentiated Union. When they subside, perhaps as a result of increasing geopolitical uncertainty involving the US and China, the EU might take important steps to integrate further.

Next to the importance of rifts between member states, the functional pressure to integrate may increase in the coming years. Pressing policy issues such as climate change, pandemics, and geopolitical instability require even more cross-national coordination between European countries. As we have outlined in Chapter 12, EU institutions have proposed ambitious plans for a European Green Deal. The European Green Deal aims to transform the EU from a high- to a low-carbon economy by aiming to ensure net zero carbon emissions by 2050, and a 50–5 per cent cut in emissions by 2030 compared with 1990 levels. While the implementation of the European Green Deal will require substantial policy change at the EU level and the approval of national parliaments, it may jump start another wave of integration in Europe. Even if member states may be wary of taking further integrative steps, one country's exposure to climate change is shaped by the behaviour of other countries.

The EU clearly faces difficult challenges in the years ahead. In the past, journalists, politicians, and scholars have all questioned the ability of the EU to weather the various challenges it has faced, from the banking and government debt crises, to various waves of immigration and refugees and Brexit. However, the EU has proved remarkably resilient in the face of crisis over the years. In fact, the EU is traditionally forged by crisis. The solutions that European political leaders tend to find are not always elegant; they often resemble a process of 'muddling through' rather than thorough and once-and-for-all problem-solving. But cooperation across European nations continues and shows little sign of abating.

When we think about the resilience of the EU, it is also important to think about what yardstick we use. Just like it is difficult to judge democracy within the EU, it is also difficult to judge its performance. Can we judge the policy performance of the EU only in those areas where it has the exclusive authority to act, like in the case of trade or monetary policy, or should we see the policy performance of the EU as a combination what EU institutions and member states institutions do? Even though clear differences exist in the policy outcomes we observe across EU member states, when we compare Europe to other parts of the world, like the United States, these differences may seem less big. When we think of the political response to the coronavirus outbreak, for example, it becomes clear that, even though individual EU member states reacted differently to the crisis, partly due to differences in healthcare systems and fiscal space, compared to the United States, we see the outlines of a European-type response. All European countries implemented government-led measures to slow the spread of the virus, such as closing schools, banning large gatherings, and closing down parts of their economy, but they combined these interventions with government-assisted programmes to prevent job losses. While the coordination provided by EU institutions on the health side was quite limited, due to the lack of EU policy authority in this area (see Chapter 12), the EU assisted member states in their efforts to prevent mass employment. The European Commission introduced a new instrument for temporary support to mitigate unemployment risks, which allows for a financial assistance up to 100 billion Euro in the form of loans from the EU to affected member states. This response stands in stark contrast to the United States response where unemployment rose sharply without government-assisted schemes to allow people to remain in work. These different policy responses reflect different policy traditions when it comes to the government's role in the economy and social rights of citizens.

14.6 **Summary**

This chapter, and indeed this book, has explored ongoing issues of politics within Europe. The EU, as a supranational organization, has played a particularly significant role in the development of political systems in post-war Europe. However, the EU and the member states that comprise it continue to confront questions about democracy in the face of both European and global challenges. Following the global financial crisis beginning in 2008 and coronavirus crisis of 2020, Europe stands at a crossroads, where countries must collectively decide either to pursue much deeper cooperation, or to return powers to nation-states. While we do not know exactly what European cooperation and European politics will look like in the years and decades to come, we can be relatively confident that states of Europe will remain a tightly interconnected group of wealthy democracies, likely to be at the heart of solutions to global problems.

 For additional material and resources, including multiple-choice questions, web links, and more, please visit the online resources: **www.oup.com/he/devries1e**

Glossary

Abstract review: A type of judicial review where a constitutional court can assess the constitutionality of a law before it takes effect, usually at the request of a small set of political actors granted the right to ask for a review by the constitution.

Accommodative strategy of mainstream parties: Involves mainstream parties adopting a similar strategy to challenger parties in hopes of drawing voters away from a threatening competitor.

Accountability: Refers to citizens using the vote to sanction or reward politicians. In representative democracies, free, fair, and periodic elections are the main instrument through which voters can hold elected officials accountable for their time in office.

Adversarial strategy of mainstream parties: Involves mainstream parties competing with challenger parties by adopting an opposing position on an issue that has been mobilized by a challenger party.

Agenda control: The ability to control the parliamentary agenda and timetable.

Agenda setting: The ability to make proposals that can either be defeated or passed, but not amended.

Anticipatory representation: The notion that elected representatives base their policy platforms and behaviour on what they think their constituents will approve of at the next election, not on what they promised to do at the last election.

Attitudes: People's beliefs (likes or dislikes) about a specific individual, ideas, or objects.

Backbencher: A member of parliament who does not hold a leadership role or a major legislative office.

Belief system: A configuration of attitudes and ideas in which the elements are bound together by some form of constraint or functional interdependence (Converse, 1964, 207).

Bicameral parliament: A parliament with two distinct legislative chambers involved in parliamentary deliberations and decision-making.

Bipolar party system: A multiparty system where parties are divided into two ideological blocs that form relatively stable coalitions.

Cabinet: At the national level, a cabinet consists of the prime minister and ministers. In the European Commission, it is called the College of Commissioners.

Cabinet portfolios: Policy jurisdictions that are under the responsibility of cabinet ministers.

Cadre party: An elite-driven party type that developed in European parliaments, with a minimal extra-parliamentary organization. Also known as elite or caucus party.

Candidate-centred system: A system in which electoral rules and parties' candidate selection rules create incentives for candidate-centred behaviour of elected representatives, such as promoting personal views in speeches and votes and constituency service.

Cartel party: A type of political party that, according to Katz and Mair (1995), uses the resources of the state to maintain its position within the political system.

Catch-all party: A type of political party that seeks to attract voters from different points of view and ideologies. It has a large and heterogeneous membership.

Centralization: Centralization is the process by which policy authority is concentrated at the national level, within the national government.

Centrifugal party systems: According to Sartori (1976), these are systems where the political parties tend to move away from the centre.

Centripetal party systems: According to Sartori (1976), these are systems where the political parties tend to move towards the centre.

Chain of delegation: The pathway, as defined by the political institutions of a country, through which political authority is passed from one actor or set of actors to another. See also Delegation.

Challenger party: A party that does not have government experience (De Vries and Hobolt, 2020).

Christian Democratic party family: A party family that is rooted in the church–state cleavage. Parties locate themselves on the centre-right on the left–right dimension while adopting more traditionalist value policies.

Civic duty: The notion that most people derive some non-instrumental utility from voting mostly due to compliance with social norms.

Civil law: The basis for the legal systems of most European countries. In this system, judges are expected to make their rulings by referencing a series of legal codes that set out the basis of all law.

Cleavage: A societal division in which the groups involved are conscious of their collective identity and have organizational expression, such as a political party that expresses the views of the group. See also Cleavage theory.

Cleavage theory: A theory by Lipset and Rokkan (1967) about the origins of European party systems as based in historical developments, such as the national revolutions, the Reformation, and the Industrial Revolution, that produced enduring lines of conflict that continue to shape political structure, political organization, and the content of political conflict.

Closed-list PR: A proportional representation (PR) electoral system that allocates seats to political parties in proportion to the vote shares received. Parties nominate candidates on party lists and seats for each party are filled in a top-down sequence on the list. Voters can only cast a vote for a party list and cannot change the order in which candidates appear on the list.

Coalition agreement: A written agreement published after coalition formation that contains the coalition compromise on a range of policy issues and that is supposed to constrain the future actions of coalition partners and ministers.

Coalition compromise: The notion that policy represents a compromise among the policy preferences of the parties in government.

Coming-together federalism: A type of federalism whereby previously independent political entities come together in a bigger territorial unit in order to benefit from pooling authority to improve their economic and security situation.

Committee of Regions: An EU advisory body. The Committee of Regions is a political assembly of regional and local representatives across the EU.
It safeguards the principle of subsidiarity so that policy decisions are taken and implemented closer to the citizen.

Common law: The basis of the legal systems in the UK and Ireland, as well as other non-European democracies including the United States. Rather than referring to legal code, as done in civil law systems, judges are expected to make reference to case law and legal precedent.

Communism: A political and economic doctrine that aims to replace private property and a profit-based economy with public ownership and communal control of the major means of production and the natural resources of a society. Communism builds on the writings of Karl Marx who tended to use the terms communism and socialism interchangeably, but later communism has become associated with a more radical and revolutionary form of socialism.

Comparative advantage: The theory of comparative advantage holds that under the condition of free trade, an agent will produce more of a good for which the relative marginal cost prior to trade is lower compared to others.

Comparative statics: In game theory, analysts can perform a comparative statics analysis once a game is solved. This means that the analyst can predict if equilibrium strategies of actors change if particular elements of the payoffs change.

Compulsory voting: A system in which citizens are legally required to vote in elections.

Concrete review: A type of judicial review where a constitutional court assesses the constitutionality of a law on the basis of a particular case that is brought before it. Any citizen has the ability to bring a case that makes a constitutional argument about the validity of a law.

Congruence: The fit between the policy preferences of citizens and the policy positions of their representatives. For instance, assuming a single policy dimension, it can be conceived as the ideological distance between the median voter and the policy position of the government.

Conservatism: A political ideology that views politics in terms of a traditional social order and hierarchy that should be preserved. While several strands of conservatism exist, they generally advocate the preservation of a range of political and social institutions, such as constitutional monarchy, parliamentary government, private property, and the church, with the aim of securing social stability and continuity.

Consolidated democracy: A country that has a long history of democracy and is highly unlikely to revert back to an authoritarian form of government.

Constitution: A set of higher order laws and norms that regulates the interactions between political actors and sets out basic rights.

Constitutional monarchy: A system of government where a hereditary monarch serves as a head of state, but possesses very little or no political power. The monarch, instead, is a figurehead and a representative of the state, while all political authority rests with the elected head of government.

Constitutional review: The process by which a constitutional or supreme court can evaluate the constitutionality of a law and strike down any laws that it deems to be unconstitutional. Constitutional review can either be abstract or concrete.

Constructive vote of no confidence: A motion in parliament in which a parliamentary majority nominates a replacement candidate for prime minister. If the vote is successful, the prime minister and the cabinet resign and the replacement candidate is elected prime minister.

Convergence: Party system convergence involves the process whereby parties adopt similar policy positions, often in the centre of a dominant political dimension of contestation, such as the left–right dimension in European politics.

Copenhagen criteria: A set of criteria with respect to democratic and economic development set out by the EU that prospective member states must meet in order to be considered for membership.

Core: The set of status quo points that cannot be changed by the political actors. In a veto player situation, this is the unanimity core, also known as the pareto set.

Core state powers: This refers to (1) resources deriving from the monopoly of legitimate coercion and taxation of a state based on coercive capacity, fiscal capacity, and the administrative capacity needed to manage, implement, and enforce public laws and policies, and (2) how important certain policy areas are for defining a state as a sovereign entity, generally referring to state survival and national security.

Costs of voting: The efforts that voters need to endure in order to cast a ballot in an election, such as transportation to the voting booth or getting informed about political parties (or candidates).

Council of the European Union: This represents the governments of each of the member states at the ministerial level and is one of the main decision-making bodies of the EU, together with the European Parliament.

Court of Justice of the European Union: This court upholds the rule of EU law. It ensures that EU law is applied in the same way in all EU member states, and settles legal disputes between national governments and EU institutions. In certain circumstances, it can be used by individuals, companies, or organizations to take action against an EU institution, if they feel that their rights were infringed upon.

Credible commitment: A credible commitment is a promise made by a political actor that, given the political situation, the actor has a very strong incentive to keep. Therefore all other actors can safely believe that promises will be upheld.

Cross-cutting issues: Issues not clearly aligned with the dominant left–right dimension, such as European integration or the environment.

Cross-cutting cleavages: When political fault-lines, such as class, religion, or regional identity, that characterize the most important lines of political conflict in a political system are largely uncorrelated with each other.

Cue-taking: This refers to voters, in particular partisan ones, taking cues from political parties and adopting the same position on an issue.

Cultural dimension: A dimension structuring electoral competition around non-economic issues, such as issues related to immigration, identity, nationalism, European integration, and multiculturalism.

Cyclical majority: A group of rational actors is incapable of making a rational group decision when the collective

preference ordering is intransitive, that is each policy alternative can be beaten by another proposal in a pairwise majority contest. Initially formulated by Condorcet, this situation can occur in a spatial model in multiple dimensions and is known also as the Chaos Theorem.

De facto federalism: Refers to the degree to which a country resembles a federal state in practice, even when it cannot be classified as federal based on its constitution.

De jure federalism: Refers to the extent to which regional authority is constitutionally recognized and cannot be unilaterally abolished by the central government.

Dealignment: A process whereby a large portion of the electorate abandons its previous partisan (political party) affiliation, without developing a new one to replace it. It is contrasted with realignment.

Decentralization: The process by which the authority of national governments over policy-making is transferred to regional governments.

Deepening of European integration: The process of delegating more and more powers from the national to the supranational level.

Delegate model of representation: Representatives are delegates of voters and meant to simply follow the expressed preferences of their constituents.

Delegation: In a principal–agent relationship, a person or a group (the principal) delegates authority to make certain decisions or represent the principal to another person or group (the agent). Delegation constitutes the essence of a representative democracy.

Democracy: See Minimalist and Maximalist conceptualizations of democracy, Liberal democracy, Direct democracy.

Democratic backsliding: A gradual decline in the quality of democracy caused by the state-led weakening of political institutions that sustain the democratic system, such as an independent judiciary and a free press.

Democratic deficit in the EU: A term used to argue that the EU institutions and their decision-making procedures suffer from a lack of democracy.

Descriptive representation: The notion that elected representatives resemble the electorate on certain characteristics, such as gender and ethnicity.

Devolution: The process by which a unitary state grants more authority to regional governments, but holds the right to revoke these rights.

Direct democracy: See Referendum.

Direct effect: In European law, the notion that (some) rights in EU treaties and EU law confer rights directly on EU citizens, and not just on member state governments. Thus, EU citizens can rely directly on EU law in a court of law.

Dismissive strategy of mainstream parties: A strategy that involves mainstream parties seeking to ignore the issue mobilized by the challenger party. By not taking a position, the mainstream party signals to voters that the issue lacks merit.

Disproportionality of electoral systems: A measure for the deviation from the proportionality principle of the seat–votes relationship in an electoral system on the basis of an aggregation of the differences between seat and vote shares for each political party.

District magnitude: The number of candidates to be elected in each electoral district. In case of single seat district (plurality) elections, the district magnitude is 1. In case of proportional representation, the district magnitude is greater than 1. Under proportional representation (PR), the district magnitude can therefore act as an informal electoral threshold, since it is more difficult for parties to gain seats under PR if only a few seats are available in each electoral district.

Dominant party systems: A system with one large party with a more than absolute majority of votes and seats and limited alternation of government.

Duverger's Law: Duverger suggested that single member district plurality favours a two-party system, a relationship that has become known as Duverger's Law. Duverger also hypothesized that double-ballot majority systems (like in France) tends to produce multipartism, and that proportional representation tends to lead to a fragmented party system. The reasons for Duverger's Law are mechanical (large parties are favoured over small parties) and strategic (voters do not want to cast wasted votes in plurality elections).

Dynamic representation: The notion that elected representatives change their positions in the same direction as public opinion over time. See also Responsiveness.

Early warning mechanism on subsidiarity ('yellow card mechanism'): A national parliament of an EU member state may object to an EU legislative proposal if it deems the principle of subsidiarity has been violated. If one-third of the national parliaments raise an objection the European Commission must review the proposal. This is commonly referred to as the 'yellow card'.

Economic and Monetary Union (EMU): Involves the coordination of economic and fiscal policies, a common monetary policy, and a common currency, the Euro within the EU. While all EU member states take part in the economic union, only some member states have adopted the Euro and thus are part of the Euro area.

Economic voting: The idea that voters use their evaluations of past economic performance evaluations to reward or punish an incumbent government in elections.

Effective number of parties (ENP): A measure that captures both the number and the size of parties in a system. The concept was introduced by Laakso and Taagepera (1979) to present an adjusted number of political parties in a country's party system, weighted by their relative strength (votes or seats).

Electoral accountability: See Accountability.

Electoral formula: The set of mathematical rules that determine how votes cast get transferred into parliamentary seats.

Electoral manifesto: A public declaration of the general political aims and specific policy proposals and pledges issued by a political party ahead of an election campaign.

Electoral system: A collection of rules, or institutions, that govern the nature of elections within a country. An electoral system comprises rules on who can vote, who can stand as a candidate, how candidates' names appear on the ballot or if they do at all, and how votes get counted and turned into seats in parliament.

Electoral threshold: All proportional representation systems have an electoral threshold, leading to some form of disproportionality. Thresholds can be formal and be written into constitutions or electoral law (e.g. requiring parties to clear a certain percentage of the votes cast to gain any seats) or they can be natural as a consequence of the specific design of PR (e.g. a low district magnitude).

Electoral volatility: A measure of the degree of change in vote choice between elections shown as the change in the vote shares between elections averaged across all political parties.

Entrepreneurial party: A type of party that is the extra-parliamentary initiative of a political entrepreneur. It has minimal formal organization with hierarchical control by the leadership and the membership is largely irrelevant. One example is the business-firm party.

Ethnic minority: An ethnic group that differs from the dominant ethnicity of a country, based on a real, or assumed, common origin and cultural legacy that collectively ties members of that group, rooted in race, religion, culture, geography, immigration status, or a combination of these.

European Central Bank: The central bank of the EU member states that have adopted the Euro as their official currency. Its main task is to maintain price stability in the Eurozone in order to preserve the purchasing power of the Euro.

European Coal and Steel Community: Predecessor organization of the EU with six founding member states (Belgium, France, Italy, Luxembourg, the Netherlands, and West Germany) created after the Second World War to regulate their industrial production under a centralized authority. It was formally established in 1952 by the Treaty of Paris. The European Coal and Steel Community allowed its members to pull down tariff barriers, abolish subsidies, fix prices, and raise money for reconstruction by imposing levies on steel and coal production.

European Commission: An EU institution with the mandate of protecting the general interest of the EU by proposing and enforcing legislation as well as by implementing policies and the EU budget. It is the only European institution that can propose legislation.

European Council: An EU institution that sets the EU's overall political direction and priorities, traditionally by adopting 'conclusions' during European Council summits which identify issues of concern and actions to take. It is led by a president and comprises of the national heads of state or government as well as the President of the European Commission.

European Communities: The set of international treaties that initially provided the rules for what is nowadays known as the European Union. The European Communities included the European Coal and Steel Community (ECSC), which started in 1952, as well as the European Atomic Energy Community (EAEC or Euratom) and the European Economic Community (EEC), both of which began in 1958. See also: European Economic Community.

European Economic Community: Created by the Treaty of Rome which entered into force in 1958, it set out the contours of the EU's Single Market in Europe and the constitutional framework for the European polity. The European Economic Community (EEC) established key EU institutions such as the European Commission, Council of Ministers, and the European Court. It also founded the Customs Union and established the four freedoms—free movement of people, goods, services, and capital—that guide the constitutional framework for the Single Market to this day. The six founding members were Belgium, France, Italy, Luxembourg, the Netherlands, and West Germany. The EEC was renamed the European Community in 1993 when the European Union was formally founded. With the Treaty of Lisbon, the institutional framework of the EC was consolidated into the European Union and it formally ceased to exist.

European integration: The process of delegating authority from the national to the supranational level in the European Union through treaties that are adopted unanimously among the member states of the European Union and ratified in national parliaments or referendums. In addition, integration can occur through the daily work of European institutions (see also Liberal intergovernmentalism, neofunctionalism, and supranationalism).

European Parliament: The legislative chamber of the European Union that consists of directly elected members who represent EU citizens. The European Parliament elects the President of the European Commission following a proposal by the European Council.

European Union: The supranational political system in Europe to which member states have delegated policy authority through the European treaties. Its precursors were the European Coal and Steel Community and the European Economic Community. Amongst others, the EU stands for the promotion of peace, a single market, economic and monetary union, freedom and justice without internal borders, and cultural and linguistic diversity.

Euroscepticism: Opposition to the political cooperation in Europe, the institutions of the European Union, and/or the process of European integration.

Exclusive competences of the EU: Policy areas in which policy can only be decided at the EU level, and not at the national level.

Federalism: Systems are considered as federal when two levels of government rule the same land and people, each level has at least one area of action in which it is autonomous, and there is some guarantee (even through merely a statement in the constitution) of the autonomy of each government in its own sphere (Riker, 1964). See also De facto federalism, de jure federalism, coming-together federalism, and holding-together federalism.

Flexible-List PR: Electoral system that allocates seats to political parties in proportion to the vote shares received. The order of candidates on the party list is partly determined by parties and partly by voters.

First-past-the-post: Single-member plurality electoral system in which the candidate receiving the most votes (but not necessarily the majority of votes) is elected.

Fiscal decentralization: The degree to which a regional, rather than central, government is able to collect a share of the tax revenue.

Focal point: In game theory, a mechanism that helps players choose between two equilibrium outcomes.

Formateur: A politician who is appointed to lead the formation of a coalition government, usually the prime minister designate. Some national constitutions make the leader of the largest party the default formateur, whereas others provide the head of state with the opportunity to appoint a formateur.

Franchise: The right to vote in elections, and it is a core feature of democracy. It was expanded from primarily male landholders to all citizens over time.

Fragmentation: The number of parties in a party system. This is often weighted by the size of parties, see Effective number of parties.

Freezing hypothesis: Lipset and Rokkan's observation that West European party systems in the 1960s, with only few exceptions, reflected the cleavage structures of the 1920s.

Fundamental equation of politics: A formula introduced by Plott capturing basic insights from the institutionalist perspective of politics: political outcomes are a function of actors' preferences and political institutions.

Game theory: The formal study of strategic decision-making. A game (e.g. delegating power to a bureaucracy) is defined by actors, their strategy sets, and their payoffs. Actors are the players in the game (e.g. political parties), a strategy is a complete description of what a player can do at every possible point in the game, regardless of whether a particular move actually occurs. A strategy set is a set of all possible strategies available to a player. Payoffs define what players receive at each outcome of the game. A game is solved to find optimal strategies for all players such that no player has an incentive to deviate from it.

Gatekeeping: In the study of parliaments, this refers to the ability of a political actor to prevent a proposal from being placed on the parliamentary agenda for a vote.

Gender quota: In elections, this is a requirement that women must make up a certain percentage of candidates in party quotas (through the party-controlled candidate selection process).

Green party family: A party family that emerged out of the ecology social movement of the late 1970s and 1980s. Parties take left-wing stances economically and emphasize environmental protection.

Heresthetics: According to Riker, a political strategy by which a political actor seeks to manipulate the context and structure of a debate or a decision-making process in order to be more likely to win.

Holding-together federalism: A type of federalism whereby the central government of a given country chooses to decentralize its power to subnational governments in order to diffuse secessionist pressures.

Ideology: A belief system, including a wide range of political attitudes that are consistent with one another given the political context (e.g. socialism).

Indifference curve: In a two-dimensional spatial model, an indifference curve represents the set of policy alternatives between which a political actor is indifferent. When indifference curves are drawn through the status quo, the curve demarcates the boundary between policies that an actor prefers over the status quo and those that make the actor worse off. All points inside this indifference curve are points that are preferred by the actor over the status quo because they are closer to her ideal point.

Informateur: A person, often a former politician, who tries to mediate between parties to form a coalition government.

Infringement proceedings: Legal proceedings in the European Union that occur when the European Commission believes that a member state government may be violating EU law. Infringement proceedings could lead to the Commission taking a member state to court, but they are typically resolved before the Court of Justice of the European Union makes a ruling.

Inside lobbying: An interest group strategy that aims to influence policy-making through direct meetings with decision-makers.

Institutions: Political institutions are the rules and norms that govern interactions between actors in politics or any social setting.

Integration–demarcation dimension: A second 'cultural' dimension that structures political competition in many European countries. This pits the losers of globalization who are wary of immigration and European integration against the winners who embrace process of migration and political integration in Europe.

Interest group system: Interest group systems can be pluralist, in which any interest group can compete for attention of policy-makers, or corporatist, in which selected interest groups (trade unions and business organizations) have privileged access to policy-makers.

Investiture vote: Constitutionally mandated confirmatory vote in parliament of the prime minister before she can take office.

Issue competition: A theory of party competition that argues that parties seek to influence what issues voters think about when making electoral choices to gain an electoral advantage. The strategy is to campaign on issues that they 'own', i.e. where voters consider them competent, in order to ensure that voters place greater weight on those issues in the ballot box.

Issue entrepreneurship: A strategy by which parties mobilize issues that have been largely ignored in party competition and adopt a policy position on the issue that is substantially different from the mainstream status quo.

Issue ownership: The perception among voters that for a given issue there is one party that is much more competent in carrying out the desired objective than others.

Judicial review: See Constitutional review

Kelsenian Court: The most common system of courts in European states where the constitutional court is separate from the regular court system and only hears constitutional cases. The regular courts system is topped by a supreme court, and if any cases in the regular courts touch on constitutional issues, they must be sent to the constitutional court.

Left–right dimension: A conflict dimension that structures political competition in most European countries. The classic left–right dimension juxtaposes more state intervention in the economy and greater redistribution (Left) and free market with less state involvement, redistribution, and spending (Right).

Liberal democracy: A democratic system of government in which individual rights and freedoms are officially recognized and protected, and the exercise of political power is limited by the rule of law.

Liberal intergovernmentalism: A theory of European integration, which suggests that the type and degree of integration we observe can be explained by the national interests of member states. According to this view, member states remain in control over the process of integration and will always protect their sovereignty. The EU is an international regime for effective policy coordination among member states to obtain preferred policy outcomes that they otherwise could not achieve.

Liberalism: A political ideology based on the notion of the fundamental rights to life, liberty, and property. While several strands of liberalism exist, they all generally support civil rights, democracy, secularism, gender equality, racial equality, internationalism, freedom of speech, freedom of the press, and freedom of religion.

Liberal party family: A party family that is on the centre-right economically (fiscally conservative), but adopts a more progressive stance on the cultural dimension (socially liberal).

Majoritarian electoral system: Election of one candidate in each electoral system, either by plurality (first-past-the-post) or two-round run-off.

Majority rule: A decision rule in which the policy alternative that musters a majority beats alternative proposals. Democratic decision-making usually employs majority rule (e.g. in elections or legislative decision-making). In some instances, supermajority rule is employed (e.g. in the Council of the European Union where member states decide by a so-called qualified majority).

Manichaean: A dualistic worldview of the struggle between a good, spiritual world of light, and an evil, material world of darkness, inspired by the religious thought of Manichaeaism founded by the Iranian prophet Mani.

Mass party: A party type with a large and homogeneous membership base, often representing social groups, such as workers, where party leadership is formally accountable to members.

Maximalist conceptualization of democracy: Definitions of democracy that, in addition to electoral constestion, focus on other participatory

aspects of democracy, as well as guarantees of basic rights and rule of law.

Median voter: In a uni-dimensional political space, the median voter is the person who is precisely in the middle of the political spectrum.

Median voter theorem: The median voter theorem demonstrates that for a uni-dimensional spatial model the ideal point of the median voter will win against any alternative in a pairwise majority rule contest. This means that this position is privileged over other preferences.

Michigan model of voting: A theory of voter choice stressing the importance of partisanship in shaping policy preferences, candidate evaluations, and vote choices.

Minimal winning coalition: A coalition government which does not have more parties than required for parliamentary majority. Out of all minimal winning coalitions, the one that has the lowest number of surplus seats is known as the minimum winning coalition.

Minimalist conceptualization of democracy: Definitions of democracy that focus on the presence of free and fair electoral contestation between two or more candidates or parties.

Ministerial autonomy: The policy discretion available to ministers due to their informational advantage provided by expertise present in the ministerial bureaucracy.

Minority government: A government whose cabinet parties do not command a parliamentary majority.

Mixed electoral system: Electoral system that combines proportional representation and first-past-the-post and voters have two votes, one for a party list and one for a candidate in a local electoral district. A mixed system can lead to proportional outcomes (only party vote matters for party seat shares) or more majoritarian outcomes (seats are added up from both electoral tiers separately).

Model of politics: A theoretical simplification of real-world political situations using a set of assumptions and statements. Models serve various purposes: they may provide insights into general political problems, generate causal hypotheses that can be tested, or highlight counter-intuitive predictions that go against common wisdom.

Moderate pluralism: A multiparty system where parties adopt non-extreme centrist positions.

Modernization theory: A theory of democratization that suggests that countries only democratize once they have reached a certain level of economic and social development. Citizens must be sufficiently wealthy and educated in order to support democracy.

Movement party: A party type that grows out of a social movement organized around a single issue or a set of issues. The membership base is actively involved in decision-making.

Multiparty system: A system with several parties in parliament, with none approaching a parliamentary majority. They are characterized by alternation of government between parties and a high frequency of coalition government.

Multilevel governance: Policy authority which is shared and structured between political actors situated at different territorial levels of government, most notably the supranational and subnational level.

Mutual recognition: The principle of EU law under which member states must allow goods that are legally sold in another member state to also be sold in their own territory. Established in the Cassis de Dijon ruling by the Court of Justice of the EU in 1979.

Nash equilibrium: When each actor cannot benefit by changing a strategy given what the other actors are doing, this constitutes a Nash equilibrium, named after the Nobel Prize-winning mathematician John Nash.

Neofunctionalism: A theory of European integration which highlights the functional nature and the importance of the new supranational actors for the process of integration. It pro poses that integration starts in those policy areas in which countries deem cooperation necessary (e.g. coal and steel). Over time, however, countries would realize that more transfer of power is necessary in other areas to reach the desired goals. This process is known as spillover (see also Spillover).

Niche party: Non-mainstream party, such as green, radical right, and regionalist parties. According to Meguid (2008), they cross-cut existing cleavages and disregard economic issues, focusing instead on a small range of topics.

Open-list PR: Electoral system that allocates seats to political parties in proportion to the vote shares received. Parties nominate unranked candidates on party lists, and voters cast preference votes for candidates. This form of PR gives more prominence to individual politicians than in closed-list PR.

Ordinary legislative procedure: The standard way of law-making in the EU involving a proposal by the European Commission and approval by the Council (qualified majority) and the Parliament (majority). The procedure was known as the co-decision procedure in the EU Treaties until it was renamed in the Treaty of Lisbon to reflect its general applicability to most policy areas.

Outside lobbying: An interest group strategy that aims to influence policy-making through public campaigns for particular causes, including demonstrations and street protests.

Paradox of voting: The observation that the level of actual voter turnout is inconsistent with an expectation based on the notion of a rational, self-interested voter.

Pareto set: see Core.

Parliamentary policing: The institutional strength of parliaments to scrutinize and amend government bills before passage.

Parliamentary system: A democratic regime type based on mutual dependence between the legislature and the executive. In a parliamentary system the formation of government (executive) occurs within parliament (legislature). The government needs the support of a parliamentary majority to pass bills.

Partisanship: The loyalty of voters to a specific political party (also Party identification or party attachment). It can act as a perceptual screen, where an emotional attachment to a specific political party originating from family socialization during early childhood filters out unfavourable information about the party, or as a running tally, where loyalty to a specific political party is based on a continued assessment of how it has performed.

Party-centred system: A system in which electoral rules and parties' candidate selection rules create incentives for party-centred behaviour of elected representatives, such as party loyalty in legislative speeches and votes.

Party family: A cross-national grouping of like-minded parties, often sharing a similar ideology, voter base, and similar origins.

Party leader: A politician who leads a political party. Party leaders often compete in elections as lead candidates on top of a party list. Leaders of government parties frequently hold cabinet positions or parliamentary party leader positions, while leaders of opposition parties typically lead the parliamentary party delegation.

Party system: A set of parties that compete and cooperate with the aim of increasing their influence on government and policy and their appeal to voters. Party systems are often classified on the basis of the number and the size of parties (fractionalization) and the ideological distance between them (polarization).

Personal vote: The personal vote refers to the amount of support a particular candidate for office receives due to her own personal characteristics, rather than the characteristics of the party to which she belongs.

Pivotal: The likelihood that the action of an individual is going to change the outcome of an election.

Pluralism: The view that power is not concentrated in the hand of a single party or societal interest, but that political power and influence are distributed across multiple groups. Robert Dahl established the pluralist theory of democracy according to which political outcomes are enacted through competitive groups.

Polarization: In party systems, polarization refers to the ideological distribution of parties in the party system. This is generally conceptualized along a single ideological continuum, such as left–right. The greater the variance of party positions, the higher the levels of polarization.

Polarized pluralism: A multiparty system which is highly polarized.

Policy competence in the EU: The degree to which member states have granted the EU different levels of authority over different policy areas. The exercise of EU policy competence is subject to two fundamental principles: proportionality and subsidiarity.

Policy positions: Revealed preferences over policy alternatives of political actors (e.g. candidates or political parties).

Policy responsiveness: See Responsiveness.

Policy stability: Inability in a political system to change the legislative status quo.

Political fragmentation: See Fragmentation and Effective number of parties.

Political party: An institutionalized coalition of people who are policy-seeking and organize to gain control of public office by winning elections.

Political representation: Elected politicians (agents) act and speak for of the represented (principals).

Politics: A subset of human behaviour in which individuals use power to influence decisions that affect themselves and society as a whole. Politics focuses on the process of political decision-making involving the activities of political actors (e.g. voters, members of parliament, governments).

Pooling of sovereignty: Joint decision making among the principals themselves, consisting of the rules under which member states make decisions, how those decisions are ratified, and the extent to which they are binding.

Populism: A thin-centred ideology that divides society into two homogeneous and antagonistic groups: 'the pure people' on the one side and 'the corrupt elite' on the other.

Post-materialism: A theory by Inglehart (1977) that posits that, when people's material needs are taken for granted in their formative years, they are likely to privilege post-material values like the environment, gender equality, democracy, self-expression, and human rights, over material concerns.

Precedent: The notion, in common law countries, that a legal ruling can establish case law that judges subsequently ruling in similar cases can rely on and are expected to follow.

Preferences: Citizens hold preferences over policies or political candidates. When faced with a choice (e.g. several policy proposals or candidates), citizens compare and rank these choices in order of preference based on their attitudes and values.

Preliminary ruling procedure: The process in the EU where national court judges can ask the Court of Justice of the EU (CJEU) for an opinion on national case that touches on aspects of European law. It is the procedure through which the CJEU has ruled on many of its most important decisions.

Presidential system: A democratic regime type based on mutual independence between the legislature and the executive. Both parliament and the president have separate electoral mandates and their own legitimacy.

Principal–agent relationship: see Delegation.

Principle of proportionality: The content and scope of EU action may not go beyond what is necessary to achieve the objectives of the EU treaties.

Prisoners' dilemma: The prisoners' dilemma in game theory refers to a paradox in which two individuals acting in their own self-interest do not produce the optimal outcome. It is set up in such a way that both players choose to protect themselves at the expense of the other player. As a result, both players find themselves worse off than if they had cooperated with each other.

Promissory representation: The notion that elected representatives base their policies on what they promised to do at the last election.

Proportional representation (PR): Electoral system that allocates parliamentary seats to parties in proportion to the votes received.

Prospective voting: The notion that citizens vote for a political party (or candidate) based on the policy proposals that this political party (or candidate) aims to implement in the future.

Proximity model of voting: A model rooted in spatial theory that assumes that parties and voters can be located on a single ideological dimension, and that voters are expected to vote for the party that most closely resembles their own position.

Qualified majority voting (QMV): A voting rule within the European Council and Council of the European Union in which decisions are taken when a double majority approves. The double majority is defined as the support of 55 per cent of member states representing 65 per cent of the EU's population.

Radical left party family: A party family rooted in the communist tradition. Parties are on the extreme left on the economic dimension and are typically critical towards the capitalist system and advocate a strong role of the state in the economy.

Radical right party family: A party family that takes extreme positions on a cultural dimension. Parties typically take nationalist, xenophobic, and anti-democratic stances.

Rational choice institutionalism: A theory of comparative politics that when applied to European integration views it as a function of both the actions and interests of EU member state governments and the actions and interests of supranational actors. Institutionalism studies the consequences of political institutions for policy-making: that is, how member states and supranational actors take decisions in the EU's political system and what it means for the potential for policy change.

Rationality: The notion that individuals have complete and transitive preferences orderings over a set of outcomes, that is, they can compare all alternatives and put them into a consistent ranking.

Realignment: A large and durable shift in a political system's configuration of voters' partisan identifications and political parties' vote shares. Relates to the argument that, while traditional cleavages are weakening in electoral politics, a new divide (or set of divides) have become more salient and provide structure to the political system and to voting behaviour.

Referendum: A popular vote on an issue. Referendums may be mandatory on some matters according to constitutional provisions, but in most instances governments can decide whether to hold one or not. Some systems also allow for citizen-initiated referendums (initiatives).

Regional government: Legislative and executive institutions responsible for authoritative decision-making in a coherent subnational territorial entity.

Regionalist party family: A party family that arose out of the centre–periphery cleavage. Parties advocate more devolved powers to their regions or even secession.

Regulatory state: A political entity that pursues policy objectives through regulatory and deregulatory means, rather than direct intervention and redistribution.

Reinforcing cleavages: When social categories that people exhibit, such as class, religion, or regional identity, that characterize the most important lines of political conflict in a political system, are highly correlated with each other.

Representation: See Political representation.

Republic: A system of government where the head of state is directly or indirectly elected (in contrast with a constitutional monarchy). In a parliamentary republic, the head of state is usually indirectly elected and has little power. In a semi-presidential system, the head of state is directly elected and has more political power.

Responsiveness: A political system is responsive if policy shifts with the position of voters. Parties are responsive if they change their policy positions in line with changes in public opinion.

Retrospective voting: The notion that voters sanction or reward a political party (or candidate) on their evaluations of the past policy performance of this political party (or candidate) and vote accordingly in elections.

Second order national elections: Elections that are considered to be less important than first order (usually national parliamentary) elections by both citizens and political parties, usually because they do not lead to the composition of a national government. Both local and European elections are considered second order national elections.

Semi-presidential system: A democratic regime type with a popularly elected president with a fixed term who exists alongside a prime minister and cabinet who are responsible to a legislative majority in parliament.

Shadowing ministers: Coalition parties can install a junior minister in a ministry to monitor actions of a minister who is a member of another coalition party.

Shared competences in the EU: Policy areas in which member states can act, but only if the EU has chosen not to.

Shirking: This occurs when an agent does not act in the interest of the principal. In politics, shirking of an agent may, for instance, lead to different policy outcomes than the principal desires.

Signal responsiveness: The notion that elected representatives behave in a way that signals that they are responsive to voter preferences, even though it does not necessarily imply actual policy responsiveness.

Single market: The single market in Europe, which seeks to guarantee the four freedoms, the free movement of goods, capital, services, and persons, within the European Union. It encompasses all EU member states, and has been extended to Iceland, Liechtenstein, and Norway through the Agreement on the European Economic Area and to Switzerland through bilateral treaties.

Single Transferable Vote: Proportional representation electoral system in which voters rank candidates in multi-seat electoral districts. Candidates are elected if they clear a quota. If no candidate clears the quota, the one with the fewest votes is eliminated and the votes are transferred to other candidates determined by the back-up preferences of the voters until a candidate receives enough votes to clear the quota. The system is used in Ireland.

Single-party system: A political system where only one political party is allowed to hold power. Also known as a one-party state.

Social cleavage: See Cleavage.

Social democratic party family: A party family rooted in the class cleavage and linked to trade unions. Parties locate themselves on the centre-left on the left–right dimension while adopting more progressive value policies.

Social group identification: A person's sense of who they are based on their group membership, such as social class or religious groups.

Social norms: A perception of what is acceptable group conduct.

Socialism: A political ideology that views politics in terms of a class struggle. While several strands of socialism exist, they generally advocate collective or governmental ownership and administration of the means of production and distribution of goods.

Sovereignty: A political entity is considered sovereign when it has the sole authority to make decisions on policies.

Spatial model of politics: A model that simplifies real-world politics by focusing on the preferences of political actors (such as candidates, political parties, or governments) in a spatial way, where larger distances between actors equal larger policy differences. Spatial models furthermore model the effect of political institutions and produce predictions about political outcomes or strategies of political actors. Spatial models can be uni- or multidimensional. According to spatial models of party competition, parties compete by adopting policy positions close to voters. Voters care only about which party will enact policies closest to their preferences and they vote for the candidate closest to their own policy location

Special competences in the EU: Policy areas in which the EU can take special measures to ensure that member states coordinate their activities. One key example of the EU's special competences is Common Foreign and Security Policy in which a High Representative of the Union for Foreign and Security Policy represents the EU.

Spillover: A term used in neofunctionalist theory of European integration to describe the process whereby the transfer of authority to the supranational level in one policy area encourages the transfer of authority in other areas to reach the desired goals. Specifically, functional spillover is used to explain the way in which integration in one policy area, for example, coal and steel, creates pressure for integration in further areas, such as currency exchange rates, whereas political spillover is used to explain the importance of supranational and subnational actors in the integration process, as they create further pressure for more integration to pursue their interests.

Stare decisis: The Latin term, meaning 'stand by things decided', used in common law countries to describe the legal doctrine that obligates courts to fol-

low historical cases when making a ruling on a similar case, in other words that precedent matters. Judges are expected to consider and abide by previous decisions.

Status quo: The current policy in place, usually in the form of an adopted and implemented law.

Strategy: See Game theory.

Subnational government: See Regional government.

Subsidiarity: The principle that policy should be made by the level of government closest to the citizens, given the level of coordination and cooperation required to effectively govern in that policy area. Within the EU, it means that the EU can only take action if the goals of a particular policy proposal are better achieved at the EU level than at the member state level.

Substantive representation: The notion that policies adopted by elected representatives reflect the preferences of voters.

Supporting competences in the EU: Policy areas in which the EU may not adopt laws that lead to a EU-wide harmonization of national laws or regulations.

Supranational organization: A supranational organization is a political organization that exists above the level of the nation-state to which member state governments have delegated to policy authority.

Supranationalism: A theory of European integration that assumes that the process of integration has a transformative and self-reinforcing dynamic that goes beyond the control of member states. Neofunctionalism is one prominent example of a supranationalist theory of integration.

Supremacy of EU law: The notion in EU law that higher order European law takes precedence over (and negates) national law when the two are in conflict. It was established by the Court of Justice of the European Union over several rulings, but most notably in the Costa v. ENEL case.

Surplus majority government: A government that includes more parties than are strictly necessary to command a parliamentary majority.

Symbolic representation: The notion that representatives 'stand for' the represented.

Theory: A set of logically coherent assumptions that, by simplifying the complex world to focus on specific features and interactions, allow researchers to make comparisons, offer explanations, and engage in generalizations. Researchers talk about building theoretical models that allow them to focus on specific aspects of the political and social world.

Thermostatic model of representation: A theory of representation where a responsive public adjusts its preferences for policy as a response to government actions. When policy increases (decreases), the preference for more policy will decrease (increase), other things being equal. In turn, policy-makers are also responsive to changing public opinion.

Transaction costs: The costs associated with doing business, i.e. the time it takes to gather relevant information and make decisions.

Transitive preferences: The notion that a person who prefers choice option x to y and y to z must prefer x to z.

Trustee model of representation: Representatives are trustees of voters and meant to follow their own judgement and understanding of the best action to pursue in the interest of their constituents.

Turnout: The number of citizens who vote in an election.

Two-dimensional policy space: Party competition structured along two dimensions, e.g. an economic and a noneconomic 'cultural' dimension.

Two-party system: Two parties with a combined vote share of at least around 80 per cent. Alternation between parties in government, normally single-party government.

Two-round system: A majoritarian electoral system in which the single-member district winner is determined in two rounds, where only a limited number of candidates can enter the second round of elections given their performance from the first round. The system is used in France.

Unanimity: In the EU, unanimity refers to a decision-making rule that requires agreement of all member states. When it comes to voting, the principle of 'constructive abstention' applies whereby a member state can abstain in a vote where unanimity is required without thereby blocking the success of the vote.

Unicameral parliament: A parliament with only one legislative chamber involved in parliamentary deliberations and decision-making.

Unconsolidated democracy: A newly formed democracy that has a relatively high likelihood of reverting back to an authoritarian form of government.

Unitary states: Within unitary states the central government is ultimately supreme. While the central government may delegate powers to subnational level, it holds the legal right to revoke these rights.

Valence competition: Party competition based on voters' evaluations of non-policy characteristics, such as competence, leadership traits, etc.

Valence issue: An issue that is uniformly liked or disliked among the electorate, as opposed to a position issue on which opinion is divided. Corruption is an example of a valence issue, since that is an issue uniformly disliked by voters and parties associated with corruption tend to be unpopular.

Veto player: Any actor that has the authority to veto, or block, a proposed change. Veto players are defined by constitutions (institutional veto players) and political competition and elections (partisan veto players). The number of veto players and ideological distance between them affects the ability of a political system to change policy.

Vote of confidence: A motion in parliament in which the head of government asks for the confidence of a parliamentary majority. If the prime minister loses the vote, the cabinet resigns.

Vote of no confidence: A motion in parliament in which a parliamentary majority can withdraw its confidence in the government. If the vote is successful, the cabinet resigns.

Voting: A method for an electorate to make a collective decision of which political party (or candidate) should rule following an election campaign (in elections) or on a specific issue (in referendums).

Welfare state: A social system in which the state undertakes some responsibility for providing basic social and economic welfare for its citizens. We can distinguish between different types of welfare states based on the level of decommodification they provide. Decommodification here is understood as the extent to which individuals can maintain a livelihood without reliance on the market.

Widening of European integration: The process of enlarging the EU to include more and more member states. Also refered to as 'enlargement'.

Yellow card mechanism: See Early warning mechanism on subsidiarity.

Bibliography

Abou-Chadi, Tarik, and Markus Wagner. 2019. "The Electoral Appeal of Party Strategies in Postindustrial Societies: When Can the Mainstream Left Succeed?" *Journal of Politics* 81(4): 1405–1419.

Abou-Chadi, Tarik, and Markus Wagner. 2020. "Electoral Fortunes of Social Democratic Parties: Do Second Dimension Positions Matter?" *Journal of European Public Policy* 27(2): 246–272.

Acemoglu, Daron, Suresh Naidu, Pascual Restrepo, and James A. Robinson. 2019. "Democracy does Cause Growth." *Journal of Political Economy* 127(1): 47–100.

Adams, James, and Lawrence Ezrow. 2009. "Who do European Parties Represent? How Western European Parties Represent the Policy Preferences of Opinion Leaders." *Journal of Politics* 71(1): 206–223.

Adams, James, Lawrence Ezrow, and Christopher Wlezien. 2016. "The Company You Keep: How Voters Infer Party Positions on European Integration from Governing Coalition Arrangements." *American Journal of Political Science* 60(4): 811–823.

Adams, James, Michael Clark, Lawrence Ezrow, and Garrett Glasgow. 2004. "Understanding Change and Stability in Party Ideologies: Do Parties Respond to Public Opinion or to Past Election Results?" *British Journal of Political Science* 34(4): 589–610.

Adams, James, Michael Clark, Lawrence Ezrow, and Garrett Glasgow. 2006. "Are Niche Parties Fundamentally Different from Mainstream Parties? The Causes and the Electoral Consequences of Western European Parties' Policy Shifts, 1976–1998." *American Journal of Political Science* 50(3): 513–529.

Adams, James, Samuel Merrill, and Bernard Grofman. 2005. *A Unified Theory of Party Competition: A Cross-National Analysis Integrating Spatial and Behavioral Factors.* Cambridge; New York: Cambridge University Press.

Adams, James, Simon Weschle, and Christopher Wlezien. 2020. "Elite Interactions and Voters' Perceptions of Parties' Policy Positions." *American Journal of Political Science*. Advance online publication.

Akkerman, Agnes, Cas Mudde, and Andrej Zaslove. 2014. "How Populist are the People? Measuring Populist Attitudes in Voters." *Comparative Political Studies* 47(9): 1324–1353.

Aldrich, John H. 1993. "Rational Choice and Turnout." *American Journal of Political Science* 37(1): 246–278.

Amt für Statistik, Berlin-Brandenburg. 2017. "Stimmzettel." <https://www.wahlen-berlin.de/wahlen/Bu2017/stimmzettel/WK83m.pdf> (Accessed on 24 August 2017).

Anderson, Brilé, Tobias Böhmelt, and Hugh Ward. 2017. "Public Opinion and Environmental Policy Output: A Cross-National Analysis of Energy Policies in Europe." *Environmental Research Letters* 12: 114011.

Armingeon, Klaus, Virginia Wenger, Fiona Wiedemeier, Christian Isler, Laura Knöpfel, David Weisstanner, and Sarah Engler. 2018. "Comparative Political Data Set 1960–2016." <www.cpds-data.org>.

Arzheimer, Kai, and Carl Berning. 2019. "How the Alternative for Germany (AfD) and their Voters Veered to the Radical Right, 2013–2017." *Electoral Studies* 57(1): 90–102.

Bäck, Hanna, and Marc Debus. 2019. "When do Women Speak? A Comparative Analysis of the Role of Gender in Legislative Debates." *Political Studies* 67(3): 576–596.

Bäck, Hanna, Marc Debus, and Jochen Müller. 2014. "Who Takes the Parliamentary Floor? The Role of Gender in Speech-Making in the Swedish Riksdag." *Political Research Quarterly* 67(3): 504–518.

Bailer, Stefanie, Mikko Mattila, and Gerald Schneider. 2015. "Money Makes the EU Go Round: The Objective Foundations of Conflict in the Council of Ministers." *Journal of Common Market Studies* 53(3): 437–456.

Bakker, Ryan, Catherine E. De Vries, Erica Edwards, Liesbet Hooghe, Seth Jolly, Gary Marks, Jonathan Polk, Jan Rovny, Marco Steenbergen, and Milada Anna Vachudová. 2015. "Measuring Party Positions in Europe: The Chapel Hill Expert Survey Trend File, 1999–2010." *Party Politics* 21(1): 143–152.

Bakker, Ryan, Liesbet Hooghe, Seth Jolly, Gary Marks, Jonathan Polk, Jan Rovny, Marco Steenbergen, and Milada Vachudová. 2020. "2019 Chapel Hill Expert Survey." <www.chesdata.eu>.

Bawn, Kathleen, and Frances Rosenbluth. 2006. "Short Versus Long Coalitions: Electoral Accountability and the Size of the Public Sector." *American Journal of Political Science* 50(2): 251–265.

BBC. 2018. "Jean-Claude Juncker: EU Superstate Claims are Nonsense." <https://www.bbc.com/news/uk-politics-43058087> (Accessed on 27 July 2020).

Bednar, Jenna. 2009. *The Robust Federation: Principles of Design.* Cambridge: Cambridge University Press.

Benedetto, Giacomo, Simon Hix, and Nicola Mastrorocco. 2020. "The Rise and Fall of Social Democracy, 1918–2017." *American Political Science Review*.

Benson, David, Viviane Gravey, and Andrew Jordan. 2016. "Environmental Policy." In *European Union Politics*, ed. Michelle Cini and Nieves Pérez-Solórzano Borrogán. Oxford: Oxford University Press.

Bird, Karen, Thomas Saalfeld, and Andreas M. Wüst. 2010. *The Political Representation of Immigrants and Minorities: Voters, Parties and Parliaments in Liberal Democracies*. London: Routledge.

Bischof, Daniel, and Markus Wagner. 2017. "What Makes Parties Adapt to Voter Preferences? The Role of Party Organization, Goals and Ideology." *British Journal of Political Science* 50(1): 1–11.

Bittner, Amanda. 2011. *Platform or Personality? The Role of Party Leaders in Elections*. Oxford: Oxford University Press.

Black, Duncan. 1948. "On the Rationale of Group Decision-Making." *Journal of Political Economy* 56(1): 23–34.

Blais, André, and Marc André Bodet. 2006. "Does Proportional Representation Foster Closer Congruence between Citizens and Policy Makers?" *Comparative Political Studies* 39(10): 1243–1262.

Blumenau, Jack. 2019. "The Effects of Female Leadership on Women's Voice in Political Debate." *British Journal of Political Science*. Advance online publication.

Bochsler, Daniel. 2010. "Xenophobic Voters, or Just Strategic Failure? The Anti-Immigrant Vote in Switzerland as a Condorcet Paradox." <https://poliscizurich.wordpress.com/2010/11/29/xenophobic-voters-or-just-strategic-failure/>.

Boix, Carles. 1999. "Setting the Rules of the Game: The Choice of Electoral Systems in Advanced Democracies." *American Political Science Review* 93(3): 609–624.

Börzel, Tanja A. 2000. "Why There is No 'Southern Problem': On Environmental Leaders and Laggards in the European Union." *Journal of European Public Policy* 7(1): 141–162.

Börzel, Tanja A. 2005. "Mind the Gap! European Integration between Level and Scope." *Journal of European Public Policy* 12(2): 217–236.

Börzel, Tanja A., Tobias Hofmann, Diana Panke, and Carina Sprungk. 2010. "Obstinate and Inefficient: Why Member States do Not Comply with European Law." *Comparative Political Studies* 43(11): 1363–1390.

Brader, Ted, Lorenzo De Sio, Aldo Paparo, and Joshua A. Tucker. 2020. ""Where You Lead, I Will Follow": Partisan Cueing on High-Salience Issues in a Turbulent Multiparty System." *Political Psychology* 41(4): 795–812.

Broder, David S. 2000. *Democracy Derailed: Initiative Campaigns and the Power of Money*. San Diego: Houghton Mifflin.

Browne, Eric C., and Mark N. Franklin. 1973. "Aspects of Coalition Payoffs in European Parliamentary Democracies." *American Political Science Review* 67(2): 453–469.

Browne, Eric C., John P. Frendreis, and Dennis W. Gleiber. 1984. "An "Events" Approach to the Problem of Cabinet Stability." *Comparative Political Studies* 17(2): 167–197.

Budge, Ian, and Dennis Farlie. 1983. *Explaining and Predicting Elections: Issue Effects and Party Strategies in Twenty-Three Democracies*. London; Boston: Allen & Unwin.

Budge, Ian, Hans-Dieter Klingemann, Andrea Volkens, Judith Bara, and Eric Tanenbaum. 2001. *Mapping Policy Preferences. Estimates for Parties, Electors, and Governments 1945–1998*. Oxford: Oxford University Press.

Burke, Edmund. 1790/1987. *Reflections on the Revolution in France*. Indianapolis: Hackett.

Caiani, Manuela, and Paolo Graziano. 2018. "Europeanisation and Social Movements: The Case of the Stop TTIP Campaign." *European Journal of Political Research* 57(4): 1031–1055.

Cain, Bruce, John Ferejohn, and Morris Fiorina. 1987. *The Personal Vote: Constituency Service and Electoral Independence*. Cambridge, MA; London: Harvard University Press.

Campbell, Angus, Philip E. Converse, Warren E. Miller, and Donald E. Stokes. 1960. *The American Voter*. New York: John Wiley & Sons.

Campbell, Rosie. 2004. "Gender, Ideology and Issue Preference: Is There Such a Thing as a Political Women's Interest in Britain?" *British Journal of Politics and International Relations* 6(1): 20–44.

Campbell, Rosie, Philip Cowley, Nick Vivyan, and Markus Wagner. 2019. "Legislator Dissent as a Valence Signal." *British Journal of Political Science* 49(1): 105–128.

Canovan, Margaret. 1999. "Trust the People! Populism and the Two Faces of Democracy." *Political Studies* 47(1): 2–16.

Carey, John M., and Matthew S. Shugart. 1995. "Incentives to Cultivate a Personal Vote: A Rank Ordering of Electoral Formulas." *Electoral Studies* 14(4): 417–439.

Carey, John M., and Simon Hix. 2011. "The Electoral Sweet Spot: Low-Magnitude Proportional Electoral Systems." *American Journal of Political Science* 55(2): 383–397.

Carroll, Royce, and Gary W. Cox. 2007. "The Logic of Gamson's Law: Pre-Election Coalitions and Portfolio Allocations." *American Journal of Political Science* 51(2): 300–313.

Carrubba, Clifford J., Matthew Gabel, and Charles Hankla. 2008. "Judicial Behavior under Political Constraints: Evidence from the European Court of Justice." *American Political Science Review* 102(4): 435–452.

Chan, Alexsia T., and Beverly K. Crawford. 2017. "The Puzzle of Public Opposition to TTIP in Germany." *Business and Politics* 19(4): 683–708.

Cheibub, José A., Jennifer Gandhi, and James R. Vreeland. 2010. "Democracy and Dictatorship Revisited." *Public Choice* 143(1): 67–101.

Clark, William R., and Matt Golder. 2006. "Rehabilitating Duverger's Theory: Testing the Mechanical and Strategic Modifying Effects of Electoral Laws." *Comparative Political Studies* 39(6): 679–708.

Clarke, Nick, Will Jennings, Jonathan Moss, and Gerry T. Stoker. 2018. *The Good Politician: Folk Theories, Political Interaction, and the Rise of Anti-Politics.* Cambridge: Cambridge University Press.

Clayton, Amanda, Diana Z. O'Brien, and Jennifer M. Piscopo. 2019. "All Male Panels? Representation and Democratic Legitimacy." *American Journal of Political Science* 63(1): 113–129.

Colomer, Josep M. 2005. "It's Parties that Choose Electoral Systems (or, Duverger's Laws Upside Down)." *Political Studies* 53(1): 1–21.

Coman, Emanuel Emil. 2019. "When Left or Right do Not Matter: Ideology and Spending in Central and Eastern Europe." *Research and Politics* 6(1): 1–9.

Converse, Philip. 1964. "The Nature of Belief Systems in Mass Publics." In *Ideology and Discontent*, ed. David E. Apter. Vol. 5. New York: Free Press, 206–261.

Coppedge, Michael, John Gerring, Carl H. Knutsen, Staffan I. Lindberg, Jan Teorell, David Altman, Michael Bernhard, M. Steven Fish, Adam Glynn, Allen Hicken, Anna Lührmann, Kyle L. Marquardt, Kelly McMann, Pamela Paxton, Daniel Pemstein, Brigitte Seim, Rachel Sigman, Svend-Erik Skaaning, Jeffrey Staton, Steven Wilson, Agnes Cornell, Lisa Gastaldi, Haakon Gjerløw, Nina Ilchenko, Joshua Krusell, Laura Maxwell, Valeriya Mechkova, Juraj Medzihorsky, Josefine Pernes, Johannes von Römer, Natalia Stepanova, Aksel Sundström, Eitan Tzelgov, Yi-ting Wang, Tore Wig, and Daniel Ziblatt. 2019. "Varieties of Democracy (V-Dem) Project [Country-Year/Country-Date] Dataset v9." <www.v-dem.net>.

Coppedge, Michael, John Gerring, Carl Henrik Knutsen, Staffan I. Lindberg, Jan Teorell, David Altman, Michael Bernhard, M. Steven Fish, Adam Glynn, Allen Hicken, Anna Luhrmann, Kyle L. Marquardt, Kelly McMann, Pamela Paxton, Daniel Pemstein, Brigitte Seim, Rachel Sigman, Svend-Erik Skaaning, Jeffrey Staton, Steven Wilson, Agnes Cornell, Nazifa Alizada, Lisa Gastaldi, Haakon Gjerløw, Garry Hindle, Nina Ilchenko, Laura Maxwell, Valeriya Mechkova, Juraj Medzihorsky, Johannes von Römer, Aksel Sundström, Eitan Tzelgov, Yi-ting Wang, Tore Wig, and Daniel Ziblatt. 2020. "Varieties of Democracy (V-Dem) Project [Country-Year/Country-Date] Dataset v10." <www.v-dem.net>.

Court of Justice of the European Union. 2018. "Annual Report 2018: Judicial Activity." <https://curia.europa.eu/jcms/upload/docs/application/pdf/2019-04/_ra_2018_en.pdf>.

Cox, Gary W. 1997. *Making Votes Count: Strategic Coordination in the World's Electoral Systems.* Cambridge; New York: Cambridge University Press.

Cox, Gary W., and Mathew D. McCubbins. 1993. *Legislative Leviathan: Party Government in the House.* Cambridge: Cambridge University Press.

CPI. 2020. "Transparency International's Corruption Perceptions Index (CPI)I.".

Culpepper, Pepper D. 2010. *Quiet Politics and Business Power: Corporate Control in Europe and Japan.* Cambridge: Cambridge University Press.

Dahl, Robert A. 1971. *Polyarchy; Participation and Opposition.* New Haven: Yale University Press.

De Vries, Catherine E. 2007. "Sleeping Giant: Fact or Fairytale? How European Integration Affects National Elections." *European Union Politics* 8(3): 363–385.

De Vries, Catherine E. 2018. *Euroscepticism and the Future of European Integration.* Oxford; New York: Oxford University Press.

De Vries, Catherine E., and Erica E. Edwards. 2009. "Taking Europe to its Extremes: Extremist Parties and Public Euroscepticism." *Party Politics* 15(1): 5–28.

De Vries, Catherine E., and Hector Solaz. 2017. "The Electoral Consequences of Corruption." *Annual Review of Political Science* 20(1): 391–408.

De Vries, Catherine E., and Isabell Hoffmann. 2019. "Great Expectations. The New European Commission, its Ambition and European Public Opinion. *eupinions* 2019(2)." <http://aei.pitt.edu/102424/>.

De Vries, Catherine E., and Sara B. Hobolt. 2020. *Political Entrepreneurs: The Rise of Challenger Parties in Europe.* Princeton: Princeton University Press.

De Vries, Catherine E., Wouter Van der Brug, Marcel H. Van Egmond, and Cees Van der Eijk. 2011. "Individual and Contextual Variation in EU Issue Voting: The Role of Political Information." *Electoral Studies* 30(1): 16–28.

Dinas, Elias, and Ksenia Northmore-Ball. 2020. "The Ideological Shadow of Authoritarianism." *Comparative Political Studies* 53(12): 1957–1991.

Downs, Anthony. 1957. *An Economic Theory of Democracy*. New York: Harper & Row.

Döring, Holger, and Philip Manow. 2019. "Parliaments and Governments Database (ParlGov): Information on Parties, Elections and Cabinets in Modern Democracies. Development Version." <www.parlgov.org>.

Druckman, James N., and Michael F. Thies. 2002. "The Importance of Concurrence: The Impact of Bicameralism on Government Formation and Duration." *American Journal of Political Science* 46(4): 760–771.

Druckman, James N., Lanny W. Martin, and Michael F. Thies. 2005. "Influence without Confidence: Upper Chambers and Government Formation." *Legislative Studies Quarterly* 30(4): 529–548.

Duch, Raymond M., and Randolph T. Stevenson. 2008. *The Economic Vote: How Political and Economic Institutions Condition Election Results*. New York: Cambridge University Press.

Dür, Andreas, and Gemma Mateo. 2016. *Insiders Versus Outsiders: Interest Group Politics in Multilevel Europe*. Oxford: Oxford University Press.

Dür, Andreas, David Marshall, and Patrick Bernhagen. 2019. *The Political Influence of Business in the European Union*. Ann Arbor: University of Michigan Press.

Duverger, Maurice. 1951. *Les Partis Politiques*. Paris: Colin.

Duverger, Maurice. 1970. *Institutions Politiques et Droit Constitutionnel*. 11th ed. Paris: Presses Universitaires de France.

Elgie, Robert. 1999. *Semi-Presidentialism in Europe*. Oxford: Oxford University Press.

Emanuele, Vincenzo. 2015. "Dataset of Electoral Volatility and its Internal Components in Western Europe (1945–2015)." <http://dx.doi.org/10.7802/1112>.

Emanuele, Vincenzo, Davide Angelucci, Bruno Marino, Leonardo Puleo, and Federico Vegetti. 2019. "Dataset of Electoral Volatility in the European Parliament Elections since 1979." <http://dx.doi.org/10.7802/1905>.

Erikson, Robert S., Michael B. MacKuen, and James A. Stimson. 2002. *The Macro Polity*. Cambridge: Cambridge University Press.

Esping-Andersen, Gøsta. 1990. *The Three Worlds of Welfare Capitalism*. Princeton: Princeton University Press.

EU Integrity Watch. 2020. "Integrity Watch—EU Lobbyists." <https://www.integritywatch.eu/organizations> (Accessed on 27 July 2020).

European Commission. 2016. "Accession Criteria." <https://ec.europa.eu/neighbourhood-enlargement/policy/glossary/terms/accession-criteria_en>. (Accessed on 26 July 2020).

European Commission. 2017. "European Citizens' Initiative: Commission Registers 'Stop TTIP' Initiative." <https://ec.europa.eu/commission/presscorner/detail/en/IP_17_1872> (Accessed on 27 July 2020).

European Commission. 2019a. "Eurobarometer 90.3, ZA7489." ZA7489, dataset version 1.0.0, doi:10.4232/1.13254.

European Commission. 2019b. "The European Green Deal." <https://eur-lex.europa.eu/legal-content/EN/TXT/?uri=CELEX:52019DC0640> (Accessed on 27 July 2020).

European Commission. 2019c. "Infringement Decisions." <https://ec.europa.eu/atwork/applying-eu-law/infringements-proceedings/infringement_decisions/> (Accessed on 1 June 2019).

European Commission. 2020a. "EU Enlargement." <https://ec.europa.eu/info/policies/eu-enlargement_en> (Accessed on 26 July 2020).

European Commission. 2020b. "Eurobarometer 92.3, ZA7601." ZA7601, dataset version 1.0.0, doi:10.4232/1.13564.

European Environment Agency. 2018. "Approximated Estimates for Greenhouse Gas Emissions." <https://www.eea.europa.eu/data-and-maps/data/approximated-estimates-for-greenhouse-gas-emissions> (Accessed on 26 July 2020).

European Environment Agency. 2019. "Indicator Assessment: Waste Recycling." <https://www.eea.europa.eu/data-and-maps/indicators/waste-recycling-1/assessment-1> (Accessed on 26 July 2020).

European Parliament. 2019. "Women in the European Parliament (Infographics)." <https://www.europarl.europa.eu/news/en/headlines/society/20190226STO28804/women-in-the-european-parliament-infographics> (Accessed on 26 July 2020).

European Social Survey. 2002. "ESS Round 1: European Social Survey Round 1 Data (Version 6.6)." doi:10.21338/NSD-ESS1-2002.

European Social Survey. 2004. "ESS Round 2: European Social Survey Round 2 Data (Version 3.6)." doi:10.21338/NSD-ESS2-2004.

European Social Survey. 2006. "ESS Round 3: European Social Survey Round 3 Data (Version 3.7)." doi:10.21338/NSD-ESS3-2006.

European Social Survey. 2008. "ESS Round 4: European Social Survey Round 4 Data (Version 4.5)." doi:10.21338/NSD-ESS4-2008.

European Social Survey. 2010. "ESS Round 5: European Social Survey Round 5 Data (Version 3.4)." 10.21338/NSD-ESS5-2010.

European Social Survey. 2012. "ESS Round 6: European Social Survey Round 6 Data (Version 2.4)." doi:10.21338/NSD-ESS6-2012.

European Social Survey. 2014. "ESS Round 7: European Social Survey Round 7 Data (Version 2.2)." doi:10.21338/NSD-ESS7-2014.

European Social Survey. 2016. "ESS Round 8: European Social Survey Round 8 Data (Version 2.1)." doi:10.21338/NSD-ESS8-2016.

Eurostat. 2020a. "Healthcare Resource Statistics—Beds." <https://ec.europa.eu/eurostat/statistics-explained/index.php/Healthcare_resource_statistics_-_beds> (Accessed on 26 July 2020).

Eurostat. 2020b. "Healthy Life Years Statistics." <https://ec.europa.eu/eurostat/statistics-explained/index.php?title=Healthy_life_years_statistics> (Accessed on 26 July 2020).

Evans, Geoffrey. 2006. "The Social Bases of Political Divisions in Post-Communist Eastern Europe." *Annual Review of Sociology*, 245–270.

Evans, Geoffrey, and James Tilley. 2017. *The New Politics of Class: The Political Exclusion of the British Working Class*. Oxford: Oxford University Press.

Evans, Geoffrey, and Nan Dirk De Graaf. 2013. *Political Choice Matters: Explaining the Strength of Class and Religious Cleavages in Cross-National Perspective*. Oxford: Oxford University Press.

Evans, Geoffrey, and Stephen Whitefield. 1993. "Identifying the Bases of Party Competition in Eastern Europe." *British Journal of Political Science* 23(4): 521–548.

Feld, Lars P., and Stefan Voigt. 2003. "Economic Growth and Judicial Independence: Cross-Country Evidence Using a New Set of Indicators." *European Journal of Political Economy* 19(3): 497–527.

Ferland, Benjamin. 2016. "Revisiting the Ideological Congruence Controversy." *European Journal of Political Research* 55(2): 358–373.

Ferrera, Maurizio. 1996. "The 'Southern Model' of Welfare in Social Europe." *Journal of European Social Policy* 6(1): 17–37.

Finke, Daniel, Thomas König, Sven-Oliver Proksch, and George Tsebelis. 2012. *Reforming the European Union: Realizing the Impossible*. Princeton: Princeton University Press.

Fiorina, Morris P. 1981. *Retrospective Voting in American National Elections*. New Haven: Yale University Press.

Føllesdal, Andreas, and Simon Hix. 2006. "Why There is a Democratic Deficit in the EU: A Response to Majone and Moravcsik." *Journal of Common Market Studies* 44(3): 533–562.

Ford, Robert, and Will Jennings. 2020. "The Changing Cleavage Politics of Western Europe." *Annual Review of Political Science* 23: 295–314.

Fortunato, David. 2017. "The Electoral Implications of Coalition Policy Making." *British Journal of Political Science* 43(1): 1–23.

Fortunato, David. 2021. *The Cycle of Coalition*. Cambridge Cambridge University Press.

Fortunato, David, and Randolph T. Stevenson. 2013. "Perceptions of Partisan Ideologies: The Effect of Coalition Participation." *American Journal of Political Science* 57(2): 459–477.

Franchino, Fabio, and Christopher Wratil. 2019. "Representing the Compromise: How Institutions Serve Government Support Coalitions in European Union Policy Making." *European Journal of Political Research* 58(4): 1129–1151.

Franklin, Mark N. 2004. *Voter Turnout and the Dynamics of Electoral Competition in Established Democracies since 1945*. Cambridge: Cambridge University Press.

Franklin, Mark N, and Sara B Hobolt. 2011. "The Legacy of Lethargy: How Elections to the European Parliament Depress Turnout." *Electoral Studies* 30(1): 67–76.

Funk, Patricia. 2010. "Social Incentives and Voter Turnout: Evidence from the Swiss Mail Ballot System." *Journal of the European Economic Association* 8(5): 1077–1103.

Gallagher, Michael. 1991. "Proportionality, Disproportionality and Electoral Systems." *Electoral Studies* 10(1): 33–51.

Gallego, Aina. 2015. *Unequal Political Participation Worldwide*. Cambridge: Cambridge University Press.

Gamson, William A. 1961. "A Theory of Coalition Formation." *American Sociological Review* 26(3): 373–382.

Garrett, Geoffrey, R. Daniel Kelemen, and Heiner Schulz. 1998. "The European Court of Justice, National Governments, and Legal Integration in the European Union." *International Organization* 52(1): 149–176.

Gerber, Elisabeth R. 1999. *The Populist Paradox: Interest Group Influence and the Promise of Direct Legislation*. Princeton: Princeton University Press.

Gibson, Edward L. 2005. "Boundary Control: Subnational Authoritarianism in Democratic Countries." *World Politics* 58(1): 101–132.

Gibson, Edward L. 2013. *Boundary Control: Subnational Authoritarianism in Federal Democracies*. Cambridge: Cambridge University Press.

Gilens, Martin. 2012. *Affluence and Influence: Economic Inequality and Political Power in America*. Princeton: Princeton University Press.

Golder, Matt, and Gabriella Lloyd. 2014. "Re-evaluating the Relationship between Electoral Rules and Ideological Congruence." *European Journal of Political Research* 53(1): 200–212.

Golder, Sona N. 2006. *The Logic of Pre-Electoral Coalition Formation*. Columbus, OH: Ohio State University Press.

Green, Jane, and Sara B. Hobolt. 2008. "Owning the Issue Agenda: Party Strategies and Vote Choices in British Elections." *Electoral Studies* 27(3): 460–476.

Green, Jane, and Will Jennings. 2017. The Politics of Competence: Parties, *Public Opinion and Voters*. Cambridge: Cambridge University Press.

Green-Pedersen, Christoffer. 2019. *The Reshaping of West European Party Politics: Agenda-Setting and Party Competition in Comparative Perspective*. Oxford: Oxford University Press.

Grzymala-Busse, Anna. 2002. *Redeeming the Communist Past: The Regeneration of Communist Successor Parties*. Cambridge Cambridge University Press.

Gschwend, Thomas, Michael F. Meffert, and Lukas F. Stoetzer. 2017. "Weighting Parties and Coalitions: How Coalition Signals Influence Voting Behavior." *Journal of Politics* 79(2): 642–655.

Haas, Ernst B. 1958. *The Uniting of Europe: Political, Social, and Economic Forces, 1950–1957*. Stanford, CA: Stanford University Press.

Hagemann, Sara, Sara B. Hobolt, and Christopher Wratil. 2017. "Government Responsiveness in the European Union: Evidence from Council Voting." *Comparative Political Studies* 50(6): 850–876.

Hager, Anselm, and Hanno Hilbig. 2020. "Does Public Opinion Affect Political Speech?" *American Journal of Political Science*. 64(4): 921–937.

Hainmüller, Jens, and Dominik Hangartner. 2019. "Does Direct Democracy Hurt Immigrant Minorities? Evidence from Naturalization Decisions in Switzerland." *American Journal of Political Science* 63(3): 530–547.

Hakhverdian, Armen. 2010. "Political Representation and its Mechanisms: A Dynamic Left–Right Approach for the United Kingdom, 1976–2006." *British Journal of Political Science* 40(4): 835–856.

Hamilton, Daniel S. 2014. "Transatlantic Challenges: Ukraine, TTIP and the Struggle to Be Strategic." *Journal of Common Market Studies* 52(S1): 25–39.

Haughton, Tim, and Kevin Deegan-Krause. 2021. *The New Party Challenge*. Oxford Oxford University Press.

Hawkins, Kirk A., Scott Riding, and Cas Mudde. 2012. "Measuring Populist Attitudes." *Political Concepts Committee on Concepts and Methods Working Paper Series* 55: 1–35.

Healy, Andrew, and Neil Malhotra. 2013. "Retrospective Voting Reconsidered." *Annual Review of Political Science* 16(1): 285–306.

Heisenberg, Dorothee. 2005. "The Institution of 'Consensus' in the European Union: Formal Versus Informal Decision-Making in the Council." *European Journal of Political Research* 44(1): 65–90.

Herron, Erik S., R. Pekkanen, and Matthew S. Shugart. 2018. "Terminology and Basic Rules of Electoral Systems." In *The Oxford Handbook of Electoral Systems*, ed. Robert J. Pekkanen, Erik S. Herron, and Matthew S. Shugart. Oxford: Oxford University Press, 1–20.

Hinich, Melvin J., and Michael C. Munger. 1997. *Analytical Politics*. New York: Cambridge University Press.

Hix, Simon, and Michael Marsh. 2007. "Punishment or Protest? Understanding European Parliament Elections." *Journal of Politics* 69(2): 495–510.

Hix, Simon, and Abdul Noury. 2016. "Government–Opposition or Left–Right? The Institutional Determinants of Voting in Legislatures." *Political Science Research and Methods* 4(2): 249–273.

Hix, Simon, Giacomo Benedetto, and Nicola Mastrorocco. 2020. "Replication Data for: Giacomo Benedetto, Simon Hix and Nicola Mastrorocco (2020). The Rise and Fall of Social Democracy, 1918–2017." <https://doi.org/10.7910/DVN/WTYLTK>.

Hobolt, Sara B. 2009. *Europe in Question: Referendums on European Integration*. Oxford: Oxford University Press.

Hobolt, Sara B. 2016. "The Brexit Vote: A Divided Nation, a Divided Continent." *Journal of European Public Policy* 23(9): 1259–1277.

Hobolt, Sara B., and Catherine E. De Vries. 2015. "Issue Entrepreneurship and Multiparty Competition." *Comparative Political Studies* 48(9): 1159–1185.

Hobolt, Sara B., and Catherine E. De Vries. 2016a. "Public Support for European Integration." *Annual Review of Political Science* 19(1): 413–432.

Hobolt, Sara B., and Catherine E. De Vries. 2016b. "Turning Against the Union? The Impact of the Crisis on the Eurosceptic Vote in the 2014 European Parliament Elections." *Electoral Studies* 44: 504–514.

Hobolt, Sara B., and Robert Klemmensen. 2008. "Government Responsiveness and Political Competition in Comparative Perspective." *Comparative Political Studies* 41(3): 309–337.

Hobolt, Sara B., and Jae-Jae Spoon. 2012. "Motivating the European Voter: Parties, Issues and Campaigns in European Parliament Elections." *European Journal of Political Research* 51(6): 701–727.

Hobolt, Sara B., and James Tilley. 2014. *Blaming Europe? Responsibility without Accountability in the European Union*. Oxford: Oxford University Press.

Hobolt, Sara B., and James Tilley. 2016. "Fleeing the Centre: The Rise of Challenger Parties in the Aftermath of the Euro Crisis." *West European Politics* 39(5): 971–991.

Hobolt, Sara B., Jae-Jae Spoon, and James Tilley. 2009. "A Vote Against Europe? Explaining Defection at the 1999 and 2004 European Parliament Elections." *British Journal of Political Science* 39(1): 93–115.

Hobolt, Sara, Thomas J. Leeper, and James Tilley. 2020. "Divided by the Vote: Affective Polarization in the Wake of the Brexit Referendum." *British Journal of Political Science*.

Hoffmann, Stanley. 1966. "Obstinate or Obsolete? The Fate of the Nation-State and the Case of Western Europe." *Daedalus* 95(3): 862–915.

Homola, Jonathan. 2019. "Are Parties Equally Responsive to Women and Men?" *British Journal of Political Science* 49(3): 957–975.

Hooghe, Liesbet, and Gary Marks. 2001. *Multi-Level Governance and European Integration*. Lanham, MD: Rowman & Littlefield.

Hooghe, Liesbet, and Gary Marks. 2018. "Cleavage Theory Meets Europe's Crisis: Lipset, Rokkan, and the Transnational Cleavage." *Journal of European Public Policy* 25(1): 109–135.

Hooghe, Liesbet, Arjan H. Schakel, and Gary Marks. 2010. *The Rise of Regional Authority: A Comparative Study of Forty-Two Democracies*. London: Routledge.

Hooghe, Liesbet, Gary Marks, and Carole J. Wilson. 2002. "Does Left/Right Structure Party Positions on European Integration?" *Comparative Political Studies* 35(8): 965–989.

Hopkin, Jonathan, and Caterina Paolucci. 1999. "The Business Firm Model of Party Organisation: Cases from Spain and Italy." *European Journal of Political Research* 35(3): 307–339.

Horowitz, Donald L. 1990. "Presidents vs. Parliaments: Comparing Democratic Systems." *Journal of Democracy* 1(4): 73–79.

Hotelling, Harold. 1929. "Stability in Competition." *Economic Journal* 39(153): 41–57.

Huber, John D. 1989. "Values and Partisanship in Left–Right Orientations: Measuring Ideology." *European Journal of Political Research* 17(5): 599–621.

Huber, John D., and Charles R. Shipan. 2000. "The Costs of Control: Legislators, Agencies, and Transaction Costs." *Legislative Studies Quarterly* 25(1): 25–52.

Høyland, Bjørn, Sara B. Hobolt, and Simon Hix. 2017. "Career Ambitions and Legislative Participation: The Moderating Effect of Electoral Institutions." *British Journal of Political Science* 49(3): 491–512.

IDEA, International. 2020. "IDEA Voter turnout database."

Indridason, Indridi H., and Gunnar Helgi Kristinsson. 2013. "Making Words Count: Coalition Agreements and Cabinet Management." *European Journal of Political Research* 52(6): 822–846.

Inglehart, Ronald. 1977. *The Silent Revolution*. Princeton: Princeton University Press.

Inter-Parliamentary Union. 2020. "Women in National Parliaments." <http://archive.ipu.org/wmn-e/classif-arc.htm> (Accessed on 27 July 2020).

Ipsos-Mori. 2020. "Issues Index Archive." <https://www.ipsos.com/ipsos-mori/en-uk/issues-index-archive> (Accessed on 27 July 2020).

Jagers, Jan, and Stefaan Walgrave. 2007. "Populism as Political Communication Style." *European Journal of Political Research* 46(3): 319–345.

Jensen, Christian B. 2007. "Implementing Europe: A Question of Oversight." *European Union Politics* 8(4): 451–477.

Jordan, Andrew J., and Duncan Liefferink. 2004. *Environmental Policy in Europe: The Europeanization of National Environmental Policy*. London: Routledge.

Kaltwasser, Cristóbal R., Robert Vehrkamp, and Christopher Wratil. 2019. "Europe's Choice. Populist Attitudes and Voting Intentions in the 2019 European Election." *Bertelsmann Policy Brief* 01.2019. <https://www.bertelsmann-stiftung.de/de/publikationen/publikation/did/policy-brief-12019-europes-choice>.

Kam, Christopher J. 2009. *Party Discipline and Parliamentary Politics*. Cambridge: Cambridge University Press.

Katz, Richard S., and Peter Mair. 1995. "Changing Models of Party Organization and Party Democracy: The Emergence of the Cartel Party." *Party Politics* 1(1): 5–28.

Kedar, Orit. 2009. *Voting for Policy, not Parties: How Voters Compensate for Power Sharing*. Cambridge; New York: Cambridge University Press.

Kedar, Orit, Liran Harsgor, and Raz A. Sheinerman. 2016. "Are Voters Equal under Proportional Representation?" *American Journal of Political Science* 60(3): 676–691.

Kelemen, R. Daniel. 2011. *Eurolegalism*. Cambridge, MA: Harvard University Press.

Kelemen, R. Daniel. 2017. "Europe's Other Democratic Deficit: National Authoritarianism in Europe's Democratic Union." *Government and Opposition* 52(2): 211–238.

Kelemen, R. Daniel. 2020. "The European Union's Authoritarian Equilibrium." *Journal of European Public Policy* 27(3): 481–499.

Kelemen, R. Daniel, Anand Menon, and Jonathan B. Slapin. 2014. "Wider and Deeper? Enlargement and Integration in the European Union." *Journal of European Public Policy* 21(5): 647–663.

Kirchheimer, Otto. 1966. *The Transformation of the Western European Party Systems*. Princeton: Princeton University Press, 177–200.

Kitschelt, Herbert. 1994. *The Transformation of European Social Democracy*. Cambridge: Cambridge University Press.

Klingemann, Hans-Dieter, Andrea Volkens, Judith Bara, Ian Budge, and Michael McDonald. 2006. *Mapping Policy Preferences II: Estimates for Parties, Electors, and Governments in Eastern Europe, European Union and OECD 1990–2003*. Oxford: Oxford University Press.

Klüver, Heike. 2012. "Informational Lobbying in the European Union: The Effect of Organisational Characteristics." West European Politics 35(3): 419–510.

Klüver, Heike. 2013. Lobbying in the European Union: Interest Groups, Lobbying Coalitions, and Policy Change. Oxford: Oxford University Press.

Klüver, Heike, and Hanna Bäck. 2019. "Coalition Agreements, Issue Attention, and Cabinet Governance." Comparative Political Studies 52(13–14): 1995–2031.

Klüver, Heike, and Jae-Jae Spoon. 2016. "Who Responds? Voters, Parties and Issue Attention." British Journal of Political Science 46(3): 633–654.

Klüver, Heike, and Jae-Jae Spoon. 2020. "Helping or Hurting? How Governing as a Junior Coalition Partner Influences Electoral Outcomes." Journal of Politics 82(4): 1231–1242.

Klüver, Heike, and Radoslaw Zubek. 2018. "Minority Governments and Legislative Reliability: Evidence from Denmark and Sweden." Party Politics 24(6): 719–730.

Knill, Christoph, and Andrea Lenschow. 2000. Implementing EU Environmental Policy: New Directions and Old Problems. Manchester: Manchester University Press.

Knill, Christoph, and Andrea Lenschow. 2005. "Compliance, Competition and Communication: Different Approaches of European Governance and their Impact on National Institutions." Journal of Common Market Studies 43(3): 583–606.

König, Thomas, and Thomas Bräuninger. 2004. "Accession and Reform of the European Union: A Game-Theoretical Analysis of Eastern Enlargement and the Constitutional Reform." European Union Politics 5(4): 419–439.

König, Thomas, and Lars Mäder. 2014. "The Strategic Nature of Compliance: An Empirical Evaluation of Law Implementation in the Central Monitoring System of the European Union." American Journal of Political Science 58(1): 246–263.

Krauss, Svenja, and Corinna Kroeber. 2020. "How Women in the Executive Influence Government Stability." Journal of European Public Policy. Advance online publication.

Kreppel, Amie, and Buket Oztas. 2017. "Leading the Band or Just Playing the Tune? Reassessing the Agenda-Setting Powers of the European Commission." Comparative Political Studies 50(8): 1118–1150.

Kriesi, Hanspeter, Edgar Grande, Romain Lachat, Martin Dolezal, Simon Bornschier, and Timotheos Frey. 2008. West European Politics in the Age of Globalization. Cambridge; New York: Cambridge University Press.

Krook, Mona L. 2009. Quotas for Women in Politics: Gender and Candidate Selection Reform Worldwide. Oxford: Oxford University Press.

Krook, Mona L., and Diana Z. O'Brien. 2012. "All the President's Men? The Appointment of Female Cabinet Ministers Worldwide." Journal of Politics 74(3): 840–855.

Krook, Mona L., Joni Lovenduski, and Judith Squires. 2009. "Gender Quotas and Models of Political Citizenship." British Journal of Political Science 39(4): 781–803.

Laakso, Markku, and Rein Taagepera. 1979. "'Effective' Number of Parties: A Measure with Application to West Europe." Comparative Political Studies 12(1): 3–27.

Laclau, Ernesto. 2005. On Populist Reason. London: Verso.

Laver, Michael. 2003. "Government Termination." Annual Review of Political Science 6(1): 23–40.

Laver, Michael. 2014. "Measuring Policy Positions in Political Space." Annual Review of Political Science 17(1): 207–223.

Laver, Michael, and Kenneth A. Shepsle. 1996. Making and Breaking Governments: Cabinets and Legislatures in Parliamentary Democracies. Cambridge; New York: Cambridge University Press.

Laver, Michael, Kenneth Benoit, and John Garry. 2003. "Extracting Policy Positions from Political Texts Using Words as Data." American Political Science Review 97(2): 311–331.

Leemann, Lucas, and Isabela Mares. 2014. "The Adoption of Proportional Representation." Journal of Politics 76(2): 461–478.

Leemann, Lucas, and Fabio Wasserfallen. 2016. "The Democratic Effect of Direct Democracy." American Political Science Review 110(4): 750–762.

Lewis-Beck, Michael S. 1990. Economics and Elections: The Major Western Democracies. Ann Arbor University of Michigan Press.

Lührmann, Anna, Seraphine F. Maerz, Sandra Grahn, Nazifa Alizada, Lisa Gastaldi, Sebastian Hellmeier, Garry Hindle, and Staffan I. Lindberg. 2020. "Autocratization Surges – Resistance Grows. Democracy Report." Varieties of Democracy Institute (V-Dem).

Lijphart, Arend. 1992. Parliamentary Versus Presidential Government. Oxford: Oxford University Press.

Lijphart, Arend. 1997. "Unequal Participation: Democracy's Unresolved Dilemma Presidential Address, American Political Science Association, 1996." American Political Science Review 91(1): 1-14.

Lijphart, Arend. 2012. Patterns of Democracy: Government Forms and Performance in Thirty-Six Countries. 2nd ed. New Haven Yale University Press.

Linz, Juan J. 1990. "The Perils of Presidentialism." *Journal of Democracy* 1(1): 51–69.

Linz, Juan J., and Alfred C. Stepan. 1996. "Toward Consolidated Democracies." *Journal of Democracy* 7(2): 14–33.

Lipset, Seymour M. 1959. "Some Social Requisites of Democracy: Economic Development and Political Legitimacy." *American Political Science Review* 53(1): 69–105.

Lipset, Seymour M., and Stein Rokkan. 1967. *Party Systems and Voter Alignments: Cross-National Perspectives.* New York: Free Press.

Locke, John. 1690/1980. *Second Treatise of Government.* Indianapolis: Hackett.

Lowe, Will, Kenneth Benoit, Slava Mikhaylov, and Michael Laver. 2011. "Scaling Policy Preferences from Coded Political Texts." *Legislative Studies Quarterly* 36(1): 123–155.

Lundell, Krister, and Lauri Karvonen. 2003. "A Comparative Data Set on Political Institutions." *Abo Akademi*, Department of Political Science, Finland.

Lynch, Julia. 2020. *Regimes of Inequality: The Political Economy of Health and Wealth.* Cambridge: Cambridge University Press.

Macron, Emmanuel. 2019. "For European Renewal." <https://www.elysee.fr/emmanuel-macron/2019/03/04/for-european-renewal.en> (Accessed on 27 July 2020).

Mainwaring, Scott. 1993. "Presidentialism, Multipartism, and Democracy: The Difficult Combination." *Comparative Political Studies* 26(2): 198–228.

Mair, Peter. 2013. *Ruling the Void: The Hollowing of Western Democracy.* London: Verso.

Majone, Giandomenico. 1998. "Europe's 'Democratic Deficit': The Question of Standards." *European Law Journal* 4(1): 5–28.

Manin, Bernard. 1997. *The Principles of Representative Government.* Cambridge: Cambridge University Press.

Mansbridge, Jane. 1999. "Should Blacks Represent Blacks and Women Represent Women? A Contingent 'Yes.'" *Journal of Politics* 61(3): 628–657.

Mansbridge, Jane. 2003. "Rethinking Representation." *American Political Science Review* 97(4): 515–528.

Martin, Lanny W., and Georg Vanberg. 2005. "Coalition Policymaking and Legislative Review." *American Political Science Review* 99(1): 93–106.

Martin, Lanny W., and Georg Vanberg. 2011. *Parliaments and Coalitions: The Role of Legislative Institutions in Multiparty Governance.* Oxford: Oxford University Press.

Martin, Lanny W., and Georg Vanberg. 2013. "Multiparty Government, Fiscal Institutions, and Public Spending." *Journal of Politics* 75(4): 953–967.

Martin, Lanny W., and Georg Vanberg. 2014. "Parties and Policymaking in Multiparty Governments: The Legislative Median, Ministerial Autonomy, and the Coalition Compromise." *American Journal of Political Science* 58(4): 979–996.

Martin, Lanny W., and Georg Vanberg. 2020a. "Coalition Government, Legislative Institutions, and Public Policy in Parliamentary Democracies." *American Journal of Political Science* 64(2): 325–340.

Martin, Lanny W., and Georg Vanberg. 2020b. "What you See is Not Always What you get: Bargaining Before an Audience under Multiparty Government." *American Political Science Review* 114(4): 1138–1154.

Marx, Karl. 1867. *Das Kapital.* Hamburg: Otto Meissner Verlag.

Matland, Richard E., and Donley T. Studlar. 1996. "The Contagion of Women Candidates in Single-Member District and Proportional Representation Electoral Systems: Canada and Norway." *Journal of Politics* 58(3): 707–733.

Matsusaka, John G. 2005. "Direct Democracy Works." *Journal of Economic Perspectives* 19(2): 185–206.

Matthijs, Matthias, and Kathleen McNamara. 2015. "The Euro Crisis' Theory Effect: Northern Saints, Southern Sinners, and the Demise of the Eurobond." *Journal of European Integration* 34(2): 229–245.

McDonnell, Duncan, and Marco Valbruzzi. 2014. "Defining and Classifying Technocrat-Led and Technocratic Governments." *European Journal of Political Research* 53(4): 654–671.

McKelvey, Richard D. 1979. "General Conditions for Global Intransitivities in Formal Voting Models." *Econometrica* 47(5): 1085–1112.

Mbaye, Heather A. D. 2001. "Why National States Comply with Supranational Law: Explaining Implementation Infringements in the European Union, 1972–1993." *European Union Politics* 2(3): 259–281.

Meguid, Bonnie M. 2008. *Party Competition between Unequals: Strategies and Electoral Fortunes in Western Europe.* Cambridge; New York: Cambridge University Press.

Müller, Wolfgang C., and Kaare Strøm. 1999. *Policy, Office, or Votes? How Political Parties in Western Europe Make Hard Decisions.* Cambridge: Cambridge University Press.

Moore, Barrington. 1966. *Social Origins of Dictatorship and Democracy; Lord and Peasant in the Making of the Modern World.* Boston: Beacon Press.

Moravcsik, Andrew. 1998. The Choice for Europe: Social Purpose and State Power from Messina to Maastricht. Ithaca, NY: Cornell University Press.

Moravcsik, Andrew. 2002. "Reassessing Legitimacy in the European Union." *Journal of Common Market Studies* 40(4): 603–624.

Mudde, Cas. 2004. "The Populist Zeitgeist." *Government and Opposition* 39(4): 541–563.

Müller, Wolfgang C, and Kaare Strøm. 2008. "Coalition Agreements and Cabinet Governance." In *Cabinets and Coalition Bargaining: The Democractic Life Cycle in Western Europe.* Oxford: Oxford University Press, 159–199.

Neto, Octavio Amorim, and Gary W. Cox. 1997. "Electoral Institutions, Cleavage Structures, and the Number of Parties." *American Journal of Political Science* 41(1): 149–174.

Norris, Pippa. 1985. "Women's Legislative Participation in Western Europe." *West European Politics* 8(4): 90–101.

North, Douglass C., and Barry R. Weingast. 1989. "Constitutions and Commitment: The Evolution of Institutions Governing Public Choice in Seventeenth-Century England." *Journal of Economic History* 49(4): 803–832.

O'Brien, Diana Z. 2019. "Female Leaders and Citizens' Perceptions of Political Parties." *Journal of Elections, Public Opinion and Parties* 29(4): 465–489.

OECD. 2016. *International Migration Outlook 2016.* Technical report. Paris: OECD.

O'Grady, Tom. 2019. "Careerists Versus Coal-Miners: Welfare Reforms and the Substantive Representation of Social Groups in the British Labour Party." *Comparative Political Studies* 52(4): 544–578.

O'Grady, Tom, and Tarik Abou-Chadi. 2019. "Not So Responsive After All: European Parties do Not Respond to Public Opinion Shifts across Multiple Issue Dimensions." *Research and Politics* 6(4): 1–7.

Olson, Mancur. 1965. *The Logic of Collective Action: Public Goods and the Theory of Groups.* Cambridge, MA: Harvard University Press.

Olson, Mancur. 1993. "Dictatorship, Democracy, and Development." *American Political Science Review* 87(3): 567–576.

Panebianco, Angelo. 1988. *Political Parties: Organization and Power.*; New York: Cambridge University Press.

Passarelli, Gianluca. 2020. Preferential Voting Systems: *Influence on Intra-Party Competition and Voting Behaviour.* London: Palgrave Macmillan.

Pedersen, Mogens N. 1979. "The Dynamics of European Party Systems: Changing Patterns of Electoral Volatility." *European Journal of Political Research* 7(1): 1–26.

Petrocik, John R. 1996. "Issue Ownership in Presidential Elections, with a 1980 Case Study." *American Journal of Political Science* 40(3): 825–850.

Phillips, Anne. 1995. *The Politics of Presence.* Oxford: Oxford University Press.

Pilet, Jean-Benoit, Alan Renwick, Lidia Núñez, Elwin Reimink, and Pablo Simón. 2016. "Database of Electoral Systems." <www.electoralsystemchanges.eu>.

Pitkin, Hanna F. 1967. *The Concept of Representation.* Berkeley, CA: University of California Press.

Plott, Charles R. 1967. "A Notion of Equilibrium and its Possibility under Majority Rule." *American Economic Review* 57(4): 787–806.

Plott, Charles R. 1991. "Will Economics Become an Experimental Science?" *Southern Economic Journal* 57(4): 901–919.

Polk, Jonathan, Jan Rovny, Ryan Bakker, Erica Edwards, Liesbet Hooghe, Seth Jolly, Jelle Koedam, Filip Kostelka, Gary Marks, Gijs Schumacher, Marco Steenbergen, Milada Vachudová, and Marko Zilovic. 2017. "Explaining the Salience of Anti-Elitism and Reducing Political Corruption for Political Parties in Europe with the 2014 Chapel Hill Expert Survey Data." *Research and Politics* 4(1): 1–9.

Powell, Eleanor N., and Joshua A. Tucker. 2014. "Revisiting Electoral Volatility in Post-Communist Countries: New Data, New Results and New Approaches." *British Journal of Political Science* 44(1): 123–147.

Powell, G. Bingham. 2000. *Elections as Instruments of Democracy: Majoritarian and Proportional Visions.* New Haven: Yale University Press.

Powell, G. Bingham. 2009. "The Ideological Congruence Controversy: The Impact of Alternative Measures, Data, and Time Periods on the Effects of Election Rules." *Comparative Political Studies* 42(12): 1475–1497.

Proksch, Sven-Oliver, and Jonathan B. Slapin. 2006. "Institutions and Coalition Formation: The German Election of 2005." *West European Politics* 29(3): 540–559.

Proksch, Sven-Oliver, and Jonathan B. Slapin. 2012. "Institutional Foundations of Legislative Speech." *American Journal of Political Science* 56(3): 520–537.

Proksch, Sven-Oliver, and Jonathan B. Slapin. 2015. The Politics of Parliamentary Debate: Parties, *Rebels and Representation.* Cambridge: Cambridge University Press.

Proksch, Sven-Oliver, Will Lowe, Jens Wäckerle, and Stuart Soroka. 2019. "Multilingual Sentiment Analysis: A New Approach to Measuring Conflict in Legislative Speeches." *Legislative Studies Quarterly* 44(1): 97–131.

Prosser, Christopher. 2016. "Calling European Union Treaty Referendums: Electoral and Institutional Politics." *Political Studies* 64(1): 182–199.

Przeworski, Adam, and John Sprague. 1986. *Paper Stones: A History of Electoral Socialism*. Chicago: University of Chicago Press.

Przeworski, Adam, Michael E. Alvarez, José A. Cheibub, and Fernando Limongi. 2000. *Democracy and Development: Political Institutions and Well-Being in the World, 1950–1990*. Cambridge; New York: Cambridge University Press.

Rae, Douglas W. 1967. *The Political Consequences of Electoral Laws*. New Haven: Yale University Press.

Rasch, Bjørn E., Shane Martin, and José A. Cheibub. 2015. *Parliaments and Government Formation: Unpacking Investiture Rules*. Oxford: Oxford University Press.

Reif, Karlheinz, and Hermann Schmitt. 1980. "Nine Second-Order National Elections: A Conceptual Framework for the Analysis of European Election Results." *European Journal of Political Research* 8(1): 3–44.

Rico, Guillem, and Eva Anduiza. 2019. "Economic Correlates of Populist Attitudes: An Analysis of Nine European Countries in the Aftermath of the Great Recession." *Acta Politica* 54(3): 371–397.

Riker, William H. 1964. *Federalism: Origin, Operation, Significance*. Boston: Little Brown.

Riker, William H. 1975. "Federalism." In *Handbook of Political Science 5: Governmental Institutions and Processes*, ed. Fred I. Greenstein and Nelson W. Polsby. Reading, MA: Addison-Wesley, 93–172.

Riker, William H. 1986. *The Art of Political Manipulation*. New Haven: Yale University Press.

Riker, William H., and Peter C. Ordeshook. 1968. "A Theory of the Calculus of Voting." *American Political Science Review* 62(1): 25–42.

Roberts, Andrew. 2006. "What Kind of Democracy is Emerging in Eastern Europe?" *Post-Soviet Affairs* 22(1): 37–64.

Rokkan, Stein. 1970. *Citizens, Elections, Parties: Approaches to the Comparative Study of the Processes of Development*. New York: David McKay.

Rooduijn, Matthijs, Stijn Van Kessel, Caterina Froio, Andrea Pirro, Sarah De Lange, Daphne Halikiopoulou, Paul Lewis, Cas Mudde, and Paul Taggart. 2019. "The PopuList: An Overview of Populist, Far Right, Far Left and Eurosceptic Parties in Europe." <www.popu-list.org>.

Röth, Leonce, and André Kaiser. 2019. "Why Accommodate Minorities Asymmetrically? A Theory of Ideological Authority Insulation." *European Journal of Political Research* 58(2): 557–581.

Rovny, Jan. 2012. "Who Emphasizes and Who Blurs? Party Strategies in Multidimensional Competition." *European Union Politics* 13(2): 269–292.

Rovny, Jan. 2014. "Communism, Federalism, and Ethnic Minorities: Explaining Party Competition Patterns in Eastern Europe." *World Politics* 66(4): 669–708.

Ruedin, Didier. 2020. "Regional and Ethnic Minorities." In *The Oxford Handbook of Political Representation in Liberal Democracies*. Oxford: Oxford University Press.

Rustow, Dankwart A. 1970. "Transitions to Democracy: Toward a Dynamic Model." *Comparative Politics* 2(3): 337–363.

Samuels, David, and Matthew S. Shugart. 2010. *Presidents, Parties, and Prime Ministers: How the Separation of Powers Affects Party Organization and Behavior*. Cambridge: Cambridge University Press.

Sartori, Giovanni. 1976. *Parties and Party Systems: A Framework for Analysis*. Cambridge.; New York: Cambridge University Press.

Schakel, Wouter. 2019. "Unequal Policy Responsiveness in the Netherlands." *Socio-Economic Review*. doi: 10.1093/ser/mwz018.

Scharpf, Fritz W. 2015. "Political Legitimacy in a Non-Optimal Currency Area." In *Democratic Politics in a European Union under Stress*, 19–47.

Schattschneider, Elmer E. 1960. *The Semisovereign People; A Realist's View of Democracy in America*. 1st ed. New York: Holt, Rinehart & Winston.

Schelling, Thomas C. 1960. *The Strategy of Conflict*. Cambridge, MA: Harvard University Press.

Schimmelfennig, Frank, and Ulrich Sedelmeier. 2004. "Governance by Conditionality: EU Rule Transfer to the Candidate Countries of Central and Eastern Europe." *Journal of European Public Policy* 11(4): 661–679.

Schimmelfennig, Frank, Dirk Leuffen, and Berthold Rittberger. 2015. "The European Union as a System of Differentiated Integration: Interdependence, Politicization and Differentiation." *Journal of European Public Policy* 22(6): 764–782.

Schleiter, Petra, and Edward Morgan-Jones. 2010. "Who's in Charge? Presidents, Assemblies, and the Political Control of Semipresidential Cabinets." *Comparative Political Studies* 43(11): 1415–1441.

Schmitt, Hermann, Evi Scholz, Iris Leim, and Meinhard Moschner. 2008. "The Mannheim Eurobarometer Trend File 1970–2002 (ed. 2.00)." European Commission [Principal investigator]. ZA3521 Data file Version 2.0.1, doi:10.4232/1.10074.

Schmitt, Hermann, Sara B. Hobolt, Wouter van der Brug, and Sebastian A. Popa. 2019. "European Parliament Election Study 2019, Voter Study." <www.europeanelectionstudies.net>.

Schneider, Christina J. 2019. *The Responsive Union: National Elections and European Governance*. Cambridge: Cambridge University Press.

Schulte-Cloos, Julia. 2018. "Do European Parliament Elections Foster Challenger Parties' Success on the National Level?" *European Union Politics* 19(3): 408–426.

Schumpeter, Joseph A. 1942. *Capitalism, Socialism, and Democracy*. New York and London: Harper & Brothers.

Schwindt-Bayer, Leslie A., and William Mishler. 2005. "An Integrated Model of Women's Representation." *Journal of Politics* 67(2): 407–428.

Serdült, Uwe, Norina Frehner, Irina Lehner, and Louis Gebirstorf. 2018. "Centre for Research on Direct Democracy." <www.c2d.ch>.

Shapiro, Martin. 1981. *Courts: A Comparative and Political Analysis*. Chicago: University of Chicago Press.

Shugart, Matthew S. 2005. "Comparative Electoral Systems Research: The Maturation of a Field and New Challenges Ahead." In *The Politics of Electoral Systems*, ed. Michael Gallagher and Paul Mitchell. Oxford: Oxford University Press.

Shugart, Matthew S., and John M. Carey. 1992. *Presidents and Assemblies: Constitutional Design and Electoral Dynamics*. Cambridge; New York: Cambridge University Press.

Shugart, Matthew S., and Martin P. Wattenberg. 2003. *Mixed-Member Electoral Systems: The Best of Both Worlds?* Oxford: Oxford University Press.

Slapin, Jonathan B. 2009. "Exit, Voice, and Cooperation: Bargaining Power in International Organizations and Federal Systems." *Journal of Theoretical Politics* 21(2): 187–211.

Slapin, Jonathan B. 2015. "How European Union Membership Can Undermine the Rule of Law in Emerging Democracies." *West European Politics* 38(3): 627–648.

Slapin, Jonathan B., and Sven-Oliver Proksch. 2008. "A Scaling Model for Estimating Time-Series Party Positions from Texts." *American Journal of Political Science* 52(3): 705–722.

Slapin, Jonathan B., and Sven-Oliver Proksch. 2010. "Look Who's Talking: Parliamentary Debate in the European Union." *European Union Politics* 11(3): 333–357.

Smets, Kaat, and Carolien van Ham. 2013. "The Embarrassment of Riches? A Meta-Analysis of Individual-Level Research on Voter Turnout." *Electoral Studies* 32(2): 344–359.

Sojka, Aleksandra, Jorge Díaz-Lanchas, and Frederico Steinberg. 2020. *The Politicisation of Transatlantic Trade in Europe: Explaining Inconsistent Preferences Regarding Free Trade and the TTIP*. LSE Europe in Question Discussion Paper Series 151. London: LSE.

Somer-Topcu, Zeynep. 2015. "Everything to Everyone: The Electoral Consequences of the Broad-Appeal Strategy in Europe." *American Journal of Political Science* 59(4): 841–854.

Sørensen, Rune. 2019. "The Impact of State Television on Voter Turnout." *British Journal of Political Science* 49(1): 257–278.

Soroka, Stuart N., and Christopher Wlezien. 2010. *Degrees of Democracy: Politics, Public Opinion, and Policy*. Cambridge: Cambridge University Press.

Spoon, Jae-Jae. 2011. *Political Survival of Small Parties in Europe*. Ann Arbor: University of Michigan Press.

Spoon, Jae-Jae, Sara B. Hobolt, and Catherine E. De Vries. 2013. "Going Green: Explaining Issue Competition on the Environment." *European Journal of Political Research* 53(2): 363–380.

Stepan, Alfred, and Cindy Skach. 1993. "Constitutional Frameworks and Democratic Consolidation: Parliamentarianism Versus Presidentialism." *World Politics* 46(1): 1–22.

Stepan, Alfred C. 1999. "Federalism and Democracy: Beyond the US Model." *Journal of Democracy* 10(4): 19–34.

Stimson, James A., Michael B. MacKuen, and Robert S. Erikson. 1995. "Dynamic Representation." *American Political Science Review* 89(3): 543–565.

Stokes, Donald E. 1963. "Spatial Models of Party Competition." *American Political Science Review* 57(2): 368–377.

Stone Sweet, Alec. 2000. *Governing with Judges: Constitutional Politics in Europe*. Oxford; New York: Oxford University Press.

Strøm, Kaare. 1990. *Minority Government and Majority Rule*. Cambridge: Cambridge University Press.

Strøm, Kaare, Wolfgang C Müller, and Daniel Markham Smith. 2010. "Parliamentary Control of Coalition Governments." *Annual Review of Political Science* 13: 517–535.

Stubager, Rune. 2010. "The Development of the Education Cleavage: Denmark as a Critical Case." *West European Politics* 33(3): 505–533.

Svolik, Milan. 2008. "Authoritarian Reversals and Democratic Consolidation." *American Political Science Review* 102(2): 153–168.

Taggart, Paul. 1998. "A Touchstone of Dissent: Euroscepticism in Contemporary Western European Party Systems." *European Journal of Political Research* 33(3): 363–388.

Taggart, Paul. 2000. *Populism: Concepts in the Social Sciences*. Buckingham: Open University Press.

Tavits, Margit. 2009. *Presidents with Prime Ministers: Do Direct Elections Matter?* Oxford: Oxford University Press.

Tavits, Margit, and Natalia Letki. 2009. "When Left is Right: Party Ideology and Policy in Post-Communist Europe." *American Political Science Review* 103(4): 555–569.

The Comparative Study of Electoral Systems. 2020. "CSES Module 5 Second Advance Release [Dataset and Documentation]. May 14, 2020 Version." <www.cses.org>.

Thies, Michael F. 2001. "Keeping Tabs on Partners: The Logic of Delegation in Coalition Governments." *American Journal of Political Science* 45(3): 580–598.

Thomson, Robert, Terry Royed, Elin Naurin, Joaquín Artés, Rory Costello, Laurenz Ennser-Jedenastik, Mark Ferguson, Petia Kostadinova, Catherine Moury, François Pétry, and Katrin Praprotnik. 2017. "The Fulfillment of Parties' Election Pledges: A Comparative Study on the Impact of Power Sharing." *American Journal of Political Science* 61(3): 527–542.

Tilly, Charles. 1990. *Coercion, Capital, and European States, AD 990–1990.* Oxford; Cambridge, MA: B. Blackwell.

Toshkov, Dimiter D. 2017. "The Impact of the Eastern Enlargement on the Decision-Making Capacity of the European Union." *Journal of European Public Policy* 24(2): 177–196.

Toshkov, Dimiter D. 2020. "55 Years of EU Legislation." <http://www.dimiter.eu/Eurlex.html>. (Accessed on 26 July 2020).

Tsebelis, George. 1995. "Decision Making in Political Systems: Veto Players in Presidentialism, Parliamentarism, Multicameralism and Multipartyism." *British Journal of Political Science* 25(3): 289–325.

Tsebelis, George. 2002. *Veto Players: How Political Institutions Work.* New York: Russell Sage Foundation.

Tsebelis, George, and Geoffrey Garrett. 2001. "The Institutional Foundations of Intergovernmentalism and Supranationalism in the European Union." *International Organization* 55(2): 357–390.

Tsebelis, George, and Jeannette Money. 1997. *Bicameralism.* Cambridge; New York: Cambridge University Press.

Tucker, Joshua A. 2006. *Regional Economic Voting: Russia, Poland, Hungary, Slovakia, and the Czech Republic, 1990–1999.* Cambridge; New York: Cambridge University Press.

Vachudová, Milada. 2005. *Europe Undivided: Democracy, Leverage, and Integration after Communism.* Oxford; New York: Oxford University Press.

Valdini, Melody E. 2019. *The Inclusion Calculation: Why Men Appropriate Women's Representation.* Oxford: Oxford University Press.

Van Haute, Emilie, Emilien Paulis, and Vivien Sierens. 2018. "Assessing Party Membership Figures: The MAPP Dataset." *European Political Science* 17: 366–377.

Vatter, Adrian, and Julian Bernauer. 2009. "The Missing Dimension of Democracy: Institutional Patterns in 25 EU Member States between 1997 and 2006." *European Union Politics* 10(3): 335–359.

Verba, Sidney, Kay Lehman Schlozman, and Henry E. Brady. 1995. *Voice and Equality: Civic Voluntarism in American Politics.* Cambridge, MA: Harvard University Press.

Volkens, Andrea, Werner Krause, Pola Lehmann, Theres Matthieß, Nicolas Merz, Sven Regel, and Bernhard Weßels. 2019. "The Manifesto Data Collection. Manifesto Project (MRG/CMP/MARPOR). Version 2019b." <https://doi.org/10.25522/manifesto.mpds.2019b>.

Wängnerud, Lena. 2006. "A Step-Wise Development: Women in Parliament in Sweden." In *Women in Parliament: Beyond Numbers,* ed. Julie Ballington and Azza Karam. IDEA Handbook. Rev. version, 238–248.

Weber, Max. 1978. *Economy and Society: An Outline of Interpretive Sociology.* Berkeley, CA: University of California Press.

Weeks, Ana Catalano. 2018. "Why are Gender Quota Laws Adopted by Men? The Role of Inter- and Intraparty Competition." *Comparative Political Studies* 51(14): 1935–1973.

Weingast, Barry R. 1997. "The Political Foundations of Democracy and the Rule of Law." *American Political Science Review* 91(2): 245–263.

Whitefield, Stephen. 2002. "Political Cleavages and Post-Communist Politics." *Annual Review of Political Science* 5(1): 181–200.

Winzen, Thomas. 2017. *Constitutional Preferences and Parliamentary Reform: Explaining National Parliaments' Adaptation to European Integration.* Oxford: Oxford University Press.

Wlezien, Christopher. 1995. "The Public as Thermostat: Dynamics of Preferences for Spending." *American Journal of Political Science* 39(4): 981–1000.

Wlezien, Christopher, and Stuart N. Soroka. 2012. "Political Institutions and the Opinion-Policy Link." *West European Politics* 35(6): 1407–1432.

Wratil, Christopher. 2018. "Modes of Government Responsiveness in the European Union: Evidence from Council Negotiation Positions." *European Union Politics* 19(1): 52–74.

Ziblatt, Daniel. 2017. *Conservative Parties and the Birth of Democracy.* Cambridge: Cambridge University Press.

Index

Note: tables, figures, and boxes are indicated by an italic *t.*, *f.*, and *b.* following the page number.